Wissenschaftliche Untersuchungen
zum Neuen Testament · 2. Reihe

Herausgeber / Editor
Jörg Frey

Mitherausgeber / Associate Editors
Friedrich Avemarie · Judith Gundry-Volf
Martin Hengel · Otfried Hofius · Hans-Josef Klauck

215

Morten Hørning Jensen

Herod Antipas in Galilee

The Literary and Archaeological Sources
on the Reign of Herod Antipas
and its Socio-Economic Impact on Galilee

Mohr Siebeck

MORTEN HØRNING JENSEN, born 1972; 2001 M. Theol. (cand.theol.) from the University of Aarhus, Denmark; 2005 Ph.D.; 2006–2008 Postdoc from the Carlsberg Foundation, University of Aarhus.

ISBN 3-16-148967-5
ISBN-13 978-3-16-148967-9
ISSN 0340-9570 (Wissenschaftliche Untersuchungen zum Neuen Testament, 2. Reihe)

Die Deutsche Bibliothek lists this publication in the Deutsche Nationalbibliographie; detailed bibliographic data is available in the Internet at *http://dnb.ddb.de*.

The book was printed by Gulde-Druck in Tübingen on non-aging paper and bound by Buchbinderei Held in Rottenburg/N.

Printed in Germany.

For Jeanette

Acknowledgements

In 2000/01 I was given the opportunity to spend the academic year at the Hebrew University of Jerusalem as a graduate student. While initially pursuing the catchphrase *'The Quest for the Historical Jesus,'* I somehow ended up in 'Galilee.' In retrospect, this was a fortunate 'detour' that also kept me busy throughout the succeeding period of PhD study at the Faculty of Theology, University of Aarhus, Denmark in 2002–5. Not only has the issue of Roman Galilee provided an unrivalled opportunity for training in the classical deeds of source-oriented history writing, with a focus on such interesting areas as archaeology, Josephus studies, New Testament studies and rabbinica, but it also opened the door to a vibrant international research community in which – obviously – youth and ignorance are no hindrance to a warm welcome!

When currently publishing a revised edition of my dissertation, *Herod Antipas in Galilee,* submitted in August 2005, there is therefore a list of persons that I genuinely need to thank for their help and guidance. As my email archive reveals, a large number of scholars have taken time to discuss various issues with me, provided me with the unique opportunity to read through unpublished manuscripts, or even – outstandingly – commented on one or more chapters. I wish to thank Sean Freyne, Jürgen Zangenberg, Douglas Edwards, Steve Mason, Jonathan L. Reed, James F. Strange, Mordechai Aviam, Mark A. Chancey, John Dominic Crossan, Andrea M. Berlin, Danny Syon, David Hendin, Morgan Kelly, James S. McLaren, Milton Moreland, Douglas E. Oakman, Carolyn Osiek, Anders Runesson, Donald T. Ariel, Uriel Rappaport, Peter Richardson, Halvor Moxnes, Marianne Sawicki, John S. Kloppenborg, Nikos Kokkinos, Svend Fodgaard Jensen, Gunnar Haaland, Monika Bernett, Haim Gitler, Moshe Hartal, Yizhar Hirschfeld, and my colleagues at the Department of New Testament Studies.

A special thanks goes to my doctoral advisor, Per Bilde, for his continuous guidance and sincere interest in my project. During a year-long tutorial on Josephus' *Antiquities* 18 I profited tremendously from his great classical wisdom; and thanks to his consistently thorough response, each and every page of what follows benefited from his 'red-inked' error corrections and suggestions for improvement. For what remains of errors and shortcomings, I have solely myself to blame.

I also wish to express my sincere appreciation to the editor of the WUNT II series, Jörg Frey, for inviting me to present my dissertation at a conference in Munich as well as for accepting it for publication, to Jesper Tang Nielsen for mentioning my work to Jörg Frey, and to Henning Ziebritzki and the editorial staff of Mohr Siebeck Publishing House for competent guidance throughout the process of preparing the manuscript for publication.

I also want to express my gratitude to the research foundation known as Forskningsrådet for kultur og kommunikation, which has covered the main expense of my three-year employment as a PhD student; and to the Faculty of Theology, University of Aarhus, for providing me with such superior facilities for a PhD programme. Participation in several international conferences and three seasons of digging in the campaign in Tiberias directed by Yizhar Hirschfeld was made possible through the generous support of Aarhus Universitets Forskningsfond, Knud Højgårds Fond, Frimodt-Heineke Fonden, Brorsons rejselegat and Torben & Alice Frimodts Fond, for which I am deeply grateful.

I wish to conclude by explaining why this entire project is dedicated to Jeanette – the love of my life. The completion of the project has demanded a number of working hours beyond what is reasonable – not to mention periods during which I was abroad, leaving her alone with the responsibility for caring for our three children, Johanne, Benjamin and Oliver, and for this I am deeply grateful. At the same time, I have experienced a warm concern from her for the subject matter of this dissertation. During our visits to Israel together, we have both learned to treasure the historical, geographical and archaeological scenery behind the books of our Bible.

Aarhus, May 2006   Morten Hørning Jensen

Table of Contents

Part I: Settings

Part II: Sources

Part III: Assessment

Abbreviations and Preliminary Remarks

All translations of written texts and epigraphic material are, unless otherwise indicated, facilitated by the author. Greek and Latin texts are taken from the Loeb Library if nothing else is noted. The texts from the New Testament follow the Nestle-Aland 27th edition.

When referring to individuals from antiquity, I generally prefer the names that are commonly used in the research, though they may not reflect the actual names used in antiquity. Thus, Herod the King is referred to as 'Herod the Great,' though this term is only used in *Ant.* 18.103, 133 and 136, where it might just translate as "the elder" (cf. Feldman 1965, 89, note c and Richardson 1999, 12). Similarly, I refer to Herod the Tetrarch as Herod Antipas or just Antipas, although every coin and inscription we have uses the designation 'Herod the Tetrarch.'

In general, the book and the bibliography are formatted by following *The SBL Handbook of Style* (ed. P.H. Alexander et al., 3rd edition 2003) using its prescriptions regarding abbreviations of biblical books, ancient authors, ordinary abbreviations etc. In general, abbreviations apart from common ones are avoided, with the exception of the following:

ESI:	Excavations and Surveys in Israel.
IEJ:	The Israel Exploration Journal.
LS:	*A Greek-English Lexicon*, compiled by Henry George Liddell and Robert Scott, 9th edition with supplements (1996), electronic version by Logos Bible Software.
NA 27:	*Novum Testamentum Graece*. Edited by E. Nestle and B. et K. Aland, 1993.
NEAEHL:	E. Stern, ed. 1993. *The New Encyclopedia of Archaeological Excavations in the Holy Land.* 4 Vols. Jerusalem: Carta, The Israel Exploration Society.
PG:	*Patrologia Graeca.* Edited by J.-P. Migne. 162 vols. Paris, 1857–1886.
TJC:	Meshorer, Y. 2001. *A Treasury of Jewish Coins: From the Persian Perod to Bar Kokhba.* Jerusalem: Yad Ben-Zvi Press.

The time periods used follow *The Oxford Encyclopedia of Archaeology in the Near East* (edited by Eric M. Meyers, 1997), the article "Periodization" (Herr 1997):

Hellenistic period:	332 – 63 BCE.
Roman Period:	63 BCE – 135 CE.
Middle Roman period:	135 – 250 CE.

Late Roman period: 250 – 325 CE.
Byzantine period: 325 – 640 CE.

References to figures concern the figures at the back of the present volume. Besides these essential figures, the book's accompanying website found at the url: www.herodantipas.com features the *Herod Antipas in Galilee Image Gallery* containing additional images grouped in the following categories: Tiberias, Sepphoris, Yodefat, Cana, Capernaum, Gamla, Scythopolis, Hippos, Caesarea Maritima and Picturesque Galilee. Most of the figures are also displayed in colour in the Image Gallery.

Tables and Figures

Full-colour versions of the figures are accessible on the website www.herodantipas.com.

Part I

Settings

Chapter 1

Approaching Herod Antipas

1.1 All Roads Lead to Galilee…

During the last three decades, the question of "Roman Galilee" has become an issue of intense interest, and the quest for its historical, cultural, political and religious secrets has had a magnetic attraction, uniting different fields of research such as historical Jesus research, Josephus research, research on Rabbinic Judaism, and archaeological field work. Broad 'roads of interest' lead to Galilee from each of these areas of study.

Although Galilee has always been an area of focus to some extent, at least for New Testament research,[1] this recent scholarly enterprise is an entity of its own catalyzed by two important factors. First, in 1980 Sean Freyne published his seminal work, *Galilee from Alexander the Great to Hadrian 323 B.C.E. to 135 C.E.: A Study of Second Temple Judaism* (Freyne 1980b). Freyne's study provided, for the first time ever, a thorough one-volume investigation of the historical, cultural, political, economic and religious conditions of Hellenistic and Roman Galilee. Second, based on the socio-archaeological paradigm of 'New Archaeology' (cf. section 5.2), large-scale archaeological investigations were launched. In the 1970s, the 'Meiron Project' surveyed and excavated sites mainly in Upper Galilee.[2] In 1981, the director and co-director of this project, Eric

---

[1] Ever since Byzantine times, Galilee has attracted pilgrims as described in the travel reports of Egeria and elsewhere (cf. Wilkinson 1977; Wilkinson 1981). The European re-occupation of Palestine in the 19th century brought Galilee back into focus through several new travel reports authored by E. Renan, Condor & Kitchener and others (Renan 1991; Conder and Kitchener 1881, cf. the instructive presentations in Shepherd 1987; Freyne 2000c, 2–7 and Moxnes 2001b, 26–33). In the early 20th century, the question of the ethnicity of the Galileans created a fierce debate between those who followed Schürer's thesis of the Galileans as recently converted Itureans (cf. below), which taken to the extreme meant that Jesus was detached from Judaism since the "Galiläa heidnisch war", which means that "Jesus kein Jude war" (W. Grundmann, quoted after Freyne 1995, 599), and A. Alt, who argued that there was a continued Israelite presence in Galilee (Alt 1953, see further Bilde 1980; Freyne 2000c, 8–9 and Moxnes 2001b, 33–34).

[2] A list of the excavated sites during the Meiron project can be found in Meyers, Strange and Groh 1978, 7. The final reports are presented in the series *Meiron Excava-*

M. Meyers and James F. Strange, published the small, but influential book, *Archaeology, The Rabbis, and Early Christianity*, in which they summarized the impact which the archaeological fieldwork should have on studies of the social and cultural background for the Jesus movement as well as the rabbinical movement. The impact of archaeology on traditional text-based historical studies of Galilee became even more evident through the largest single excavation in Galilee, which began in 1983 and continues today: the excavation of Sepphoris conducted by teams from the University of South Florida, Duke University and the Hebrew University (cf. section 5.4).

Consequently, the question of 'the social world of Galilee' became a topic of discussion at international conferences conducted under the auspices of the Society of Biblical Literature (SBL) and others. Four papers were published in the 1988 edition of the SBL seminar papers (Lull 1988). In 1989, the first international conference on Galilee was held at Kibbutz Hanaton in Galilee. The papers from this event were published in Levine 1992, covering questions related to Josephus, the New Testament, and archaeological and rabbinic studies. In 1996, the second international Galilee conference was held at Duke University in connection with an exhibit of archaeological finds from Sepphoris at the North Carolina Museum of Art. The papers from this conference were published in Meyers 1999, and a beautifully illustrated book with instructive articles accompanied the exhibit (Nagy 1996). In the meantime, Galilee had again been discussed at the SBL, and four papers focusing specifically on the relationship between archaeology and the historical Jesus quest were published in Lovering 1994. In 1997, an important collection of articles was presented in the festschrift to James F. Strange, *Archaeology and the Galilee: Texts and Contexts in Graeco-Roman and Byzantine Periods* (Edwards and McCollough 1997a). As will become clear below, several independent articles as well as monographs were published in the same period. Most recently, a research programme entitled "Galilee, Ethnicity and Identity in Ancient Galilee" was hosted by the University of Wuppertal and Yale University, including several conferences and a major final publication yet to be published (Attridge, Martin and Zangenberg Forthcoming).

---

tion Project Reports (ed. Eric M. Meyers), counting a total of six volumes covering the four main excavations of Khirbet Shema, Meiron, Gush Halav and Nabratein (all sites in Upper Galilee). See also Hanson 1980, 51 and Meyers 1997, 57–58 for additional lists of the excavated sites.

1.1.1 Historical Jesus Research

At the same time as the interest in Galilean studies began to spread, the so-called third quest for the historical Jesus gradually evolved. Compared with the two earlier 'quests' or phases, this third quest is marked by a clear interest in establishing a 'plausible' context around Jesus through which he needs to be interpreted (cf. Meier 1991, 167–195; Wright 1996, 85–86; Theißen and Winter 1997; Holmén 1999 and others). Freyne states as an example: "The Bultmann era of New Testament scholarship did not encourage research into the Palestinian background of either Jesus or his movement. Nor indeed did the so-called new quest for the historical Jesus, inaugurated by Ernst Käsemann in his now famous lecture of 1953, generate any particular attention in that direction either" (Freyne 2000c, 20). In contrast, the recent development in the historical Jesus research incorporates new material from the archaeological excavations and textual sources shedding light on first-century Palestine. Consequently, "there has been an explosion of interest in all aspects of the social world of first century Palestine" (Freyne 1994, 75, cf. also Wright 1996, 84–85; Reed 2000, 7).

Thus it is obvious that the descriptions of the social and cultural conditions of first-century Galilee constitute an important factor in the most recent historical Jesus research. As noted by Jonathan L. Reed: "Since descriptions of the realities in Galilee to a large extent determine the interpretation of Jesus' teachings and his life, it is not surprising that the renewed quest has witnessed variously shaded Galilees to make the competing descriptions of the historical Jesus more credible" (Reed 2000, 8). Similarly, Freyne states: "The quest for Jesus is rapidly in danger of becoming the quest for the historical Galilee" (Freyne 1994, 76). As the primary locus for the historical Jesus, Galilee provides *the* historical context, which has the potential to verify or undermine certain proposals about the historical Jesus. Incisively, Andrew Overman notes how Galilee has become "fodder and fuel for the Quest for the historical Jesus... Galilee is quickly emerging – in certain circles – as epiphenomenal to the Quest for the historical Jesus" (Overman 1997, 67).

1.1.2 Four Important Issues

The discussion within this lively and voluminous debate on Ancient Galilee has focused on several key questions, of which four stand out.[3] First, it

---

[3] It is not possible here to conduct a comprehensive investigation of the research history of the Galilean research as I was able to do in my MA thesis, *Galilæa på Jesu tid: En præsentation og vurdering af de sidste to årtiers Galilæa-forskning* ('Galilee at the Time of Jesus: A Presentation and Evaluation of the Last Two Decades of Galilean Research', Jensen 2002b). A summary of the archaeological contributions can also be found

has been discussed if Galilee was a special hotbed for revolutionary tendencies, and if the term οἱ Γαλιλαῖοι as used by Josephus in his *Life*
should be interpreted as a technical term for revolutionaries. In short, the
proposal of interpreting οἱ Γαλιλαῖοι as "a particular rebel group" (Loftus
1974, 183, cf. Zeitlin 1974; Loftus 1977–1978) did not resist the closer
analyses performed by Feldman, Freyne and Armenti, who argue that the
term is used mainly geographically by Josephus with an occasionally reference to the rural population as opponents to the city-dwellers of Tiberias
and Sepphoris (cf. Freyne 1980a; Feldman 1981–1982; Armenti 1981–
1982 and Feldman 1996, 111–113, cf. further section 3.3.8). In the context
of Galilean research, the connected question of Galilee as a hotbed for
revolutionaries has mainly been discussed by Freyne and Horsley. Aimed
at the view of Horsley (Horsley 1979a; Horsley 1981), Freyne argues for a
relatively quiet and stable Galilee with Antipas as a buffer against direct
Roman rule, describing the few known upheavals as Hasmonean resistance
to Herodian rule (Freyne 1980b, 190–192; Freyne 1988a; Freyne 1988b,
163–167). Of Horsley's many publications on this topic, Horsley 1988 (re-
produced in Horsley 1995c) is interesting as a direct answer to Freyne. In
this publication he agrees that Galilee did not witness a long-standing organized (zelotic) resistance group. However, building on Hobsbawn's idea
of 'social bandits' defined as "a prepolitical form of social protest against
particular local conditions and injustices" (Horsley 1995c, 259, cf.
Hobsbawn 1969), Horsley maintains that Galilee witnessed such groups
concerned with "righting wrongs" (Horsley 1988, 185).[4]

Second, the question of the origins of the Galileans has been debated as
an inherited unsolved issue from the earlier nineteenth and twentieth centuries debates between E. Schürer, who argued that the Galileans were
Iturean tribes converted by the Hasmoneans (cf. Schürer 1901, 275–276;
Schürer 1907, 9–12, for instance), and A. Alt, who argued that the Galileans were remnants of the old Israelite tribes (Alt 1953, 363–435). On the
basis of new archaeological surveys, such as Zvi Gal's survey on Iron Age
settlements in Galilee (Gal 1992), and M. Aviam's on settlement patterns
in the Late Hellenistic and Early Roman periods (Aviam 1993), this discussion seems to have been settled in favour of a third solution, namely
that the Galileans consisted largely of newcomers from Judea, who moved
to the area shortly before, during and after the Hasmonean takeover under
Aristobulos (cf. Freyne 1997a, 72; Freyne 2000a, 177ff.; Freyne 1999, 42;

---

in Overman 1993, and a bibliographical survey has been conducted in Meyers et al. 1995.
Shorter but highly instructive overviews can also be found in Freyne 1994; Freyne 2000c
and Reed 2000, 1–22.

[4] For a more thorough treatment, see Jensen 2002b, 13–18, 75–76.

Reed 1999; Reed 2000, 23–61 and others). This seems to be the case, even though Richard A. Horsley has maintained the thesis of Alt (cf. Horsley 1995c, 19–61; Horsley 1996, 15–27; Horsley 1999 and others), and scholars arguing for a Jesus inspired by Cynic philosophy still operate within the old paradigm of Schürer (cf. below).[5]

Third, the most intensively debated issue concerns the question of the cultural milieu of Galilee. Freyne's study from 1980 advocated a picture of Galilee as a quiet, rural, isolated Jewish area with close connections to Jerusalem, to which the reign of Antipas brought stability and protection against "direct Roman intervention" (Freyne 1980b, 69, cf. Freyne 1988b, 155–156). The archaeological excavations conducted in both Upper and Lower Galilee have led archaeologists to describe the cultural ethos of Galilee in a radically different way from Freyne. In an early article on "Galilean regionalism", Meyers stated that a "more cosmopolitan atmosphere" prevailed in Lower Galilee (Meyers 1976, 95, cf. Meyers 1979, 689). Strange proposed that the expanding urban civilisation of Rome had resulted in an "Urban Overlay" of Galilee manifested most clearly in Sepphoris (Strange 1992c, 32, cf. Strange 1991). Richard A. Batey and Andrew J. Overman, assistants of Strange in the Sepphoris excavations, advanced this idea even further, stressing the "cosmopolitan atmosphere" of Sepphoris (Batey 1984, 251, cf. Batey 1991, 56), determining that "life in lower Galilee in the first century was as urbanized and urbane as anywhere else in the empire" (Overman 1988, 168, cf. also Overman 1993, 47). In turn, this picture of a cosmopolitan first-century Galilee has played a role in the historical Jesus research as one of the arguments for a Jesus inspired by Cynic philosophy, presented by (among others) F. Gerald Downing (cf. Downing 1987; Downing 1988; Downing 1992), John Dominic Crossan (Crossan 1991; Crossan 1997; Crossan 1999; Crossan and Reed 2001),[6] and not least Burton L. Mack, who has boldly described Galilee as "an epitome of Hellenistic culture on the eve of the Roman era" (Mack 1988, 66) and as "a no-man's-land" (Mack 1993, 53, cf. Mack 1997).

As summarized in Jensen 2002a, important studies by Jonathan L. Reed, Sean Freyne, Richard Horsley, Eric M. Meyers and most recently Mark Chancey have contributed significantly to this discussion to an extent that

---

[5] For a more thorough treatment, see Jensen 2002b, 11–12, 20–21, 76–78, 83–86.

[6] The works of Crossan represent an interesting development in this question. Even as early as *'The Historical Jesus'* he tried to keep a balance by describing Jesus as a "peasant Jewish Cynic" (Crossan 1991, 421). In *'The Birth of Christianity'* this is recalled, and criticizing Batey and others, Crossan concludes that "new evidence" is needed to settle the case (Crossan 1999, 215). Finally, in his book co-authored with Jonathan L. Reed, *Excavating Jesus,* Jesus is described as one of "those first-century apocalypticists and/or protesters" (Crossan and Reed 2001, 174).

has largely settled the issue in their favour. Unless new material data is presented, Galilee in the *Early* Roman period was not 'as Hellenized as anywhere else', but instead possessed a Jewish culture similar to that of Judea and a level of urbanization not comparable with larger urban centres such as Caesarea Maritima and Scythopolis. To summarize, their arguments are centred on the following four points:[7] (a) The population density of Lower Galilee was not as high as suggested by some (cf. Reed 1992; Reed 1994a; Reed 1994b; Reed 1999; Reed 2000, and Crossan and Reed 2001). (b) Several cultural/religious identity markers are traceable in the archaeological data that clearly point to a predominantly Jewish population of Lower Galilee, such as Jewish ritual baths, *mikvaot* (מקוות), widespread use of limestone vessels, lack of pig bones, Jewish religious symbols like incense shovels, special burial customs including use of *loculi* and a high percentage of Hasmonean coinage (cf. Meyers and Chancey 2000; Chancey 2001; Chancey 2002b; Aviam 2004a; Reed 2000, 100–138; Crossan and Reed 2001, 165–172; Freyne 1997a and others).[8] (c) In contrast, the identity markers expected of a highly romanised and urbanised area are missing (cf. Meyers and Chancey 2000, 27–28; Reed 2000, 123–131; Reed 1994b, 215; Horsley 1996, 59 and others). (d) It is necessary to pay close attention to the archaeological stratigraphy, since Galilee experienced a great political and cultural change around the Bar Kochba rebellion leading to a much heavier presence of Roman soldiers and Roman administration (cf. Meyers 1997; Meyers and Chancey 2000; Chancey 2003 and most recently Chancey 2005, 43–70, for instance). Based on this, the thesis of a Cynic-like Jesus has often been rejected as unwarranted or even impossible due to the material culture (cf. Horsley 1994, 127; Horsley 1999, 57–64 Freyne 1997a; Reed 2000, 135; Betz 1994; Aune 1997; Marshall 1997 and others).

Fourth, the issue of how the internal relationship between town and village should be pictured in Ancient Galilee has been debated with increasing intensity. When it gradually became evident that at least early-first-century Galilee did not possess the kind of Greco-Roman culture known from other places at that time, the focus shifted to an investigation of what *then* went on in this period, on an internal socio-economic level. Galilee did perhaps experience some radical changes with the advent of its first lo-

---

[7] Much of this will be dealt with in detail in chapter five.

[8] It should be noted that Horsley contests the assumption that ethnicity and religion can be traced in archaeological data (cf. Horsley 1996, 108ff.). Though a valid point of caution, the implications of the identity markers are not overstated (cf. Chancey 2001, 139 and others). The argument based on identity markers concerns first and foremost the accumulated amount of material, which taken together is assumed to offer "a reliable indicator of Jewish religious identity" (Reed 1999, 100).

cally placed ruler for many years, Herod Antipas. It is possible to trace exactly how this question has attracted growing attention, and how Herod Antipas has increasingly become 'a factor of explanation and verification' of the various presentations of his Galilee. To this we now turn.

1.2 Urban-Rural Relations – Conflict or Harmony?

1.2.1 Two Pictures of Galilee

The short survey above has made two things clear. First, archaeology has acquired an increasingly vital role in the discussion. The question of the origin and ethnic character of the Galileans has been advanced due to new material data, just as the question of the cultural conditions of Galilee largely involved a discussion of the archaeological findings. Second, as briefly mentioned, the main focus has shifted from a comparison of Galilee with the wider Roman world to a more localized discussion of the urban-rural relations of early-first-century Galilee in the wake of Antipas' programme of urbanization. However, while it is agreed that archaeology must be incorporated on an equal footing with texts,[9] and that 'the question of Antipas' is a vital key to understanding the socio-economic conditions of early-first-century Galilee, no consensus has been reached on how to depict his Galilee. As pointed out by Halvor Moxnes, two pictures have evolved. *Either* Antipas is viewed as a buffer against direct Roman rule and exploitation, thereby providing a good basis for trade and mutual enrichment of both urban and rural areas (a 'picture of harmony'); *or* Antipas is depicted as a typical tyrant extracting heavy taxes from his region for the financing of his building programme, which resulted in economic upheaval with increasing indebtedness and tenancy (a 'picture of conflict', cf. Moxnes 1998, 107; Moxnes 2001a). Thus, the Galilean research is currently in a state of impasse on this important question. In the following, these two pictures will be presented, and a possible way out of the impasse will be discussed.

---

[9] The most important archaeological contributions to the discussion are: (a) The excavations of Sepphoris and Tiberias. (b) Excavations of rural sites in Lower Galilee like Yodefat, Cana, Capernaum, Gamla and others. (c) Studies of specific items and subjects such as David Adan-Bayewitz's neutron activation analyses of pottery (from here of, NAA, cf. Adan-Bayewitz and Perlman 1990; Adan-Bayewitz and Wieder 1992; Adan-Bayewitz 1993 and note 10), and studies of coin distributions like Richard S. Hanson's of Tyrian coinage in Upper Galilee (Hanson 1980) and the very recent study by D. Syon of the general coin distribution pattern in Upper and Lower Galilee (Syon 2004). Chapters five and six are devoted to a discussion of these issues.

1.2.2 'A Picture of Harmony' – Reciprocal Urban-Rural Relations

As mentioned above, in his early works Freyne describes the reign of Antipas as a buffer against direct Roman rule and influence (cf. Freyne 1980b, 69, 192; Freyne 1988b, 155–156). Freyne does not deny that such a Hellenistic-style monarchy meant heavy taxes, or that there was great pressure on the small landowners. However, the peace and stability provided by Antipas is viewed as a more important factor than the high tax burden, which had been a basic fact of life since Ptolemaic rule (cf. Freyne 1980b, 186). As early as in his book from 1988, Freyne footnotes T.F. Carney's sociological study, *The Shape of the Past: Models in Antiquity* (Carney 1975, cf. Freyne 1988b, 156 note 47), and it is made clear that the new way of life in the cities led to a clash with the more homogenous life in the villages (Freyne 1988b, 146). In these early works, however, it is important for Freyne to stress that life in the rural areas went on relatively undisturbed by events occurring in the cities, and that we have no evidence of a socio-economic recession in Galilee either under Antipas or even immediately before the war of 66–70 CE:

It is now time to ask whether or not this Galilean economy had within it those alienating forces as far as the majority of Galileans are concerned, which are so often assumed to have been operative in the background to Jesus' ministry. Here attention must be drawn to the conclusions arrived at in the previous study of Galilee, namely, that the province was not at the time of the first revolt seething with disaffection and in a state of revolutionary turmoil. (Freyne 1988b, 161–162, cf. also p. 152)

Thus, while Freyne describes the cities as potentially disruptive forces for life in the rural areas, he does maintain in his early works that life in rural Galilee fared better than elsewhere due to the peaceful reign of Antipas.

This view is supported and expanded by several of the archaeologists working in Sepphoris, such as Eric M. Meyers, D. Edwards, J. Strange and J. Reed. With various nuances they describe the urban-rural situation as a reciprocal relationship marked by interaction, trade and mutual enrichment. Meyers admits that Antipas' building programme

...had an enormous impact on everyday life. Numerous villages, farms, and hamlets were now called upon to provide food for the growing populations of the cities, and the fertile lands nearby, which until now had sustained independent, self-subsistent farmers, were now transformed into places where products were grown on a much larger scale for cash. (Meyers 1997, 62)

However, this development is not perceived as overtly negative. As "centers of consumption" (Meyers 1997, 62), the cities also provided new markets, and with reference to Adan-Bayewitz's NAA analyses,[10] Meyers states that "the data surely indicates a continuum of positive interaction between city and town in the Early Roman period. Theories that suggest that urban centers exploit the surrounding countryside are to be soundly rejected on the basis of archaeological evidence alone" (Meyers 1997, 61). Instead, "the Galilean context of Jesus was such that both its incipient urbanism and its predominantly rural village culture could live in harmony. City and town were economically interlinked as we have demonstrated from ceramics" (Meyers 1997, 64).

James F. Strange also deduces from the NAA analyses of Adan-Bayewitz to a reciprocal trade pattern. Furthermore, he argues that the internal road grid of Galilee was far more developed than described in earlier investigations, which "hardly seemed to allow the traveller of the first century access to Galilee" (Strange 1997a, 39, cf. Strange 1994a, 82 and Strange 2000a, 393), providing the necessary logistics for "a highly developed, local trade network in Galilee" (Strange 1997a, 39). Strange substantiates this claim with references to mainly unpublished studies of wine presses, glass production of Sepphoris, and subsequent rabbinical traditions, which all point to a Galilean culture with highly specialised production centres for "olives, barley, wine, fish, herbs, and flax, and for finished products such as cloth, clothing, dye-stuffs, basketry, furniture, breads, perfumes, and metal fittings" (Strange 1997a, 41). Strange's point is "that an extensive specialized agricultural and industrial production implies a vigorous trade network" (Strange 1997a, 42). Thus, "we must give up the view that there is a sharp distinction between city dwellers and the peasants in the countryside" (Strange 1997b, 300). Finally, Strange includes analyses of New Testament metaphors and parables pointing at a complex setting "that uses urban as well as rural metaphors" (Strange 1992c, 47, cf. also Strange 2000aa).

On a similar basis, Jonathan Reed uses Adan-Bayewitz's analyses as an indicator of how Sepphoris functioned as a "lucrative market thereby compensating for the relatively lengthy overland transport" (Reed 1994b, 218). In this way, mutually beneficial interaction between the rural production centres of Shiknin and Kefar Hananya, for instance, and the market centres of Sepphoris and Tiberias was a fact of life. Reed advances this proposal

---

[10] In short, neutron activation analysis can determine "a site-specific manufacturing provenience to the majority of the common pottery" (Adan-Bayewitz and Wieder 1992, 189) by revealing the specific chemical profile of the clay. The result of the 350 analyzed potsherds points to the conclusion that the major part of the common pottery of Galilee was produced in Kefar Hananya, Shiknin or Nahf. However, the excavations at Yodefat revealed that the same kind of pottery was produced there, and the former conclusions might have to be reconsidered (private communication with M. Aviam).

through analyses of the Q material. He notices that the urban market system appears in Luke/Q in the form of plazas, city gates, banks, courts and prisons as well (Luke/Q 7:25, 7:32, 10:10, 11:43, 12:57–59, 13:24, 13:26, 14:21, 19:23). Likewise, no direct rejection of either Sepphoris or Tiberias is uttered as in the case of Capernaum, Bethsaida and Chorazin (Luke/Q 10:11–14), which is why they "cannot be described as the locus of animosity for the Jesus movement, nor likely for Galilean society in general" (Reed 2000, 99). Instead the urban metaphors "suggest that urban-rural contacts were not uncommon, which raises the question of whether Jesus can be placed exclusively in a village context, first around Nazareth and then around Capernaum, or whether he did, in fact, visit Tiberias or Sepphoris" (Reed 2000, 99).

At the very same time, Reed almost contradictorily states that the urbanization process under Antipas meant a spiral of increased monetization and taxation, and a change from polycropping to monocropping, which in the end meant increased new pressures on the peasant population (Reed 2000, 83–89). The object of self-sufficiency became problematic under Antipas, "polycropping inevitably waned, as monocropping was required to produce higher yields and satisfy tax demands." Thus, "an asymmetrical exchange of goods increased", which again "facilitated the trend of peasants selling their land to pay off their taxes in cash, and then staying on their land as tenants or indentured servants paying rent, or simply leaving their land to ply an artisan trade and eke out an existence" (Reed 2000, 87). Thus, while no direct denunciation of the great cities of Galilee is found in the New Testament material:

Antipas's building of Sepphoris and Tiberias and the accentuation of social stratification and asymmetrical exchange created considerable stress on the population. It is not surprising that Jesus' proclamation of the Kingdom of God alluded to and directly addressed some of these concerns created by Antipas's kingdom building. (Reed 2000, 220)[11]

Douglas R. Edwards has presented new arguments for a mutually beneficial urban-rural interaction via his archaeological field work at Sepphoris, Yodefat and Kfar Cana (cf. section 5.5), and via utilization of Ian Hopkins' study, "The City Region in Roman Palestine", which applies 'the central place theory' to Ancient Palestine by outlining how the cities had an encircled network of smaller villages and towns that were related via trade and administration (cf. Hopkins 1980, 19). Edwards matches this description of the urban-rural relationship with the NAA analyses of Adan-Bayewitz, asserting that "this suggests that a reciprocal market relationship between

---

[11] As discussed below, this picture of the negative influence of Antipas on rural life is expanded further in Crossan and Reed 2001.

village and city existed" (Edwards 1988, 174, cf. Edwards 1992, 56–57). Furthermore, "villages and rural areas in Lower Galilee had the advantage of markets for their own produce as well as the ability to buy goods not readily available in their own village markets" (Edwards 1988, 176). Edwards does not deny, however, that both economic growth and depression were a part of the Galilean economy. Actually, while the initial phase of Antipas' building activity might have "boosted the local economy" (Edwards 1992, 63), a depression possibly occurred when this activity was completed in the 20s CE and intensified further by Antipas' failures in his foreign policy leading to the destruction of his army in the battle with the Nabateans (cf. Edwards 1992, 62–65). The crucial point, however, is that such a decline would have had an impact on both rich and poor, and thus "created an atmosphere of perceived if not real decline in the standard of living of both the elite and peasant classes" (Edwards 1992, 64). Rather than depicting a sharp dividing line between the urban and rural sphere, Edwards sees a close interaction including a common destiny on the economic level.

This argument is continued in an article written in association with P. Richardson. While it is accepted that some degree of hostility was felt between the classes (Richardson and Edwards 2002, 265), the archaeological material speaks against the presumed rural-urban animosity implied in the work of R. Horsley and others. For one thing, virtually no fortresses are attested in Galilee in the Herodian period, which suggests "that banditry was not as endemic as some have suggested" (Richardson and Edwards 2002, 254). Furthermore, while it is accepted that heavy urbanization would imply exploitation of peasants, it is argued that the archaeological evidence does not reveal any heavy urbanization in the first century:

The more important movements towards urbanism in the east were earlier, in the late Hellenistic period (roughly the second century B.C.E), and later, in the middle Roman period (the second century C.E.)... Both Sepphoris and Tiberias were fairly modest cities in the first century, only a fraction of the later second- and third-century cities. (Richardson and Edwards 2002, 254–255)

On the contrary, it is argued on the basis of the excavations in Yodefat that "rural village life expanded and improved at the same time that urbanization was proceeding at Sepphoris and Tiberias... Decline in village life, abandonment of houses, and reduction of opportunities does not seem apparent" (Richardson and Edwards 2002, 265). Finally, Richardson and Edwards also assert that the monetization of the period is exaggerated since most of the coins circulating were Hasmonean with "relatively few Herodian" coins in play (Richardson and Edwards 2002, 255). Instead they argue in accordance with Andrea M. Berlin that the resistance of the Galileans is best attested in the private sphere as the kind of 'covert resistance' expressed in reclamation of traditional culture insisting on using special forms of pottery, special kinds of coins, intensive focus on ritual purity etc. (Richardson and Edwards 2002, 248ff.).[12]

In a forthcoming article, Edwards reinforces his thesis of a vibrant and dynamic rural Galilee. With reference to a new field study of settlement dynamics in Upper Galilee (Frankel et al. 2001), he states against Horsley that

...villages were neither static nor generally long-lived. In the upper Galilee alone over a quarter of villages went out of existence in the transition from the Hellenistic to the Roman period... This makes difficult the oft-cited maxim that villages served as repositories for long held traditions. So-called "little traditions" may develop but as likely reflect the memories of new settlers on the land. (Edwards Forthcoming, 12–13)

Instead it is concluded:

Early Roman Galilean villages participated in the economic opportunities and dangers inherent in a Mediterranean system. They operated fully within a vibrant economic environment under Herod Antipas that witnessed an expansion in population, agricultural activity and a variety of structures ranging from public buildings, to frescoed private dwellings to olive presses and specialty goods like ceramics, stone vessels or dove production. Transactions through storage or distribution occurred on a variety of levels that included market activity. Agrarian transactions in wheat and oil, wages of artisans and agricultural workers, and even taxes contributed to a dynamic economy. Villagers as well as urban dwellers participated in the benefits as well as the risks of that economy. (Edwards Forthcoming, 13)

The same picture of Galilee is presented by the Israeli archaeologist M. Aviam, who has conducted archaeological field work and surveys in Galilee for 25 years. The results have been summarised in a new book (Aviam 2004b) and in the important article, "First Century Jewish Galilee: An Archaeological Perspective" (Aviam 2004a). One of Aviam's main points is to understand Early Roman Galilee in the light of the Hasmonean takeover of Galilee, which left a dramatic impact on the material data. Up until that time, a special kind of vessel, which he names "Galilean coarse ware" was particularly common in Upper Galilee (cf. the map in Aviam 2004a, 9). However, it disappears by the end of the second century BCE, thus strongly suggesting that it was "produced by the pagan population in Galilee during the Persian and Hellenistic periods" (Aviam 2004a, 7, cf. Frankel et al. 2001, 61f, 132). To summarize, according to Aviam the Hasmonean takeover meant three things: (a) a rise in the number of settlements: "In the reign of Alexander Jannaeus, or perhaps even earlier, under

---

[12] The question of 'covert resistance' and the work of Berlin will be discussed in section 7.2.2.

Judah Aristobulus, Jewish settlements began to spring up all over the Galilee" (Aviam 1993, 453, cf. also Frankel et al. 2001, 126–140 for Upper Galilee specifically); (b) the beginning of mass production of olive oil in large installations: "The Hasmoneans repopulated Galilee with Jewish inhabitants, among them Judaeans, who probably brought with them the knowledge of olive cultivation and the new technology of the mechanized oil press" (Aviam 2004b, 56); and (c) widespread use of Hasmonean coinage, which is by far the most common form of coinage throughout the Early Roman period (cf. Aviam 2004a, 14).

Another important point for Aviam concerns the Galilee of Antipas. Two things are noted. On the one hand, the development of urban areas of Galilee was carried out, since Antipas, unlike Herod the Great, invested in the area. Thus, "a great change took place in Galilee in the first century CE. Herod Antipas built "Hellenistic-Roman"-style cities in the tradition of his father's activities" (Aviam 2004a, 15). Aviam asserts that "archaeological excavations have uncovered significant remains from the first century CE in both capitals of Galilee" (Aviam 2004a, 16). In the case of Tiberias, Aviam refers to the theatre, which he thinks might be first century (contrary to the excavator, cf. section 5.3.2), the monumental round towers and the cardo in Tiberias. In the case of Sepphoris, Aviam refers to the theatre, the foundation of the cardo, and the first stage of the aqueduct (Aviam 2004a, 16). On the other hand, Aviam argues that the period of Antipas was a period of peace and prosperity: "His 39–year reign was peaceful and probably contributed much to the expansion and strengthening of both structures and society in general. During these days the town of Yodefat spread downhill and reached its maximum size" (Aviam 2004b, 315, cf. Aviam 2004a, 21ff.). This assertion is, according Aviam, supported archaeologically by the fact that virtually no fortresses existed in Galilee in this period (cf. Aviam 2004b, 103ff.).[13]

---

[13] A recent study by Karl-Heinrich Ostmeyer also argues for a relatively stable and quiet Galilee during the period of Herod Antipas: "Alles in allem zeichnete sich die Herrschaft des Antipas durch außergewöhnliche Stabilität aus, und das „sub Tiberio quies" des Tacitus (Hist. 5,9) trifft insbesondere für seine Tetrarchie zu" (Ostmeyer 2005, 156), and against the trend in the newest Jesus research, Ostmeyer concludes: "Die Entwicklungen in der neueren Galiläaforschung geben Anlass, verbreitete Klischees zu überdenken. Das Umfeld Jesus präsentiert sich weit weniger spektakulär, als vielfach vorausgesetzt wird. Die Bevölkerung Galiläas war keine von den Römern unterdrückte und von Großgrundbesitzern ausgebeutete Masse; von einem Dahinvegetieren einer hungerleidenden Mehrheit am Rande des Existenzminimums kann keine Rede sein" (Ostmeyer 2005, 168).

1.2.3 'A Picture of Conflict' – Parasitic Urban-Rural Relations

It is evident from the examination above that the scholars arguing for 'a picture of harmony' rely heavily on the archaeological material; and indeed most of them have conducted one or more excavations in Galilee. As will become evident below, the advocates of 'a picture of conflict' to a larger extent utilize various sociological models when interpreting the material data. This is true of Sean Freyne (in his later works), M. Moreland, Richard L. Horsley, J.D. Crossan and William E. Arnal, whose arguments will be evaluated as representatives of the picture of Early Roman Galilee that stresses conflict, hostility and a spiral or slide of increasing debt and tenancy.

Several of Sean Freyne's later works concentrate on the urban-rural relationship, and in these works he changes his overall view of the political and economic situation of Antipas' Galilee (cf. especially Freyne 1992; Freyne 1995; Freyne 1997b). In his article from 1992, "Urban-Rural Relations in First-Century Galilee: Some Suggestions from the Literary Sources", Freyne distinguishes between what he calls orthogenetic cities and heterogenetic cities. While the former represent a static conservative tradition, the latter represent a new type of economic system and a world view based on foreign ideas (cf. the table in Freyne 1992, 77). Based mainly on literary sources, Freyne categorizes Sepphoris and Tiberias as the heterogenetic type – or at least this is how they were perceived in the local rural community. Though he sees it as an exaggeration to describe the rural-urban relationship as "uniformly hostile", he argues "that the rural animosities toward the cities were deep-seated and permanent" (Freyne 1992, 83). In Galilee there were two distinctive environments, and "each had its own identity, values, and norms" (Freyne 1992, 90).

With the article from 1995, Freyne incorporates an increased amount of archaeological data in the discussion, specifically the excavations in Sepphoris, Adan-Bayewitz's NAA analyses and Hanson's study of Tyrian coinage in Upper Galilee. On the one hand, Freyne acknowledges that these studies seem to document an extensive trade that was "both inter-regional and inter-ethnic" (Freyne 1995, 602), and that they "suggest a pattern of co-operation between the city and the villages in the hinterland that would appear to rule out any idea of tension between them" (Freyne 1995, 605). Likewise, the lack of pagan religious symbols in the first-century stratum of Sepphoris, combined with its market facilities, gives an impression of the city that does not support the idea of it being "a hostile centre for Jewish peasants" (Freyne 1995, 605). Therefore, "Sepphoris, on the basis of this evidence, could not be seen as a typical "consumer" city parasitically related to its hinterland, since it provided a market outlet for the village wares" (Freyne 1995, 605). On the other hand, however, Freyne spends the rest of the article relating the archaeological findings to textual material. Archaeological material is not "the 'hard' facts" (Freyne 1995, 598), but is in need of interpretation as well, and "at this point, a more general model of urban-rural relations can help in sorting out and interpreting the data, rather than simply juxtaposing discrete pieces of evidence" (Freyne 1995, 605). Drawing most of his material from Josephus' *Life*, Freyne concludes that

> ...the picture emerging from this discussion is one in which considerable tensions can be presupposed between Sepphoris and Tiberias on the one hand, and the Galilean rural hinterland on the other. This is essentially because they represented two very different value systems which could not easily co-exist, since the success of the one was dependent on the destruction of the other." (Freyne 1995, 609)

This, in turn, is exactly why Jesus avoided the two centres of Herodian ideology and world view. Freyne thus changes his earlier presentation of first-century Galilee that downplayed the amount of urban exploitation of the peasants and the amount of social banditry seen as features much more present in Judea than in Galilee (Freyne 1988b, 163–167, for instance).

The debate between an archaeological- and a textual-oriented approach is continued in Freyne's article from 1997, "Town and Country Once More" (Freyne 1997b). Questioning the proposed objectivity of archaeological data, and the arguments for a high interaction between city and village as argued by James F. Strange, Freyne states, on the basis of the literary evidence, that

> ...both Sepphoris and Tiberias functioned heterogenetically as far as Galilean peasants were concerned, not because they were gentile enclaves in a Jewish hinterland..., but because, as Herodian centres, they represented an intrusion to a more traditional way of life, by a new type of Hellenised (or Romanised) Jew who was prepared to collaborate with an alien Roman system as its power-brokers. (Freyne 1997b, 50)

Thus, Herod Antipas is placed right at the centre of Freyne's view of the historical Jesus. In another article from 1997, "Galilean Questions to Crossan's Mediterranean Jesus" (Freyne 1997a), Freyne criticizes Crossan for the lack of an intimate perspective of what went on in Galilee in the early first century: "Antipas' reign, therefore, marked the rapid development of the Galilean economy along lines that were directly opposed to the Jewish patrimonial ideal" (Freyne 1997a, 80). In this way, it is indeed the Galilee of Antipas "which provides the best context for explaining the emergence of the Jesus movement and the particular form of social critique that it embodied" (Freyne 1997a, 90). Thus, the role of Antipas differs from that presented in his earlier works.

In the important article, "Herodian Economics in Galilee. Searching for Suitable Model", originally published in 1995, Freyne considers why it is possible to arrive at such different descriptions of the urban-rural interactions of first-century Galilee based on the same sources (Freyne 2000b, 86). To further this discussion, Freyne promotes the use of sociological models, which have the ability to make our "presuppositions explicit", as well helping "in assembling and organizing the scattered pieces of data at our disposal and in uncovering the missing links" (Freyne 2000b, 87–88). Freyne briefly considers how various models have been proposed ranging from the model of Finley describing the cities as "parasitic on the countryside in a highly exploitative way" (Freyne 2000b, 89) to the works of Hopkins, which describe the cities "as production centres, giving rise to a commercial class who were able to pay the rural population for their produce" (Freyne 2000b, 90). To Freyne, this debate highlights the need for a model which on the one hand avoids setting up rigid oppositions, and on the other does not reduce the urban-rural differences to "a meaningless tautology" (Freyne 2000b, 90). The fundamental assumption of Freyne is that in Antipas' Galilee "some further far-reaching and rapid forms of change were occurring that had a strong economic component built into them", which again provide "the immediate context in which to understand the ministry of Jesus" (Freyne 2000b, 91). During the reign of Herod the Great, Galilee seems to have been left comparatively undisturbed. Thus, "it was only with Antipas that the full effects of the Romanisation of the Augustian age were felt directly in Galilee" (Freyne 2000b, 95). In order to test the impact of the changes taking place under Antipas, Freyne introduces the model worked out by T.F. Carney (Carney 1975). It is designed to discern when 'rapid changes' occur in a society, which happens when three key elements (or 'probe zones') are affected at the same time. These are *specialisation*, *monetization*, and *attitudinal changes* in the market (cf. Freyne 2000b, 91), and it is Freyne's aim to investigate whether these three changes are traceable in the sources to early-first-century Galilee:

Regarding specialisation, Freyne finds evidence that growing market awareness occurred as a result of the refurbishment of Sepphoris and the founding of Tiberias. Though archaeological material on landowning patterns and other factors is sparse (Freyne 2000b, 99), it is assumed that the needs of these two cities could only be satisfied through an intensified agricultural production, which must have meant intensified monocropping for surplus. At the same time, Freyne does not ignore the fact that the market could have provided economic benefits for the peasants as well (cf. Freyne 2000b, 95–103).

Regarding monetization, Freyne collects the archaeological evidence for a wide use of Tyrian coins in both Upper and Lower Galilee. Though neither Tiberias nor Sepphoris struck their own coins until later, and though relatively few coins of Antipas seem to have been issued, Freyne finds evidence in the Gospels for a wide use of the smaller bronze coins in everyday life. Taken together, these things "point firmly toward a monetised economy which is dominated by trading links with Tyre, even though local trading within Galilee and with the Golan region was also thriving" (Freyne 2000b, 108).

Finally, regarding attitudinal changes in the market, Freyne refers to the later economic component in the internal upheavals during the war of 66–70 CE (cf. *Ant.* 20.181, 206–207; *Life* 63). Though matters at the time of Antipas "had not yet come to such a pass" (Freyne 2000b, 109), there are several glimpses in the Gospels of gross inequality (Matt 11:9ff.; Luke 7:25ff.; Mark 12:7ff.). Once again, Sepphoris and Tiberias are to blame: "What was new about them was that they had introduced into the heart of lower Galilee in a relatively short space of time people whose values clashed directly with those on which the Jewish peasants' lives had operated" (Freyne 2000b, 111). In conclusion, Freyne asserts that the renewal movement represented by Jesus is best understood as a reaction against the rapid changes taking place under Antipas, which the model of Carney has helped point out as the "immediate historical context" for the Jesus movement (Freyne 2000b, 113). Thus, "the proposal is that Jesus and his renewal movement are best understood as offering another set of values in addition to the two competing ones which we have seen within the social world of Antipas' Galilee" (Freyne 2000b, 112).

In Freyne's most recent book from 2004, *Jesus, A Jewish Galilean*, the exploitative role of Sepphoris and Tiberias seems to be even more pronounced:

The building projects of Herod Antipas in Galilee were inevitably a drain on the resources of the region, material as well as human. More significant than the buildings, however, was the introduction of a new element into the population who are encountered occasionally in the gospels as the Herodians. These represented new elite and retainer classes, replacing the old Hasmoneans who had resisted Herod and had paid the price eventually. The new cities, even when the majority of their inhabitants were Jewish, were alien to and parasitical on the surrounding territory. An urban culture introduced new types into the population, scribal administrators, military personnel, and others in various retainer roles, acting on behalf of the ruling elite and the native aristocracy. It also made new demands for goods and services – thereby, increasing the burden of taxation on the peasantry. This pressure from the top inevitably led to an increase in the levels of poverty, and the slide from landowner to tenant farmer to day labourers, to beggars, all characters we hear of in Jesus' parables, was inexorable. As always in such situations it is the poor who are most vulnerable, exposed to the effects of disease and dispossession. These conditions are the breeding ground for violent outbursts of hostility and pillaging, and it is no surprise to find that one of the effects of the Herodian rule was the increase of what has been described as 'social banditry'. This phenomenon has been defined as pre-political and rural-based, arising in conditions of major upset in the social equilibrium, when the official instruments of control are weak and unable to act swiftly and decisively, and its applicability to first-century Galilean conditions seems in general appropriate. (Freyne 2004, 134–135)

Thus, Freyne changes his description of Antipas from being a buffer against direct Roman rule and exploitation, to being the immediate cause of the Jesus movement due to the economic and social "slide" his programme of urbanisation created within the rural population. In contrast to his earlier descriptions, Freyne does now perceive the impact of Antipas' reign as an *inevitable* factor of drainage of resources with "social banditry" as the consequence much in line with what was argued by Horsley (as also noted in Freyne 2004, 136–139).[14]

Milton Moreland has presented an investigation similar to that of Freyne, only utilizing another sociological model worked out by James C. Scott (Scott 1976).[15] According to Moreland, Scott's model is more in line with Finley's view of the parasitic nature of the urban environment, than with Hopkin's description of a reciprocal urban-rural relationship (Moreland 2002b, 1, note 1). Scott's model is centred on four key elements, which together describe the peasant ideology as:

(1) an overarching desire for safety; (2) a need for risk-sharing measures; (3) a generally negative impact of administrative urban centers on their agrarian villages; and (4) a common lack of overt resistance measures against the new administrative controls. (Moreland 2004, 39)

The result of Moreland's application of this model to Early Roman Galilee is highly interesting, since it suggests that the model's implied indicators of parasitic urban-rural relations were not present in early-first-century Galilee, which fared better than elsewhere: Regarding the 'safety-first' principle, the peasants of Galilee were 'blessed' with very fertile lands, a mild climate, trade opportunities of small-scale artisan production, and fishing opportunities for those living next to the lake. Moreland states with reference to Fiensy 1991 and Safrai 1994: "While certainly not risk-free, the Galilean peasant had several options available during times of extreme conditions that would have provided a very basic safety net" (Moreland 2004, 42). Regarding risk-sharing measures, Moreland asserts that Galilee was organised around a network of villages, which remained intact even

---

[14] In all fairness, it must also be noted that Freyne warns against a heavy reliance on sociological models, and instead seeks at "employing sociology as a tool to provoke interesting questions rather than to provide a framework for a re-telling of the Jesus story in its Galilean setting" (Freyne 2004, 17).

[15] Moreland has published his findings in two articles, Moreland 2001; Moreland 2004, of which the last is based on a unpublished paper presented at the annual SBL meeting 2003 (Moreland 2002b). In the forthcoming number of *Semeia*, Moreland will present his views in a rewritten form (Moreland Forthcoming).

after the establishment of Sepphoris and Tiberias. Such a setting provided a good environment for a common risk-sharing among the peasants, including their patrons as well, as long as they lived in the area. Regarding the impact of the urban centres, Moreland states that though they potentially meant an "increase in taxation, administrative structures, absentee landlordism, a gradual monetization of the economy, and shifts in the traditional forms of peasant farming... there are signs that suggest a substantial amount of stability prevailed in the region, at least from the late 20s to the late 50s CE" (Moreland 2004, 42). Moreland backs this observation by stressing the lack of evidence of fortresses in the region from this period, the lack of evidence of major natural disasters, the lack of evidence of extreme wealth on display in either Sepphoris or Tiberias, and finally the lack of evidence of major peasant revolts. Finally, regarding the overt means of resistance, Moreland concludes that the regular overt mode of social banditry did not exist in Galilee during the Antipas period. Actually, Scott has observed that urbanization in the short run "is generally a condition of more prosperous economic times" (Moreland 2004, 43). Thus, Moreland balances his description between the picture of conflict given by Horsley and others, and the picture of trade and mutual enrichment given by Edwards and others, pointing out that "we must avoid overstating the types and extent of exploitation in Early Roman Galilee. No doubt the peasants were oppressed, but to claim that they were pressed to the limits of survival is not supportable" (Moreland 2002b, 14).[16]

In a series of articles and books, Richard A. Horsley has contributed to the study of the socio-economic conditions of Ancient Galilee. Important points in his vast production concern the following three issues: (a) In several of his early works, Horsley deals with the political conditions of ancient Israel. As discussed above (cf. section 1.1.2), Horsley agrees with Freyne and others that no structured rebel group of zealots was formed right up until the war. Instead there was a pre-political unorganized mode of resistance among the peasants occupied by "righting wrongs" (Horsley 1988, 185), i.e. "social banditry". This early work is mostly confined to detailed studies of Josephus (Horsley 1979b; Horsley 1979a; Horsley 1981; Horsley 1984; Horsley and Hanson 1985; Horsley 1988; Horsley 1986; Horsley 1993). (b) Horsley later expanded this approach by adopting in-

---

[16] At one point, Moreland even aligns his own views concerning the archaeological material describing the urban-rural interaction with those of Edwards and Adan-Bayewitz in contrast to Horsley, Crossan and others (cf. Moreland 2001, 565). He nevertheless maintains that "the growth and development of Sepphoris and Tiberias in the Early Roman period must have been consequential for the ecomomic conditions of the Galilee," not least due to their ideological impact, which "disturbed the world view of the Galilean residents" (Moreland 2001, 568).

sights from social sciences, underlining the elite's exploitation of the peasant class by extracting the surplus (outspoken in Horsley 1989 and a permanent part of the later works). (c) In an array of works including several
articles (Horsley 1994; Horsley 1995b; Horsley 1995a; Horsley 1999) and
two monographs (Horsley 1995c; Horsley 1996), Horsley focuses on first-
century Galilee as the background for his picture of the historical Jesus
movement. In these works, the input from archaeology becomes increasingly dominant (especially in Horsley 1996), and the material culture is
spoken of as "a whole new source of information" (Horsley 1996, viii).
Besides a critical hermeneutical debate with the archaeologists on the interpretation of the archaeological material (cf. below), Horsley investigates
what kind of setting first-century Galilee provides for the historical Jesus.
Much effort is devoted to defending A. Alt's thesis of the Galileans as
remnants of the old Israelite tribes, and to refuting the picture of a highly
cosmopolitan Galilee (cf. section 1.1.2).

A prominent issue in all of Horsley's works concerns the urban-rural relationship. On a three-fold basis, Horsley strongly criticizes the idea of a
reciprocal relationship including heavy trade and interaction. First, Horsley
rejects the proposed implications of the NAA analyses of Adan-Bayewitz
and the findings of Tyrian coins in Upper Galilee. With regard to the latter,
Horsley insists that it takes a process of interpretation to proceed from the
finds of artefacts such as coins to a conclusion that the trade between Tyre
and Galilee was profitable (Horsley 1994, 105). Tyrian coins seem to have
been the standard monetary unit in the Levant, used even in the temple.
Thus, "if Tyre was a major supplier of money in the Levant, then the inci-
dence of Tyrian coins in Upper Galilee would have been nothing unusual
and would not imply trade with Tyre" (Horsley 1996, 69). Regarding
Adan-Bayewitz's analyses of pottery, Horsley acknowledges the method's
ability to expose a pattern of distribution, and thus a pattern of trade. However, there are several modifiers. Most importantly, pottery is not a good
indicator of wide-scale trade, since good clay was restricted to special areas, making trade and transport of pottery an obvious necessity (Horsley
1996, 72). Furthermore, Horsley finds indicators in the Rabbinical material
implying that the distribution of pottery did not take place under conditions
similar to a modern open-market system, but through a fixed-price system
without much contact between supplier and buyer (Horsley 1996, 71;
Horsley 1995b, 224). Therefore it is unlikely "that we can extrapolate from
the distribution of Kefar Hananya pottery to a more general system of
commercial and cultural interaction" (Horsley 1994, 111), underlined also
by the fact that "the appearance of the pottery varies inversely with dis-

tance from Kefar Hananya itself, not Sepphoris or Tiberias" (Horsley 1995b, 224).[17]

Second, as already mentioned, Horsley has analysed Josephus in an attempt to find evidence of any upheaval and social unrest. While admitting that the sources do not justify a description of Galilee as the place for a long-standing zealot resistance group, there is evidence of a pre-political wave of social banditry. Horsley sees the upheavals in Galilee as a result of the Roman suppression:

> The activities of Hezekiah and his brigands can be easily understood as the product of fifteen years of social disruption and dislocation caused by the Roman conquest and re-organization of Palestine, and the ensuing civil war in Palestine as well as in the Roman Empire (including the struggles among Hasmonean factions). (Horsley 1988, 188)

In turn, this meant great hostility between city and village. Thus, Horsley concludes with references to Josephus' *Life* that "far from suggesting cultural continuity, the literary evidence for Galilee at the time of Jesus indicates sustained tension and even overt conflict between cities and the Galilean peasantry" (Horsley 1995b, 225).

Third, these conclusions based on Josephus are substantiated by the introduction of sociological models. Horsley does not portray trade as a factor of importance in the rural environment of first-century Galilee. Self-sufficiency was the primary principle (Horsley 1996, 70). This coupled with Finley's description of the city as "the consumer city" paves the way for a substantiation of a hostile urban-rural relationship. Galilee's new city centres would have struck at the core of village life through a spiral of taxes, loans and indebtedness, namely the ability to uphold a self-sufficient life through polycropping. This precisely underlines the crucial effect of Antipas' urbanization programme, which "would have meant an unusually heavy economic burden on the Galilean and Perean peasantry" (Horsley 1994, 110). In this way "Antipas intensified the structural political-economic conflict in Galilee" (Horsley 1996, 36).

Consequently, this view of a heavy economic stress in the wake of Antipas' reign is emphasized in three recent books concerned with the historical Jesus and the New Testament, in which Antipas is interpreted as *the* decisive factor, which explains why Jesus formed a renewal and protest movement (Horsley and Silberman 1997; Horsley and Draper 1999;

---

[17] This is noted by Adan-Bayewitz himself: "However, although Kefar Hananya ware is plentiful throughout the Galilee, a decrease in the relative quantities of Kefar Hananya ware is evident with the increasing distance from the manufacturing centre" (Adan-Bayewitz and Perlman 1990, 158). For the same reason, Crossan also finds the NAA analyses of little use in establishing an argument for intensive trade through market centres in Tiberias and Sepphoris (Crossan 1999, 224–225).

Horsley 2001). Antipas was essentially "Remaking the Galilee" (Horsley and Silberman 1997, 22), a view advanced by the following four arguments: (a) Antipas' new cities, described "as centers of Roman-Hellenistic culture" (Horsley and Draper 1999, 58), hit the central nerve of the old established life:

> For Jesus and his Galilean neighbors and kinsfolk, Antipas's programs of city-building and tax collection were not simply dangerous threats to their livelihoods and time-honored techniques of farming and fishing: they posed an unprecedented attack on the very basis of the village culture that they and their ancestors had faithfully maintained for hundreds of years. (Horsley and Silberman 1997, 26)

(b) Following this, it is stated without much argument that "the impact of Antipas' direct rule in Galilee, both political-economic and cultural, *must have* been intense, particularly during the generation of Jesus and his followers" (italics added), since

> ...it would be a projection of early modern times to imagine that the Galilean peasants received any mutual benefits from these cities suddenly imposed on the landscape or even that they interacted in any active way with Sepphoris and Tiberias – other than rendering up their produce in taxes, of course." (Horsley and Draper 1999, 58–59)

Without citing the sources, it is claimed that, "the evidence drawn from rabbinic literature and from legal documents of the period suggests that rural indebtedness dramatically increased throughout the Herodian period, with desperate farmers seeking loans from the officials of the Herodian administration and the priestly aristocracy" (Horsley and Silberman 1997, 28). (c) The bronze coins of Antipas are also interpreted as expressing Antipas' own political ambitions and messianic dreams:

> With a palm branch stamped on one side (calling to mind biblical descriptions of the fertility of the Land of Israel) and a Roman laurel wreath on the other (symbolizing the *auctoritas* and *dignitas* of the world-conquering Emperor Tiberius), the coins issued by Herod Antipas gave symbolic expression to his own political ambitions and messianic dreams. (Horsley and Silberman 1997, 22)

In this way "Antipas believed that his people's best route to salvation was through aggressive economic development, not religious fundamentalism", so, "if anyone was seeking the Kingdom of God, Antipas was eager to show that the era of its fulfilment had arrived" (Horsley and Silberman 1997, 35–36). (d) Finally, as a result of Antipas' economic pressure, his reorganization of the established way of life and the religious overtones in his rule, a reaction of resistance and renewal was produced from below and manifested in John the Baptist and Jesus: "It cannot be coincidental... that the prophet John the Baptist condemned Antipas (*Ant.* 18.116–119) and that Jesus and his movement emerged in Galilee under Antipas" (Horsley and Draper 1999, 59). In contrast to Antipas, "Jesus did not believe that the Kingdom of God would arrive with fire and brimstone. And he was convinced that he would not need aqueducts, palaces, coins, marble columns, or soldiers to utterly remake Galilee" (Horsley and Silberman 1997, 42). Thus, according to Horsley, Jesus is best interpreted in the light of the old northern Israelite tradition of social resistance against the unjust ruler as explicitly manifested in the prophet Amos (cf. Horsley 2001, 35–36; Horsley and Draper 1999, 59).

John Dominic Crossan is another historical Jesus scholar who utilizes sociological models to interpret the sources. Crossan is well aware of the potential problems involved in using models, but does so "to eliminate the danger of imposing presuppositions from advanced industrial experience on the world of an ancient agrarian empire" (Crossan 1991, 44–45). In his study, *The Historical Jesus* (1991), Crossan confines his use of models to the work of Gerhard Lenski, which according to Crossan balances between a functional tradition and a conflict tradition, i.e., between an approach emphasizing the interests that unite city and village (functional) and the interests that divide them (conflict, cf. Crossan 1991, 44). In his later work, *The Birth of Christianity*, Crossan incorporates more models, especially the work of John H. Kautsky, into what he calls "the Lenski-Kautsky model" (Crossan 1999, 152). This shifts the emphasis to the conflict approach. While Lenski's model divides the ancient agrarian society into two different strata with several sub-classes, Kautsky's model distinguishes between a traditional and a commercializing agrarian society. From Lenski, Crossan concludes that social inequality between the two different strata is enlarged through three things: urbanization, monetization and scribalization. In a society marked by a growing emphasis on these three things, the lowest class in the low stratum, "the expendable class", will have a steady supply of people being forced down from the classes just above, such as landless peasants and workless artisans (cf. Crossan 1999, 153). A society marked by these forces is, in the terms of Kautsky, commercialized: "In a traditional agrarian empire, the aristocracy takes the *surplus* from the peasantry; in a commercializing agrarian empire, the aristocracy takes the *land* from the peasantry" (Crossan 1999, 157). In conclusion, Crossan states that "the Lenski-Kautsky model indicates that peasant resistance escalates as rural commercialization encroaches on the traditional peasant way of life, breaches the safety net of kinship relations and village contacts, and changes the land from inalienable family inheritance to negotiable business commodity" (Crossan 1999, 166). In connection with this, Crossan stresses that the term "peasant" is neither neutral nor a mere synonym for "farmer". While the concept of a farmer may denote a rural, independent, isolated small-plot landowner, a peasant is defined as a rural small-plot landowner or tenant paying for the consumption of the city. "A peasant is, quite simply, an *exploited* farmer" (Crossan 1999, 158). In relation to Kautsky, Crossan denounces any talk about mutuality in the urban-rural relationship and states (in italics) that "*peasants and cities go hand in hand. They are the necessarily twin sides of an oppressive or exploitative system*" (Crossan 1999, 218). Thus, this "model warns us against presuming that new cities are good news for the local peasants" (Crossan 1999, 218–219).

Against the background of these sociological considerations, Crossan enters into a debate with Galilean archaeologists in a three-fold way. First, Crossan rejects Batey's placing of Jesus in a "romantic urban environment" (Crossan 1999, 215). Likewise, both Strange's and Meyers' unproblematic view of the urban-rural relationship is denounced. They fail to account for the distinct implication of the word 'peasant' in contrast to 'farmer', and by leaving out insights from cross-cultural anthropology they miss the fact that "the quite predictable result of commercialization through urbanization... is heightening tension between peasant and city" (Crossan 1999, 217).

Second, in *The Birth of Christianity* (Crossan 1999, 223–230) as well as in an article awaiting publication, "The Relationship between Galilean Archaeology and Historical Jesus Research" (Crossan Forthcoming), Crossan engages in a debate with Adan-Bayewitz on how to interpret the socio-economic implications of his NAA analyses in the same way as Horsley. While Crossan accepts the analyses' prediction of trade between rural production centres and urban market centres, he rejects this as proof of the existence of "entrepreneurial potters" and "enhanced traders" (Crossan Forthcoming, 3). Adan-Bayewitz fails to take the consequence of the cross-cultural ceramic anthropological study of Dean Arnold, which he cites. According to Crossan's reading of Arnold, potters were not part of a trade boom, but on the contrary part of the class into which indebted and now landless peasants fell: "those village ceramicists were not daring entrepreneurs but desperate farmers" (Crossan Forthcoming, 3). Thus, Crossan strongly opposes the proposal of Adan-Bayewitz that his analyses imply a rejection of urban-peasant exploitation (cf. Adan-Bayewitz and Perlman 1990, 171–172). Instead, according to Crossan, the utilization of cross-cultural anthropology should have warned against such "romantic generalizations" (Crossan 1999, 229).

Third, Crossan applies his cross-cultural approach to the archaeological findings in Sepphoris and Tiberias. Not surprisingly, Crossan considers the impact of such two new cities on the relatively small area of Galilee to be rather dramatic. Crossan does not, however, seem to be consistent in his writings. In *The Historical Jesus,* Crossan almost seems to agree with the proposals of Overman, Edwards and Meyers that no "cultural split" existed between the rural areas and the two cities (cf. Crossan 1991, 19). In *The Birth of Christianity,* Crossan questions the description given by Overman and others stating that Roman urbanization meant a slide, which "dislocated the traditional peasant way of life and pushed individuals from poverty into destitution, from small landowner into tenant farmer, from tenant farmer into day-laborer, and from day-laborer into beggar or bandit" (Crossan 1999, 223). The same view is presented in Crossan's book co-authored with Reed, *Excavating Jesus.* While it is maintained in agreement with the earlier investigations of Reed that Galilee did not experience any extreme form of urbanization (cf. Crossan and Reed 2001, 54), the impact of the urbanization process of Antipas is nevertheless described as having been profound:

Estates grew and tenancy increased as economies of scale for cash crops were created. More currency in the Galilean economy facilitated taxation, which funded Antipas's urbanization. The kingdom was being commercialized. Architectural grandeur increased at one end of Galilean society by making poverty increase at the other. Countryside and city, then taxes and frescoes. (Crossan and Reed 2001, 70)

Antipas is thus again placed right in the centre as 'the factor of explanation' of why Jesus 'happened' with a striking similarity to the ideas presented beforehand by Horsley and partly Freyne. The opening question in *Excavating Jesus* is: "Why did Jesus happen when and where he happened?" (Crossan and Reed 2001, xviii, cf. also Crossan and Reed 2001, 80). The answer is that 'they happened' as a direct response to the commercialized kingdom of Antipas, which in every single element was in opposition to Jesus' kingdom of God:

Romanization meant urbanization meant commercialization and, especially with the establishment of Tiberias by the early 20s C.E., the new *Pax Romana's* economic boom struck Lower Galilee fully and forcibly. If we think of covenant rather than commerce, would an Amos have said anything very different to Antipas at Tiberias in the first century than he said to Jeroboam II at Samaria in the eighth century long before? (Crossan and Reed 2001, 114–115)

Based on what are believed to be the earliest layers of Q and on the Gospel of Thomas, Antipas is portrayed as a foil for Jesus against whom Jesus reacted by establishing a totally oppositional community (cf. Crossan and Reed 2001, 135 and elsewhere). In the conclusion of the book, the answer to the initial question is summarized:

The power of the Kingdom of Rome, miniatured in the tetrarchy of Antipas in Galilee, was confronted by the Kingdom of God... It was not a military confrontation... It was, instead, a programmatically non-violent resistance but, emphatically, it confronted present economic, social, and political realities. (Crossan and Reed 2001, 274)

In his book, *Jesus and the Village Scribes: Galilean Conflicts and the Setting of Q,* William E. Arnal has investigated the political, sociological and economic background for the Jesus movement in a similar way to Horsley and Crossan. Arnal also focuses on the hypothetical document Q, and derives its existence from an immediate crisis in the Q community of Galilean origin. To prove this, the central chapter of his book is devoted the "the socioeconomics of Roman Galilee".[18] Beginning with the introduction, the urbanization programme of Antipas is identified as the background for the alleged Q crisis:

> The immediate material context for the rise of the Jesus movement, Q included, is one of socioeconomic crisis. This crisis was caused by a deliberate effort to restructure the northern Galilean local economy along lines more conducive to a monetized Roman imperial economy oriented to both trade and booty. Galilean isolation from the coast had allowed the region a measure of autonomy both social and economic, and thus had, to a degree, allowed geography and the technological limits of ancient transport to put a natural brake on the extent to which the region could be exploited by whatever political power happened to control it. Antipas's foundation of new cities within Galilee, however, most especially Tiberias, put an end to this autonomy and caused significant social and economic changes. It was the foundation of cities and the consequent loss of local autonomy, rather than widespread poverty, Roman military oppression, or rampant Hellenization, that most marked the period and region with which we are concerned. (Arnal 2000, 10–11 cf. also p. 101)

Arnal aims at presenting an in-depth analysis of Antipas' Galilee compensating for earlier Q studies, which to his mind are too broad and imprecise (cf. Arnal 2000, 100). In four subsections, Arnal investigates a number of earlier studies of the written and archaeological sources concerning life in Ancient Galilee, and arrives at the following four conclusions. First, agriculture was by far the most important factor of the ancient Roman society. As noted by Josephus (*War* 3.42–43), Galilee provided good and fertile conditions for such an industry (Arnal 2000, 107).

Second, Arnal stresses that trade, travel and transport were complicated matters in an ancient inland community such as Galilee: "It was ineffective and uneconomical, except in the instance of rare, extremely small, or specialized items, to transport goods for any significant distance over land" (Arnal 2000, 118). Arnal states that this general conclusion is confirmed by the NAA analyses of Adan-Bayewitz. Like Crossan and Horsley, Arnal does not accept the socio-economic implications of the NAA analyses proposed by Adan-Bayewitz himself, which according to Arnal presuppose a modern market model (cf. Arnal 2000, 124). At the same time, Arnal pic-

---

[18] A similar investigation can be found in J. Kloppenborg Verbin's book, *Excavating Q,* in which a central chapter is titled: "Reading Q in the Galilee" (cf. Kloppenborg Verbin 2000).

tures a certain amount of local trade. The existence of pottery from Shiknin and Kefar Hananya in Sepphoris, as well as the description in Josephus of John of Gischala's export of olives to Tyre (*War* 2.591–92 and *Life* 74–75), indicate some kind of trade. "Thus, at the very least, and in contrast to Horsley's conclusions, there appears to have been a fairly elaborate network in place, in spite of technological and geographical difficulties, to channel produce and other goods to the main cities, as well as throughout the region" (Arnal 2000, 127). In conclusion of this sub-section, Arnal makes two points. On the one hand, Galilee at the time of Antipas was marked by a closed economy:

These observations suggest that... trade, especially open trade, need not have been a major factor in their (the two Galilees) economies. Some trade in basic but specialized necessities undoubtedly took place, and surplus product may have been used to acquire the odd luxury or imported good... But the Galilees were marked, in spite of what movement of goods took place, by a closed economy. (Arnal 2000, 132)

On the other hand, building on Safrai 1994, Arnal states that there is evidence for a change to a more open economy during the later Mishnaic period, providing funds for a large-scale synagogue building project throughout the region. "Thus there appears to have been a change in trading patterns over time, a movement from a closed economy to a (more or less) open one" (Arnal 2000, 133 with reference to Safrai 1994, 423).

Third, Arnal focuses on monetization and debt. Evaluating Safrai's survey of hoards (Safrai 1994, 399–401), Arnal states that it can be demonstrated that the use of coins increased from the first century and onwards. Hoards from Migdal and Huara have no coins earlier than 74 CE. "The stark paucity of first-century copper city coins, not only in hoards but in general, does reflect a relatively unmonetized Galilee in the first century" (Arnal 2000, 136). Still, Arnal seems to contradict this statement as well as his description of the economy of Galilee as 'closed' during the period of Antipas, when he proceeds and claims that it was Antipas who monetized Galilee: "The Galilean economy was not especially monetized by the time Antipas came to power but became increasingly so from that point onward, and did so as a result of, or at least with the encouragement of, deliberate political policy" (Arnal 2000, 138). This resulted in increasing debt and tenancy, a conclusion for which Q itself delivers the bulk of the evidence (cf. Arnal 2000, 140).

Fourth, Arnal considers the impact of cities and urbanization. Building on the sociological model of Kautsky, Arnal advocates a parasitic function of the consumer city. However, without presenting much archaeological data or discussion of what kind of cities Sepphoris and Tiberias were during the time of Antipas, Arnal states that they required "a complete reorientation of the Galilean economy toward surplus production and cash cropping (with attendant stimulation of trade and monetization) simply to feed their inhabitants" (Arnal 2000, 147). This impact was especially severe in the case of Tiberias. With a note to Kautsky, Arnal sums it up:

> The moment that the brand-new city of Tiberias went up, however, there would have been a sudden and dramatic effect on the countryside around the lake, and, to a lesser degree, in Upper Galilee. In particular, we would expect this region to experience a drift of goods toward the city (with attendant social effects at the village level), a (forcible) reorientation of agriculture toward urban consumption, progressive monetization of the economy, more frequent use of hired labor, greater efficacy in the extraction of taxes and other dues, incremental concentration of land with resultant tenancy and loss of small-holdings, cash cropping and specialization, greater trade, and a noticeable polarizing of the divide between the relatively wealthy and the very poor. (Arnal 2000, 149–150)

Thus, Arnal adds to the picture of an increasing amount of conflict in the Galilee of Antipas with a deterioration of the urban-rural relationship, just as he emphasizes that Antipas is the immediate background for the Jesus movement and the slightly later Galilean Q community.

1.2.4 The Question of Sociological Models

The outline above of different pictures of Galilee and its urban-rural relationship has illustrated the crucial importance sociological models tend to have on historical reconstruction. Therefore, before a preliminary assessment can be reached, the question of sociological models will have to be examined more closely. Since the 1970s, the use of sociological models and anthropological studies has been increasingly adopted within studies of the New Testament and early Christianity. In short,[19] this enterprise has traceable roots back to "Die Religionsgeschichtliche Schule" (most notably to Ernst Troeltsch) and in the so-called "Chicago School of social analysis" (most notably to Shirley Jackson Case, cf. Martin 1999, 125ff.; Horrell 2002, 4–7), as well as to the regular studies in sociology and anthropology from Max Weber and onwards. Recently, a group titled "The Social Description of Early Christianity" was formed by Leander E. Keck and Wayne A. Meeks under the auspices of the SBL. With interruptions it has been running ever since only now titled "The Social History of Formative Judaism and Christianity" (cf. Osiek 1989, 268). The approach represented by this group is often labelled "social historical". In 1983 another group was formed entitled "Social Sciences and the New Testament Interpretation", eventually to be headed by Bruce J. Malina and John Pilch. This

---

[19] Introductions to the history of and approaches to sociological studies of the New Testament can be found in Osiek 1989; Holmberg 1990; Garrett 1992; Elliott 1993; Hanson and Oakman 1998, xvii-17; Martin 1999; Horrell 1999; Mulholland 2001; Horrell 2002; Turcotte 2002; Blasi 2002; Osiek 2003; deSilva 2004 and others.

group, also known as "the context group", focuses more specifically on the application of social-science models to the data (Osiek 1989, 269), and has been very productive publishing many books and articles.[20] This approach is often labelled "social-scientific". The differences between these two groups with regard to how models should be implemented are followed by a second difficulty, namely *which* kind of model to utilize. Finally, a third problem has been raised in the context of Galilean studies, namely *whether* cross-cultural models resting on data from a different period and a different area should be utilized at all.

Social-Scientific Criticism (SSC) is marked by the use of an explicit model, since the lack of this element would imply the use of an unrealized implicit and anachronistic model derived from our modern society that differs in vital respects from Israel in the Roman period. In the words of Hanson and Oakman: "The use of explicit models is vital to a social-scientific approach... The alternative to employing an explicit model is not working without presuppositions, but employing an implicit model" (Hanson and Oakman 1998, 10, cf. also Esler 2000, 112–113). In a ten-point description of the SSC approach found in Elliott 1993, 36–59, the reason for this is emphasized. Since "social-scientific critics presuppose that all knowledge is socially conditioned and perspectival in nature", it is implied that "the method of analysis must include means for *distinguishing and clarifying the differences between the social location of the interpreter and the social location of the authors and objects to be interpreted*" (Elliott 1993, 36–37). These "means" are theories and models, since "social models are 'maps' that organize selected prominent features of social terrain" (Elliott 1993, 43). Furthermore, a model is described as having a cognitive as well as a heuristic function, which serve "as vehicles for discovery" and "prompt the search for patterns, correlations, and coherency among masses of material" (Elliott 1993, 44).

The approach of 'social historians' is also marked by the use of sociological models, but in a more subdued and cautious manner. One of its advocates, Carolyn Osiek, describes the difference from the social-scientific approach saying that social historians "work at a lower level of abstraction, focusing more on particularity and the interrelationship of social facts, letting the models arise from the ancient texts themselves" (Osiek 1989, 270). Osiek herself lists five objections to an imprudent use of models (Osiek

---

[20] A partial selective list of their many publications includes: Elliott 1993; Hanson 1989b; Hanson 1989a; Hanson 1990; Hanson 1994; Esler 1994; Oakman 1994; Rohrbaugh 1996; Malina 1996; Hanson and Oakman 1998; Pilch 2001; Malina 2001; Stegemann, Malina and Theißen 2002.

1989, 275–276)[21]: (a) The distance in time naturally prevents live observations – the method preferred in regular sociological studies. (b) On top of
this comes the question of how representative our samples of early Christian life and other issues are, taking into consideration the biases of the
texts. (c) There is a further problem related to the aims and focuses of the
texts, since "religious documents are not meant to yield social information" (Osiek 1989, 276). They do not intend to provide the sort of information modern sociological studies are concerned with. (d) It is questionable
how valid it is to perform not only cross-cultural studies, but also studies
that compare material from very different time periods. (e) It is an open
question whether models are inherently limiting and deterministic: "Does
social-science analysis reduce all human culture to the material and economic? Does it function to reinforce a deterministic interpretation of the
dynamic of religious faith?" (Osiek 1989, 276). In conclusion, Osiek states
that social analysis

...used rigidly and exclusively... can isolate us from the text rather than join us to it, by
stressing differences and destroying links. But used in conjunction with historical, literary, and liberation methods, it promises to yield good fruit for the harvest of biblical interpretation." (Osiek 1989, 278)[22]

That is why this approach avoids the word "scientific", preferring to label
the approach as heuristic or hermeneutic (cf. Martin 1999, 131). Anthony
J. Blasi, also from the social historian's group, summarizes this as follows:

In the light of these dilemmas, one should be cautious about social sciences in inquiry
into ancient Christianity. Contemporary social scientific concepts and models are not
"cookie cutters" that can stamp out preestablished shapes in an otherwise formless dough
of ancient information. The social scientific concepts and models are not "answers" to be
substituted for missing evidence but questions. (Blasi 2002, 78)[23]

---

[21] David G. Horrell lists a few similar reservations against the use of models in SSC in
a debate with Philip F. Esler on how to approach ancient sources. See Horrell 2000, 93–
94 and Esler 2000.

[22] Carolyn Osiek has continued the debate with the social scientists, and in a paper
from the Annual SBL Congress in 2003, Atlanta, she performs a critical comparison of
their method of approach with sociologists working on ancient Roman history, concluding that they incorporate the findings of anthropology "with a great deal more caution
than biblical scholars, largely because they have so much more data to go on, and so often do not find the theories or models confirmed there" (Osiek 2003, 13). The same thing
is stated by Horrell in his debate with Esler: "However, anthropologists writing on the
Mediterranean (and elsewhere) in recent years seem to describe their method more in
terms of the humanistic taks of *interpreting* than the 'scientific' one of adopting and test-
ing models" (Horrell 2000, 89).

[23] Naturally, the proponents of a social-scientific approach have reacted to such a

Even if a consensus were to be reached as to how to incorporate models and data, there is still a second question of what model to use. This is an-other area of dispute, and generally speaking two types of model have been utilized in Biblical studies, namely a structural-functionalist model and a conflict model. Drawing on Malina, Osiek writes that "structural function-alism assumes that all the social forces interacting in a given situation work together to create balance or equilibrium, so that when one factor dis-rupts harmony, the others adjust to restore it" (Osiek 1989, 272). Accord-ing to Hanson and Oakman, this approach is based on the philosophical tradition of idealism (Hanson and Oakman 1998, 9). Changes occur when needed. The conflict model, on the other hand, understands the forces at work in a society conceptually differently: "...change is a regular element of social life, producing constant levels of social constraint, so that con-flict, reaction to constraint, rather than consensus or balance is the glue of social life and the cause of change" (Osiek 1989, 272). This approach fo-cuses on the power relations of society, and according to Hanson and Oakman it has close relations to the Marxist materialist tradition (Hanson and Oakman 1998, 9).

As mentioned above, a third problem concerns the very question of the legitimacy of cross-cultural models in Galilean studies. In this connection, Marianne Sawicki's book, *Crossing Galilee: Architectures of Contact in the Occupied Land of Jesus*, is interesting because it voices a three-fold criticism of the way sociological models are applied to the study of first-century Galilee: (a) The models chosen are outdated and abandoned in the regular sociological research; especially the "honour and shame" model, which imports general Mediterranean cultural identity into Palestine, and the "Lenski-Kautsky model", which imports Marxist materialist western ideas on economic constructions (Sawicki 2000, 5–6). In this respect, Bib-lical scholars like Crossan (Sawicki 2000, 66–67), Malina and the Context Group (Sawicki 2000, 75ff.) are outdated since the "social scientists today recognize that earlier "cross-cultural" models covertly generalized Western categories and Western concerns, and were therefore blind to much that was unique and distinctive about particular peoples" (Sawicki 2000, 6). Crossan's utilization of the Lenski-Kautsky model is an example of such a generalization, with the model's inherent conceptions being accepted with-

characterization by stressing that models and data should be read together in a way that does not rank models over data. Hanson and Oakman formulate it this way: "The goal of modelling is not to force data into a preconceived mold or pigeonhole... The idea is to account for the available data, not dispense with data that does not conform to a precon-ceived model... one should work back and forth from data to model and back to data" (Hanson and Oakman 1998, 10–11).

out proof from Galilee itself: "The possibility remains that Galilean farm-workers had mutually beneficial relations with city-dwellers. Data must still be collected from the archaeological record and the textual record in order to pare down that possibility to slime or nil" (Sawicki 2000, 67). (b) Cross-cultural comparisons are inherently reductionstic when confining human activity to "arrows of causality", where "any given state is sup-posed to be completely predictable and explainable" (Sawicki 2000, 6). However, "systems theory cannot adequately interpret individual or collec-tive creative agency" (Sawicki 2000, 6). (c) There is not enough awareness of the fact that models do not deliver new data. According to Sawicki, sys-tems introduce "a priori" a causality "without regard to the particular soci-ety that happens to be under investigation" (Sawicki 2000, 65). In this way, the utilized models carry "the risk of importing its own interest into the ancient materials and mixing them with data" (Sawicki 2000, 37).[24]

In chapter seven we will return briefly to the question of models, but for the time being it can be concluded that the issue of sociological models presents several problems: (a) Within the Galilean research, the different use of models seems to predetermine the different views on the urban-rural relationship. (b) The research on models in connection to Biblical studies is itself divided as to which approach to take on the crucial question of how to relate data and models. (c) There are several different models at hand, and again it is obvious that different models produce different out-comes. (d) Finally, it is debatable whether it is at all appropriate to apply cross-cultural models to a Biblical time period. Consequently, as discussed in the next chapter, the present investigation utilizes a contextual source-oriented approach, which initially focuses on the sources available and thereafter applies an appropriate model, since the models otherwise seem to have a deterministic influence on the results.[25]

---

[24] In opposition to this, Sawicki presents her own approach to first-century Galilee as "a spatial interpretation of Galilee, couched in terms of the indigenous logic of circula-tion" (Sawicki 2000, 61), which "is not a new modelling; it is a discernment of the an-cient modelling" (Sawicki 2000, 62). This indigenous-oriented modelling, based on texts and archaeology, has a central focus on Herod Antipas: "When Jesus was a young man, Antipas re-mapped and re-landscaped Galilee. Tiberias, his new capital, diverted the Babylonian tourist traffic across the Lake and into Galilee. Antipas effectively re-designed the Sea of Galilee into a little Aegean Sea... Herod Antipas turned the Jordan into a little Tiber" (Sawicki 2000, 4, cf. also p. 92–94, 145–147 and 158). In my opinion, Sawicki's own reconstruction of first-century Galilee, though important and provocative, falls short on a number of issues, and does not manage to provide a convincing source-based argumentation for its hypothesis of a spatial reoriented Galilee under Antipas. This will become evident as the investigation proceeds (cf. also the review by M. Moreland, Moreland 2002a).

[25] Cf. also Horrell's reservations when he states: "The problem with starting with a

1.3 Research on Herod Antipas

As demonstrated above, Herod Antipas has become a vital 'factor of explanation' in the Galilean research focusing on the socio-economic conditions of the Early Roman Galilee as a background for the historical Jesus. However, two problems are evident. First, virtually every possible scenario describing the impact of Antipas on the region has been suggested. Thus the question of Antipas is at present at an impasse, as is the question of the urban-rural relationship to which it is closely related. Second, there seems to be a lacuna in the Galilean research concerning the rather fragmentary way Antipas and the sources of his reign are treated. It turns out that no study has so far devoted the space needed to examine the entire body of sources available in a thorough manner with an explicit methodology. Therefore we now turn to the research on Antipas outside the Galilean studies in order to see if it has obtained a more uniform picture.

1.3.1 German Research of the Nineteenth and Early Twentieth Century

As part of the impressive research enterprise in Germany in the ninetienth and early twentieth century, three scholarly studies of Herod Antipas were published. In 1873, M. Brann published a long article on Herod Antipas in connection with a study of the sons of Herod. In 1901, E. Schürer published the last edition of his *Geschichte des jüdischen Volkes im Zeitalter Jesu Christi*, one chapter of which is devoted to Antipas. Finally, W. Otto wrote the entry on Antipas in *Paulus Real-Encyclopädie der Classischen Altertumswissenschaft* published in 1913 in the *Supplementband II*.[26]

Brann's investigation is important as a point of reference for later studies. It is formed more or less as a lengthy paraphrase of the various sources, and examines the life of Antipas sequence by sequence, discussing issues like chronology and the specific meanings of Greek terms. Perhaps the most important thing to note is the outspoken judgment of Antipas' character as slack, lazy, and extremely phlegmatic: "Schon in seiner

---

model is that – despite Esler's protestations – it can lead the researcher to view the evidence in a particular way, or to assume that a certain pattern of conduct must be present. Ignoring the vast cultural differences over both space and time in 'the Mediterranean', a model of Mediterranean social interaction can be used as a kind of 'trump card', which *per se* demonstrates that a particular interpretation must be right, whether or not there is evidence in the text to support it" (Horrell 2000, 90–91). For this reason, Horrell also sees the need to adopt a "contextual and specific rather than a generalized" method of approach (Horrell 2000, 94).

[26] Besides these three studies, William M. Willett published a book entitled *Herod Antipas* in 1866, which is formed as a well-written paraphrase of the various sources on Antipas and the Roman emperors at the time (Willett 1866).

Jugend charakterisert er sich so, wie er sein ganzes Leben hindurch geblieben ist, als schlaff, träge und äußerst phlegmatisch" (Brann 1873, 306). This description is based on his relation to Herodias, which is described as one of dewy-eyed love if not mere stupidity:

> Herodes, von blinder Leidenschaft befangen, gab diesen verfänglichen Punkt nach, ohne zu bedenken, daß er dadurch selber seinem Throne eine hauptstütze raube, ohne zu überlegen, daß er sich den mächtigen und gefährlichen Nachbar zum persönlichen Feinde mache." (Brann 1873, 409)

In a final assessment, Brann states that the fall of the rotten reign of Antipas was grounded in immoral lust as well as greediness: "Durch Sinnlichkeit und Unsittlichkeit war der Grund zum Sturze gelegt worden, Habsucht und Herrschgier hatten den morschen Bau im Nu zusammenstürzen gemacht" (Brann 1873, 474).

Emil Schürer's, *Geschichte des jüdischen Volkes im Zeitalter Jesu Christi*, represents an institution in itself, to which any succeeding inquiry into the historical background of the New Testament is indebted. In the 1970s it was retranslated into English in an updated and rewritten form. In the paragraph on Herod Antipas (section 17.2), however, the new English version is very close to the German original providing mostly updated references to literature (cf. Schürer 1901, 431–449; Schürer 1973, 340–353). The main thrust of Schürer's work is the processing of a vast amount of written material, to which the notes generously refer. The text itself is formed as a rather straightforward treatment of the sources in a chronological manner with a slight touch of the 'moral history writing' as seen in the case of Brann. Thus Schürer describes Antipas saying: "Seinem Charakter nach war Antipas ein ächter Sohn des alten Herodes, klug, ehrgeizig und prachtliebend, nur weniger thatkräftig als der Vater" (Schürer 1901, 432). While Schürer's synopsis of the sources concerning the life of Antipas is fine, the continued value of Schürer's work is found in the footnotes such as his discussion of the connotations of the designation of Antipas as a fox (ἀλώπηξ) in Luke 13:32 (note 5), his discussion of who the four Herodian princes mentioned in Philo *Legat.* 300 might be (note 15), his discussion of the identity of Herodias' former husband (note 19), the several notes spent on the chronology of Antipas' last years in office (note 37–46, note 34–42 in the English edition), as well as his discussion of the information in Dio that Antipas was put to death by Caligula (note 47, note 43 in the English edition).

W. Otto's entry in *Pauly-Wissowa* represents the ultimate in-depth investigation of the written sources concerning the life of Antipas. This entry was not to be surpassed in thoroughness before the dissertation of Hoehner (1972). The account of Otto is influenced by the 'Quellen Kritik' of its time searching for the sources within the source. Following this, Otto tries to chart the sources on Antipas available for Josephus, whom he presumes to have been an uncreative compiler. Otto states that Josephus "über das Regiment der Herodessöhne nur ganz aphoristisch berichtet" because his main sources ran out: "Zwei der Hauptquellen des Josephus für Herodes I., Nikolaos von Damaskos und der jüdische Anonymus, haben offenbar beide Zeit nicht behandelt" (Otto 1913, 172). Otto criticizes the suggestion by Täubler that Josephus should have had access to a particular source on Antipas, a "Memoiren des Herodes Antipas", since he would in that case have provided more information on the entire reign of Antipas and not just the final years as in the case of *Ant.* 18.101ff. Thus, "die eine wirklich genaue Schilderung in § 101ff. muß ihm demnach vielmehr gerade indirect zugeflossen sein. Welches hier die Primärquelle ist, bleibe noch unentschieden" (Otto 1913, 174). In the rest of his essay, Otto performs an investigation similar to that of Schürer, focusing on the following things: a careful analysis of all the sources available, an investigation of the Jewish and the Hellenistic considerations of Antipas marked by the pre-Hengel incompatibility between the two, a careful consideration of chronological issues, and finally a moral assessment of the character of Antipas.

Regarding Antipas' Hellenistic and/or Jewish disposition, Otto finds both Hellenistic and Jewish elements in the reign of Antipas. The Hellenistic elements consist primarily of two things: First, when Antipas adopted the family name, Herod, instead of his personal name, Antipas, he linked himself to "die Traditionen der großen hellenistischen Dynastien" (Otto 1913, 171).[27] Second, there is Antipas' love for luxury manifested in the magnificent building of Tiberias through which he revealed that he was "ganz auf den Bahnen des Vaters" (Otto 1913, 175). Otto states that precisely the foundation of Tiberias is for "die Stellung des Tetrarchen zum Judentum und zum Hellenismus charakteristisch" (Otto 1913, 175). Otto points to five things illustrating Antipas' Hellenistic tendencies in connection with Tiberias: (a) The fact that Tiberias was built on graves directly prohibited by the Jewish laws, (b) the use of images of animals in the palace and the building of a stadium, (c) the way the city was governed with an "echt hellenistische Verfassung mit βουλή und den einschlägigen Beamten." This way "Die Einrichtung der Haupstadt als echt griechische πόλις zeigt uns schon die Beibehaltung der hellenistischen Verwal-

---

[27] It is worth noting that while Hoehner, Kokkinos and others assert that this did not happen until after the banishment of Archelaos (Hoehner 1972, 109; Kokkinos 1998, 233), Otto finds that it must have taken place from the outset of Antipas' reign: "Antipas hat im Anschluß an seine Einsetzung als Tetrarch seinen Namen geändert" (Otto 1913, 170, with reference to *War* 2.167). A recent coin find might prove Otto be right in this case (cf. section 6.4.1).

tungsmaximen des Vaters" (Otto 1913, 176), (d) the way in which Antipas acted in no other way than "alle hellenistischen Herrscher" (Otto 1913, 176), when he used force to relocate the inhabitants of the city, and (e) Otto finally adds the two inscriptions found at Cos and Delos as proof of the Hellenistic flavour of Antipas. At the same time, four things point to a certain favourable disposition towards the Jews in the reign of Antipas, who had "durchaus nicht mit dem Judentum gebrochen" (Otto 1913, 177): (a) It is believed that the synagogue in Tiberias was built by Antipas (*Life* 277), (b) the way he travels to Jerusalem for the Jewish feasts (Luke 23:7ff, *Ant.* 18.121, 241), (c) the way he rejected Pilate's introduction of golden shields in Jerusalem (*Legat.* 299–305), (d) and finally, the way he avoided images on his coins and only introduced the name of the emperor at the end of his reign, which can be explained as a way to please Gaius.

Regarding the chronological issues, Otto tries to date the second marriage of Antipas, which he finds "sehr strittig" (Otto 1913, 179). Without excluding the possibility of a later dating, he proposes that it took place at the beginning of the reign of Tiberius, when a trip was probably conducted (Otto 1913, 178–183).

Finally, regarding the moral assessment of Antipas, Otto is much more positive than Brann, whose description of Antipas as 'ruhiger', 'schlaffer' and 'träger' is rejected. Instead, Antipas is portrayed as an able ruler who only misjudged the situation a couple of times, thereby losing his good relationship to Aretas when he ousted Aretas' daughter in favour of Herodias, and to Vitellius after the peace negotiations on Euphrates when he informed Tiberius about the meeting behind Vitellius' back. Moreover, Antipas did not possess the "Tatkraft und Energie wie sein Vater" and is instead, in Otto's view, characterized as a "ἀγαπῶν τὴν ἡσυχίαν", a lover of quietness (Otto 1913, 189, with reference to *Ant.* 18.245, cf. *War* 2.182). Likewise, in contrast to his father, he is nowhere described as cruel. However, on one point Otto moralizes and evaluates Antipas in a very negative way, namely in the case of his second marriage to Herodias, which is taken as a sign of true Herodian kinship full of "Leidenschaftlichkeit und Sinnlichkeit" and "Rücksichtslosigkeit" (Otto 1913, 189–190). Still, the final assessment of Otto is positive: "Ein seines bedeutenden Vaters unwürdiger Sohn ist Herodes Antipas anscheinend nicht gewesen; auch daß ein Mann wie Tiberius ihn besonders geschätzt hat, spricht zu seinen Gunsten" (Otto 1913, 190).

1.3.2 Popular Scholarly Works

During the mid twentieth century, three popular scholarly books were released that either focused solely on Antipas (Harlow 1954), or treated him as a part of the Herodian family (Jones 1938 and Perowne 1958). While none of them discusses new sources or delivers a more thorough study than the preceding German studies, they do attract some interest for their more or less well-argued presentation and interpretation of the figure of Antipas.

The book by the ancient historian A.H.M. Jones, *The Herods of Judaea*, published in 1938, is worth noting mainly for its exceptional storytelling. It is based predominantly on Josephus, and since Josephus spends little time on Antipas, Jones' section on Antipas is fairly short as well (pp. 176–83, 195–6). It is significant that Jones makes no attempt to present an articulated moral assessment of Antipas, at least in the negative sense. Instead, Jones notices that "Antipas was the ablest of Herod's sons" (Jones 1938, 176), since he governed the most difficult areas, where inhabitants

...descended from the pagan inhabitants of these regions, who had been forcibly converted by the Hasmonaean kings... That he managed to remain on tolerably good terms with his subjects – and there is no evidence of serious unrest save Strabo's apocryphal story of his impeachment in A.D. 6 – is, therefore, strong testimony to his tact and firmness. (Jones 1938, 176)

In 1953 Victor E. Harlow published a book devoted to Herod Antipas with the title *The Destroyer of Jesus*, designed as a historical inquiry into the life of Antipas from the perspective of his relationship to Jesus. In general, the book contains little of current value. It tends to be speculative and overly dramatic, as well as tending to resort to psychological descriptions. An example of Harlow's speculative tendencies can be seen when he asserts, without any references, that "probability is high that from his infancy he was brought up as a completely orthodox Jew" (Harlow 1954, 46). Harlow's tendency to resort to psychological speculation is in certain cases downright repelling. In connection with Antipas' execution of John the Baptist, Harlow asserts that

...in that act Herod Antipas showed the lack of fibre frequently characteristic of individuals of widely mixed ancestry... The lack of complete physical adjustment in individuals whose blood is as widely mixed as was that of Herod is nearly always a foundation for the lack of firm and correct action in moral crises, especially when the physical mixture is accentuated by clashing racial mores. (Harlow 1954, 142)

Having said this, the book advances one thesis which is still worth considering, namely that Antipas was the most active person behind the conviction of Jesus. Pilate was "merely an instrument who carried out the judgment of Jesus' legal prince" (Harlow 1954, 202). The main argument is an alternative translation of Luke 23:15. Instead of translating ἀλλ' οὐδὲ Ἡρῴδης in the normal way, "neither has Herod" (found Jesus to be guilty), Harlow translates "but not so Herod" (Harlow 1954, 230). Though in no way conclusive, Harlow's proposal is interesting and it will be dealt with to a greater extent in chapter four.

Finally, a book by Stewart Perowne, *The Later Herods: The Political Background of the New Testament,* was published in 1958. Although utilizing more sources than just Josephus, the part on Antipas is very short and without any startling suggestions as in the case of Harlow. The picture of Antipas is one of a firm and eager ruler characterized as "an ambitious schemer" (Perowne 1958, 50).

1.3.3 Recent Research on Antipas

In recent times, three important studies have been published on Antipas. The first to appear was a short but admirably thorough article by F.F. Bruce, "Herod Antipas, Tetrarch of Galilee and Peraea" (1963). In the course of 18 pages, Bruce manages to evaluate and discuss the available sources on the life of Antipas, with the exception of the archaeological and numismatic material. The general view of Antipas expressed by Bruce is one of a good and able ruler, who managed to stay in office for 43 years without any known riots or revolts in his area except for the events around John the Baptist, Jesus, and perhaps Judas, though this riot in 6 CE seems to have been a Judean matter (Bruce 1963, 8). Bruce examines Antipas' life chronologically, discussing several important historical questions along the way: (a) Mark and Matthew's incorrect use of the term 'βασιλεύς' about Antipas (Mark 6:14, 22, 25, 26, 27; Matt 14:9, cf. though 14:1) is explained as a translation issue since the Aramaic *malka* was used in a more broad and imprecise sense (cf. Bruce 1963, 9). (b) Bruce also enters into the discussion of the identity of Herodias' former husband. Unlike Kokkinos (cf. below), Bruce denies that the Slavonic version of Josephus can be trusted since it "confuses her first husband with Philip the Tetrarch, and has no claim on our credence" (Bruce 1963, 10). (c) Dealing with the New Testament passages, Bruce finds Luke to be most valuable having an "independent and fuller information about the Herod family" (Bruce 1963, 10), whereas the passage of Antipas' birthday in Mark is designated as a "colourful story" (Bruce 1963, 11). According to Bruce, "it is unlikely that Mark's account depends on anything like direct eyewitness testimony. It had simply come to be known that John's execution was somehow a sequel to Antipas's birthday party in that year" (Bruce 1963, 13). It is further discussed where this party took place. Mark 6:21 seems to imply that it took place in Galilee, since the invited guests included τοῖς μεγιστᾶσιν αὐτοῦ καὶ τοῖς χιλιάρχοις καὶ τοῖς πρώτοις τῆς Γαλιλαίας but none from Perea. Bruce suggests the banquet was held in Tiberias. In addition, referring to Sherwin-White, it is noted how the entire setting of the birthday is described as a typical oriental banquet of the Roman petty princes (Bruce 1963, 12). Likewise, the identity of the dancing girl is discussed. It is noted that Mark 6:22 does not say it was Salome. In fact, Bruce finds that to be unlikely, since she would have been an adult at the time and no κοράσιον, since she was able to marry Philip the Tetrarch (*Ant.* 18.137). Instead Bruce opts for the weightiest manuscript tradition reading, τῆς θυγατρὸς αὐτοῦ Ἡρῳδιάδος, "his daughter Herodias" implying that Herod and Herodias had a daughter called Herodias. Most translations choose the alternative of the critical apparatus reading, τῆς θυγατρὸς αὐτῆς τῆς Ἡρῳδιάδος, "Herodias' own daughter" (cf. note 83). Finally, Bruce presents an interesting discussion of the relationship between Antipas and Pilate in connection with the trial in Luke 23. One issue that has been disputed in Roman legal studies is whether an indicted person belonged under the jurisdiction of the place he originated, or the place he was charged. Bruce concludes that "the probability is that Pilate was in no way bound to refer the case of Jesus to Antipas, but did so as a courteous gesture" (Bruce 1963, 16), a courtesy Antipas returned by sending Jesus back and thereby confirming Pilate's primacy in the matter. In this way Bruce explains how the case of Jesus could result in reconciliation between the two, as mentioned in Luke 23:12. Bruce also explains the previously bad relationship as a result of the massacre on Galilean pilgrims mentioned in Luke 13:1, and as a result of the episode of the votive shields recorded by Philo (*Legat.* 300).

The only scholarly dissertation devoted entirely to Antipas so far is Harold Hoehner's, *Herod Antipas* (1972)! The book is formed as a classical historical biography with an elaborate and exhaustive discussion of an impressive amount of sources totalling seventeen pages when indexed. As such, it still maintains its value, and the discussion in chapter four below on the New Testament sources is particularly indebted to Hoehner's efforts. However, two considerations compromise his work. First, its main weakness is an outspoken lack of methodological awareness. In a two-page introduction (Hoehner 1972, 1–2) covers the research history and then moves on to the first chapter on Antipas' youth. No space is devoted to a discussion of Josephus as a writer of history, for instance, and no effort is made to understand the different sets of texts in their own framework before filtering out the short passages on Antipas.[28] In this sense, it is characteristic that in his lengthy discussion of all the sources, Hoehner confines himself to a one-and-a-half page conclusion, since his overall aim is to de-

---

[28] This is also noted by J.C.H. Lebram in a review of the book: "Man muß an Hoehners Buch die Frage stellen, ob der historische Wert der Quellen richtig beurteilt ist. Josephus schreibt weder eine Biographie des Antipas, noch scheint ihm eine solche vorzuliegen... Herodes Antipas ist als unbedeutender orientalischer Potentat geschildert, ambivalent und abhängig von seiner Frau, keiner großen Entwürfe fähig" (Lebram 1973, 234–235).

liver an unbiased presentation and discussion of the material, and not a certain perspective that needs an elaborate conclusion. Second, a more excusable weakness is the book's lack of archaeological material in the discussion. In 1972 such material was in short supply, and there was no tradition for incorporating it on an equal footing as there is today. In this respect, Hoehner's dissertation is outdated.

Of the many important observations in Hoehner's study, the following should be noted. First, Hoehner's general assessment of Antipas is one of a "good ruler", whose "wise administration contributed to a tranquil life in Galilee and Peraea" (Hoehner 1972, 57–58). This conclusion is based on the lack of reports of uprisings in Antipas' area, and on his long reign. In addition, the actions taken against John the Baptist, and to some extent Jesus, are credited as acts of a far-sighted ruler able to strike the seeds of disturbances before they could unfold (Hoehner 1972, 264). Likewise, he seemed "to have been much milder than Herod the Great" (Hoehner 1972, 264) and not so greedy for power. In conclusion, Hoehner states: "He was an able ruler. He lived peaceably with his people. Except for Agrippa II, he reigned longer than any other Herod. All of this to his credit" (Hoehner 1972, 265). Second, in addition to his description of Antipas as a good ruler, Hoehner adds a psychological description of him as "basically a coward" (Hoehner 1972, 201). According to Hoehner, four things point to "his ambivalence of character" (Hoehner 1972, 202): (a) He was reluctant to place a claim to the throne, (b) he did not face the daughter of Aretas with his wish to marry Herodias, (c) he hesitated to imprison and kill John the Baptist, and was forced to do so by Herodias, (d) and he was ambivalent in seeking the rank of a king (cf. Hoehner 1972, 169). Hoehner also asserts that Antipas could easily have condemned Jesus if he so desired (cf. Luke 13:31), but did not do so out of an ambivalent reluctance (cf. Hoehner 1972, 202).

In 1998 Nikos Kokkinos published his dissertation, *The Herodian Dynasty: Origins, Role in Society and Eclipse,* which aims at a fresh assessment of the entire Herodian house and its internal relations, questioning several standard views in the research. Basically, Kokkinos argues for a hypothesis showing Herod the Great to be "*Phoenician* by descent, *Hellenized* by culture, *Idumaean* by place of birth, *Jewish* by official religion, *Jerusalemite* by place of residence, and *Roman* by citizenship" (Kokkinos 1998, 351). It is within such a highly complex setting of an oriental dynasty that we find Antipas. Though the treatment of Antipas is relatively short (cf. in particular Kokkinos 1998, 229–335), the following important hypotheses are advanced. First, Kokkinos discusses what role Antipas might have played in Jerusalem. Accepting the historical value of Luke 23, he rejects the proposal that Antipas' encounter with Jesus in Jerusalem was an unhistorical allusion to Psalms 2:1–2. Instead, Kokkinos argues that it is highly possible that Antipas was present in Jerusalem during the Passover, as depicted also in the Gospel of Peter and in Jerome's commentary on Matthew 7.223 (cf. Kokkinos 1998, 195, note 82). Antipas' good connections with the priests of Jerusalem and the Jewish nation as such may also be derived from Philo's story of votive shields (*Legat.* 299–305). In a dispute with Pilate, four Herodian princes were dispatched to bring charges against Pilate before Tiberius. Their names are not provided, but of the ten sons of Herod, four were already dead, Archelaos was out of the picture, and only Antipas and Philip were at this point in office as rulers. Kokkinos thus agrees with the standard view that Antipas was part of the delegation (cf. Kokkinos 1998, 195, note 80, cf. the discussion in chapter four).

Second, Kokkinos proposes an interesting hypothesis on the marriages of Herodias crediting the Slavonic version of Josephus, which designates Herodias' former husband to be Philip the Tetrarch.[29] It has long been noted that it is difficult to match the information provided by Josephus (*Ant.* 18.136f and 18.109–115) with the information in the Gospels (Mark 6:17; Matt 14:3; Luke 3:19). Kokkinos' solution discredits Josephus' information in 18.136 that Herodias left Herod, son of Herod the Great and Mariamme II (daughter of Simon the high priest) to marry Antipas, and that her daughter with Herod, Salome, married Philip the Tetrarch. Instead, Kokkinos argues that Antipas was Herodias' third husband. He believes that Herodias left Herod, her first husband, long before she married Antipas, to whom she must have been married fairly late, since this marriage was the alleged reason for Aretas' attack on Antipas around the time Tiberius died (37 CE). According to Kokkinos, Herodias' second husband was the Philip mentioned in the Gospels, who was none other than Philip the Tetrarch. Kokkinos argues that when Philip died in 33, Herodias looked for a way to hold on to the territory, and by marrying Antipas, she hoped that Tiberius would let her keep her former property. When Agrippa I, her brother, was later named king of Philip's (and her own) former territory, she orchestrated the fatal journey to Rome to ask Gaius for kingship that eventually led to the exile of both herself and Antipas. Thus, the marriage was politically motivated and not guided by blind love (cf. Kokkinos 1998, 264–271). The main problem with this hypothesis is that it disregards what Josephus clearly states in *Ant.* 18.109–110 and 18.136, namely that Herodias was married to Herod, son of Mariamme II, and it was the daughter of Herodias, and not Herodias herself, who married Philip. Although Josephus seems to have encountered a lack of sources for this pe-

---

[29] According to Hoehner, but not noted by Kokkinos, this solution has been suggested earlier by A. Parrot (Hoehner 1972, 133).

riod, it would represent a serious error on his part if he was not correctly informed of the identity of Philip the Tetrarch's wife. A second problematic consequence of the hypothesis is that the death of John, and subsequently Jesus, will have to be dated as late as 36 CE, after the death of Philip. The standard solution has been either to prefer Josephus over Mark and Matthew, or to combine the evidence proposing that Herodias' first husband was named Herod-Philip (cf. Hoehner 1972, 131–135; Krieger 1994, 51–56; Gillman 2003, 40).

Finally, it should be mentioned that the sources on Antipas in the New Testament material have been treated separately in a number of both older and recent studies. Some of them examine the entire New Testament material on Antipas, some concentrate on the relationship between Antipas and John the Baptist, and some examine solely the traditions rendered in Luke. These investigations will be treated in chapter four.

Chapter 2

Procedure of the Investigation

2.1 Research Area

In the preceding chapter, an attempt was made to clarify the broader context and research area of the problem under investigation. It has been argued that while Roman Galilee in broad terms has been a central issue of
the historical Jesus research for some time, the question of Herod Antipas
has gradually emerged as a central issue of the Galilean research. Four
points were noted as particularly important in this connection.

First, more than 25 years of intensive research has produced some consensus on certain issues. The question of the cultural character of Early
Roman Galilee has been elucidated considerably as more and more material data has become available and refined detailed studies have been conducted. It turns out that unless new material data is unearthed, it can be
safely concluded that the Galilee of Antipas was *not* as Hellenized as anywhere else in the Roman world.

Second, archaeological data has come to play an ever-increasing role in
the various historical reconstructions of life in Roman Galilee. While archaeological excavations played hardly any role in the early works of
Freyne, for instance, it is now often the most recent discoveries or specialized studies that advance a certain area of discussion such as the question
of the origins of the Galileans, the cultural question, and the question of
the urban-rural relationship. As noted by Freyne, "it is to the developments
in the archaeological realm that one can reasonably look for the most important advances" (Freyne 2000c, 26). Therefore, any upcoming study
needs to consider archaeological data on an equal footing with textual
sources. However, important methodological problems are connected to
this enterprise, as will be discussed in chapter five.

Third, the clarification of Roman Galilee's cultural character has paved
the way for a refined focus of the most important factor in order to understand life in first-century Galilee, namely the urban-rural relationship. This
important question has been discussed intensively for the last 10 to 15
years, but no consensus has been reached yet. Two pictures of Early Galilee and its urban-rural relationship have evolved, and at present the research is more or less stranded at an impasse on this issue. The preceding

discussion has demonstrated that the question of how to utilize sociological models or whether to utilize them at all plays an important role.

Fourth, the investigation above has finally pointed out how important Herod Antipas is for the various conceptions of first-century Galilee. Antipas has emerged as *the* decisive factor of explanation of the socio-economic realities of early-first-century Galilee. However, closely related to the divergent views of the urban-rural relationship, several pictures of Antipas have been presented ranging from him being a buffer against direct Roman rule, safeguarding peace and prosperity, to him being the direct cause of the social and economic 'slide' through his programme of urbanization funded by monetization and taxation. At this end of the spectrum, Antipas is presented as a foil for the two prophets or protesters, Jesus and John, and as an explanation as to why they "happened" in his areas within such a short time. Interestingly, none of the Galilean investigations above make any attempt to treat all the available sources to the reign of Antipas systematically with an explicit methodology. Rather, they often deduce straightforwardly from the passages in Josephus concerning Antipas' building activities, for instance, via a specific model to a certain picture of his impact bolstered with brief surveys of the archaeological material. For this reason, the research on Antipas in a non-Galilean context was examined in order to explore whether a different picture emerged. It turned out that only a few detailed investigations have been conducted. The last presentation covering the entire source body is the dissertation by H. Hoehner published in 1972. Although this study is very helpful in many regards, its continued value is compromised by its lack of an explicit methodology in its treatment of written sources, and the vast amount of archaeological material unearthed since its publication.

2.2 Main Problem

The preceding introduction has clarified that within the larger context of Galilean issues one of the main problems is: what was the relation between the reign of Herod Antipas and the socio-economic conditions of early-first-century Galilee?

This central question is accompanied by four difficulties. First, a deadlock seems to have evolved on how to describe Antipas and his influence on early-first-century Galilee. Mutually contradictory pictures of his influence have been proposed. Second, in general the sources on the reign of Antipas are not treated thoroughly enough, which has actually resulted in a lacuna in the research. Third, there is an unresolved dilemma concerning the use of models. It is clear that nearly all supporters of the picture of conflict utilize models from cross-cultural anthropology or socio-scientific criticism, while the opposite is true for supporters of a picture of harmony. Finally, it must be acknowledged that our sources on Antipas and his impact on Galilee are not overwhelming and many questions are left unanswered. It is therefore an open question whether or not our main problem *can* be answered. It is perfectly possible in our case that the conclusion might be that the sources are either insufficient or too diverse to really warrant a plausible reconstruction of the impact of the reign of Antipas on socio-economic conditions in Galilee.

2.3 Methodology

The present investigation seeks to deal with these difficulties by choosing a source-oriented method of approach. It proposes that all the sources on the reign of Antipas need to be examined once again and treated thoroughly on their own terms, group by group, before attempting to answer the main issue at hand. In other words, due to the lacuna in the way the sources on Antipas are treated, and due to the fact that models seem to predetermine the outcome, there is another basic question that needs to be answered before attempting to answer the main question: what do we know about Herod Antipas from the sources?

In addition, the explicit assumption is that the proper way to engage ancient sources is to read them within their own context before they are removed and reused to understand a contemporary set of questions. Accordingly, the *context* of the sources on Antipas plays a vital role. It is not sufficient to extract bits of information on Antipas from Josephus, like the above-mentioned example of him being a builder of cities. Instead Josephus' entire presentation of Antipas needs to be uncovered in its own larger framework of Josephus' presentation of the entire Herodian house. Similarly, the archaeological remains from Sepphoris and Tiberias, for instance, need to be understood within a larger regional and inter-regional perspective, just as the coins of Antipas need to be treated in the light of the broader framework of Second Temple Jewish coinage.

Such an approach does not, however, provide direct access to the past or a reconstruction of historical events as they were. It is an accepted fact of modern historical research that serious theoretical problems are connected to the act of (re)constructing past events from biased sources. Some of these problems will be addressed specifically in the two main chapters (chapter three on Antipas and Josephus, and chapter five on Antipas and archaeology). It may be noted that in the Galilean research this problem is not addressed in general. It is an established working paradigm that readings of ancient sources do allow reconstructions of the past, whose internal divergences may be solved through the principle of plausibility. The present study adopts this view, but it may be added that 'a plausible reading' is not the same as 'the right reading'. The bias of *both* the text and the reader makes it futile to look for a core of raw data within the sources, for instance. Rather, the sources will always remain contextual sources that need to be read as entities within their own framework. In this position it is regarded as possible to discern between a *plausible* reading and *wrong* or *implausible* readings. Thus, the present investigation accepts that only three options exist: (a) To argue against certain interpretations of Antipas that the source material in its own context seems to preclude. (b) To argue for a certain plausible interpretation of Antipas on the basis of the currently available source material. (c) To arrive at the conclusion that the source material is too insufficient to arrive at any conclusion.

2.4 Focus

As will quickly become apparent, such a 'source-contextual' approach to Antipas is rather laborious. For this reason it is important to note the aspects that the present study will not be able to discuss, in order to keep its distinct focus intact. First, this study is not another biographical study of Antipas such as that of Hoehner and the previous German studies. It is a study of Antipas with a specific focus on his socio-economic impact on Galilee. For this reason, chronological issues will not be dealt with in any detail. Second, this is not a study of ancient Palestinian economics *per se* such as Oakman 1986; Fiensy 1991; Safrai 1994; Pastor 1997 and Lapin 2001. It would otherwise be very helpful to conduct an economic survey specifically focusing on early-first-century Galilee. However, it is estimated that such a study could follow the present study, which will hopefully serve as a background for further investigation. Finally, this study is not a survey of the different sociological models in play, in order to evaluate which seem to work best. Such a survey would be beneficial, but will also involve further investigation. As outlined above, since the different models seem to have a determining effect on the main issue that will be examined, it is necessary to conduct a contextual survey of all the sources first. The consequence of this is, admittedly, that models will only be touched upon lightly in the subsequent assessment and discussion (cf. section 7.3.3).

In short, the present study has been provoked by the obvious ambiguity in the way Antipas is evaluated and the way the urban-rural situation is understood. Since this has to do with the way models are utilized and the lacuna in the way the sources are treated as mentioned above, the present study confines itself to a source-oriented investigation in which the context of each source is vital in order to establish a well-argued interpretation of each group of sources within its own framework. Only subsequently will the study engage in a broader historical discussion, which for reasons of space will be shorter than if the study had been conducted the other way round.

2.5 Outline

This gives the following outline and internal progression of the study: *Part I – Settings* (chapters one and two) has aimed to define the exact problem that will be examined within its larger topical context. *Part II – Sources* (chapters three to six) forms the main body of the study by investigating the sources on the reign of Antipas divided into: (a) Josephus, (b) other written sources, namely the ancient historians that touch upon the reign of Antipas and the New Testament, (c) archaeological sources divided into: Sepphoris, Tiberias, regional villages and inter-regional cities, (d) the numismatic and epigraphic sources. On this basis, *Part III – Assessment* (chapters seven and eight) will engage in a synthetic discussion with a view to determining, first, *if* the alleged impasse can be answered and then, second, *how* it may be answered. On this basis, chapter eight will conclude the investigation.

Part II

Sources

Chapter 3

Herod Antipas and Josephus[30]

3.1 Introduction

This chapter will examine the writings of Josephus from which most of our textual sources on Antipas derive.[31] The aim is to provide a literary analysis of how Josephus organizes and presents his material, since such an approach has the best prospects for further historical enquiry (cf. below section 3.2.6).

However, although Josephus is by far the most informative literary source available on Antipas, he does not describe the reign of Antipas in any profound detail. Actually, of the rulers of the Herodian house, Josephus only thoroughly presents Herod the Great and Agrippa I. His description of Antipas can be divided into three parts: (a) Material concerning the youth of Antipas and the events in Rome following the death of Herod the Great (*War* 1.646, 2.20–95; *Ant.* 17.20, 188, 224–318). (b) Material concerning the founding of Sepphoris (*Ant.* 18.27) and Tiberias (*War* 2.167–168; *Ant.* 18.36–38; *Life* 64–69). (c) Material concerning events during the reign of Antipas in *Ant.* 18.36–38, 101–125, 240–255 and *War* 2.178.181–183. This part contains the actual narratives on Antipas, with *Ant.* 18.101–125 as the central block containing stories centered on Antipas not found in *War*.[32] Altogether eight episodes are presented:

(1)   The founding of Tiberias (*War* 2.170; *Ant.* 18.36–38; *Life* 64–69).

(2)   The peace treaty with Parthia on a bridge over the Euphrates (*Ant.* 18.101–105).

(3)   Antipas' marriage to Herodias (*Ant.* 18.109–112, 136).

---

[30] An early version of parts of this chapter has been published in Jensen 2006.

[31] The edition of the Greek text of Josephus used in the following is in general Niese 1955 (editio maior) in combination with the text edition in the Loeb series (ed. J. Thackeray et al., 10 vols.). For a general introduction to the life and writings of Josephus, I refer to Attridge 1984, Bilde 1988 and Mason 2003c, 35–145.

[32] This is the reason why Daniel R. Schwartz proposes the existence of a special '*Antip*'-source available for Josephus when he wrote *Antiquities* (cf. Schwartz 1990, 8 and the table p. 38). As seen above, this suggestion is not new. Täubler also suggested that Josephus used a "Memoiren des Herodes Antipas", an idea that was rejected by W. Otto (cf. Otto 1913, 174).

(4)   The war with Aretas (*Ant.* 18.113–115).

(5)   Antipas and John the Baptist (*Ant.* 18.116–119).

(6)   Vitellius' and Antipas' preparations for war against Aretas (*Ant.* 18.120–125).

(7)   Antipas' employment of Agrippa (*Ant.* 18.148–150; *War* 2.178).

(8)   Antipas' plea for kingship and his subsequent banishment (*War* 2.181–183; *Ant.* 18.240–255).

As discussed in Part I, the contextual methodological approach utilized in this investigation demands a thorough analysis of the narrative of Josephus in order to understand why he narrated his sections on Antipas the way he did. Therefore, we need to approach his accounts on Antipas through a close reading of his treatment of the Herodian house as such. In consequence, after a brief survey of the research on Josephus as a historiographer, the subsequent investigation will examine all Josephus' writings dealing with the time beginning with Herod the Great until Agrippa I. In particular, any traceable changes from the account of *War* to the account of *Antiquities* will be emphasized. The insights gained in this way will provide a background for understanding and interpreting the account of Herod Antipas in its own inherent context. The main question is how Josephus uses his account on Antipas, and whether it is, despite its brevity, in a clear and telling way engrafted into his narrative or rather loosely attached as an incomplete *Vita* of Antipas.

3.2 Josephus as a Writer of History

Why is Josephus rather sparse when it comes to material on Antipas, and actually material on the whole period from the death of Herod the Great to the reign of Agrippa I? What lies behind his choices as to what to include and what to leave out? What is the relationship between the actual events and the narrative of Josephus? The main part of the last hundred years or more of Josephus research has centered on answering such questions. Without attempting an in-depth treatment of this highly complex issue, the following will present some of the main problems and main approaches in the research in order to reach a position from which the rest of the investigation can proceed.

3.2.1 Per Bilde

One of the main contributors to this discussion is Per Bilde. In his Danish dissertation (Bilde 1983) and in a later English general introduction to Josephus (Bilde 1988), Bilde conducts a comprehensive survey of the research up until roughly 1983. He divides the research into two, the *classi-*

cal and the *modern* approach to Josephus, to which can be added a pre-modern medieval approach marked by a non-reflective reading of Josephus at face value. Bilde advocates the credibility of the modern approach.

Bilde defines the classical conception as having a sceptical or even dismissive approach to the narratives of Josephus. Originally, this approach was prompted by a rejection of Josephus' short narrative on Jesus, the Testimonium Flavianum, at least partially. Eventually, this influenced the entire reading of Josephus, resulting in an outspoken negative approach to Josephus for his personal qualities, for him being a Flavian propagandist, for his defence of the Jewish people which was viewed as overstated, and for his attempt to cover up his own morally suspicious career (Bilde 1988, 126). Studies of the sources behind Josephus' narrative added to this image. Von Destinon launched the idea of an anonymous source, which Josephus used heavily making him not much more than an "unimaginative penpusher" (Bilde 1983, 126) attributing what he found of historical value to the sources and not to Josephus himself. Through a source-critical approach guided by a search for internal contradictions, it was thought possible to detach the Josephean imposition from the truly trustworthy historical information (cf. Bilde 1988, 126–141).[33]

In contrast to the classical conception, Bilde defines "the modern conception" in a dual manner. First, it grants Josephus a positive political, theological and national agenda, seeing him as a creative writer. Second, it finds that his writings contain genuine historical value. Regarding Josephus as a creative writer, two arguments are presented: (a) From a literary and philological point of view the works of Josephus are deemed to be coherent, thereby making it unlikely that they are a mere compilation of sources. (b) Beginning with the work of Farmer and Braun (both published in 1956), a genuine theological and political agenda is ascribed to Josephus (cf. Bilde 1988, 144ff.). Bilde adds to this picture through an analysis of the theological aspects of Josephus' writings. In an important article from 1979, "The causes of the Jewish war according to Josephus", Bilde shows how it is possible throughout the entire narrative of Josephus to find an underlying focus on why the war happened, and how the destruction of the temple could take place. The concerns of Josephus are to be found on a far deeper level than his private life and reputation alone: "His chief concern is, as we have seen, the final interpretation of the fundamental causes of

---

[33] It is noteworthy that one of the newest contributors to the Josephus studies with a 'classical approach', Daniel R. Schwartz, denies that the search for sources automatically leads to "belittlement" of Josephus: "The efforts involved in compiling – extracting, assembling, coordinating and linking – are worthy of appreciation, not belittlement" (Schwartz 1990, XIV).

the war. This concern I would understand as a vital personal problem for Josephus" (Bilde 1979, 201). Even though many concerns and threads of thought run through the narrative of Josephus, the reason for the destruction of the temple and the demolishing of Judaism is the single most important issue for Josephus, who finds the ultimate answer in 'the will of God'. Everything happened through God's intervention. It was he who selected the Roman Empire to punish the Jewish people (cf. Bilde 1979, 199 and Bilde 1988, 146, 182). This theological agenda can be found in both *War* and *Antiquities*, though it is most pronounced in *Antiquities*, where Josephus states – even in the preface – that there is a divine rule decreeing that if the law is not upheld irretrievable disasters will occur (1.14, cf. Bilde 1988, 184–185). Bilde further refers to *Apion* 2.145–219, which systematically unfolds Josephus' theology:

According to Josephus, the first and most important point in the Jewish concept of the Divine is faith in God's providence and guidance... Josephus emphasizes that by abiding by God's law, the Jewish people will live to see his blessing. When Israel abides by the law of God, it will arrive at perfect unity, harmony and peace. (Bilde 1988, 186)

This may actually also be the point of the militant nationalists, who nonetheless are rejected by Josephus for not acknowledging the Roman Empire as willed by God, who himself had given supremacy to Rome. Consequently, rebellion against Rome was rebellion against God (cf. Bilde 1988, 187 for references). In reality, Josephus thereby places himself among the Old Testament prophets and chronologists, who also present interpretations of events loaded with divine insight. Thus, through the

...gift of prophecy Josephus claims that he was able to see through the course of history and therefore he was also able to write an adequate account of the historical events... Josephus ranks himself as a priestly prophet in line with Ezekiel. He identifies himself more or less clearly with him and with Joseph, Elijah, Jeremiah, Daniel and even Esther. (Bilde 1988, 190–191)

Regarding the second point, the historical value and credibility of Josephus, Bilde states that Josephus must be understood as a sincere writer of history, based on the standards of his own time. This assertion is based in turn on two observations: (a) An 'external study' of Josephus, comparing his description of Gaius' attempt to erect his statue in the temple with Philo's description of the same event, leads Bilde to the conclusion that "it turns out that in Josephus the material appears to have been edited less heavily than with Philo" (Bilde 1988, 197, cf. Bilde 1983). Bilde further asserts that "Josephus treats his sources cautiously and meticulously" (Bilde 1988, 196). This is not to say that Josephus does not alter his sources or use them for specific purposes, but he does so with clear and traceable tendencies such as updating them with a Hellenistic touch, giving them a dramatic, pathetic and erotic tone, and by outspokenly providing his own interpretation, often of an apologetic nature (cf. Bilde 1988, 196). (b) Furthermore, an 'internal study' of the coherency throughout the works of Josephus leads Bilde to conclude that all major shifts in focus can be explained as a result of their different purposes. Indeed, Bilde finds the classical conception "simply absurd" (Bilde 1988, 178). It does not make sense that Josephus portrays himself as a heroic freedom fighter in *War* if it is supposed to be a work of Flavian panegyric; or that he portrays himself as a coward without control in *Life*, if it is intended to be a nationalistic work. Instead Bilde states that "from *War* to *Ap.*, we encounter the same basic view as I have attempted to demonstrate in the review of each individual work" (Bilde 1988, 178).

Thus, Josephus can be ascribed "a nearly passionate historical interest" (Bilde 1988, 197), and in conclusion Bilde asserts:

> Josephus is certainly a creative author with artistic ambitions as well as obvious political and theological intentions. Yet, the rather surprising conclusion of recent investigations is that, at the same time, he remains loyal towards his sources as far as their substance, main contents and their most essential data are concerned. (Bilde 1988, 196)

3.2.2 James S. McLaren

A completely different evaluation of Josephus is found in James S. McLaren's study, *Turbulent Times?* (McLaren 1998), in which McLaren evaluates some of the prominent contributions to the study of Josephus, as well as undertaking a case study of Josephus' description of the fall of Jerusalem. Basically, McLaren finds Josephus' work to be so shaped by his own "*interpretative framework*" that the real historical background, "*the subject matter*" (McLaren 1998, 59), is almost impossible to recover. McLaren defines Josephus' interpretative framework as two strands of thought pervading the entire presentation. One is Josephus' description of the affairs before the war as a time of increasing turmoil. Another is his way of describing the war as inevitable (McLaren 1998, 201, 291). This interpretative framework of increasing turmoil and an inevitable war,

> ...controls the entire choice of subject matter and, therefore, the overall picture that is being conveyed. We must now contend with the possibility that although we can make conclusions and observations regarding what Josephus narrates, what we can conclude is, in itself, the product of an interpretation. In other words, the picture being used to understand the first century CE in Judaea may not necessarily provide the reader with a 'full' or 'balanced' representation of what was happening in the territory. In effect, our major resource for examining the period is itself a constructed picture. (McLaren 1998, 67)

This is in itself not a new insight. Even T. Rajak and Bilde in no way deny that Josephus is describing the events from a certain perspective. What is new is the radical way McLaren presents his thesis by actually rejecting all previous research as flawed: "It is a central tenet of this study that all the existing discussion within scholarship that purports to establish independence from Josephus's interpretation is fundamentally flawed" (McLaren 1998, 17). Instead Josephus' own claim as being a trustworthy writer of history is totally rejected:

We are left, therefore, with a situation where Josephus's notion of objective 'truth' in relation to writing history should be rejected. It is not possible to extract the commentary of Josephus and to assume that we possess a bare description of historical facts. (McLaren 1998, 124)

On this basis, McLaren examines other works by Josephus scholars, and finds none that are able to escape Josephus' 'interpretative framework': "Despite the claims of independence they continue to undertake their reconstructions of Judaea within the interpretative framework established by Josephus" (McLaren 1998, 183). Even the most critical approach to Josephus remains, according to McLaren, "conceptually dependent on Josephus" (McLaren 1998, 201):

There are no half measures here – everything Josephus records is the result of his choice to include the material... Josephus's two pillars – a society racked by conflict and escalating turmoil, and a belief that the revolt was to be explained as an inevitable climax to the escalation of conflict – are borrowed by scholarship primarily because they have not been recognized as expressions of his interpretation. In other words, the most fundamental element of Josephus's narrative has become the framework for all contemporary discussion of the first century CE. (McLaren 1998, 201)

In order to bolster this claim, McLaren divides the scholarship into three categories based on their approach to the bias or the apologetic aims of Josephus. One is taken by Rajak, Bilde and Steve Mason, which is characterised by a positive view of the trustworthiness of Josephus as a writer of history despite his biases. Another is found in the works of Moehring, who is so critical that Josephus becomes almost useless for historical purposes. Finally, a third middle position, held by the vast majority of scholars, views the bias of Josephus as a kind of enemy that must be found and ruled out, after which access can be gained to a reliable fund of historical information. Even this is not possible:

The alleged removal of Josephus's bias does not leave the reader with a restored narrative of the actual situation. It is a fallacy to believe that Josephus's bias can be separated from the narrative and that a 'core' of historical events is then left over. To siphon out the bias is to remove the entire narrative" (McLaren 1998, 235).

It might seem that McLaren's approach forces him to give up the use of Josephus in a historical reconstruction of the first century. But that is actually not so. Through a three-fold *case study approach,* McLaren finds it possible to use recorded incidents in a historical reconstruction. First one has to identify and isolate each incident, then evaluate them separately, and then finally bring them together in a new synthesis which is only then detached from the interpretive framework of Josephus (McLaren 1998, 252ff.).

The question is, however, how such an approach differs from other scholars' way of trying to remove the bias of Josephus from the real historical 'subject matter'. Since the twin-pillars of Josephus' framework are the results of McLaren's own analyses, in what way would such an approach promise more objectivity? In a critical review, Lorenzo DiTommaso suggests that "McLaren fails to acknowledge the many potential pitfalls involved when kernels of historical fact are identified and segregated from their larger narrative contexts" (DiTommaso 1999, 361). Sharply formulated by DiTommaso, the question to McLaren must be: "In what manner is this balkanizing of the data so as to "cut through" the narrative framework any different from previous attempts to utilize Josephus as a historical source by ascertaining and then side-stepping his bias?" (DiTommaso 1999, 361). Thus, the question is whether McLaren in this way has found any safer way to establish historical probability or just another way that is equally subjective.

A further question is to what extent it is preferable to cut the narrative of Josephus into pieces, and thus lose insights from literary analyses of the composition of the narrative itself. Josephus definitely had access to more material than he incorporated, as in the case of Antipas. Thus it seems necessary to analyze why he chose to narrate the way he did. The only way to do that is through a close reading of the incidents in their context, and not as separate cases. The question remains then, if a close reading of the entire narrative of Josephus will provide a sense of his aims, theology and apologetic concerns, and if it is possible from there to proceed to historical questions.

3.2.3 Uriel Rappaport

One example out of many regarding the 'bias approach' to Josephus can be found in Uriel Rappaport's article, "Where was Josephus Lying – in his *Life* or in the *War*?", in which the historical trustworthiness of Josephus is discussed by focusing on the events in Galilee during the war. Most often, Josephus is the only source for the events he describes, so he is difficult to validate. However, in the case of the events in Galilee during the war, Josephus has provided two narrations of the same period, allowing us "to use comparative methodology for research on the revolt" (Rappaport 1994, 279), even though both descriptions "are marred by similar weakness – his involvement in the events he describes; his personal, partisan, national and political interests; his apologetics and his subservience to his Roman patrons" (Rappaport 1994, 279).

Josephus' two versions differ when it comes to his own role, which is described in *War* as being very active, but in *Life* as being subdued and downplayed. There are three obvious solutions to this. Either the description in *War* can be preferred, or the description in *Life* can be preferred, or the third option is that the differences can be downplayed and described as the consequence of the different purposes of the two descriptions. Rappaport enters into this discussion through a focus on the bias of Josephus. Can anything be said on what motivated him in each of the descriptions to render the story the way he did? If so, it is supposedly possible to bypass the bias of Josephus and thus get closer to the actual events.

Rappaport's thesis is that in the 70s Josephus wrote as a Flavian panegyrist and draws a picture of himself as the heroic general, whom Vespasian was eventually able to defeat. In the 90s, the scene had changed. Josephus came under attack from the Jewish community for being responsible for the destruction of Galilee. Charges were brought forward especially by Justus of Tiberias. This forced Josephus to produce a much less self-flattering but more truthful description:

Evidently Josephus could not stick to his story in the *War*, which substantiated Justus' accusations. He chose to admit, to some measure the truth, which suited his actual present interest, though it did not support his own self-image... The hidden truth about his activity in Galilee in 66–67 is that in reality he did not possess much authority in Galilean affairs and that he sided with the moderates. This fact, which he preferred not to disclose in public in the seventies when he wrote the *War*, he admitted in *Life* § 175 because it served him better in the nineties than in the seventies" (Rappaport 1994, 283).

However, the question is whether Rappaport in this estimation can claim anything else than just possibility and not probability. His evaluation is based solely on internal evidence in Josephus, since no external evidence exists. On top of this comes the fact that the argumentation is not entirely coherent. On the one hand, Rappaport states that "in *War* the pressure on Josephus to distort the truth was much greater than in *Life*" (Rappaport 1994, 286), since he wrote on behalf of the Flavian house. On the other hand, he thinks that in *Life* "Josephus was forced to disclose the truth, to save his reputation, or even his neck" (Rappaport 1994, 287). Why would this new type of pressure not produce a similar condition in which Josephus felt obliged to alter the truth? Thus, all merits aside, Rappaport's thesis lacks a convincing ground to rest on and seems dependent on a historical reconstruction which is impossible to verify.

3.2.4 Steve Mason

Some of the most important recent contributions to this discussion are those provided by Steve Mason. In four new articles (Mason 2003b; Mason 2005b; Mason 2003a; Mason 2005a), Mason considerably expands his earlier analyses of Josephus' literary aims (cf. Mason 1998, 64, note 2) and applies his findings on the relationship between Josephus' narrative and history.

The earlier part of Mason's work concerns a rejection of the classical view of Josephus as a highly source-dependent, uncreative writer. According to Mason, the scholarly tradition "has tended to do everything with Josephus except read his works coherently" (Mason 1998, 64). On the basis of a full-scale analysis, Mason rejects the proposal by Laqueur and later by Seth Schwartz that Josephus wrote *Antiquities* and *Life* to please the rabbinic movement at Yavneh or other Jewish communities in the Diaspora and to defend himself (Mason 1998, 66). Instead, Mason concludes that they are written for a gentile audience:

We may conclude with some confidence, then, that Josephus's aim in Antiquities/Life is to provide a handbook of Judean law, history and culture for a Gentile audience in Rome that is keenly interested in Jewish matters. In spite of its ramblings and changes in style, the book has a coherent and powerful message. It is not primarily a defensive work; it is not directed at Diaspora Jews; it does not target either the Yavnean rabbis or the 'Roman government' on their behalf; it is not a vague 'apologetic for Gentiles'; it is not even simply a work of theological history. Josephus has an immediate and serious purpose in mind, a need to meet, a question to answer. His audience desires a comprehensive but readable summary of the Judean constitution and philosophy: origins, history, laws and culture. (Mason 1998, 101)

In his recent articles, this line of argument is substantiated by investigations into the structure of *Antiquities* and its audience and reception in Flavian Rome. As a point of departure, Mason notes that every point of the classical view has in principle been rejected (Mason 2003b, 563, note 21). Josephus must be understood as a highly intelligent and creative writer. This statement is substantiated by the following four arguments:

First, the twenty books of *Antiquities* are not a loose compilation of sources. Instead, they are narrated in a highly intelligent manner forming a chiasmus around the fall of the first temple and the role played by the prophet and priest Jeremiah, and the prophet Daniel (cf. Mason 2003b, 567–568).

Second, Mason further investigates the initial audience of the writings of Josephus. Once it is established that Josephus was a creative writer, it is only logical to investigate how his work might have been received and read: "My goal here is to press further and ask how his works were read in Flavian Rome... Did he leave signals for his audience that there was more for them to discover than he had plainly said?" (Mason 2005a, 244–245). A comparison with Roman historiography shows that Josephus includes the same style of personal and moral assessment that had been fashionable since Cicero: "In keeping with his moral quest, Josephus tells the story of Judean history through the lives of great individuals" (Mason 2003b, 570). Mason notes how Josephus in this way tries

...to achieve balance in his moral assessments, and to render his characters plausible human beings with conflicting drives toward good and evil. Such a rounded psychological analysis, with its resulting ambiguities, was a hallmark of Roman historiography. (Mason 2003b, 571)

Josephus even manages to say something positive about Herod the Great, as well as about Samson, Salomon, Gaius and others.

Third, and connected to a special feature of Roman historiography, Mason points out how Josephus mastered the use of irony as "the art of safe criticism" (Mason 2005b). Mason distinguishes between 'text-dependent' and 'audience-dependent' irony, where the latter is only detected by the intended audience (cf. Mason 2005a, 249–251). On the basis of the non-controversial observation that Josephus' works initially circulated between the elite of Rome,[34] Mason argues that all his writings contain a subtle criticism of the Flavian house. Even *War*, generally seen as a Flavian panegyric chronicle, when viewed against the anti-Judean politics of Rome in the 70s, contains a subtle, but very direct critique of the Flavian version of the war events. According to Josephus, it was not Titus who had the power to destroy the temple, but the Jewish God himself, who acted through Titus, thereby giving Titus the rather unflattering role of a puppet (for instance *War* 5.391ff., cf. Mason 2005a and Mason 2005b). The hidden critique is even more remarkable in *Antiquities*, which was published exactly in the years when Domitian executed other intellectual critics of his reign (in the year 93 or 94 Mason 2003b, 560). Even so, it contains a more profound criticism of Flavian Roman society, namely of the constitution itself.

Fourth, Mason finally argues that Josephus' ability as a creative and independent writer shows in the way he organizes his narration around the central theme of the Jewish constitution, which Josephus himself describes as an aim of his writings (*Ant.* 1.5ff.; 20.229, 251, 261; *Apion* 2.188, 222, 226, 272–273, 287, cf. Mason 2003b, 574). The ideal constitution, accord-

---

[34] In a recent published article, H. Cotton and W. Eck argue, though, that Josephus was probably isolated from the better part of the Roman elite at the time he published *Antiquities*. Consequently, this work may have circulated less among the Roman elite than assumed by Mason (cf. Cotton and Eck 2005).

ing to Josephus, is to be found in the early priestly and aristocratic leadership of both Israel and Rome, by contrast with the later rule of kings and princes. Josephus provides an abundance of examples in an attempt to prove that the latter will always lead to tyranny. Tyranny was at the top of the list of horror scenarios that could befall a state. Mason refers to Plato, Aristotle, Polybius, Dionysius besides Herodotus, who state that even the best man empowered with absolute rule will become a tyrant who "skews the traditional laws, violates women, and executes without a trial" (Mason 2003b, 579).[35] In this way, Josephus establishes a parallel between the constitutional crisis of Israel under Herod the Great, for instance, and the similar crisis of Rome under Tiberius and Gaius. Consequently, Mason argues against the scholars who view the two long digressions on Tiberius and Gaius in *Ant.* 18 and 19 as redundant material inserted by Josephus to rival the renowned twenty volumes of Dionysius' *Antiquitates Romanae*. Instead, Mason interprets them as part of a subtle critique of the system of *principes* that eventually led to a constitutional crisis exemplified with the awkward story of how Tiberius was forced to appoint Gaius as his successor. Thus, while Josephus could not utter a direct critique of the Flavian house, he could in this way indirectly ridicule the entire Roman constitution of emperors.[36] When Josephus could speak more freely, as in the case of Herod the Great, his contempt for the system of kings and absolute rulers is far more outspoken.[37] In conclusion, Mason states:

We have little choice, it seems to me, but to conclude that he wished not only to praise the Judean constitution before his inquisitive Roman audience, but also to comment on

---

[35] Cf. also Mason 2001, 28 note 124, where he refers to Diodorus Siculus for the view that tyranny was among the three greatest evils that could befall a state along with sedition and war.

[36] Mason especially finds Josephus' subtle critique stated in the speech of Gnaeus Sentius Saturninus in the Senate (*Ant.* 19.167–184). Sentius blames the internal Roman misery on Julius Caesar (19.173ff.), who was the first to destroy democracy (καταλύσει τῆς δημοκρατίας), violate the common law (τὸν κόσμον τῶν νόμων), and place himself above order. He did this to such a degree that there was no evil thing which did not thwart the city (οὐκ ἔστιν ὅ τι τῶν κακῶν οὐ διέτριψεν τὴν πόλιν). And *all* who succeeded him (ἁπάντων οἳ ἐκείνῳ διάδοχοι) likewise departed from the custom of the fathers (τοῦ πατρίου) by killing noble men, for instance, until it finally reached its peak with Gaius, who acted with tyranny (τυραννίς) against both men and gods. One may add that these three indictments for (a) departing from the law and ancient order, (b) acting with tyranny without any moderation, and (c) being the ultimate reason for the destruction of the civil order mirror *exactly* the ones Josephus cast upon Herod the Great, the Herodian house (except Agrippa) and the Fourth Philosophy, as we shall also see below.

[37] Mason points out how Josephus forms his narrative on Herod the Great with an inclusion of negative evaluations through the warnings of the aristocrats of Jerusalem in 14.165 and the judgments of the elders in 17.304 (cf. Mason 2003b, 582).

Roman affairs – as directly as any writer would dare at this point in Domitian's reign. (Mason 2003b, 589)

The important question remains of how Mason evaluates Josephus as a writer of history; and unlike Bilde, Mason's high view of Josephus as a creative writer is not followed by a positive view of him as an accurate writer of history. Instead, Mason finds Josephus so present in his narrative that no original subject matter can be detached and freed from his bias. Therefore the idea that original reliable sources can be found through contradictions is rejected. This is the topic of Mason's important study, "Contradiction or Counterpoint? Josephus and Historical Method" (Mason 2003a), in which Mason rejects the 'bias research' and the more direct use of Josephus as a historical source with a triple argument: First, our questions are not the same as those asked by Josephus:

We might ask about the social and economic relations between Galilee and Jerusalem or between villages and cities in Galilee, or about the outlook of Ananus II or Eleazar son of Ananias. In the service of his own questions, to be sure, Josephus occasionally comments upon such issues, but he does not ask *our* questions, therefore does not marshal the evidence known to him (no doubt considerable) and argue methodically from it. (Mason 2003a, 185)

Therefore, in the absence of any other evidence, we cannot retrieve more information from Josephus simply by asking other questions and rearranging his material. Second, the consequence is that *if* no other material is available, then one hypothesis cannot be proven more probable than another on grounds other than mere "taste" (Mason 2003a, 187). Third, we must realize that

Josephus' shaping of his material is not limited to programmatic sections, such as prologue, speeches, remarks, and epilogues, but affects his very words, phrases, and syntax...We have no way to transmogrify selected pieces of it into something more neutral, to decode it, disinfect it, or distill from it a residue of factual statements. That would require magic or alchemy, not history. Though they are histories by ancient standards of genre, his narratives contain much of the dramatic, tragic, and poetic. It is not possible to detach even one item or case from 'Josephus' framework', for that framework is pervasive and fully wrought, animating all of its constituent atoms. (Mason 2003a, 186)

To some extent, in this recent contribution Mason advocates a view similar to that of McLaren, something which he also acknowledges (Mason 2003a, 183). However, this only goes for the rejection of the 'bias research'. Mason does not follow McLaren in his proposed 'case study approach':

When McLaren comes to recover the concealed back-story of these case studies, now truly without any guidance from Josephus, he is understandably in the realm of speculation, left trying to convert a string of mere possibilities into a probability. (Mason 2003a, 183)

Instead, Mason outlines a proper way of using Josephus for the purpose of history by drawing attention to two things. First, we should realize that "the journey is the destination" (Mason 2003a, 187). Hypotheses can have heuristic purposes without aiming at probability, and from there we can find ways to relate our hypotheses to other similar and relevant material in other parts of the Roman world. Second, Mason calls for a shift in Josephus research. Rather than focusing on the events behind the narrative, we should focus on the narrative itself. Not only from a literary perspective, but also from the historical perspective of an immediate reception in Flavian Rome. This way a wide array of contextual sources can be utilized in the efforts aimed at "recovering in depth a real person in a concrete context" (Mason 2003a, 188).[38]

Finally, it must be noted that Mason's argumentation against the search for contradictions and unbiased kernels of trustworthy information is primarily aimed at the (many) cases where Josephus is our only source. Mason's point is that in these cases, where it is not possible to compare Josephus' statements with other sources describing the same event, the step beyond 'heuristic questions' to 'plausible conclusions' is always mediated by taste. In the opposite cases, where other material is available, Josephus' narratives should naturally be utilized on an equal footing with the entire array of sources at hand. However, they should always be regarded as creative contributions which should be utilized through a contextual perspective.[39]

3.2.5 Klaus-Stefan Krieger

Finally we turn to Klaus-Stefan Krieger's comparative study of *Antiquities* 18–20 and *War* 2 as presented in his dissertation, *Geshichtsschreibung als Apologetik* (Krieger 1994) and in a shorter article from an SBL conference (Krieger 2000). Krieger provides a comprehensive analysis of the relationship between *Ant.* 18–20 and *War* 2 in order to trace the aims and purposes of Josephus, which in turn provides important input for the discussion of Josephus as a writer of history. Two things are brought to our attention. First, *Antiquities* uses *War* as both a source and an outline. The order of events is very close, as seen from the table in Krieger 2000, 7ff. However, more stories are included in *Antiquities*. Second, generally speaking, the

---

[38] In a forthcoming publication, Sean Freyne has responded to the challenge of Mason by opting for a more pragmatic approach, granting Josephus a general historical value based on the cases where his overall description concurs with both archaeological findings and the Gospels (Freyne Forthcoming).

[39] Mason's translation of *Life* in the new Brill series illustrates this procedure through its abundance of notes with references to contextual material, as well as several appendices including a thorough overview of the archaeological sites in Galilee (Mason 2001).

stories from *War* incorporated in *Antiquities* have a different flavour. In the SBL article, Krieger illustrates this with the story of Pilate and the shields in Jerusalem. While the incident in *War* is rendered quite directly without any comments, in *Antiquities* it is used as part of the assessment of the bad Roman procurators. There is a different ideological background and setup in the two stories.

The *Antiquities* aims to elicit sympathy for the Jews. Josephus stresses that the only zeal of the Jews is keeping the traditional Jewish customs. For the observance of the Mosaic Law – in the case of the first conflict with Pilate the avoidance of images – they do not want to fight, but they are ready to die a martyr's death. (Krieger 2000, 5)

A number of other examples are given that (taken together) enable Krieger to disclose what he finds to be the apologetic aims of Josephus:

Als Ergebnis können wir festhalten: Flavius Josephus schreibt die Geschichte seines Volkes, um zu verteidigen... Josephus' Beschäftigung mit jüdischer Geschichte kann daher zutreffend als apologetisch ausgerichtete Historiographie beschrieben werden. (Krieger 1994, 326)

Josephus does write history as this was done in his day and age, but with an implied apologetic purpose: "Er treibt Historiographie nach allen Regeln der antiken Kunst, und er tut dies ganz und gar aus apologetischem Interesse" (Krieger 1994, 338).

The apologetic defence concerns four groups: the Jewish people, the Romans, himself, and finally the Jewish God. Krieger finds that the apology for the Jewish people "beherrscht Josephus' literarisches Werk" (Krieger 1994, 327). Josephus tries to prove, even in *War,* that "nur ein kleiner Teil der Juden den Aufstand initiiert und getragen hat; die Mehrheit auch des palästinischen Judentums wird als romtreu oder zumindest den Krieg ablehnend vorgestellt" (Krieger 1994, 327). This trend is strengthened in *Antiquities*. Likewise, Josephus defends the Romans. In *War* we find a defence of the Flavians. The temple was destroyed against the will of Titus. In *Antiquities* the focus is different. Here Josephus builds pairs, differentiating between

...den „schlechten" Statthaltern Judäas und den „guten" Legaten Syriens sowie zwischen „guten" Kaisern – in AJ 18–20 Tiberius und v.a. Claudius – und „schlechten" Kaisern, v.a. Caligula... Selbst der Anschlag eines judenfeindlichen Kaisers, des Caligula auf den Tempel, wird von einem Römer, Petronius, mit Gottes Hilfe vereitelt. (Krieger 1994, 328)

Krieger also briefly notes that Josephus is highly concerned about how his own role will be understood by his readers – not only in *Life* but also in *War*. Finally, Josephus tries to give a theological defence to explain how the Jewish God could allow the destruction of the temple.

In die gleiche Richtung zielt die Geschichtstheologie des Josephus: Gott hat sich von seinem Volk abgewendet und sein Heiligtum verlassen, weil die Aufständischen Torahver-
letzungen begangen und ihr Heil bei den Waffen statt im Vertrauen auf Gottes Beistand
gesucht haben. Josephus sucht eine theologische Deutung für die Zerstörung Jerusalems
und des Tempels und baut dabei auf Interpretationen auf, die im Judentum bereits für die
Eroberung des Ersten Tempels gefunden worden waren: Die Katastrophe ist Strafe Gottes
für den Ungehorsam der Israeliten. (Krieger 1994, 329)

The reason why God abandoned his people is clear: "Gott strafte sein
Volk, weil im Aufstand gegen Rom die Torah wieder und wieder gebrochen und das Heiligtum entweiht wurde" (Krieger 1994, 338).

Krieger thus presents the same positive view of Josephus' abilities as a
writer as Mason and Bilde. Krieger is not looking for the sources within
the narrative, but searching for the overall tendency of Josephus on the basis of which the credibility and probability can be evaluated. The question
is, however, if Krieger in his literary analyses avoids the inherent risk of
such analyses to conflate the material into a picture which substantiates a
specific hypothesis. To my mind, this is what happens gradually in what is
otherwise a profound discussion. In order to emphasize the difference between *War* and *Antiquities*, Krieger states several times that all the procurators are bad in *Antiquities*, whereas only the last ones in *War* are described in a similar manner by Josephus: "In AJ sind nicht nur die letzten
beiden, sondern alle Präfekte und Prokuratoren Judäas schlechte Statthal-
ter. Sie alle sind unfähig, korrupt, ausbeuterisch, brutal oder judenfeind-
lich" (Krieger 1994, 330). However, this claim does not withstand a closer
inspection, since most of the procurators in *Antiquities* are merely mentioned without any further information. The same applies to *War*. Likewise, the portrayal of Antipas at the end is too generalized and one-sided.
Krieger wants to show a difference between the positive picture given of
Philip and that given of Antipas, although they are not directly contrasted
by Josephus. In this way Krieger emphasizes the events around Herodias
and John the Baptist, whereas Antipas' positive relations to Tiberius and
Rome are overlooked.

3.2.6 Approaching Josephus

As already mentioned, this investigation does not claim to be in-depth or
conclusive. Only a small fraction of the comprehensive research on
Josephus as a writer of history has been brought into play as a representative selection with a special emphasis on the topic we are treating in general. The aim has nevertheless been to provide a feeling of the problems
we face in using Josephus for historical purposes. As tentative conclusions,
the following may be said: first, the approaches searching for contradictions in the sources and McLaren's re-shaped edition in his 'case study approach' are marred by the internal contradiction of trying to recover his-

torical material from Josephus through external and debatable, if not contingent, standards. As discussed in the treatment of Rappaport's approach, this methodology will not provide a more solid ground to judge the historical subject matter on than that of personal "taste", to use Mason's phrase.

Second, on the contrary, it is accepted that Josephus must be viewed as a creative writer. Though he naturally used sources extensively, he did this in an intelligent manner. Therefore, literary analyses of the entire narrative are warranted, as seen in the work of Bilde, Mason, Krieger and others.

Third, a literary analysis of Josephus should still be keenly aware of the problem of how to take account of the many different strands of thought in and purposes behind his narratives, which is why care must be taken not to conflate the picture in order to present a coherent image (cf. also Mason 1998).

Fourth, the most important question remains of how to move from literary analyses to historical facts. At least it is possible to follow Mason when he argues that absolute safe ground is reached when the quest for historical plausibility is exchanged for a series of heuristic questions, at least, when Josephus is our only source. Following Bilde and Krieger, however, it is further accepted that the Josephean narrative can be compared to the historical standards of its day, including the careful treatment of the sources that have been incorporated. Bilde even argues, on the basis of a study of the geographical excurses, that Josephus to some extent mastered what even today would be considered a valid historical methodology (Bilde 1994).

To sum up, this means that it is more fruitful to read the narrative of Josephus using a method of '*Tendenzkritik*' searching for the broader narrative framework, than using a method of 'contradiction' searching for the sources in the source. Though we should be more careful than Krieger, for instance, in defining Josephus' *Tendenz* beforehand, and though we should try not to conflate the picture, reading the individual stories from the larger perspective is a promising method. Josephus is thus *one* historical voice, which should first be read on its own terms, and then read alongside all other available material of the period under investigation. The first step, the literary analysis, will be performed in what follows. And the second step, the historical inquiry, will be performed in Part III.

3.3 The Context

3.3.1 *Antipater, the Founder of the Herodian Dynasty*

The Herodian house is introduced with Antipater, the father of Herod the Great. In *War* he is introduced in 1.123 and described as an old enemy of

Aristobulos and as a wealthy Idumean, a principal of his nation (πρωτεύων τοῦ ἔθνους). His marriage to the Arabian Cypros and his friendship with the king of Arabia is noted as well (1.181–182), as is his personal and courageous aid to Caesar during his campaign in Egypt, for which he was generously awarded Roman citizenship, exemption from taxes and other honours and marks of friendship (τιμῆς καὶ φιλοφρονήσεως, 1.194). In this period, Antipater is described as the actual ruler of the Jewish nation (*War* 1.203). In the passage following the assassination of Antipater by poison, Josephus describes him as an energetic man (δραστήριος ἀνὴρ, 1.226).

In *Antiquities*, the picture of Antipater is somewhat different from that presented in *War*. On the one hand, Antipater is called a rebel (στασιαστής, 14.8), who looked jealously at Aristobulos (ὑφοράω, 14.11), and therefore constantly brought charges against him before Hyrcanos (ἑκάστης ἡμέρας πλαττόμενος καὶ διαβάλλων, 14.14). On the other, Josephus still informs us of Antipater's military aid of Caesar in Egypt and the way he is rewarded for this (14.133–139); and when Antipater dies, Josephus evaluates him even more positively than in *War* describing him as a man distinguished for piety and justice (εὐσεβείᾳ τε καὶ δικαιοσύνῃ διενεγκὼν) committed to his country (περὶ τὴν πατρίδα σπουδῇ, *Ant.* 14.283).

Thus a development from *War* to *Antiquities* is traceable, though not unequivocally so. The appearance of the Herodian house is clearly in itself ambiguous to Josephus. On the one hand, it was an aid to Hyrcanus and helped to keep the Jewish nation on good terms with Rome. It even produced good rulers like Phasael, who in *War* as well as in *Antiquities* is described as a mild and fair ruler of Jerusalem (*War* 1.206–207; *Ant.* 14.161–162). On the other hand, problems emerged with Herod, as we shall now see.

3.3.2 Herod the Great

The description of Herod the Great is the longest sequence on a single person in Josephus (*War* 1.204–673 and *Ant.* 14.158–17.199). From *War* to *Antiquities*, Josephus changed his narrative on at least two points. First, the structure was changed from being thematic in *War* to being chronological in *Antiquities*.[40] Second, and most notable, is the fact that Josephus is more judgmental in *Antiquities*. Through several editorial remarks (cf. 14.274;

---

[40] In *War*, the surrounding political history is concentrated into one section (going from 1.204 to 1.400), then follows the story of Herod's building activities (1.401–428), after which, following a minor digression on Herod's physical constitution (1.429–34), Herod's close family tragedies are presented (1.435–664).

15.266–267, 328; 16.150–159; 17.180–181, 191–192; 18.127–129 and more), he advances a negative judgment of Herod. Gideon Fuks has pointed out six instances in which Herod is judged by Josephus for his attitude towards the Jewish religion (Fuks 2002). Fuks' list, however, is not comprehensive and can be increased to at least eighteen incidents in which Josephus, either directly by himself or indirectly through some pious Jews, accuses Herod of being a transgressor of the law (παρανομία, e.g. *Ant.* 14.167; 15.243, 266, 328; 16.4; 17.150, 304), a transgressor of the ancestral traditions (τὰ πάτρια, e.g. *Ant.* 15.277, 281), customs and practices (ἔθος, e.g. *Ant.* 15.267, 268, 274, 288, 328, 365), of being impious (ἀσέβεια/ἀσεβής, e.g. *Ant.* 15.275; 16.402; 17.1, cf. also *Ant.* 15.182, 267, 288, 365), and of being a cruel (ὠμότης, e.g. *War* 1.534; *Ant.* 17.191) tyrant (τυραννικός/τυραννίς, e.g. *War* 2.84; *Ant.* 14.165; 16.4; 17.304) not marked by the necessary 'moderation' (μέτριος, e.g. *Ant.* 15.182).

In a sum, Herod offends in a three-fold way. First, in his relations to his Hasmonean family in-laws. Second, by being too *philorhomaios*, too friendly towards the Roman establishment through games and lavishly built temples, in which way he transgressed the ancestral laws by innovations that were foreign and destructive to Jewish practices and customs. Third and finally, by being a cruel tyrant who lacked any kind of moderation. In two crucial passages, Josephus even blames Herod for being partly responsible for the ultimate destruction of Jerusalem and the temple (cf. 15.267 and 15.281). To Josephus, Herod was an innovator who inflicted things on the Jews that were not previously known. This will now be demonstrated as we work our way through *Antiquities* books 14–17, analyzing the narrative structure of the works of Josephus. References to *War* will be given showing both similarities and dissimilarities.

(1) In both *War* and *Antiquities*, the first recorded official appearance of Herod is his appointment as commander of Galilee (*War* 1.203ff.; *Ant.* 14.158ff.). Both texts describe him in a positive manner as an active young man (δραστήριος, *War* 1.204, νέος, *Ant.* 14.158). Likewise, in both texts he is praised by the Syrians as a restorer of peace and wealth (Ἡρώδης ὡς εἰρήνην αὐτοῖς καὶ τὰς κτήσεις ἀνασεσωκώς, *War* 1.205, cf. *Ant.* 14.160) upon his neutralizing Ezekias, who had plundered their area. But in Jerusalem, the news of Herod's activities in Galilee is not welcomed. In *War* some "malicious" (βάσκανοι) persons rose up (ἐρεθίζω) against Herod in the court of Hyrcanus, accusing him of violating the Jewish law (παρὰ τὸν τῶν Ἰουδαίων νόμον, *War* 1.208–209). In *Antiquities*, on the other hand, the opponents of Herod are no longer described as malicious, but are now the leading men of the Jews (οἱ πρῶτοι τῶν Ἰουδαίων, *Ant.* 14.165), who, along with accusing him of transgressions of the Jewish law (παραβὰς τὸν ἡμέτερον νόμον, 14.167), also brought a new charge

against Herod for trying to establish himself as a tyrant (τυραννίς, 14.165). This is one of many typical "minor" changes occurring in the narratives on Herod between *War* and *Antiquities*.

(2)   In the paragraphs dealing with the time before Herod captured Jerusalem in 37 BCE, Josephus describes Herod in a moderately positive manner. Herod is an efficient commander capable of collecting one hundred talents in Galilee for Cassius to be used in the civil war against Octavian and Anthony (*War* 1.221; *Ant.* 14.274). In *Ant.* 14.274, however, we have one of the editorial remarks advancing a negative judgment of Herod, who "thought it to be sensible to nurse (friendship) with the Romans and to take care of their goodwill on the pain of others" (σῶφρον γὰρ ἔδοξεν αὐτῷ Ῥωμαίους ἤδη θεραπεύειν καὶ τὴν παρ᾽ αὐτῶν κατασκευάζειν εὔνοιαν ἐκ τῶν ἀλλοτρίων πόνων). Still, Herod's abilities as a soldier and commander appeared to be valuable during the many internal fights for power, and his efforts to free Jerusalem from the enemies of Hyrcanos finally made him "beloved by everyone (in Jerusalem) for his success" (πᾶσιν ἀγαπητὸς ὢν ἐπὶ τῷ κατορθώματι, *War* 1.240), and they crowned his head with wreaths (στεφάνοι, *Ant.* 14.299). His marriage with Mariamme, the daughter of Hyrcanos, was sealed, and the people of Jerusalem seemed to have accepted Herod (*War* 1.241). This peaceful situation was not to last. In both *War* and *Antiquities*, we immediately learn of resistance against Herod and Phasael grounded in discontent with their de facto reign on behalf of Hyrcanos. In both accounts, we are told three times of how the leading Jews (Ἰουδαίων οἱ δυνατοί, οἱ ἐν τέλει Ἰουδαίων) approached Anthony to accuse the brothers, who for their part had secured themselves through large bribes (cf. *War* 1.242, 243–244, 245ff.; *Ant.* 14.301ff., 324ff., 327ff.). Interestingly, in *Antiquities*, Josephus tells us how Herod tried to spare the lives of the Jews from being killed by Anthony (*Ant.* 14.236).

(3)   As already noted, the two accounts on Herod are not structured in the same manner. Following the chronological order of *Antiquities*, the next examples concern Herod's relationship to his Hasmonean family in-laws. *Antiquities* 15.23ff. describes Herod's murder of the son of Alexandra and the brother of Mariamme, Aristobulos, who is pictured as utmost good or beautiful (κάλλιστον, 15.23, 25, 51). Especially interesting is the description of his appearance as a high priest in the temple. People rejoiced over the sight of him, since, as Josephus adds, "...by his appearance, he displayed completely the rank of his descent" (περὶ τὸ γένος ἀξιώματος πλεῖστον ἐν τῇ μορφῇ διαφαίνων, 15.51). In *War*, Josephus just briefly mentions how Herod had the young high priest killed (*War* 1.437). Thus, a clear distinction is made between Herod and the royal Hasmonean family,

which Josephus further unfolds throughout the rest of his account in *Antiquities*.

(4)   The next example of domestic trouble is the execution of Hyrcanos. The account in *Antiquities* is much more extensive than the account in *War*, and provides another clear example of the way in which Josephus altered his description by inserting personal evaluations and editorial remarks. While *War* briefly recounts the way in which Herod had Hyrcanos put to death on suspicion of conspiracy (1.433–434), *Antiquities* provides two accounts of the events to underline the cruelty of it as well as a final obituary on Hyrcanos (15.161–182). Along the way, Hyrcanos is said to be the only one left of royal rank (ἀξιώματος βασιλικοῦ) and more worthy of the kingdom than Herod (ἄνδρα τυχεῖν τῆς βασιλείας ἀξιώτερον, 15.164), while Herod clearly is the one to blame. Hyrcanos is described as gentle and moderate (ἐπιεικὴς καὶ μέτριος), while Herod was neither just nor pious (οὔτε δίκαιον οὔτ᾽ εὐσεβὲς, 15.182). Once again, Herod is contrasted with the Hasmonean family and judged by Josephus as impious, unjust and as having one of the clear marks of tyranny, i.e. lack of moderation.

(5)   After describing the events around the battle at Actium (*Ant.* 15.183–201), Josephus returns to Herod's problems with his Hasmonean family in-laws (15.202). First in line is Herod's beloved wife, Mariamme. The account of the events leading to her execution is much longer in *Antiquities* (15.202–246) than in *War* (1.438–444), and it is also changed according to the same pattern as found above. In *War*, no obvious judgmental statements are uttered. In *Antiquities* we learn of a subsequent infectious disease (λοιμώδης νόσος, 15.243) killing both some of the people and some of Herod's friends, and which was thought to be from God due to the lawless acts (παρανομία, 15.243) inflicted on Mariamme. In *War*, Herod's act is motivated by jealousy alone (ζηλοτυπία, *War* 1.443).

(6)   Surprisingly, the mother of Mariamme, Alexandra, is not mentioned in *War*. In *Antiquities* she plays a vital role in the prolonged problems of the Herodian house. The general picture of Alexandra is not flattering, and when she is executed in 15.247–252, a positive appraisal does not follow, as in the case of Hyrcanos and Mariamme. However, in the succeeding paragraphs we are told of Herod's execution of the sons of Baba, who were from the Hasmonean royal lineage as well (15.263). This step is harshly commented on by Josephus, who states that by now no one was left alive from the family of Hyrcanos, and *therefore* no one was left to prevent his unlawful acts (μηδενὸς ὄντος ἐπ᾽ ἀξιώματος ἐμποδὼν ἵστασθαι τοῖς παρανομουμένοις, 15.266). Again a clear distinction is made between Herod and the Hasmonean royal lineage.

(7)　This development is commented on by Josephus in the highly important summarising editorial statement in paragraph 15.267: (a) because of the executions (διὰ τοῦτο), Herod forsook even more the customs of the fathers (μᾶλλον ἐξέβαινεν τῶν πατρίων ἐθῶν); (b) with foreign practices he changed the ancient way of living that had been inviolable (ξενικοῖς ἐπιτηδεύμασιν ὑποδιέφθειρεν τὴν πάλαι κατάστασιν ἀπαρεγχείρητον οὖσαν); and (c) therefore, Josephus states, by these means no little evil wrongdoing happened at a later time (ἐξ ὧν οὐ μικρὰ καὶ πρὸς τὸν αὖθις χρόνον ἠδικήθημεν), because what had earlier brought about piety in the people was neglected (ἀμεληθέντων ὅσα πρότερον ἐπὶ τὴν εὐσέβειαν ἦγεν τοὺς ὄχλους). In a profound way, Josephus directly connects the reign of Herod to the fall of the temple, and as mentioned above, the question of why the temple was destroyed is one of the most central issues for Josephus altogether. It is highly notable that Herod is presented as one of the causes of this (cf. also 15.281), as is the Fourth Philosophy (*Ant.* 18.1–10, cf. below).

(8)　This summarising statement is exemplified in the following paragraphs, where Herod is judged for the establishment of athletic contests and for building a theatre and an amphitheatre in Jerusalem. Both actions are said to be foreign according to Jewish practice (κατὰ τοὺς Ἰουδαίους ἔθους ἀλλότρια, *Ant.* 15.268). Again it is highly interesting to note the different flavour of *War.* 1.404 mentions Herod's building of the temple at Paneion without any comments. Likewise, 1.415 mentions the setting up of games in Caesarea without any negative remarks, and 1.426–428 even benefits Herod as a saviour of the Olympic Games in Greece. In *Antiquities*, however, Josephus clearly condemns both the games and the buildings. In 15.274–76 games involving wild animals and gladiators are rejected as a dissolution of the customs held in esteem by the Jews (κατάλυσις τῶν τιμωμένων παρ' αὐτοῖς ἐθῶν), and as impiety (ἀσεβής) exemplified in the display of trophies (τρόπαια) thought to bear images (εἰκόνες) forbidden by the custom of the fathers (πάτριος).[41] With admiration Josephus tells us how the Jews of Jerusalem accused Herod of bringing trophies into the city and thus transgressing their custom (πάτριον αὐτοῖς, 15.277). Although Herod was able to calm down most of the Jews by showing how the trophies did not hide actual images, but were made out of plain wood (15.279–280), some maintained that the actions of Herod were one way of destroying the customs which would be the beginning of evil events (τὸ καταλύεσθαι τὰ πάτρια μεγάλων ἡγούμενοι ἀρχὴν κακῶν, 15.281). This is another ill-disguised connection of the reign of

---

[41] Interestingly, in *Ant.* 19.335–337 Josephus praises Agrippa for arranging games and spectacles including gladiatorial fights.

Herod to the destruction of the temple (cf. 15.267). For this reason these people saw it as their sacred duty (ὅσιος, 15.281) to find a way to have Herod executed with daggers, since in reality he was not a king but a true enemy of the entire people (πολέμιον φαινόμενον τοῦ παντὸς ἔθνους, 15.281), who had introduced customs against their will (πρὸς βίαν, 15.281). When caught by Herod, Josephus recounts with admiration how the conspirators openly held their act to be both good and pious (καλῶς καὶ σὺν εὐσεβείᾳ), since the common customs (τῶν κοινῶν ἐθῶν) are worthy for all Jews either to keep or to die for (ἢ φυλάττειν ἢ θνήσκειν, 15.288).

(9)   However, as in the case of Antipater, Josephus also provides some genuinely positive stories about Herod even in *Antiquities*, like his aid to the people under a severe drought (15.303–316). Even though Herod himself was financially ruined by the drought, he found a way to buy grain by using his ornamental gold to issue coins. This act of goodness (εὔνοια, 15.308) actually reversed the attitude of the people. Likewise, the rebuilding of the temple (*Ant.* 15. 380–425, *War* 1.401–402) seems to be evaluated positively. Josephus even includes a speech of Herod, in which he twice states how he became king by the will of God (σὺν τῇ τοῦ θεοῦ βουλήσει, 15.383, ἐγὼ μὲν ἄρχω θεοῦ βουλήσει, 15.387). In addition, we learn about how Herod fought for the rights of the Jews in the Diaspora (16.58–62) as well as about two tax cuts (15.365, 16.63–65).

(10)   *War* 1.422–425 and *Ant.* 15.326–330 outline Herod's building activities in the Greek cities. Once again, a notable development between the two is traceable. While *War* just gives an account and then moves on, *Antiquities* provides an interpretation and a critical judgment. According to Josephus, Herod's activities in pagan cities were directed by his love of honour (φιλοτιμίας) and his paying court or homage (τῆς θεραπείας, 15.328) to Caesar and the powerful Romans. Because of this, as Josephus continues, "he was forced to leave the customs (ἐκβαίνειν τῶν ἐθῶν ἠναγκάζετο) and to re-value many of the laws (πολλὰ τῶν νομίμων παραχαράττειν) by building cities driven by love of honour (φιλοτιμία) and by erecting temples" (15.328).

(11)   A similar charge against Herod is given in *Ant.* 15.365–372. The background is actually positive: Herod had the taxes cut by one-third. But, as Josephus adds, this was done to quell resistance in the people, to whom the works of Herod seemed to be a way of "destroying their godly way of life and a way of changing their habits" (λυομένης αὐτοῖς τῆς εὐσεβείας καὶ μεταπιπτόντων τῶν ἐθῶν, 15.365). Details are then provided of the way Herod jealously watched his people, and he is pictured as a true tyrant.

(12) *Antiquities* 16 opens with an accusation against Herod for being a cruel tyrant. A new law against theft is commented on by Josephus not as a kingly act, but one of a tyrant (οὐ βασιλικῶς ἀλλὰ τυραννικῶς) against the law (παράνομος, 16.4). In connection with Mason's analysis of Josephus' general anti-monarchial and aristocratic conservatism, it is important to notice that Herod is portrayed as an intruder and innovator.[42] His new law had no precedent (νόμον οὐδὲν ἐοικότα τοῖς πρώτοις, 16.1). Herod shares this condemnation of introducing innovations with the Fourth Philosophy, as we shall see (18.1–10).

(13) Much of book 16 is devoted to the two sons of Mariamme, Alexander and Aristobulos, who according to Josephus were persons that "did not lack royal rank in appearance" (βασιλικοῦ κατὰ τὰς μορφὰς ἀξιώματος οὐκ ἀποδέοντες, 16.7), although Josephus also criticizes their behaviour in a couple of instances (*Ant.* 16.67, 254, 399). It is nonetheless Herod who is held solely responsible for their execution, which is described as the "decisive proof of his impiety impossible to punish" (ἀσεβείας τεκμήριον ἀνυποτιμήτου, 16.402). Book 17 opens with an even harsher assessment of Herod, describing the plot hatched by him and his son Antipater against the two sons of Mariamme as the highest ungodliness (ἀσεβείᾳ τε τῇ ὑστάτῃ), exposing them to divine vengeance (ἀλαστορίᾳ, 17.1). Once again, it is striking that the religious assessment is new compared with *War*, describing it only as a cruel act without further religious implications (ὠμότης, 1.534).

(14) In *Ant.* 16.150–159 we find another of the very important summarising statements of Josephus (cf. 15.266 and elsewhere). This time with an outspoken "I" (ἐγώ, 16.152, μοι, 16.159). Josephus delves into the double-sided nature of Herod as a man who is both beneficent (εὐεργεσία, 16.150) and unjust in his harsh punishments (τὰς τιμωρίας καὶ ἀδικίας, 16.151), as well as being a stranger to all kinds of moderation (πάσης μετριότητος ἀλλότριον, 16.151). Josephus finds an explanation in Herod's love of honour (φιλότιμος, 16.153). Everything he did was based in his desire for fame. But as Josephus finally states, "the Jewish nation is by law alienated against such things, and habituated to love what is rightful before what leads to honour" (τό γε μὴν Ἰουδαίων ἔθνος ἠλλοτρίωται νόμῳ πρὸς πάντα τὰ τοιαῦτα καὶ συνείθισται τὸ δίκαιον ἀντὶ τοῦ πρὸς δόξαν ἠγαπηκέναι, 16.158). Thus, once again Herod is portrayed as a cruel tyrant and as a transgressor of the ancient law and tradition.

(15) Before the execution of Antipater and the death of Herod, Josephus tells the story of the golden eagle in the temple. In this case, the two ver-

---

[42] Cf. Mason 2003b, 577ff., with special reference to Sentius' speech in the Senate, *Ant.* 19.167–184.

sions (*War* 1.648–655; *Ant.* 17.149–167) are quite similar without any new outspoken critical remarks in the latter, though it is much longer. The two leaders of the uprising, Judas and Matthias, are called "most learned" (λογιώτατοι) and interpreters of the law of the fathers (ἐξηγηταὶ τῶν πατρίων νόμων, *Ant.* 17.149). They instructed their students to pull down what the king had built against the law (παρὰ νόμον τοῦ πατρίου κατεσκεύαστο ἔργα ὑπὸ τοῦ βασιλέως ταῦτα καθελόντες), and thus be rewarded according to the law for their brave deeds of piety (εὐσεβείας ἀγωνίσματα παρὰ τῶν νόμων φέρεσθαι, 17.150). For, as Josephus explains, Herod had, against the law (παρὰ τὸν νόμον, 17.151), erected a golden eagle in the temple, although the law forbids images. Therefore the leaders exhorted their students to safeguard the way of the fathers (τοῦ πατρίου, 17.152), and to suffer a holy death if necessary. When caught and interrogated, they defended themselves by referring to the law and to Moses (17.159), making a firm stand resembling the boldness of Mattathias in 1 Maccabees. A furious Herod burned them all alive. The story corresponds with all the others depicting Herod as both a cruel tyrant and a transgressor of the law, and as one who did not safeguard the Jewish way of life.

(16) Just before the death of Herod, two more examples are given of his cruelty, namely his attempt to create sorrow in the country upon his death by having the leading men killed (*War* 1.659–660, *Ant.* 17.174–181), and his execution of his son Antipater (*War* 1.663–664, *Ant.* 17.187). In the two accounts of the attempted killing of the leading men, we once again find a notable difference with *Antiquities*, providing us with an inserted personal editorial remark of Josephus, which judges Herod as not having any humanity (οὐδὲν ἀνθρώπειον, 17.180).

(17) When Herod finally dies, another editorial remark is inserted in *Antiquities*, evaluating him harshly by saying that he was "a man cruel to all on an equal basis" (ἀνὴρ ὠμὸς εἰς πάντας ὁμοίως), a man who was "easy to anger but above justice" (ὀργῆς μὲν ἥσσων κρείσσων δὲ τοῦ δικαίου, 17.191). In the parallel passage of *War*, no accusation is levelled of either cruelty or impiety – just a note saying that he was unlucky in his private life (1.665).

(18) Josephus does not stop accusing Herod even after his death. For instance, during the trial in Rome after the death of Herod, he is depicted as a tyrant and not a king by the Jewish delegation (οὐ βασιλέα λέγοντες ἀλλὰ τῶν πώποτε τυραννησάντων ὠμότατον ἐνηνοχέναι τύραννον, *War* 2.84), a man who had, besides torture and other forms of cruelty, transgressed the ancestral laws, and "in general the Jews had endured more misfortune from Herod in the few years than they had suffered in all the time since they returned from Babylon" (καθόλου δὲ πλείους

ὑπομεμενηκέναι τὰς ἐξ Ἡρώδου συμφορὰς ἐν ὀλίγοις ἔτεσιν Ἰουδαίους ὧν ἐν παντὶ τῷ χρόνῳ μετὰ τὴν ἐκ Βαβυλῶνος ἀναχώρησιν ἔπαθον, *War* 2.86). The same charges are found in the parallel passage in *Ant.* 17.299–310. Second, in connection with the introduction of Agrippa I in *Ant.* 18.126, Josephus inserts a genealogy aimed at praising Agrippa in contrast to Herod. In the editorial remark found in 18.127–129, Josephus states that within less than a hundred years, the lineage of Herod (τοὺς Ἡρώδου ἀπογόνους) was destroyed by the deity (ὁ θεῖος), with the single exception of Agrippa. This fact is said to be important for the story of Josephus, since it contains a godly demonstration (παράστασιν ἔχειν τοῦ θείου, 18.127) of how the only thing that matters is piety towards the deity (πρὸς τὸ θεῖον εὐσεβειῶν, 18.127).

To summarize, it is thus quite clear that, while Josephus has many good things to say about Herod's Hasmonean family in-laws and especially the two sons by Mariamme, he severely accuses Herod, as well as Herod's father Antipater, and Herod's first son, Antipater, of committing three crimes, which ultimately are connected. Herod is accused of his crimes against the Hasmonean family, of his cruelty in general, and of his transgressions against the law and tradition. It is further interesting to note the way in which Josephus develops his presentation from *War* to *Antiquities*. While the negative evaluation of Herod is not absent in *War*, it is clearer in *Antiquities*, especially in the many editorial remarks. What Josephus especially seems to emphasize in *Antiquities* is how Herod disturbed the old practices, customs and traditions of the Jews with innovations that eventually led to the destruction of the temple and Jerusalem (*Ant.* 15.267, 281). Thus, Josephus' portrait of Herod's kingship closely mirrors the three indictments against the Roman *principes* in the speech of Sentius' in the Senate (*Ant.* 19.167–184, cf. above section 3.2.4).

3.3.3 Archelaos

The same accusations of being impious, of acting against the law and of being a cruel tyrant are levelled against Archelaos as well. In this instance, the two accounts of Josephus more or less follow the same scheme and contain the same view on Archelaos, though *Antiquities* is slightly more outspoken with a final comment by Josephus clearly accusing Archelaos of transgressing the law (17.341). The account of Archelaos' rule falls into three parts: (1) the period following the death of Herod and the massacre in the temple, (2) the trial in Rome, (3) his marriage to Glaphyra and final downfall.

(1) After the death of Herod, Archelaos takes over. The people force him to promise to be a better king than his father (ἀμείνων, *War* 2.3, εὔνοιά, *Ant.* 17.203). He is presented with three demands that he accepts:

tax cuts, abolition of duties, and liberation of prisoners (*War* 2.4; *Ant.* 17.204–205). However, some people also wanted those whom Herod had burned alive in the golden-eagle episode to be honoured. Even though Archelaos initially accepts the demand and tries to set up negotiations (*Ant.* 17.208–209), violent disturbances evolve ending in a massacre of pilgrims in the temple during the Passover. 3,000 people are reported killed in the temple by the soldiers of Archelaos (*War* 2.12; *Ant.* 17.218).

(2) This incident proved fatal for Archelaos. During the trial before Augustus on the wills of Herod, Archelaos is rebuked first by the delegation supporting Antipas and later by the Jewish delegation, who wanted direct Roman rule. The allegations include cruelty (ὠμότης, *War* 2.31, 88–89; *Ant.* 17.230, 313), a tyrannical nature (τῆς φύσει τυραννίδος, *Ant.* 17.237), impiety and lawbreaking (παρανομηθεῖσιν, *War* 2.32, δυσσέβεια, *Ant.* 17.237, 313), as well as an accusation of making himself king (*War* 2.26–30; *Ant.* 17.230). He had demonstrated that he was a true son of his father (*War* 2.89; *Ant.* 17.312). The accusations of cruelty and impiety are especially striking. They are exemplified with reference to the massacre of pilgrims in the temple during the Passover, making it an act of sacrilege beyond what even Herod had ever done. Josephus recaptures the speaker of Antipas' party this way:

Especially he made the slaughter around the temple look terrible in his pleading and the impiety of it, since it was done during an ongoing feast, and in what manner they were slain as sacrifices themselves. Some were strangers, others were locals. The temple was filled with corpses, (an act) not done by a foreigner, but by one who had raised himself to the act of being a so-called lawful king, just in order to be able to fulfil his tyrannical nature in an act of injustice hated by all men (μάλιστα δὲ τὴν σφαγὴν τῶν περὶ τὸ ἱερὸν ἐδείνου τῷ λόγῳ καὶ τὴν δυσσέβειαν ὡς ἑορτῆς τε ἐνεστηκυίας καὶ ἱερείων ἐν τρόπῳ σφαχθεῖεν ἔνιοι μὲν ξένοι οἱ δὲ ἐγχώριοι πλησθείη δὲ τὸ ἱερὸν νεκρῶν οὐχ ὑπ' ἀλλοφύλου ἀλλὰ τοῦ καὶ μετὰ νομίμων ὀνομάτων τῆς βασιλείας ἐφιεμένου τῆς πράξεως ὅπως δυνηθείη πληρῶσαι τῆς φύσει τυραννίδος τὴν πᾶσιν ἀνθρώποις μεμισημένην ἀδικίαν, *Ant.* 17.237).

(3) Before his last word on Archelaos, Josephus inserts into both his accounts the lengthy story of "the Alexander fake" (*War* 2.101–110; *Ant.* 17.324–338). This insertion has an important function in the overall narrative by bolstering Josephus' message that the true royal heritage is to be found in the Hasmonean remnants of Mariamme. Her two sons with Herod were so popular in the Diaspora that a man resembling Alexander was able to convince the Diaspora Jews that he actually was Alexander, providing hopes of restoring the old glory of the Hasmoneans. Following this rather peculiar insertion, Josephus explains how the reign of Archelaos came to an end. Both accounts reveal how a group of leading Samaritans and Jews, united for the occasion, travelled to Rome to accuse Archelaos of governing with cruelty and tyranny (τὴν ὠμότητα αὐτοῦ καὶ τυραννίδα, *Ant.*

17.342, cf. *War* 2.111). *Antiquities* further adds an accusation against Archelaos for breaking the law (τοῦ πατρίου παράβασιν, 17.341) by marrying Glaphyra, since she had already been married to his half-brother Alexander, the son of Mariamme. Finally, in both *War* and *Antiquities*, the
downfall of Archelaos is underlined by the dreams he and his wife
Glaphyra had just before they went to Rome to receive their banishment.
As pointed out by J.W. van Henten, the two dreams function as divine verdicts on Archelaos' ungodly way of life and prepare the reader for a new
era in Judea without Herodian rule by the will of God (van Henten 2003).

3.3.4 The Fourth Philosophy

The downfall of Archelaos and the inauguration of direct Roman rule in
Judea provoked a rebellion led by Judas of Gamala (*Ant.* 18.4) or the Galilean (*War* 2.118). In *War*, Judas is introduced as a "sophist" with a party of
his own (οὗτος σοφιστὴς ἰδίας αἱρέσεως) not resembling anything else
among the Jews (ἦν δ᾽ οὗτος σοφιστὴς ἰδίας αἱρέσεως οὐδὲν τοῖς ἄλλοις
προσεοικώς, 2.118), and consequently contrasted to the three other philosophies (2.119–161). In *Antiquities*, the shift from Archelaos to Roman
rule is marked with a new book, and 18.1–10 are among the most important paragraphs in Josephus' entire narrative, presenting his interpretation
of reasons, fault and who to blame for the catastrophe of Jews in its total-
ity. Again some very illuminating additions are traceable compared with
the account provided by *War*.[43] We are introduced to the two basic options
of response to the Roman takeover of Palestine. One is represented by the
high priest Joazar, who is able to calm down some of the Jewish resistance
to foreign rule including the census in connection with taxation (18.3). The
other is represented by Judas from Gamala and his helper Sadduc the
Pharisee. Initially, Josephus seems to describe their programme in a
straightforward manner, namely that they initiated a rebellion (ἀπόστα-
σις), because the census and taxation (ἀποτίμησις) were unacceptable,
since it would lead to slavery, and that the deity (τὸ θεῖον) would honour
such goals and be a helper in the unavoidable rebellion and bloodshed to
come (*Ant.* 18.4–5; *War* 2.118). However, the account here in *Ant.* 18 adds
an editorial remark in which Josephus presents his own interpretation of
the Fourth Philosophy (18.6–10):

(1)   Judas and his party caused every kind of misery: "There was no
evilness that did not come forward from these men, more than speakable,

---

[43] The importance of these comments is highlighted by the fact that the presentation of
the Fourth Philosophy is both historically questionable (cf. McLaren 2001), and not in-
ternally coherent, since 18.23–24 seems to describe Judas and his followers in a positive
manner, being almost identical with the Pharisees (cf. Krieger 1994, 20–28).

and it filled up the people (κακόν τε οὐκ ἔστιν οὗ μὴ φυέντος ἐκ τῶνδε τῶν ἀνδρῶν καὶ περαιτέρω τοῦ εἰπεῖν ἀνεπλήσθη τὸ ἔθνος, *Ant.* 18.6).

(2)   These evils are defined by four instrumental datives in 18.7: (a) "by wars coming in that does not cease in having violence" (πολέμων τε ἐπαγωγαῖς οὐχ οἷον τὸ ἄπαυστον τὴν βίαν ἔχειν), (b) "by removing of friends, who could have eased the pains" (ἀποστέρησιν φίλων οἳ καὶ ἐπελαφρύνοιεν τὸν πόνον), (c) "by the formation of great gangs" (λῃστηρίων τε μεγάλων ἐπιθέσεσιν), (d) and "by the destruction of the principal men" (διαφθοραῖς ἀνδρῶν τῶν πρώτων).

(3)   Furthermore, Josephus judges the motives of these people to be of a personal nature for private gain (18.7b).

(4)   He also blames them for being the ultimate reason for famine and civil war: "From this rose sedition and killing of fellow citizens" (ἐξ ὧν στάσεις τε ἐφύησαν δι᾽ αὐτὰς καὶ φόνος πολιτικός, 18.8a).

(5)   But not least he blames them for being the reason for the final fall of the temple (κατασκαφαί μέχρι δὴ καὶ τὸ ἱερὸν τοῦ θεοῦ ἐνείματο πυρὶ τῶν πολεμίων ἥδε ἡ στάσις, 18.8b).

(6)   Finally, Josephus adds that this was nothing but an innovation compared with the tradition of the fathers (τῶν πατρίων καίνισις, 18.9) introducing ideas otherwise unknown. In contrast, only the three other philosophies of Jews, which Josephus describes in the following paragraphs, can claim true heritage.

In the light of what was said about Herod, Antipater and Archelaos, Josephus' treatment of the Fourth Philosophy is quite revealing. We are left in no doubt as to what Josephus' opinion is. Not even Herod the King is so harshly evaluated, though *Ant.* 15.267 comes close. Furthermore, there is another interesting similarity. Both the Herodian house and the Fourth Philosophy represented the introduction of practices and ideas unknown to Judaism at an earlier state, which is one of the things that Josephus highly disregards (cf. Mason 2003b, 577ff.). As in the case of Herod, the Fourth Philosophy is charged with the same the three indictments of Sentius' speech in the Senate for (a) departing from the law and ancient order, (b) acting with tyranny without any moderation, and (c) being the ultimate reason for the destruction of the civil order (*Ant.* 19.167–184). What separates it from Herod is that while he and Archelaos were too friendly towards the Romans and too insensitive towards the Jewish law, practice and religion, Judas and the Fourth Philosophy represent the opposite. In the end, however, both attitudes led away from the good and stable relationship to Rome, and had a direct connection to the ultimate disaster, i.e. the destruction of the temple.[44]

---

[44] In *Ant.* 20.166 Josephus returns to the question of the destruction of the temple and

3.3.5 Pilate

Of the seven Roman administrators in the first period from 6 to 41 CE, Pilate is the only one Josephus provides any details about. The picture given is very negative in both accounts of the three recorded episodes:

(1) In *War* 2.169–174 Pilate smuggles "the images of Caesar, which are called standards" into Jerusalem at night time (ἃς Καίσαρος εἰκόνας αἳ σημαῖαι καλοῦντα, 2.169). The Jews charged him with breaking their law (αὐτοῖς τῶν νόμων, τὰ πάτρια, 2.170–171), which forbade the making of images (δείκηλον), and followed him to Caesarea stating that they would rather die than disobey the law (ἢ τὸν νόμον παραβῆναι, 2.174). Finally, their religious zeal (δεισιδαιμονία) overwhelmed Pilate with astonishment (ὑπερθαυμάσας), leading him to give in.[45] In *Antiquities*, the story is basically narrated in the same way, but some subtle changes are notable and important.[46] The "I" of Josephus once again steps forward, and the act of Pilate is judged in a more clear and outspoken way. The transgression of *their* laws (αὐτοῖς τῶν νόμων 2.170) is changed to a transgression of *our* law (ἡμῖν τοῦ νόμου, *Ant.* 18.55). We are also told that Pilate was the first to do so (πρῶτος δὲ Πιλᾶτος, 18.56) since the former procurators did not bring any offensive signs into Jerusalem. Still, Pilate is astonished (θαυμάζω, 18.59) about their willingness to guard the laws (ἐπὶ φυλακῇ τῶν νόμων, 18.59) and removes the images from Jerusalem.

(2) On a later occasion, Pilate took money from the sacred treasury (τὸν ἱερὸν θησαυρόν, *War* 2.175, τῶν ἱερῶν χρημάτων, *Ant.* 18.60) to built an aqueduct. The two accounts (*War* 2.175–177; *Ant.* 18.60–62) are very close in this instance, though the offensive violence is once again spelled out more clearly in *Antiquities*, where disguised soldiers attack the crowd with uncontrolled force, killing many on the spot. In *War* it seems that most people died in the panic that ensued.

(3) The final act of Pilate came about when he quelled an uprising in Samaria with such an overwhelming use of force that the Samaritans sent envoys to the Roman governor of Syria, Vitellius. He had Pilate relieved of

---

how and why it happened. In another extremely important editorial remark, Josephus states that because of the brigand's violent killings, the temple became unclean. As a result, God turned away and purified the place through the fire of the Romans.

[45] This story in its entirety resembles the story of the Jews asking Petronius not to erect the statue of Gaius Caligula in the temple. Petronius was also filled with astonishment (θαῦμα, *War* 2.198) about their religious zeal, and gave in.

[46] As already noted (cf. section 3.2.5), Klaus-Stefan Krieger finds the differences between the two accounts to be rather dramatic, evolving from a more straight description of Pilate in *War* to a highly polemical and critical description in *Antiquities*, depicting Pilate as a cruel lawbreaker (cf. Krieger 2000 and Krieger 1994, 32ff.).

his duties and sent to Rome for questioning. The story is only told in *Antiquities* (18.85–89).

At this point, Josephus introduces Vitellius.[47] In contrast to Pilate, he is received in splendid fashion in Jerusalem during the Passover, where he does two things that show how "he acted according to our law" (ἐπὶ τῷ ἡμετέρῳ πατρίῳ ποιεῖται, 18.95). First, he remitted sales taxes on fruits (καρπόι, 18.90); and, second, he returned the vestments of the high priest (τὴν στολὴν τοῦ ἀρχιερέως, 18.90) to the custody of the priests on a permanent basis.

As Krieger has pointed out, Josephus deliberately pairs his characters as good and bad (cf. Krieger 1994, 332). Pilate and Vitellius function as such a pair contrasted by their level of respect for the Jewish practices, customs and laws. Like Herod and the Fourth Philosophy, Pilate is an *innovator* who does what no-one had done before him, and the result is a breakdown of the public peace and order. Vitellius, on the other hand, respects the Jewish religion in Jerusalem, and thus becomes an example of how good Roman administration and the traditional Jewish culture could coexist in harmony and peace.

3.3.6 Philip the Tetrarch

Within the line of bad Herodian rulers, Philip the Tetrarch is presented as a notable exception. Not much is told about him, though, and apart from two texts summarising his building activity (*War* 2.167–168; *Ant.* 18.27–28), Josephus just provides detail on his reign in a final obituary (*Ant.* 18.106–108). Three important things are noted: First, Philip is described as μέτριος and ἀπράγμων, moderate and easy-going. Second, he devoted all his time to his area. Finally, he is pictured as a righteous ruler ready to set up his court on the roadside if so needed to free those unjustly convicted (τοὺς ἀδίκως ἐν ἐγκλήμασι γενομένους, 18.107). The following paragraphs (18.108–126) describe Antipas in an ambiguous and rather negative way, and as Krieger notes, Josephus establishes a contrast between the two in this way:

Vor allem aber ist Philippos – und dies führt Josephus breit aus – ein gerechter und beflissener Richter für seine Untertanen und steht auch hier im Kontrast zu Herodes Antipas, der den „guten Mann" Johannes den Täufer hinrichten läßt. (Krieger 1994, 51)

Likewise, Philip stays in his area satisfied with his allotment, whereas Antipas twice travels to Rome (cf. Krieger 1994, 50).

---

[47] Cf. though an earlier "flash-forward" in *Ant.* 15.405ff. pointing to the episode narrated in 18.90–95.

3.3.7 Agrippa I

Josephus is more informative about Agrippa I (or Agrippa the Great, as he calls him) than about any other Herodian ruler apart from Herod the Great. Josephus' two accounts differ in many respects according to the same general pattern as seen above. In contrast to *War*, *Antiquities* clearly states Josephus' personal opinions. The account in *War* is also shorter, running from 2.178–222, while the account in *Antiquities* runs through 18.126–19.366, although insertions on Tiberius and the kingdom of Parthia take up some of the space. In the account in *War*, the following is notable:

(1) Agrippa is introduced as the son of Aristobulos, who had been killed by his father Herod (υἱὸς Ἀριστοβούλου ὃν ὁ πατὴρ Ἡρώδης ἀπέκτεινεν, 2.178).

(2) Instantly Agrippa is placed in opposition to another member of the Herodian house, Antipas. We are told how he came to Rome as the "accuser of Herod the Tetrarch" (κατήγορος Ἡρώδου τοῦ τετραρχοῦντος), but also how Tiberias did not approve his accusation (τοῦ δὲ μὴ προσδεξαμένου τὴν κατηγορίαν). Agrippa stayed in Rome and sought or nursed (θεραπεύω, *War* 2.178) the friendship of Gaius, son of Germanicus.

(3) 2.179–181 recounts the story of how Agrippa once openly prayed for the death of Tiberius during a party, hoping that Gaius would be made emperor instead. For this offence, Agrippa is imprisoned for six months under terrible conditions. When Gaius actually becomes emperor, he is freed and made king (βασιλεύς, 2.181) of Philip's old territory. No details are given from his period in jail, as in *Antiquities*.

(4) After a small insertion on Antipas' banishment, the next passage (2.184–203) covers Gaius' attempt to erect his statue in the temple in Jerusalem. The account is shorter than that given in *Antiquities*, and does not say anything about an intervention by Agrippa on behalf of the Jews.

(5) 2.204–217 tells the story of how Cladius became emperor, and how Agrippa played an important role in this connection as a middleman and negotiator between the senate and Caligula, for which he is eventually rewarded with all of the former areas of Herod the Great as his kingdom (2.215f).

(6) Quite surprisingly, hardly anything is said about the actual reign of Agrippa. Just how he began to encircle Jerusalem by a wall, and how he suddenly died in Caesarea. All the details contained in *Antiquities* are omitted, and there is no final obituary with final comments on his relationship to the Jewish people and religion.

In the case of Agrippa there is a noteworthy rewriting of the stories in *Antiquities*, and through a number of editorial remarks, Josephus clearly states his evaluations of the events as shown in the list below:

(1)   For one thing, Agrippa is entitled as "the Great" (Ἀγρίππας ὁ μέγας, 18.142, cf. also 17.28; 18.144).

(2)   As an introduction to Agrippa, Josephus inserts one of his outspoken "I judgments". In 18.127–129 Josephus states that within 100 years, the lineage of Herod the King was destroyed by the deity (ὁ θεῖος). This is said to be important to the history of Josephus (διὰ τὸ ἀνήκειν τῇ ἱστορίᾳ), since it serves as proof of the deity (παράστασιν ἔχειν τοῦ θείου), and demonstrates that the only thing that matters is piety towards the deity (πρὸς τὸ θεῖον εὐσεβειῶν, 18.127). This is exactly what happened to the lineage of Herod (τοὺς Ἡρώδου ἀπογόνους) with the one exception of Agrippa, who became a person of the utmost worthiness (ἀξιώτατον) and rose to great power (ἐπὶ τοσόνδε ηὐξήθη δυνάμεως, 18.129).

(3)   This bold statement is exemplified with a genealogical table (18.130–141), which can be seen as a notable enlargement of the sentence from *War* 2.178 "son of Aristobulos, who had been killed by Herod..." What Josephus really wants to demonstrate is that Agrippa is a descendant of the true and legitimate royal Hasmonean family as the son of Mariamme through Aristobulos. This lineage found its new peak with Agrippa, who eventually advanced to the pinnacle of dignity and power (ἐπὶ μέγιστον ἀξιώματός τε ἅμα προκόψειεν καὶ δυνάμεως, 18.142).

(4)   Agrippa's extravagant life in Rome led him into huge debts (18.143–146). After a short stop in Tiberias, where Antipas placed him in the office as market overseer (ἀγορανομία, *Ant.* 18.149), Agrippa returns to Rome with all his debt problems trailing behind him (18.151–167). As recounted in *War* as well, he cultivates a friendship with Gaius, but is imprisoned after openly wishing that Gaius could be emperor instead of Tiberius. At this point, in the greatest peril, resembling the situation of Joseph in Genesis, and presently Josephus himself and the Jewish nation, it is made clear to Agrippa through a couple of prophecies that he would prevail through "Divine providence" (τοῦ θείου τὴν πρόνοιαν, *Ant.* 18.197). This is not found in *War*, and together with the following examples it constitutes an interpretive overlay of Josephus.

(5)   Josephus also narrates that in three cases Agrippa took a bold stand for the religious rights of the Jews, by courageously making a stand against Gaius' attempt to erect his statue in the temple (*Ant.* 18.289ff.), by calling on Claudius to protect the Jews in Alexandria (*Ant.* 19.278–291), and by urging Petronius to punish some young men of Dora for bringing a picture of the emperor into a synagogue – something which Petronius agrees to do (*Ant.* 19.300–311).

(6)   This outer struggle for Jewish rights is reinforced by a picture of Agrippa as a sincere religious Jew making sacrifices in the temple "not ne-

glecting anything demanded by the law" (ἐξεπλήρωσε θυσίας οὐδὲν τῶν κατὰ νόμον παραλιπών, *Ant.* 19.293).

(7) At this point, Josephus steps out of the narrative with one of his editorial remarks, providing a hermeneutic key to his narrative in general. The entire story of Agrippa's fall and re-exaltation by the will of God is extrapolated to constitute proof of the hopes still ahead of the Jewish people. It is said to be "a proof of how God sometimes allows to fall what is great, and how he raises what has fallen" (ἵν' ᾖ δεῖγμα καὶ τοῦ τὰ μεγάλα δύνασθαί ποτε πεσεῖν καὶ τοῦ τὸν θεὸν ἐγείρειν τὰ πεπτωκότα, 19.294). The future hope of the restoration of the Jewish nation is an important theme for Josephus which is also outlined elsewhere, for instance in *Ant.* 19.15–16 in connection with the long digression on Gaius (19.1–211). The downfall of Gaius is said to provide "a proof of the power of God" (πίστιν τοῦ θεοῦ τῆς δυνάμεως) and that it will "comfort those who lie in destiny (i.e. bad)" (καὶ παραμυθίαν τοῖς ἐν τύχαις κειμένοις), as well as teaching anyone else that the only way to safeguard oneself is to live a life according to virtue (ἀρετῇ, 19.16). These two places (19.16 and 19.294) reveal the underlying heart and soul of Josephus' narrative. He is trying to explain why things went wrong while at the same time pointing to a way of reversing the fortunes of Israel. And as seen earlier, the impious life of Herod (15.267 and 18.127–128) as well as the impious new philosophy of Judas (18.6–10) resulted ultimately in the destruction of the temple. Agrippa is the prime counterexample in this respect.

(8) This picture is bolstered even further in Josephus' final summarising statement on Agrippa (*Ant.* 19.328–334). Josephus contrasts him with Herod, saying that "he did not resemble in his way of life the Herod who had reigned before him" (κατ' οὐδὲν Ἡρώδῃ τῷ πρὸ ἑαυτοῦ βασιλεῖ τὸν τρόπον συμφερόμενος, 19.328). Herod was evil (πονηρός) and relentless (ἀπότομος) in his punishments, as well as more gentle to the Greeks than to the Jews (19.329). Agrippa, on the other hand, is praised by Josephus for his mild, beneficent and benevolent nature (πραῢς... εὐεργετικὸς... φιλάνθρωπος, 19.330) towards all alike. Moreover, he showed himself to be an extremely religious Jew: "He stayed continuously in Jerusalem" (συνεχὴς ἐν τοῖς Ἱεροσολύμοις ἦν), and "he kept the tradition of the fathers spotlessly" (τὰ πάτρια καθαρῶς ἐτήρει). "He therefore kept himself entirely pure, and no day went by for him without the sacrifices ascribed by the law" (διὰ πάσης γοῦν αὐτὸν ἦγεν ἁγνείας οὐδ' ἡμέρα τις παρώδευεν αὐτῷ τὰ νόμιμα χηρεύουσα θυσίας, 19.331). None of this in included in *War*.

(9) An important summary of Agrippa's building activity is found in 19.335–337. Agrippa is praised for building a theatre, an amphitheatre,

baths and porticoes outside Israel. We also learn that he had people enter-tained there with spectacles (θεωρίαι) as well as paying for magnificent fights in the amphitheatre with gladiators (μονομάχοι, 19.336). On one occasion he had 1,400 criminal men (κακοῦργοι) fight against each other, and he is praised by Josephus for executing them (διαφθείρω) in a way that also amused the people (τέρψις, 19.337). It is interesting that Josephus indicts Herod for the exact same thing (15.267f).

(10) Interestingly enough, Josephus includes a couple of contrasting stories giving perspective to the picture of Agrippa: (a) A certain Jew from Caesarea, Simon, tried to have Agrippa excluded from the temple in Jeru-salem because he was not living in a holy way (οὐχ ὅσιος εἴη, 19.332); or perhaps, as one manuscript reads, he was not a native Jew (cf. Feldman 1965, 370, note c). (b) Furthermore, it seems that his death is connected to veneration of him as a god (θεός) having a nature that was beyond death (κρείττονά σε θνητῆς φύσεως, 19.345); a veneration that Agrippa did not hold ungodly to receive (ἀσεβέω, 19.346). (c) *Antiquities* also states how painful his death was, in a similar way to the death of Herod (17.168ff.). (d) Josephus does not hide the fact that some of the people of Caesarea and Sebaste celebrated the death of the king, though lamentation (οἰμωγή, 19.349) was heard in Caesarea as well. (e) Finally, Josephus openly dis-cusses Agrippa's financial problems in the final assessment of his rule (19.352).

In conclusion, the story of Agrippa is extremely important when it comes to understanding the overall intentions of Josephus. In several edito-rial remarks, Josephus directly states the difference between Herod and Agrippa. It is not that Josephus conceals Agrippa' faults, but the main point is that he presents Agrippa as the key to dealing with the precarious situation of the Jews at the time of Josephus. Agrippa is a sign of hope. If the people and the Roman authorities act according to the old rules and traditions, then the deity will punish the hubris of Herod and Gaius, for in-stance (cf. *Ant.* 19.15–16), and reverse the fortunes of the pious and right-eous (cf. *Ant.* 18.197 and 19.294).

3.3.8 Life

When using the writings of Josephus to gain insight into the reign of Herod Antipas, *Life* is also important, although it does not directly touch upon the reign of Antipas. Most of the book is concerned with the events in Galilee during the war of 66–70 CE. In this connection we are provided with some unique information on the major cities of the area, mostly Sepphoris and Tiberias, but also the neighbouring cities of Gadara, Hippos, Scythopolis and others (cf. the survey in Strange 2001).

Regarding Sepphoris and Tiberias, their internal relationship is de-scribed as one of long-standing disagreement over the primacy of Galilee, and the following may be noted:

(1)   According to Justus, "the city [Tiberias] had always been the ruler of Galilee from the time of Herod the Tetrarch, its founder, who wanted the city of the Sepphoritans to be subjected to the city of the Tiberians. This primacy was not lost under king Agrippa the father, but it was re-tained until Felix had become procurator of Judaea" (ἡ πόλις ἀεὶ τῆς Γαλιλαίας ἄρξειεν ἐπί γε τῶν Ἡρώδου χρόνων τοῦ τετράρχου καὶ κτίστου γενομένου βουληθέντος αὐτοῦ τὴν Σεπφωριτῶν πόλιν τῇ Τιβεριέων ὑπακούειν ἀποβαλεῖν δὲ τὸ πρωτεῖον αὐτοὺς μηδὲ ἐπὶ τοῦ βασιλέως Ἀγρίππα τοῦ πατρὸς διαμεῖναι δὲ καὶ μέχρι Φήλικος προεσταμένου τῆς Ἰουδαίας, *Life* 37).

(2)   Later on Tiberias, Sepphoris and Gabara are described as the three largest cities of Galilee (κατὰ τὴν Γαλιλαίαν αἱ μέγισται, *Life* 123).

(3)   In one text, Sepphoris is described as the largest city (Σέπφωριν μεγίστην τῶν ἐν τῇ Γαλιλαίᾳ πόλιν, *Life* 232).

(4)   In one other text, both Sepphoris and Tiberias are described as the largest cities of Galilee, though an important difference between them is noted. While Sepphoris lies at the very centre of Galilee (Σέπφωρις μὲν ἐν τῷ μεσαιτάτῳ τῆς Γαλιλαίας κειμένη, *Life* 346), Tiberias is located with no Jewish city next to it (μηδεμιᾶς δὲ πόλεως Ἰουδαίων παρακειμένης) only 30 furlongs (στάδιοι, *Life* 349) from Hippos, 60 from Gadara and 100 from Scythopolis. In the context Josephus uses this as an argument against Justus, saying that Tiberias could have avoided war and kept an ongoing alliance with the adjacent Roman cities (πρὸς Ῥωμαίους πίστιν φυλάττειν ῥᾳδίως ἐδύνατο, *Life* 349). This short distance to the cities of Decapolis actually meant that Justus at one time had his men attack the vil-lages of Gadara and Hippos (Γαδαρηνῶν καὶ Ἱππηνῶν κώμας, *Life* 42).

(5)   Not much is said about the buildings of Sepphoris and Tiberias. It is noted that Tiberias had a stadium (92, 331), a synagogue (277), and hot baths (85). Most important, though, is the description of Antipas' palace found in *Life* 63–69. The following can be noted: (a) Josephus is sent by the "τοῦ κοινοῦ τῶν Ἱεροσολυμιτῶν", the common or general assembly of Jerusalem[48] with the task of convincing the Tiberians to tear down the house of Herod the Tetrarch (καθαιρεθῆναι τὸν οἶκον τὸν ὑπὸ Ἡρώδου τοῦ τετράρχου, *Life* 65). (b) This well-defined assignment was given to Josephus because the palace contained images of animals (ζῴων μορφὰς), and the law speaks against the fabrication of such things (τῶν νόμων

---

[48] For discussion of the background of this phrase, see Mason 2001, 58, note 346.

οὕτως τι κατασκευάζειν ἀπαγορευόντων, *Life* 65).[49] (c) The local leaders of Tiberias, however, refused to tear down the palace. No explanation
of their resistance is given, and the reason might have been either a dispute
with Josephus over control of the city, or a regular disagreement on how to
interpret the law. (d) But a rebellious party of sailors and people in need
(τῆς τῶν ναυτῶν καὶ τῶν ἀπόρων στάσεως, *Life* 66) led by Jesus, son
of Sapphais, pre-empted Josephus and set the palace on fire. (e) Josephus
explains their actions as being caused by their desire for the precious
equipment of the palace, which had a roof made partly of gold
(κεχρυσωμένας, *Life* 66), as well as expensive furniture like a Corinthian
candelabra, royal tables and a large mass of uncoined silver, which
Josephus subsequently managed to retrieve from the rebellious party (*Life*
68–69).

Besides describing Sepphoris and Tiberias, *Life* is also important for our
purposes in connection with its use of the term "οἱ Γαλιλαῖοι". As briefly
introduced in section 1.1.2 above, it has been debated whether it should be
understood as a designation of a particular rebel group without geographical connotations. In 1974, S. Zeitlin published an article in which he argues that "the term 'Galileans' in *Vita* does not have a geographical connotation, but is an appellative name given to the revolutionaries against
Rome and the rulers of Judaea who were appointed by Rome" (Zeitlin
1974, 193).[50] While Zeitlin was not the first to argue that Galilee was a
special hotbed of rebellion (cf. the references in Freyne 1980a, 397 note 2–
3 and Feldman 1981–1982, 50), his proposal that the name 'Galileans' was
used by Josephus as a technical term for a rebel fraction called for an examination. S. Freyne was the first to test Zeitlin's hypothesis (Freyne
1980a). Shortly afterwards, two smaller articles were published by Joseph
R. Armenti and Louis H. Feldman (Armenti 1981–1982; Feldman 1981–
1982). All three studies concluded against Zeitlin, since it turned out that
Zeitlin had left out a number of references in his argumentation, and "the
omissions cover all those cases where the term cannot possibly have any

---

[49] The prohibition against images represents an important historical issue, and will be
discussed further in the numismatic discussion in section 6.2.1.

[50] In the same year, Francis Loftus published a small note about the notion in *War*
4.558 on "σύνταγμα τῶν Γαλιλαίων," the Galilean contingent, in which he argues that
this body of troops should not be understood as consisting of men from Galilee, but
rather as a particular rebel group just like other particular rebel groups in Jerusalem such
as the zealots (cf. Loftus 1974). Loftus later published an article in which he surveys the
entire body of Josephus and other relevant texts in order to prove that the reasoning behind the equation between rebel and Galilean was the many former rebellious actions in
Galilee. It is interesting to note that the timeline of Loftus is as good as blank from the
year 4 BCE to 66 CE (Loftus 1977–1978).

other meaning than a territorial one" (Armenti 1981–1982, 46, cf. also
Freyne 1980a, 397 note 1).[51] Consequently, it must be maintained that
Josephus uses, also in *Life*, the term "οἱ Γαλιλαῖοι" as a geographical designation as he does in the rest of his work (cf. the analysis in Freyne
1980a, 409–413). However, it is also obvious that Josephus refines his use
of the term in many places in *Life* – for instance, when he contrasts the
Galileans with the city dwellers of Tiberias and Sepphoris. Freyne concludes that besides geographical connotations, Josephus uses the term in
Life to designate people from the country regions (cf. 99, 102 and 206–
207, for instance), who were opposed to the major cities (cf. 30–31, 39,
97–100 and 123, for instance), while at the same time being his own loyal
supporters (cf. *Life* 84, 125, 250 and 252, for instance). The animosity is
directed against the villagers of Tiberias, Sepphoris, Gischala and Gabara
(cf. Freyne 1980a, 400–403). At the same time, there is no indication that
the Galileans were a special rebel force. Occasionally Josephus includes
women and children in the group of Galileans (cf. Freyne 1980a, 405), just
as they are distinguished from the bandits (cf. 29, 105 and 151, for instance). They are best described as patriotic rural inhabitants of Galilee
distinct from the inhabitants of the large cities of Galilee with whom tensions and bad relations became obvious during the war.

To summarize, *Life* explains how Antipas built Tiberias on the border
with the neighbouring non-Jewish areas with easy access via boat, as well
as demonstrating that at the time of the war of 66–70 CE there was an internal fight going on in Galilee between the two major cities as well as between different fractions in the population. During these upheavals, the
palace of Antipas in Tiberias was burned down because pictures of living
animals decorated its interior. Finally, it is important to note that *Life*
clearly depicts an urban-rural tension, though in a later period and under
other circumstances than those of Antipas.

3.3.9 Partial Conclusion

This survey of Josephus' writings on the Herodian house has clarified
some of Josephus' interests, in the light of which his narrative of Antipas
must be read. The following can be concluded on a preliminary basis:

First, there is a general tendency in the writings of Josephus to move
from a seemingly more detached and less personal description of events in
War, to a more settled and critical account in *Antiquities* with outspoken "I
statements" in the many editorial remarks. This is evident in several cases
concerning the life of Herod the Great, as well as in the accounts about Archelaos, the Fourth Philosophy, Philip, Agrippa and Pilate. Sometimes

---

[51] A full list can be found in Schalit 1968, 32 and Mason 2001, 281.

Josephus adds new perspectives that are not present in *War*, and at other times he expands on issues that have already been presented in *War*. After all, *War* does contain many of Josephus' personal evaluations.

Second, Josephus basically navigates between two negative positions: One too insensitive or even hostile to and brutal against the Jewish religion, law and tradition, as in the case of Herod, Archelaos and Pilate; and the other too insensitive and hostile towards Rome, as in the case of Judas and the Fourth Philosophy. In the end, both attitudes led away from 'the narrow path' granting the Jews a good and stable relationship to Rome as well as full religious freedom. Both ways are judged by Josephus as 'intruders' inflicting injustice on the old traditions of the Jews by introducing novelties hitherto unknown such as a lack of piety, ungodliness, injustice, a lack of moderation, violence and tyranny.

Third, the most crucial question for Josephus seems to be why the temple could be destroyed and with it the entire fate of the Jewish nation, and how some of that former glory can be re-erected (cf. especially *Ant.* 15.267, 281; 18.6–10; 20.166). In this connection, Josephus presents Agrippa I as a guiding light for a reversal of fortunes. His entire life, passing from hopelessness to glory through divine providence and a pious and virtuous life, resembles the hopes of Josephus for his Jewish nation.

Finally, Josephus goes to great lengths to draw a dual picture of his characters. Even Herod has some good sides, and even Agrippa has bad sides. This could reflect Josephus' wish to resemble what Mason describes as a common trend in Roman historiography (cf. Mason 2003b, 570–571), or it could reflect a keen interest in the truthful writing of history (cf. Bilde 1988, 196–197) – or, perhaps, both.

3.4 Herod Antipas in the Writings of Josephus

3.4.1 Introduction

Turning to Josephus' description of Antipas, the question is how such a broader view of the literary structure of Josephus' narrative creates a background for evaluating his account of the reign of Antipas. In the following, it will be argued that though the narrative on Antipas is comparatively short, it is precise and significant in the light of Josephus' general editorial intentions with his description of the Herodian house. Antipas is also evaluated by Josephus in the light of his relationship to Rome on the one hand, and his relationship to Jewish law, practice and religion on the other, although this is done in a less pronounced way than in the cases seen above.

3.4.2 Herod Antipas and Rome

Antipas ruled under three emperors, Augustus, Tiberias and Gaius Ca-ligula. Not much is said in the works of Josephus about the period under Augustus (4 BCE-14 CE). In *Ant.* 17.20 it is briefly mentioned that Anti-pas, together with Archelaos, 'had the living' (i.e. was raised, τροφὰς εἶχον) by a certain private man in Rome (παρά τινι ἰδίῳ). During the trial in Rome, Antipas contested Archelaos' position as the sole heir of Herod the Great (*War* 2.14–38, 80–100; *Ant.* 17.219–249, 299–323). As discussed more fully below, incorporating sources other than Josephus (cf. section 7.2.1), the appointment by Augustus as tetrarch over Galilee was less than he had hoped for (*War* 2.20–32; *Ant.* 17.224–227). According to Josephus, Augustus found that Archelaos had showed himself most worthy to have the kingdom (ἀξιώτατον εἶναι τῆς βασιλείας, *Ant.* 17.248, cf. *War* 2.37), and in defiance of Antipas' strong group of Roman supporters, Augustus finally settled for a solution involving Archelaos as the main heir with the title ethnarch, and Philip and Antipas as tetrarchs (*War* 2.93–100; *Ant.* 17.317–323). However, Josephus does not record any actual events from Antipas' reign under Augustus, apart from the fact that he remained in of-fice when Archelaos was disposed (*War* 2.167), and that he enclosed Sep-phoris with a wall (Ἡρώδης Σέπφωριν τειχίσας), made the "ornament[52] of all Galilee" (πρόσχημα τοῦ Γαλιλαίου παντὸς), and named it Auto-cratoris[53] (ἠγόρευεν αὐτὴν Αὐτοκρατορίδα, *Ant.* 18.27). Similarly, Anti-

---

[52] The word 'πρόσχημα' has the literal meaning of "screen" or "pretext", and a sec-ondary meaning of "ornament" or "outward appearance" (according to LS). According to S. Miller, the term is reserved by ancient authors to describe impregnable cities and thus entails a military connotation. For examples on the use of this designation, see Miller 1984, 57, note 286, cf. also Miller 1996, 22.

[53] It is interesting to consider what can be derived from Antipas' renaming of Sephpho-ris. According to Feldman, "Autocratoris" should be understood as the Greek equivalent of the Latin *Imperatoria,* and thus the renaming was meant to honour the Roman *Imper-ator* Augustus, just as Antipas' next city was named in honour of Tiberius. However, αὐτοκρατορίς could be translated "autonomous" as well (cf. Feldman 1965, 24, note b). Elsewhere Feldman even considers it probable that the new Autokratoris embodied a cult of Augustus (Feldman 1981–1982, 51). This is not likely, however. No trace of a temple has been found in either Sepphoris or Tiberias, which was likewise named in honour of the emperor, just as there is no mention of such an institution in either of the cities. From the time of emperor Antoninus Pius (138–161 CE), coins from Sepphoris depict Greco-Roman gods standing in a temple, and it is possible that Sepphoris had a temple by then (cf. Meyers and Chancey 2000, 24; Meshorer 1985, 37). Still, no archaeological evidence has been found of this temple either. In an important forthcoming essay, Monika Bernett suggests that the city was named in honour of Gaius Caesar, Augustus' grandson, who obtained an *imperium proconsulare* for the eastern part of the Empire in 2 BCE. Due to his untimely death, Sepphoris was soon to regain its old name (Bernett Forthcoming).

pas enclosed Betharamphtha with a wall and renamed it Ioulias after the emperor's daughter (*War* 2.168; *Ant.* 18.27).

The passages Josephus has included on Antipas (cf. the list above in section 3.1) focus instead, for the most part, on the period under Tiberius. As will become clear below, it is evident that Antipas cultivated good relations with Tiberius according to Josephus, which is demonstrated in four texts:

(1) *Ant.* 18.36–38 tells us about the founding of Tiberias and opens with the remark saying that "Herod the Tetrarch, because he had advanced much before Tiberius in regard to friendship, had a city built and named it Tiberias, after him" (Ἡρώδης δὲ ὁ τετράρχης ἐπὶ μέγα γὰρ ἦν τῷ Τιβερίῳ φιλίας προελθών οἰκοδομεῖται πόλιν ἐπώνυμον αὐτῷ Τιβεριάδα, *Ant.* 18.36). It should be noted that in his Loeb translation Feldman renders this rather freely: Antipas "advanced much *among the friends of Tiberius*" (my italics, Feldman 1965, 31). A more straightforward translation of the 'φιλία' would be "before Tiberius in regard to friendship." In both cases, however, it is clearly implied that Antipas should have gained a favourable position in the court of Tiberius through the crucial political bonds of friendship (cf. Braund 1984, 7, 23–37 and the discussion below in section 7.2.1).

(2) The good relationship with Tiberius also appears in *War* 2.178, in which Josephus notes how Tiberius turned down Agrippa when he came to Rome to accuse Antipas. We are not told what he is accused of, but perhaps the passage could be connected with *Ant.* 18.149ff., which describes how Antipas, after having placed the indebted Agrippa in the office as *agoranomos* of Tiberias, reproached him for his poverty. This infuriated Agrippa, and he left Tiberias eventually ending up in Rome, where he became a friend of Gaius. Even so, Agrippa obviously did not succeed in shaking Tiberius' trust in Antipas.

(3) Antipas' high status is further highlighted by the role he was given in the top-level political meeting between Rome and Parthia under Tiberius (*Ant.* 18.101–105).[54] The eastern border into Parthia constituted a recurring problem for Rome, as outlined by Josephus in the preceding paragraphs (18.96–100). With the mission to negotiate a peace treaty, the legate of Syria, Vitellius, was sent to meet Artabanus, who had just recaptured the throne. They met, flanked by their bodyguards, on a bridge over the Eu-

---

[54] It should be noted that there is a chronological issue associated with this meeting. Suetonius and Dio Cassius place it after the death of Tiberius. Hoehner discusses the problem in detail and follows Täubler, who favoured the chronology of Josephus, since both Suetonius and Dio Cassius were hostile towards Tiberius and therefore had an incentive to deprive him of this success (cf. Hoehner 1972, 253–254).

phrates and were able to work out an arrangement. We are told how Antipas entertained them in a luxurious tent in the middle of the bridge (18.102). Although it is not said exactly what role Antipas played during the negotiations, Antipas was able to write a letter to Tiberius so precise (ἀκριβῶς) and detailed that nothing was left for the proconsul to tell. When Vitellius later did so, Tiberius downplayed his report since matters had already been made clear (δῆλος) by Antipas (18.104–105). This upset Vitellius, but he hid his anger for a later opportunity.

(4) Finally, Antipas' good relationship to Tiberius was demonstrated when he was attacked by Aretas and had his army destroyed. Though seemingly only hearing the story from the point of view of Antipas, Tiberius took Antipas' side in this quarrel and "looked in anger on the endeavour of Aretas and wrote to Vitellius to declare war and if caught alive to lead him up in chains, or if killed to have his head sent to him" (ὁ δὲ ὀργῇ φέρων τὴν Ἀρέτα ἐπιχείρησιν γράφει πρὸς Οὐιτέλλιον πόλεμον ἐξενεγκεῖν καὶ ἤτοι ζωὸν ἑλόντα ἀναγαγεῖν δεδεμένον ἢ κτεινομένου πέμπειν τὴν κεφαλὴν ἐπ᾽ αὐτόν, *Ant.* 18.115).

However, the good relationship to Rome did not last. When Gaius became emperor and Agrippa king, the fortunes of Antipas changed. Unlike almost all the other stories about Antipas, Josephus renders the story of Antipas' downfall in both his accounts. *War* has a rather brief and concise text (2.181–183) in which we are told that Gaius' inauguration of Agrippa as king filled Herod with envy and desire (φθόνῳ τὰς Ἡρώδου τοῦ τετράρχου διήγειρεν ἐπιθυμίας, 2.181). This part is left out in *Antiquities*, where Herodias is described as the acting part. Still, *War* also states that it was she who desired a kingdom above all else (μάλιστα, 2.182), and continues by briefly recounting how Herodias eventually convinced Antipas to set sail for Rome, but how he was punished by Gaius for his greed (πλεονεξία, 2.183) and exiled to Spain.

The passage in *Antiquities* on this incident is vastly extended, covering sixteen paragraphs (18.240–255). The active role of Antipas is downplayed somewhat, and Herodias is the one orchestrating the event. She envied her brother, Agrippa, too much for his total reversal of fortunes (from pauper to king) to remain quiet (18.240–244). Antipas was unable to withstand her pressure, although he is said to be "a lover of quietness" (ἀγαπῶν τὴν ἡσυχίαν, 18.245). Herodias kept on pressing him to seek every opportunity to seize a kingdom (βασιλεία, 18.245). Eventually he set sail for Rome, but Agrippa had learned of their plan and despatched his own envoy to press charges against Antipas. Arriving at the court of Gaius, Agrippa's envoy conveyed letters indicting Antipas for "conspiracy with Sejanus against the government of Tiberius, and for having been together with Artabanus the Parthian against the government of Gaius" (ὁμολογίαν πρὸς

Σηιανὸν κατὰ τῆς Τιβερίου ἀρχῆς καὶ πρὸς Ἀρτάβανον τὸν Πάρθον ἐπὶ τοῦ παρόντος κατὰ τῆς Γαΐου ἀρχῆς, 18.250). As proof it was revealed that Antipas had collected armour for 70,000 soldiers. Since Antipas was unable to refute the existence of the armoury, Gaius "regarded the accusations for sedition to be trustworthy" (πιστὰ ἡγούμενος εἶναι τὰ ἐπὶ τῇ ἀποστάσει κατηγορούμενα, 18.252).[55] Thus, Antipas was banned to Lyon, and his property given to Agrippa.[56] Gaius offered Herodias the chance to keep her belongings, being a sister of Agrippa, but she refused and was banned as well. Josephus ends the story with an important editorial remark concluding his entire narrative on Antipas: "But God inflicted this punishment on Herodias for the envy against her brother and Herod for listening to women's light talk" (Ἡρωδιάδι μὲν δὴ φθόνου τοῦ πρὸς τὸν ἀδελφὸν καὶ Ἡρώδῃ γυναικείων ἀκροασαμένῳ κουφολογιῶν δίκην ταύτην ἐπετίμησεν ὁ θεός, 18.255). Thus, according to Josephus, Antipas maintained a good relationship with Tiberius, but finally met his destiny under Gaius Caligula.[57]

3.4.3 Herod Antipas and the Jewish Nation and Religion

Antipas' relations with his Jewish subjects were a different story according to Josephus. A picture containing substantial problems is revealed in three instances:

(1) Antipas' foundation of Tiberias in honour of Tiberius created a dual problem (*Ant.* 18.36–38, cf. also section 5.3.1-2): First, the city was inhabited by a highly questionable mob of people, a "promiscuous rabble" as L.H. Feldman translates σύγκλυδες in the Loeb edition. Though some are said to be magistrates or men in office (ἐν τέλει, 18.37), it appears from the description that most were former slaves who had hardly been set free (μηδὲ σαφῶς ἐλευθέρους, 18.38) or poor people in need (ἄνδρας ἀπόρους, 18.37) who were brought in from all over (πανταχόθεν, 18.37).

---

[55] In section 7.2.1 Antipas' relationship to Gaius will be discussed further, including whether these allegations for conspiracy are credible.

[56] As noted, according to *War* 2.183, Antipas was exiled to Spain, where he also died. Hoehner argues that by 'Λούγδουνον πόλιν τῆς Γαλλίας' (*Ant.* 18.252), Josephus is referring to Lungdunum Convenarum, a city on the border to Spain, and thus avoids a contradiction (Hoehner 1972, 262, note 1). D. Braund rejects this idea since Lugdunum in Gaul is, if not otherwise qualified, a reference to the present city of Lyon, and thus *War* might be wrong or a result of a textual corruption (Braund 1984, 177, note 76). It should also be noted that Dio (lix.18.2–3) has a statement which might be interpreted to mean that Gaius executed Antipas (cf. Schürer 1973, 353, note 43, but see Hoehner 1972, 263, note 4).

[57] Interestingly, the next paragraph describes the reign of Gaius as very positive in his first two years in office. Thus it is even more highlighted that the downfall of Antipas had nothing to do with the later despotic cruelty of Gaius (cf. 18.256).

Some were dragged there forcibly (πρὸς βίαν, 18.37). However, they are said to be "from the land subject to him" (ἐκ τῆς ὑπ' αὐτῷ γῆς, 18.37). This could imply that they were already tenants of Antipas. On the positive side, Antipas freed them in great numbers and showed himself to be a benefactor (κἀπὶ πολλοῖς ἠλευθέρωσεν καὶ εὐηργέτησεν, 18.38) by building houses "to the end", i.e. fully equipped, and adding plots of land of his own (κατασκευαῖς τε οἰκήσεων τέλεσι τοῖς αὐτοῦ καὶ γῆς ἐπιδόσει, 18.38). All of this on the single condition that they were not to leave the city again (ἀνάγκασμα τοῦ μὴ ἀπολείψειν τὴν πόλιν ἐπιθείς, 18.38). Nevertheless, a second problem concerned the fact that Antipas "knew the foundation of the city to be against the law and contrary to the Jewish ancestral tradition because it was placed on graves" (εἰδὼς παράνομον τὸν οἰκισμὸν ὄντα καὶ ἀπὸ τοῦ Ἰουδαίοις πατρίου διὰ τὸ ἐπὶ μνήμασιν, 18.38).[58] They became uprooted in great numbers when Tiberias was founded, and with an implied reference to the law (Num 19:11, 16) Josephus says that "the settlers are unclean for seven days, as the law proclaims for us" (μιαροὺς δὲ ἐπὶ ἑπτὰ ἡμέρας εἶναι τοὺς οἰκήτορας ἀγορεύει ἡμῖν τὸ νόμιμον, *Ant.* 18.38).[59]

Josephus' description of Antipas' foundation of Tiberias is thus another example of his double-sided portrait of the Herodian rulers. On the one hand, Antipas is described as a benefactor who, first, freed a lot of people, second, built them fully equipped houses and, third, even allotted them plots of land. The foundation of Tiberias seems to have been a great finan-

---

[58] As already noted, *Life* 65 describes how Antipas also broke the law, at least according to some Jews in Tiberias during the war, when he took the liberty to decorate the interior of his palace with images of living animals (ζῴων μορφὰς, cf. section 3.3.8).

[59] In an interesting essay, L. Levine discusses the various traditions about the impure condition of Tiberias in the rabbinic sources. First he notes that it is not entirely evident why Tiberias was impure, if indeed it was built upon obliterated graves, since later rabbinic law describes "possible ratifications which would have made such land usable" (Levine 1974, 168) and since Numbers 19:11–16 was applied to priests only in later periods. Also, in *Life* several events take place in Tiberias without any notice of impurity, so Levine suspects that Josephus' bad relations with the city might have influenced his accentuation of this matter. Nevertheless, in the rabbinic material several traditions attest that Tiberias was perceived as an impure place that needed to be purified, which eventually was done by the holy rabbi Simeon b. Yohai. Levine scrutinizes the traditions of this event in the Palestinian accounts, of which the edition in Genesis Rabbah 79 is the longest and most colourful, including resurrection and removal of corpses from the graves (cf. Levine 1974, 145–164). Only two versions are preserved in the Babylonian Talmud, which differ significantly in omitting any of the miraculous elements (cf. Levine 1974, 167). Although the sources differ in several aspects, Levine concludes that it is historically trustworthy that in the rabbinic period the Tiberians struggled with rumours of impurity, which they eventually chose to face directly, and that Rabbi Simeon b. Yohai eventually "became the cornerstone of the Tiberian apologetic" (Levine 1974, 183).

cial investment by Antipas. On the other hand, Josephus focuses clearly on the implied transgression of the law and explicitly states that in this case Antipas showed himself to be a transgressor of Jewish religion just like his father.[60]

(2)   The second instance in which Herod Antipas falls short according to Josephus is in his marriage to Herodias, the wife of his half-brother Herod.[61] There is more than one theory concerning the discrepancy between Josephus and the Gospels,[62] but again the primary aim of this study is to see how Josephus *uses* his sources, and the following may be noted: (a) The story (*Ant.* 18.109–115) is placed immediately after the praise of the now-deceased Philip. On some occasion Antipas visited his half-brother Herod and fell in love with his wife Herodias (ἐρασθεὶς δὲ Ἡρωδιάδος, 18.110), the sister of Agrippa the Great. (b) Antipas asked her to marry him and she accepted on the condition that his first wife, the daughter of the Nabatean king Aretas, would be expelled (ἐν ταῖς συνθήκαις ὥστε καὶ τοῦ Ἀρέτα τὴν θυγατέρα ἐκβαλεῖν, 18.110). (c) Again the deeds and doings of Antipas are described as having a two-fold problem. For one thing, this escapade turned out to be politically fatal. The subsequent paragraphs describe the way in which Aretas made war on Antipas, who suffered a severe blow, having his entire army destroyed (διεφθάρη πᾶς ὁ Ἡρώδου στρατὸς, 18.114). For another, the marriage is condemned as contravening the law (τῶν πατρίων, 18.136). As a matter of fact, Josephus constructs a parallel to Archelaos. His second marriage to Glaphyra is also deemed unholy and held against him.

(3)   The third text centered on Antipas' relations with Jewish law is placed immediately afterwards, namely his execution of John the Baptist, and is extremely significant when it comes to understanding Josephus' view of Antipas. (a) The text is a digression prompted by the destruction of Herod Antipas' army. Without any further definition, we are told that "some of the Jews thought that the destruction of the army was an act of God" (τισὶ δὲ τῶν Ἰουδαίων ἐδόκει ὀλωλέναι τὸν Ἡρώδου στρατὸν

---

[60] Klaus-Stefan Krieger goes even further and sees the story as slanderous polemics against Antipas, who Josephus points out as the only active person that had to bribe even people of very low and poor status to live there (Krieger 1994, 29–31).

[61] For a general study of the traditions concerning Herodias, see Gillman 2003.

[62] As already discussed (cf. section 1.3.3), N. Kokkinos has advanced an interesting hypothesis on how to interpret the sources on Antipas' second marriage to Herodias, and on how to understand his trip to Gaius to obtain the rank of king, in which the episodes are not seen as erotically motivated, but as a daring political attempt to obtain the tetrarchy of the deceased Philip, whose widow was Herodias (cf. Kokkinos 1998, 264–271). For the traditional view, see Krieger 1994, 51–56; Hoehner 1972, 121–143, 150–68, 257–265; Gillman 2003, 40.

ὑπὸ τοῦ θεοῦ, 18.116), which was also thought to be "very much just" (μάλα δικαίως, 18.116) as revenge for what Antipas had done against John the so-called Baptist. (b) In the following paragraph, Josephus' description of John the Baptist substantiates this judgment. He is said to be a good man (ἀγαθὸν ἄνδρα, 18.117), urging people to seek virtue (ἀρετή) and to practise justice (δικαιοσύνη) towards each other and piety (εὐσέβεια) towards God. In other words, he is described in exactly opposite terms than those used about Herod the Great and Archelaos. (c) In paragraph 118 Josephus explains the situation that made Antipas have John killed. People gathered together (συστρεφομένων) and were either "overjoyed" (ἥσθησαν) or "aroused" (ἤρθησαν)[63] to the highest degree (ἐπὶ πλεῖστον) by hearing his words. For that reason Herod feared (δείσας) that John's great influence on the people would lead to some kind of rebellion (ἐπὶ ἀποστάσει τινὶ φέροι) since it seemed that they would follow every council of his (πάντα γὰρ ἐῴκεσαν συμβουλῇ τῇ ἐκείνου πράξοντες). So Antipas held it to be much better (πολὺ κρεῖττον ἡγεῖται) to act in advance and execute him (προλαβὼν ἀνελεῖν), instead of regretting matters subsequently if he became entangled in events (τοῦ μεταβολῆς γενομένης [μὴ] εἰς πράγματα ἐμπεσὼν μετανοεῖν). From all we know of ancient bandits and messianic figures, Antipas' action is just what one would expect from a client king or local ruler (cf. section 7.2.1). (d) But in the following paragraph, Josephus judges the incident through the eyes of the Jews (this time without the qualifying "some of"). Due to Herod's ὑποψία, his "suspicion" or perhaps "jealous watch" (cf. LS II), John is brought to Machaerus and killed. The Jews had the opinion (τοῖς δὲ Ἰουδαίοις δόξαν) that as "punishment for this the destruction of the army was an act of God, who wanted to maltreat Herod" (ἐπὶ τιμωρίᾳ τῇ ἐκείνου τὸν ὄλεθρον ἐπὶ τῷ στρατεύματι γενέσθαι τοῦ θεοῦ κακῶσαι Ἡρώδην θέλοντος, 18.119). Thus, Josephus clearly describes the act of Antipas as unjust, ungodly and perhaps also an act of tyranny, although this verdict is not presented in a direct way with an editorial 'I statement' as in many other cases.

Finally, it must be said that a small notice in 18.122 balances this negative judgment of Antipas' sympathy for the Jewish religion and tradition. Josephus tells us how Vitellius, on his way to punish Aretas, yielded to the wishes of the Jews not to march through Judea with his army, since they found the images to be against the law (18.120–121). Instead, he "himself together with Herod the Tetrarch and his friends went up to Jerusalem to sacrifice to God in the traditional feasts of the Jews present there" (αὐτὸς

---

[63] For a discussion of the different manuscript tradition in this case, see Feldman 1965, 82, note d.

μετὰ Ἡρώδου τοῦ τετράρχου καὶ τῶν φίλων εἰς Ἱεροσόλυμα ἀνῄει θύσων τῷ θεῷ ἑορτῆς πατρίου τοῖς Ἰουδαίοις ἐνεστηκυίας). Naturally, it would have been of great interest if Josephus had elaborated on Antipas' religious role and function in Jerusalem after the removal of Archelaos. Since he does not do so, it is difficult to extract a firm description from this paragraph, though it does paint a picture of a positive relationship between Antipas and Jerusalem. In the next chapter, other notions on Antipas' relations to the affairs in Jerusalem will be discussed.

3.4.4 Partial Conclusion

In conclusion, Josephus describes Antipas as having close connections to the Roman emperor Tiberius. A close connection to Rome does not constitute a problem in itself, according to Josephus, if handled in the same way as Agrippa I. But as with Herod the Great, Antipas' Roman preference is coupled with an insensitive attitude towards the Jewish religion. In three cases, the foundation of Tiberias, the marriage to Herodias, and the killing of John the Baptist, Antipas is judged as a violator of the law and tradition. In particular, *Ant.* 18.101–129 is narrated as a chain of incidents, which taken together clearly build up an argument: (a) Antipas is a political fool who loses the good relationship with his nearest Roman protector, Vitellius, when informing Tiberius about the peace treaty with Parthia (101–105); (b) in contrast, his brother Philip is a just, moderate and easy-going ruler (106–108); (c) but Antipas gave in to his feelings and divorced the daughter of the neighbouring king, Aretas, which involved him in the fatal war where he lost his army (109–115); (d) this is presented as a just revenge from God because Antipas had killed a good (ἀγαθός) man who was filled with ἀρετή, δικαιοσύνη, and εὐσέβεια (116–119); (e) finally, Antipas was caught up in events. When Tiberius died, Vitellius refused to wage war against Aretas (120–125); (f) added to this, when the narratives about Antipas come to an end, his counterpart is presented: Agrippa the Great, who is magnificently introduced and directly contrasted to Herod the Great and the rest of his lineage (125–129).

However, deliberately or not, this picture does have a few cracks in it. At one point Josephus tells us how Antipas went to Jerusalem to sacrifice during the Passover (18.122). Likewise, it is not clearly stated whether or not Josephus also viewed Antipas as a τύραννος. Krieger argues that the forceful resettlement of people in Tiberias and the killing of John the Baptist are typical signs of tyranny (cf. Krieger 1994, 53, esp. note 8). However, in both cases Josephus does not say so directly, but rather softens the picture of a tyrant by letting us know, in the case of Tiberias, how Antipas took care of the resettled people (18.36–38) and, in the case of John, how he had to take action against him to prevent a possible uprising (18.118).

In this respect, the picture of Antipas is thus less pronounced than that of other members of the Herodian house, where Josephus directly states his personal opinions of the events through pronounced editorial remarks.

Nevertheless, it becomes clear in the light of the general survey of Josephus' treatment of the Herodian house that Josephus wants to present Antipas as another example of a bad Herodian ruler who was not able to safeguard the ancient and stable Jewish way of life. Antipas eventually comes to serve as a warning of how the deity punishes those not living in accordance with the law, as stated in the case of John the Baptist and in the narrative on Antipas' banishment.

3.5 Chapter Conclusions

In conclusion, this chapter has made an attempt to unfold Josephus' description of Antipas as it appears within its own context, instead of reading the stories as isolated incidents. The main question was whether Josephus' description is incoherent and incomplete, or whether it is clear and effective, when read within the larger context. As the following conclusions indicate, Josephus uses Antipas in a clear and distinct way as a part of what he intends to demonstrate.

First, the modern research on Josephus has proven how many intentions merge in the writings of Josephus. Among the most important are (a) on a profound theological level to come to terms with how the temple could be destroyed; (b) on a national-religious level to revive Jewish self-identity; and (c) on a political level to find a way to re-establish the former good relationship between Rome and the Jewish nation by pointing out how it was possible in the past to master the delicate balance between Jewish and Roman considerations, and by pointing out how both Rome and Jerusalem used to have the ideal type of aristocratic constitution freed from tyrannical kings and emperors. Thus, Josephus is constantly providing good and bad examples and is fairly easy to follow due to his intensive and consistent use of catch-words like e.g. παράνομος, ἔθος, πάτριος, ἀσεβής, εὐσεβὲς, ἀσέβεια, τυραννίς, τυραννικός, μέτριος, ὠμότης.

Second, in the context of Josephus' description of the Herodian house, Antipas is presented as one of the "tragic stories." Though perhaps not as tragic as other members due to his lack of outspoken despotic cruelty, he is, from a Josephean-Jewish perspective, one of the rulers who were too friendly with the Romans and too insensitive towards Jewish law, practice and religion. Thus, though we do not have an extensive description of Antipas, we have a clear one. Measured by Josephus' overall aims, he tells us what we need to know.

Third, one consequence of this is that Josephus' perspective on the history he is writing is different from the perspective sought and the questions asked by modern research. Josephus does not seem to ask questions "from below", focusing instead on the ruling class, relations with Rome, and the high priests and the temple. Not much is said about the financial conditions of the lower classes. The only financial element is a positive one, indicating that Antipas provided fully equipped houses together with plots of land for the forcefully rehoused settlers. Thus, Josephus does not intend to answer our set of questions.

Fourth and finally, when the picture Josephus provides of Antipas is read in conjection with Josephus' entire narrative of the Herodian house and his own disclosed intentions, the following stands out: *Antipas was by no means remarkable either in deeds or misdeeds.* In *War* he is only mentioned in occasional updates. In *Antiquities* there is more, but when Josephus' intentions are taken into account, the picture of Antipas still turns out to be rather unremarkable: (a) the foundation of Tiberias seemed to be a financial advantage for the tenant population, and the religious transgression did not prevent Josephus from freely entering the city during the war as we read in *Life*; (b) the killing of John the Baptist might have shocked those who believed in him, but was only to be expected from a local client ruler who wanted to restore calm, and is exactly what Josephus approves in other places; (c) the marriage to Herodias certainly seems to have been expensive, but only for Antipas himself without any known consequences for the population; (d) finally, Josephus is not able to come up with any real examples of cruelty or tyranny, which would otherwise have bolstered the argument he presents against the Herodian despotic rule.

Chapter 4

Herod Antipas in Other Written Sources

4.1 Introduction

While Josephus is the most informative literary source on the life and reign of Antipas, other sources contribute by adding information about events already known from Josephus, and by describing episodes otherwise unknown. The writers who mention Antipas are: Nicolaos of Damascus, a historian attached to the court of Herod the Great; the Greek geographer, historian and philosopher, Strabo (ca. 63 BCE – 21 CE); the Jewish philosopher Philo (ca. 20 BCE – 50 CE); the Roman historian Tacitus (ca. 55–117 CE); the Christian apologist Justin Martyr (ca. 100–165 CE), and the Roman historian Dio Cassius (ca. 155–235). In the New Testament Antipas is mentioned in the Gospel of Matthew, Mark and Luke as well as in Acts.[64] This material is centred on the following episodes:

(1)   The trial in Rome, and the appointment of Antipas and Philip as tetrarchs: Nicolaos (*FGrH* 90, frag. 136 §§ 8–11), Tacitus (*Hist.* 5.9).

(2)   The banishment of Archelaos and the re-appointment of Antipas and Philip: Strabo (*Geogr.* 16.2.46), Dio Cassius (LV.27.6), Justin (*Dial.* 103.4).

(3)   The votive shields of Pilate and the embassy of the four Jewish princes: Philo (*Legat.* 299–305).

(4)   Episodes mentioned in the New Testament are: (a) Antipas' execution of John the Baptist (Mark 6:14–29; Matt 14:1–12; Luke 3:18–20; 9:7–9) and (b) Antipas' interrogation of Jesus in Jerusalem (Luke 23:6–12.15, cf. also Acts 4:27) to which Antipas' general interest in Jesus and vice versa is connected (Luke 9:7–9; 13:31–33; Mark 6:14–16; 8:15; Matt 14:1–2).

---

[64] Finally, Antipas is also mentioned in some later sources with less historical value for this period, such as Hegesippus, Josippon, extra-canonical literature and Eusebius (cf. Hoehner 1972, 105–106, 245–249).

4.2 Traditions in Greek and Latin Writings

4.2.1 The Division of the Kingdom of Herod the Great

The incidents surrounding the division of Herod the Great's kingdom are briefly mentioned by Tacitus and Nicolaos. As an introduction to his account of Titus' siege of Jerusalem (*Hist.* 5.11–13), Tacitus inserts a digression on the origin of the Jewish people, the nature of their land and the latest political events leading up to the war (5.2–10). Within this list of events, it is briefly stated that "the sons of Herod ruled in three parts over a suppressed nation" (*gentem coercitam liberi Herodis tripertito rexere*, 5.9).

More information on this event may be gained from the fragments preserved of Nicolaos of Damascus' writings.[65] Fragment 136 §§ 8–11[66] describes the events after Herod's death and the trial before Augustus in Rome over Herod's wills. § 8 describes the death of Herod the Great and how a crowd of more than 10,000 rose up and rebelled (ἐπανίστημι) against his sons (in plural). When the war was over, "the successor, Archelaos, sailed to Rome on account of the entire realm" (ὁ διάδοχος Ἀρχέλαος εἰς Ῥώμην πλέων ἕνεκα τῆς ὅλης ἀρχῆς). He was accompanied by some of his brothers[67] as well as by Nicolaos himself, who Archelaos had encouraged to sail along despite his old age. Nicolaos soon discovered that Archelaos was confronted with accusations from four different groups (§ 9): first from the younger brother who laid claim to the kingdom (ὁ νεώτερος ἀδελφὸς τῆς βασιλείας ἀντεποιεῖτο). It is actually not stated explicitly that the younger brother is Antipas, as generally assumed (cf. Stern 1974, 260; Hoehner 1972, 26, note 3). It is possible that it could be Philip. Both Antipas and Philip are named only in § 11. Applying the evidence from Josephus naturally gives the impression that it must be Antipas who fought for the validity of the will granting him the entire realm

---

[65] Nicolaos of Damascus was a historian, a philosopher and a rhetorician who was employed for some time in the court of Herod the Great, serving as his primary ambassador to Rome as well as being his biographer. Upon Herod's death, he favoured Archelaos serving as his advocate during the trial in Rome (cf. Wacholder 1962, 22–36, Stern 1974, 227–233 and Malitz 2003, 1–5).

[66] The text used here is from F. Jacoby's *Die Fragmente der griechischen Historiker* band IIA, no. 90, fragment 136 (Jacoby 1926, 424–425). It is reprinted with a translation and notes in Stern 1974, 250–260.

[67] The notion 'ἄλλων ἀδελφῶν' does not specify whether Antipas would be along or not as assumed by Hoehner, who also speculates that the family fight had started already on the ship to Rome (Hoehner 1972, 20 note 5). The apparatus of Jacoby also lists two other readings, namely that Archelaos sailed to Rome "with other friends" or "with other of the brothers", which in both cases excludes both Antipas and Philip.

(cf. *War* 2.20–32; *Ant.* 17.224, cf. *War* 1.646 and *Ant.* 17.146, which specify Antipas as the *youngest* of the three). Furthermore, Archelaos is accused by all his relatives (οἱ συγγενεῖς ἅταντες κατηγόρουν αὐτοῦ),
who joined ranks with the younger brother. Finally, the last two parties ral-
lying against Archelaos were emissaries from the Greek cities of Herod
who wanted freedom under the Emperor, and emissaries representing "the
entire Jewish people" (ὅλον δὲ τὸ Ἰουδαίων ἔθνος) who accused Archelaos of killing 3,000 men in the war that had just ended. For this reason,
the Jewish people desired "to be under the Emperor" (ὑπὸ Καίσαρι εἶναι),
and if not that, then under the younger brother (ὑπο γε οὖν τῶι νεωτέρωι
ἀδελφῶι). The defence of Nicolaos (§ 10) was only directed against the
relatives of Archelaos and the Jewish people, whereas Nicolaos accepted
the Hellenistic city's wish for freedom. He did not find it fitting to contest
the younger brother because of the shared friendship (φιλία) with their father. In § 11 the verdict of Augustus is rendered, saying that a part of the
realm should be given to each of the children, though "the half part to Archelaos" (τὴν δ' ἡμίσειαν μοῖραν Ἀρχελάωι), whom he appointed ethnarch (ἐθνάρχην κατέστησεν), and who, if he prepared himself in a worthy manner (ἄξιον παρασκευάσειεν), would soon be made king (βασιλέα
ταχὺ ποιήσειν). Archelaos' two brothers, Philip and Antipas, were appointed tetrarchs (Φίλιππον καὶ Ἀντίπαν τετράρχας ἀπέδειξεν).

The description by the Nicolaos fragment of the events following the
death of Herod the Great is thus very much in agreement with Josephus'
much longer versions (*War* 2.1–100; *Ant.* 17.200–323, cf. section 4.2.1).
Josephus names Antipas as the brother who laid claim to the entire realm
backed by his relatives (*War* 2.20–32; *Ant.* 17.224–227). A Jewish delegation denounced Archelaos as king (*War* 2.80–92; *Ant.* 17.299–314), but
Nicolaos defended him strongly (*War* 2.33–38.92; *Ant.* 17.240–247.315–
316). Augustus finally gave Archelaos half of the kingdom and the title
ethnarch with the option of becoming king, while Philip and Antipas were
only appointed tetrarchs (*War* 2.93–100; *Ant.* 17.317–318).

However, one of the important details in Nicolaos, absent in Josephus,
is the Jewish delegation's acceptance of Antipas as king if they could not
be ruled directly from Rome (§ 9). This is an interesting piece of information that suggests that the Jewish opposition was directed primarily against
Archelaos, and that Antipas was viewed as milder than him. Since Nicolaos was an eye-witness to this event, and furthermore the primary source
behind Josephus' edition, there is good reason to agree with Wacholder
that Nicolaos is more precise than Josephus in this matter. Thus it seems
that "the Jewish opposition to the house of Herod was not as uncompro-
mising as one would assume from Josephus" (Wacholder 1962, 63).

4.2.2 The Downfall of Archelaos

The only recorded political event from the early years of Antipas' reign concerns his participation in the downfall of Archelaos. Josephus' two versions (*War* 2.111 and *Ant.* 17.342–344) are complemented by Strabo, Dio Cassius and Justin.

Like Nicolaos, Strabo was a Greek writer living in the first century BCE and CE (63 BCE-21 CE). His *Geographia* in 17 books is highly regarded as a source of information on life in the Roman world (Nicolas Purcell 1999, 1447). In book 16.2.44–45 Strabo describes some noteworthy places in the country of Judea such as 'Moasada' (Masada), Sodom, Gadaris, Taricheae, and the Kinnereth. In 16.2.46 Strabo shifts the focus to some of the political events in the period from Pompey to the ban of Archelaos. Surprisingly, Strabo is obviously not well-informed and makes several mistakes. He writes correctly that Pompey restored some of the land conquered by the Hasmoneans to its inhabitants (i.e. the Decapolis), but continues to say that "he appointed Herod to the priesthood" (ἀπέδειξεν Ἡρώδην τὴν ἱερωσύνην), and that "later Herod, one of his descendants, a man of the country, was transmitted into the priesthood (τῶν δ' ἀπὸ γένους τις ὕστερον Ἡρώδης, ἀνὴρ ἐπιχώριος, παραδὺς εἰς τὴν ἱερωσύνην). Strabo is thus incorrectly informed on the ancestry of the Herodian family and their relationship to the priesthood in Jerusalem. The rest of his information on Herod the Great (that Herod became king, that he mastered the relationships to Rome well, and that he executed some of his sons for conspiracy) is correct. Finally Strabo informs us that when Herod died, his successors (διάδοχοι) were ascribed a part (μερίδας) of his kingdom. Herod's will was followed by Caesar, who "honoured the sons of Herod" (τοὺς υἱοὺς ἐτίμησε τοῦ Ἡρώδου). Strabo does not name the sons as he does with Salome and her daughter Berenice, who are also said to be honoured by Caesar. Strabo also adds that it so happened that "the children of Herod were not successful, but became (involved) in charges" (οὐ μέντοι εὐτύχησαν οἱ παῖδες ἀλλ' ἐν αἰτίαις ἐγένοντο). The unfortunate destiny of the children is also explained in an 'ὁ μὲν... οἱ δε'-construction. One of them spent the rest of his life in exile (ὁ μὲν ἐν φυγῇ διετέλει), whereas "the others through paying bribes just barely found a way back with a tetrarchy assigned to each" (οἱ δὲ θεραπείᾳ πολλῇ μόλις εὕροντο κάθοδον τετραρχίας ἀποδειχθείσης ἑκατέρῳ, *Geogr.* 16.2.46). Two segments in this last part on the sons of Herod contain new information not known from any other source except Dio Cassius, who might very well be using Strabo as his source. That is how the sons were unsuccessful (εὐτύχησαν), becoming involved in accusations (ἐν αἰτίαις), and how Antipas and Philip (so it must be) just barely (μόλις) kept their tetrarchies when Archelaos was banned. It is not stated explicitly who accused who. It could be that the sons accused each other, or they may have been accused by others on common grounds. The 'ὁ μὲν... οἱ δε' construction, however, gives the impression that the three brothers were accused on common grounds, and for this reason one of them (ὁ μὲν) was exiled and the two others (οἱ δε) had to bribe their way back to their tetrarchies. If so, Strabo renders a tradition according to which Antipas was accused in the same way as Archelaos (*War* 2.111–113; *Ant.* 17.342–344). It must be noted, though, that in the same paragraph Strabo renders clearly incorrect information.

Writing two centuries later, Dio Cassius (ca. 155–235) notes that Herod of Palestine (Ἡρώδης ὁ Παλαιστῖνος) was banished beyond the Alps and had his realm confiscated because he had "received some charges from the brothers" (αἰτίαν τινὰ ἀπὸ τῶν ἀδελφῶν λαβών, LV.27.6). Dio thus spells out what Strabo does not. The source of Dio is not known, and it is plausible that it could indeed be the *Geographia* of Strabo. There is, however, as discussed by Hoehner, an alternative tradition in the codices Madicaeus and Vaticanus concerning *Ant.* 17.342 for inserting 'ἀδελφῶν' in the sentence otherwise reading "the leading men among the Jews and Samaritans... brought charges against him before the Emperor". The sentence would then read "the leading brothers among the Jews and Samaritans..." (οἱ πρῶτοι τῶν ἀδελφῶν ἀνδρῶν ἔν τε Ἰουδαίοις καὶ Σαμαρείταις). This tradition is not preferred by Niese or Loeb, and a 'καὶ' between 'ἀδελφῶν' and 'ἀνδρῶν' is missing if we are to understand it as a reference to Antipas and Philip (cf. Hoehner 1972, 103, note 5). Still, this reading together with the notion in Dio Cassius attest a tradition according to which internal quarrels in the Herodian house played a part in the downfall of Archelaos, and support the knowledge of the family quarrels in the Herodian family already abundantly known from the writings of Josephus.

Finally, Justin adds an interesting detail in his Dialogue written in the mid-second century saying that "Herod succeeded Archelaos and took over the authority (or office) assigned (to him)" (Ἡρώδου δὲ τὸν Ἀρχέλαον διαδεξαμένου λαβόντος τὴν ἐξουσίαν τὴν ἀπονεμηθεῖσαν, 103.4, cf. PG 6:716). In which way did Herod succeed Archelaos, and what kind of ἐξουσία did he gain? Hoehner argues that as an ethnarch, Archelaos had an inherent authority over his two brothers' tetrarchies as *the* representative of the Jewish people before the Emperor, a position which would then have been taken over by Antipas (Hoehner 1972, 31–33). In this context Justin tells us that Pilate sent Jesus to Antipas during his trial, and a more straightforward reading seems to be that he took over Archelaos' ἐξουσία in Jerusalem as the highest ranking Jewish ruler at the time. As discussed below (section 7.2.2), evidence suggests that Antipas administered a certain amount of power over the religious affairs in Jerusalem in cooperation with the Roman administrative supremacy. However, this rather imprecise statement by Justin can only be verified partially because Antipas did not take over the right to appoint high priests or gain custody over their vestments. According to Josephus, this right was transferred from the Herodians to the Roman administration when Archelaos was banished (cf. e.g. *Ant.* 18.26, 34–36, 95, 123). Vitellius later restored the vestments to the high priest, when he visited Jerusalem at the time of Tiberius' death, but kept the right to appoint high priests (*Ant.* 18.93–95). This right was eventually transferred to Agrippa I by Claudius (*Ant.* 19.292–298). It is interesting to note that upon Agrippa I's death this right was transferred to his brother Herod of Chalcis and later to Agrippa II, both of whom were kings outside Jerusalem (*Ant.* 20.15–16, 104, 138, 179, 196–197, 203). This makes it even more conspicuous that Antipas was not granted this promotion by the Romans as the highest ranking Jewish ruler in the Jewish territory.

4.2.3 Pilate's Votive Shields and the Jewish Embassy

Philo's *Legatio Ad Gaium*[68] contains an important story concerning Antipas. It is found in a letter written by Agrippa I to Gaius (§§ 276–329) after recovering from the initial shock he received when he heard Gaius' plans to erect his own statue in the temple of Jerusalem (§§ 261–275). In this letter, Agrippa refers to Rome's former policy towards the Jews and their temple, illustrated by two examples. The first concerns Marcus Agrippa's visit to Jerusalem during the reign of Herod the Great, during which Agrippa showed the highest respect for the Jewish temple (§§ 294–297). The second concerns Tiberius' harsh reaction to Pilate's act of placing golden shields in the palace of Herod the Great in Jerusalem (§§ 299–305). Although the shields did not display any images (μήτη μορφὴν ἐχούσας), they were set up to aggravate the people (ἕνεκα τοῦ λυπῆσαι τὸ πλῆθος, § 299). § 300 describes how four different groups reacted to Pilate's provocation. Grammatically, the subject of the action is οἱ πολλοί. When they understood (ἤσθοντο) the case, they organized a delegation against Pilate consisting of three parties besides themselves. First, "the four sons of the king, who did not stand back in dignity and good fortune to a king" (τούς τε βασιλέως υἱεῖς τέτταρας οὐκ ἀποδέοντας τό τε ἀξίωμα καὶ τὰς τύχας βασιλέων); second, other descendants (τοὺς ἄλλους ἀπογόνους); and third, those in office among themselves (τῶν παρ' αὐτοῖς τοὺς ἐν τέλει). This group met Pilate and demanded (παρεκάλουν) that the innovations (νεωτερισθὲν) should be introduced with the shields

---

[68] The text can be found in Smallwood 1961 and Colson 1962. For a discussion, see Willert 1989, 21–60, Bond 1998, 24–48 and others.

revised in order not to disturb the custom of the fathers (μὴ κινεῖν ἔθη πάτρια). Initially Pilate turned down their proposal, which made them (implicit subject) cry out (ἀνεβόησαν):

Do not revolutionize, do not make war, do not dissolve peace. Dishonour of ancient laws is not the honour of the emperor. Let not Tiberius be a pretext for your insults of the nation. He does not want to dissolve our (customs). If you say so, show for yourself an edict or a letter or something like that, that we may stop annoying you; having chosen our emissaries, we beg our master (μὴ στασίαζε μὴ πολεμοποίει μὴ κατάλυε τὴν εἰρήνην οὐκ ἔστιν ἀτιμία νόμων ἀρχαίων αὐτοκράτορος τιμή μὴ πρόφασις τῆς εἰς τὸ ἔθνος ἐπηρείας ἔστω σοι Τιβέριος οὐδὲν ἐθέλει τῶν ἡμετέρων καταλύεσθαι εἰ δὲ φής αὐτὸς ἐπίδειξον ἢ διάταγμα ἢ ἐπιστολὴν ὁμοιότροπον ἵνα παυσάμενοι τοῦ σοὶ διενοχλεῖν πρέσβεις ἑλόμενοι δεώμεθα τοῦ δεσπότου, § 301).

This threat had a great impact on Pilate, who was afraid of having all his injustices exposed (§ 302), but since he was also afraid of losing status, he refrained from removing the shields (§ 303). However, letters were sent to Tiberias, and in a harsh tone, he ordered Pilate to set up the shields in the *Augusteum* in Caesarea instead (§§ 304–305).

Three important questions arise concerning Antipas' role in this connection. First, was he among the four Jewish princes approaching Pilate? It seems certain that the episode can be placed after the execution of Sejanus in 31 CE, because the Jewish delegation could report directly to Tiberius (cf. Hoehner 1972, 197; Smallwood 1961, 305). N. Kokkinos dates the event to 33 CE. At this time so few of the ten sons of Herod were still alive that Antipas "*definitely*" was among them (Kokkinos 1998, 195, note 80).[69] Second, having established this, the question is what role Antipas played in the delegation. Hoehner proposes that "Antipas may have been the spokesman for the group, for he was the most powerful as well as the one closest to Tiberius" (Hoehner 1972, 178). Grammatically, the subject of the appeal (παρεκάλουν... ἀνεβόησαν) remains οἱ πολλοί and not the three other parties mentioned as part of the delegation. However, the use of προΐστημι as a designation of what οἱ πολλοί did with the three parties (sons, descendants and those in office) might indicate that the delegation was spearheaded by exactly these three groups.[70] Of the four sons, Antipas

---

[69] Herod himself had killed three, Antipater (son of Doris), Alexander and Aristobulos (sons of Mariamme). A fourth son had died young (*War* 1.435) and Archelaos had been banished in 6 CE (*Ant.* 17.344). The other five were Antipas, Philip, Herod (Herodias' former wife), Herod (son of Cleopatra) and Phasael (son of Pallas). Of these, only Antipas and Philip had political offices and were probably among the four (cf. also Hoehner 1972, 178; Smallwood 1961, 303).

[70] Colson translates 'προΐστημι' in the Loeb series as "having put at their head..." (Colson 1962, 151). Smallwood translates: "they chose as their spokesmen..." (Smallwood 1961, 128).

had the highest rank ruling over the most important Jewish area next to
Judea, though Philip formally had the same title. The other descendants
must be some of Herod the Great's grandchildren, who would also have a
lower ranking than Antipas (cf. Smallwood 1961, 303–304). Who, then,
are 'παρ' αὐτοῖς τοὺς ἐν τέλει' ("those in office among ourselves")?
Philo has used the term once before in § 222, and in both places it is
probably a reference to the Sanhedrin (cf. Smallwood 1961, 274, 304). It
is, however, impossible to determine who did what from the evidence in
the text, and Hoehner's proposal cannot be proved. Judging from the plural
construction in Philo, the most likely scenario indicates a close cooperation
between Antipas, the leading members of the Sanhedrin and other
Herodian descendants, who joined forces to spearhead a major delegation
sent to approach Pilate. Third, what was the complaint all about? The accusations referred to in the text are primarily of a religious nature. The act
of Pilate is called "an innovation" (νεωτερισθὲν) and a violation of the
"custom of the fathers" (ἔθη πάτρια). It is an open question why the act
was perceived as sacrilege since the shields were aniconic. According to
Smallwood, the reason might be that an "acceptance of shields which kept
the letter of the Law might create a precedent which would make the rejection of Pilate's next innovation difficult" (Smallwood 1961, 304).[71] Thus,
while the honorific inscriptions on the shields (§ 299) might have been offensive featuring the divine titles of Tiberius,[72] the complaint was probably
just as much a question of keeping the power balance in Jerusalem intact,
which Pilate had insulted with this act. Undoubtedly, Antipas' motives for
entering this dispute involved political considerations as well, since Pilate
and Antipas were the two main competitors for power in Palestine, and
thus Antipas could profit politically if Pilate was defeated.

   In conclusion, Philo presents important information in this text regarding Antipas. The tetrarch took part in the religious and political life of Jerusalem, and had a positive connection to the Sanhedrin, who chose him as

---

[71] The two confrontations known from Josephus are prompted by more clearly sacri-
legious acts by Pilate. The introduction of Roman standards in Jerusalem with attached
icons was indisputably a transgression of the Second Commandment (*War* 2.169–174;
Ant. 18.55–59). So too was the theft of money from the temple treasury spent on an aqueduct (*War* 2.175–177; *Ant.* 18.60–62), though a later discussion in the Mishnah concerns whether or not surplus from the shekel dues could be used for the city's needs (cf.
Smallwood 1961, 301 and the discussion above in section 3.3.5).

[72] Cf. the discussion by Helen K. Bond, in which she argues that Tiberius' full name
would have included his religious titles (*divi filius* and *pontifex maximus*) as known from
inscriptions and coins. "This reference to the divine Augustus would be offensive" (Bond
1998, 39).

an important part of the delegation sent to confront Pilate in order to safe-guard their religious freedom and traditions.

4.3 The New Testament

Herod Antipas' role in the New Testament has been studied as an integral part of commentaries on the Gospels, and the two main events in which Antipas features have been the focus of separate research. These two events are: (a) Antipas' execution of John the Baptist (Mark 6:14–29; Matt 14:1–12; Luke 3:18–20; 9:7–9) and (b) Antipas' interrogation of Jesus in Jerusalem (Luke 23:6–12, 15, cf. also Acts 4:27), to which Antipas' general interest in Jesus and vice versa is connected (Luke 9:7–9; 13:31–33; Mark 6:14–16; 8:15; Matt 14:1–2).[73] This list clearly reveals that Antipas is only mentioned sporadically in the New Testament. The Gospel of John does not mention him at all. Matthew only includes his response to the rumour of Jesus' ministry and his execution of John the Baptist (Matt 14:1–12).[74] Mark includes the same traditions as Matthew, as well as the warning against "the yeast of Herod" (Mark 8:15).[75] Luke, on the other hand, includes more material: Antipas is a reference point for the Jesus story (3:1); his imprisonment of John the Baptist is seen as another expression of "all the evil things he had done" (περὶ πάντων ὧν ἐποίησεν πονηρῶν ὁ Ἡρῴδης, 3:19); one of the women following Jesus, Joanna, is married to the steward (ἐπίτροπος) of Herod (8:3); Antipas is reported to have desired to meet Jesus (9:7–9), which according to the Pharisees was with the

---

[73] A more detailed classification can be found in Blinzler 1947, 6, who counts four groups: 'Herodes über Jesus' (Mark 6:14–16; Matt 14:1–2; Luke 9:7–9) – 'Jesus über Herodes' (Mark 8:15) – 'Jesus an Herodes' (Luke 13:31–33) – 'Jesus vor Herodes' (Luke 23:7–15).

[74] It may be added that G. Theißen has suggested that the reed swayed by the wind in Matt 11:7 could be a reference to Antipas (Theißen 1985; Theißen 1992, 26–39). This likely suggestion will be treated in chapter 6 in connection with the coins of Antipas (cf. section 6.4.1).

[75] Matthew and Mark are the only evangelists to include passages on 'οἱ Ἡρῳδιανοί'. Mark 3:6 mentions that the Pharisees and the Herodians planned to have Jesus killed (ἀπόλλυμι). In the parallel texts of Mark 12:13–17 and Matt 22:15–22, the two groups once again join forces against Jesus in questioning Jesus about the legitimacy of paying taxes to the Emperor. Finally a weak tradition in Mark 8:15 reads 'τῶν Ἡρῳδιανῶν' instead of the strongest tradition's 'Ἡρῴδου.' However, this is best explained as a wish to harmonize this passage with the three other passages where the Pharisees are coupled with the Herodians. Though the precise connection between the Herodians and Herod is debated, it seems undeniable that the evangelists intended some kind of relation between Antipas and the Herodians (cf. Hoehner 1972, 339).

secret intention of having him killed (13:31–33); just as Antipas plays a part in the trial of Jesus (23:6–12, 15). Finally, Antipas is mentioned in the communal prayer of Acts 4:24–30, in which he is listed alongside Pilate, the gentiles and the people of Israel as one who has gathered "against the Lord and his anointed" (κατὰ τοῦ κυρίου καὶ κατὰ τοῦ χριστοῦ αὐτοῦ, 4:26).

Though the material on Antipas in the New Testament is sparse, the research on it is abundant. In three in-depth chapters, Hoehner covers this vast research and provides meticulous discussions of the issues raised in connection with the texts (Hoehner 1972, 110–250). However, even though the main part of his dissertation is devoted to the New Testament paragraphs, he reportedly had to limit his investigation since a full investigation of Antipas' role in the trial, for instance, would have demanded a monograph of its own (Hoehner 1972, 224). The present study is even more limited in scope, with a deliberate focus on which role Antipas is given in the texts. The descriptions of Antipas in Mark and Matthew will be dealt with first, then the traditions in Luke will be examined before addressing the main question: What picture do the Gospels paint of Herod Antipas?

4.3.1 Herod Antipas and Jesus in Mark and Matthew

As mentioned above, in the Gospels of Matthew and Mark, Herod Antipas is introduced for the first time in connection with his response to the rumour of Jesus' ministry, which is linked to his execution of John the Baptist reported in a flashback. The texts in Mark 6:14–16 and Matt 14:1–2 present this as a statement, while the report in Luke (9:7–9) is slightly different because it presents Antipas' statement on Jesus as a question. In short, we are told that "Herod the Tetrarch" (Ἡρῴδης ὁ τετραάρχης, Matt 14:1) or "King Herod" (ὁ βασιλεὺς Ἡρῴδης, Mark 6:14)[76] heard of "the rumour of Jesus" (τὴν ἀκοὴν Ἰησοῦ, Matt14:1) or that "his name had become known" (φανερὸν γὰρ ἐγένετο τὸ ὄνομα αὐτοῦ, Mark 6:14). In Matthew this is followed by a statement by Antipas to his servants saying that "this is John the Baptist, he has been raised from the dead and this is why the powers work in him" (οὗτός ἐστιν Ἰωάννης ὁ βαπτιστής· αὐτὸς ἠγέρθη ἀπὸ τῶν νεκρῶν καὶ διὰ τοῦτο αἱ δυνάμεις ἐνεργοῦσιν ἐν

---

[76] Only Luke is consistent in using the title 'tetrarch' (3:19; 9:7 cf. also Acts 13:1) just like Josephus (*Ant.* 18.102, for instance). Matthew uses this correct designation in 14:1, but in 14:9 Antipas is entitled 'ὁ βασιλεὺς.' Only Mark entitles him like this (6:14, 22, 25, 26, 27). F.F. Bruce suggests that the subjects of Antipas would have entitled him with the Aramaic *malka*, which has a wider range of meaning than both *rex* and βασιλεὺς and this could explain the incorrect designation in Mark and Matthew (Bruce 1963, 9).

αὐτῷ, 14:2).[77] Mark is more elaborate, and includes statements by people other than Antipas saying that John has risen from the dead,[78] or that Jesus is Elias, or a prophet like one of the prophets (προφήτης ὡς εἷς τῶν προφητῶν, 6:15). Antipas himself states: "The one I have beheaded, John, he has been raised" (ὃν ἐγὼ ἀπεκεφάλισα Ἰωάννην, οὗτος ἠγέρθη, 6:16). It is debatable how the statements of Antipas in Mark and Matthew are to be understood (cf. Hoehner 1972, 189–190). Should they be read as remarks filled with sarcasm, or is Antipas being described as an unpredictable and capricious ruler who regretted his acts and suddenly believes in some kind of divine attestation in Jesus?

A clue to the answer to this question may be found in the way Jesus responds to Antipas, which is expressed in a three-fold way: First, while Matthew does not include any further direct stories on Antipas,[79] Mark has Jesus warning against the yeast of the Pharisees and the yeast of Herod (ὁρᾶτε, βλέπετε ἀπὸ τῆς ζύμης τῶν Φαρισαίων καὶ τῆς ζύμης Ἡρῴδου, 8:15).[80] Mark does not explain exactly what is to be avoided (as does Matt 16:12, τῆς διδαχῆς), but the statement is clearly meant to make the reader aware of an antagonistic relationship between Antipas and Jesus and his followers (cf. also 3:6). Second, the same thing seems to be expressed through the reported withdrawals of Jesus, though not in a uniform manner. Three withdrawals are reported prior to Antipas' reaction to Jesus' ministry, and ten after (cf. the detailed study in Hoehner 1972, 197–202, 317–330). The three withdrawals before are motivated by a need for solitude (Mark 1:35), the threat from the Pharisees and the Herodians (only Mark), who wanted to kill Jesus (Mark 3:7; Matt 12:15), and by the pressure from the crowds, which makes Jesus and his disciples depart (Mark

---

[77] The weak textual tradition that keeps this as a question rather as a statement (μήτι, D *pc* b f h vg[mss]) is best seen as a harmonization with Luke 9:9 (τίς δέ ἐστιν οὗτος).

[78] The textual variant of the apparatus in 6:14 reading 'ἔλεγεν' instead of the in NA 27 preferred 'ἔλεγον' actually has a better attestation and would make 'Ἰωάννης ὁ βαπτίζων ἐγήγερται ἐκ νεκρῶν καὶ διὰ τοῦτο ἐνεργοῦσιν αἱ δυνάμεις ἐν αὐτῷ' a statement by Antipas close to Matt 14:2. It speaks in favour of the plural that a singular would make verse 16 a needless repetition (cf. Hoehner 1972, 185). On the other hand, this could be exactly what makes 'ἔλεγεν' the *lectio difficilior* that should be preferred (so Achtemeier 1970, 269–270).

[79] As mentioned, G. Theißen argues that "the reed shaken by the wind" (κάλαμον ὑπὸ ἀνέμου σαλευόμενον) of Matt 11:7 is an ironic reference to Antipas. If so, Antipas is presented as the counter example as John (cf. note 74).

[80] A weak textual variant reads 'τῶν Ἡρῳδιανῶν' instead of 'Ἡρῴδου', which is best explained as a harmonization with 3:6 and 12:13. Interestingly, the parallel in Matt 16:6 reads 'Σαδδουκαίων.' Both editions of the saying possibly imply the same connotation, namely a warning against the leading groups of the society, which otherwise did not represent the same kind of 'ζύμη' (cf. Hoehner 1972, 211–213).

4:35; Matt 8:18). Matthew in particular points out that Jesus withdraws as a reaction against something. As an example, when Jesus is told that the Pharisees want to kill him we read that Jesus withdrew from that place ('Ο δὲ Ἰησοῦς γνοὺς ἀνεχώρησεν ἐκεῖθεν, 12:15). The same thing happens in the first of the ten withdrawals after Jesus is informed about Antipas' execution of John. Matthew writes that Jesus upon hearing that left in a boat for a deserted place to be on his own (Ἀκούσας δὲ ὁ Ἰησοῦς ἀνεχώρησεν ἐκεῖθεν ἐν πλοίῳ εἰς ἔρημον τόπον κατ' ἰδίαν', 14:13). Thus, according to Matthew, Jesus perceives Antipas as a threat. Mark is less pronounced, and the withdrawal following the story of the execution of John (6:31) seems to have more to do with the disciples' need for rest. Third, it is interesting that from that point onwards, when Jesus is informed about the execution of John, the character of Jesus' ministry changes in two ways: (a) Jesus is constantly on the move and most of the time outside Antipas' area with just a few short visits to lake Genesareth (Mark 6:53; Matt 14:34) and Dalmanutha or Magadan (Mark 8:10; Matt 15:39) until he reaches Capernaum one last time before setting out for Jerusalem (Mark 9:33; Matt 17:24). (b) As pointed out by Hoehner, Jesus' public preaching on the Kingdom of God virtually ceases, only to be resumed when Jesus is on his way to Jerusalem. Instead, Jesus teaches his disciples (cf. Hoehner 1972, 201, note 2). Taken together, these three points imply that an antagonistic relationship between Jesus and Antipas is indicated by Mark and Matthew. Jesus perceives Antipas as a threat and reacts accordingly.

4.3.2 *Antipas and John the Baptist in Mark and Matthew*

While Luke just notes that Antipas executed John the Baptist (9:9), Matthew and Mark describe this in detail in two passages formed as flashbacks taking up the line from Mark 1:14 and Matt 4:12 referring to John's imprisonment. These flashbacks follow immediately upon Antipas' reaction to the rumours of Jesus' ministry, as previously described.

A comparison between the two accounts reveals several similarities as well as diversities: (a) Both specify that the reason for John's imprisonment is his censure of Antipas' marriage with Herodias, the former wife of his brother Philip. (b) Both claim that the execution took place in connection with Herod's 'γενέσια', during which the daughter of Herodias fascinated Antipas with her dance making him promise to fulfil a wish for her.[81] (c) In both cases, the daughter lets her mother decide what to wish, and Herodias is the one asking for John's head. (d) Finally, both accounts close

---

[81] It is debated whether 'γενέσια' indicates Antipas' birthday or the anniversary of his accession to the throne. See Schürer 1973, 346, note 26, and also Hoehner 1972, 160, note 5.

by mentioning that the disciples of John came to collect his body for burial.

The main difference concerns the position Antipas took against John. All the accounts agree that it was Antipas who arrested John (Matt 14:3; Mark 6:17; Luke 3:20, cf. also *Ant.* 18.119), but who desired that John should be executed? Luke (9:9) and Josephus (*Ant.* 18.116) do not mention Herodias at all. Matthew states that it was Antipas' intention to kill John, but he feared to do so because the crowd regarded him as a prophet (θέλων αὐτὸν ἀποκτεῖναι ἐφοβήθη τὸν ὄχλον, ὅτι ὡς προφήτην αὐτὸν εἶχον, 14:5). Still, when John is actually killed it happens at the request of Herodias (14:8), which grieved Antipas (λυπέω) either because he did not want to kill John after all, or because he regretted the oath he had given in front of the guests (διὰ τοὺς ὅρκους καὶ τοὺς συνανακειμένους, 14:9, cf. Hoehner 1972, 158). According to Mark, on the other hand, Herodias was the one who wanted to kill John (ἀποκτεῖνω, 6:19), but was prevented from doing so by Antipas, who feared John because he knew that John was a righteous and holy man – which is why he protected him against Herodias (ὁ γὰρ Ἡρῴδης ἐφοβεῖτο τὸν Ἰωάννην, εἰδὼς αὐτὸν ἄνδρα δίκαιον καὶ ἅγιον, καὶ συνετήρει αὐτόν, 6:20). Also, Antipas gladly listened to him (καὶ ἡδέως αὐτοῦ ἤκουεν, 6:20) even though he became very disturbed/perplexed (πολλὰ ἠπόρει),[82] when he did so. Not surprisingly, Mark also narrates how saddened Antipas was when the daughter of Herodias[83] requested the head of John as fulfilment of Antipas' oath (περίλυπος, 6:26). In addition, Mark differs from Matthew by including a longer description that contains both a note on who attended the birthday party (6:21)[84], and an elaboration on how the oath was formed (6:23).[85]

---

[82] There is an important textual variant reading ἐποίει instead of the preferred ἠπόρει of NA 27. The meaning would then be that Antipas 'did many things' after he had listened to John. As discussed by Hoehner, good arguments can be advanced for both readings, though the reading of NA 27 is preferred by most commentators (Hoehner 1972, 159, note 7).

[83] There is an important textual variant in 6:22 reading αὐτῆς and not αὐτοῦ, which was actually preferred up until NA 25, and which is still the one chosen in most modern translations. Following this tradition, the translation should be: "When Herodias' own daughter came in…" A few manuscripts omit the pronoun altogether, resulting in the translation: "When Herodias' daughter came in…" But according to NA 27 the translation should be: "When his daughter Herodias came in…" This tradition has a few important manuscripts behind it, and is chosen probably because it is the more difficult reading even though αὐτῆς has a better attestation. For a discussion of this issue, and a discussion of the two other issues connected to this girl, namely what is meant by κοράσιον and whether or not she is likely to have performed such a dance in front of men, see Hoehner 1972, 151–157 and Gillman 2003, 54–55, note 6.

[84] Neither of the accounts inform us where the party took place, but Mark tells us that

The main question is what picture of Antipas Mark and Matthew intended to present to their readers. Should he be perceived as a threat, or rather as a weak, indecisive and ambivalent ruler controlled by fear of the people, of John, of his guests and of his wife? The likely answer lies somewhere in between. Both Mark and Matthew depict Antipas as a threat. Matthew clearly states that Antipas wanted to kill him (θέλων αὐτὸν ἀποκτεῖναι 14:5), and that Jesus chose to withdraw from his area (14:13). Mark states that the Herodians wanted to kill Jesus (3:6), and that Jesus himself warned against Antipas (8:15). At the same time, both paint an unflattering picture of an indecisive fearful ruler. Mark is clearest, stating that Antipas feared John as a holy and righteous man to whom he liked to listen even though he became 'perplexed' by his speeches (6:20). But both Matthew and Mark assert that when Antipas was finally forced to execute him due to his own incautious oath, he was saddened, but he was too afraid to do anything but fulfil his promise (Matt 14:9; Mark 6:26). It is possible that Antipas is perceived as dangerous precisely because he is regarded as weak, fearful and susceptible. His father is described by Matthew as an active, dangerous threat who cunningly plans to get rid of Jesus (Matt 2:3–12), and who became exceedingly infuriated when he found out he was fooled by the wise men (ἐθυμώθη λίαν, 2:16). Antipas is dangerous in another way. The line of thought in both Mark and Matthew might be that Antipas perceives Jesus to be like John (Mark 6:16; Matt 14:2). We are then told what happened to John *even though* Antipas did not really intend it. However, due to his ambiguous and unpredictable actions, driven by a susceptible nature, he had him executed anyway. The reader's next thought is consequently: "What might not happen to Jesus, then?" No wonder he leaves Antipas' area.

4.3.3 Herod Antipas and Luke – The Trial of Jesus

The Gospel of Luke includes separate traditions about Antipas, among which the Pharisees' warning of Jesus against Antipas (13:31–33) and the trial in Jerusalem (23:6–12, 15) are particularly remarkable. This material has been a subject of investigation in John A. Darr's dissertation, *Herod the Fox: Audience Criticism and Lukan Characterization,* in which an au-

---

Antipas made his banquet for his 'high persons', the officials (τοῖς μεγιστᾶσιν αὐτοῦ), for the military commanders (τοῖς χιλιάρχοις) and for the leading men of Galilee (τοῖς πρώτοις τῆς Γαλιλαίας). The last qualification gives the impression that the banquet took place in Galilee itself, most naturally in his palace in Tiberias as suggested by F.F. Bruce (Bruce 1963, 12). Josephus is the only source mentioning a specific place, namely Machaerus in Perea (*Ant.* 18.119).

[85] For a discussion of the legal aspects of oaths in ancient literature in connection with this passage, see Derrett 1965.

dience-oriented reading of the role Antipas plays in Luke-Acts is performed. In short, Darr emphasizes that Antipas was an important figure throughout the Lukan narrative. When mentioned for the first time in 3:1, the reader is alerted, and wonders what role Antipas is going to play (Darr 1998, 142). It immediately turns out to be a negative one. First, Antipas is portrayed in the classical "prophet-versus-king confrontation scene of the LXX" (Darr 1998, 157). He is a persecutor and executor of John the Baptist (3:19–20; 9:7–9), a persecutor of Jesus (9:9; 13:31–33; 23:8–12), and an evil ruler in general (3:20; 13:1). Second, Antipas is an example of those who were not able to hear, see or understand the message of Jesus. Twice the reader is informed that Antipas wants to hear Jesus and see him perform a miracle (9:9, 23:8), but "Herod is among those who, because of their abuse of power and lack of repentance, are never able truly to see and hear the revelation of God in Jesus" (Darr 1998, 212).

Luke 3:19–20

The first separate tradition in Luke on Antipas is found in 3:19–20. It is stated that when "Herod the Tetrarch" was rebuked by John because of Herodias and "because of all evil things that Herod had done" (περὶ πάντων ὧν ἐποίησεν πονηρῶν ὁ Ἡρῴδης), he added to his evil acts by imprisoning John. What does πάντων πονηρῶν allude to? Unfortunately, Luke does not provide any further examples of this asserted evil of Antipas. According to Darr, the most obvious context is found in the Old Testament tradition of prophets reproaching the king (for instance Nathan vs. David and Elijah vs. Ahab and Jezebel, cf. Darr 1998, 157–158). In this way, Luke paints a picture of Antipas as another despotic ruler.

Luke 9:7–9

Like Mark and Matthew, Luke has a sequence on Antipas' reaction to the rumour of Jesus' ministry (9:7–9). It is placed in the same context as in Mark, i.e. between the mission of the twelve disciples and the feeding of the five thousand. Three things are said about Antipas: First, the reports on the ministry of Jesus confuse him (διαπορέω, 9:7, cf. the use of ἀπορέω in Mark 6:20).[86] Second, Antipas does not know how to identify Jesus.

---

[86] It is a question what connotation διαπορέω entails. Darr argues that the word goes beyond 'puzzlement' and also implies 'restlessness' and 'a troubled mind' (Darr 1998, 165). However, only the noun 'διαπορῆμα' and not the verb 'διαπορέω' (contra Darr) has a second sense in this direction. According to LS, 'διαπορέω' means 'to be quite at a loss', 'to be in doubt', or 'to be in want', and has a second use as a stronger form of 'ἀπορέω' (to be in want, to be perplexed, to raise a difficulty). Thus, it is not implied in this verb that Antipas acted with cruelty, as suggested by Darr. Merely that he was in serious doubts and perplexed.

Rather than identifying him as John, as in Mark and Matthew, Antipas rationalizes: "I have beheaded John. Who is then he that I hear such things about?" (Ἰωάννην ἐγὼ ἀπεκεφάλισα· τίς δέ ἐστιν οὗτος περὶ οὗ ἀκούω τοιαῦτα; 9:9). Third, for this reason he seeks to see him (καὶ ἐζήτει ἰδεῖν αὐτόν, 9:9). As Darr rightly notices, this embedded remark by Luke creates a "dramatic tension" pointing forward (Darr 1998, 170). What will happen when they finally meet? Will Antipas deal with Jesus as he dealt with John?

Luke 13:31–33

The next reference to Antipas is a distinctive tradition of Luke, according to which "some Pharisees" (τινες Φαρισαῖοι) came and said to Jesus: "Move and go from this place, for Herod wants to kill you" (ἔξελθε καὶ πορεύου ἐντεῦθεν, ὅτι Ἡρῴδης θέλει σε ἀποκτεῖναι, 13:31). Jesus replies by asking them to go back and "say to that fox" (εἴπατε τῇ ἀλώπεκι ταύτῃ) that

...see, I cast out demons and accomplish healings today and tomorrow and on the third day I have been fulfilled (I am finished). Yet, it is necessary for me today and tomorrow and on the day that comes to keep going, for it is impossible to kill a prophet outside Jerusalem (ἰδοὺ ἐκβάλλω δαιμόνια καὶ ἰάσεις ἀποτελῶ σήμερον καὶ αὔριον καὶ τῇ τρίτῃ τελειοῦμαι, πλὴν δεῖ με σήμερον καὶ αὔριον καὶ τῇ ἐχομένῃ πορεύεσθαι, ὅτι οὐκ ἐνδέχεται προφήτην ἀπολέσθαι ἔξω Ἰερουσαλήμ, 13:32–33).

As thoroughly discussed by Hoehner and Darr, two important questions are connected to this pericope: First, did Antipas actually issue such a threat, or should it be understood as an invention of the Pharisees to trap Jesus? In this case, Darr's literary and Hoehner's historical analysis arrive at the same conclusion: the threat was real enough, but the intention of the Pharisees was to get Jesus out of Galilee and to Jerusalem, where the Sanhedrin could deal with him better (Hoehner 1972, 220; Darr 1998, 175–176). Darr rejects the idea that Luke's Pharisees are friendlier than the ones in the other Gospels, and points to the fact that in prior incidents they are portrayed as his active enemies (cf. the list in Darr 1998, 179). A close look at the text itself seems to verify this conclusion. Jesus accepts the threat as real, and sends the Pharisees *back* with a message, as they were connected with Herod and included in the conspiracy.

Second, what is implied in the designation "fox" (ἀλώπηξ)? According to Hoehner, two connotations can be derived from contemporary sources. On the one hand, "fox" connotes insignificance and inferiority in terms of direct power (often presented in contrast to the lion), compensated by a cunning cleverness that makes the fox a destructive animal (Song 2:15; Ezek 13:4). On the other hand, the fox was feared for its craftiness and ability to outwit other animals, as well as for its greed (cf. Hoehner 1972,

345 with references to Latin texts). Hoehner concludes that in a Jewish context it is always the first option that is presented, and concludes that "a person who is designated a fox is an insignificant or base person. He lacks real power and dignity, using cunning deceit to achieve his aims" (Hoehner 1972, 347). In other words, Hoehner reads the entire passage as a ridiculing of Antipas, who does not have the power or ability to intervene in the life of Jesus, who will move on according to his own plan and reach his final destination, Jerusalem.

Darr, for his part, emphasizes the destructive connotation of the word fox. With reference to the Song of Solomon (2:15), where the fox is designated as a destroyer of the vineyards, he argues that up until this point Antipas has revealed himself to be one of the destroyers of the vineyard of God through the execution of John. Now the shadow falls on Jesus as well. In this way Antipas is designated as another of the prophet killers, and "the fact that Jesus will not die now in Galilee at the hands of Herod is not due to Herod's inferiority or lack of courage, but rather to the divine agenda that specifies that Jesus must die in Jerusalem" (Darr 1998, 182). There is, however, no need to see the proposals of Darr and Hoehner as mutually exclusive. In Luke, Antipas is described as dangerous and has already proven his abilities beyond a doubt, but his craftiness is not that of a lion. Rather, from the evangelist's viewpoint, he was an immanent threat who with the cunning cleverness of the fox tried to get a hold of Jesus (9:7–9).[87]

Luke 23:1–15

The final episode in the Gospel of Luke concerning Antipas is also the most important. Luke is the only evangelist in the New Testament who includes a tradition according to which Jesus was sent from Pilate to Antipas for questioning, and possibly also for conviction. Five issues are to be considered. First, the prolegomena is found in 23:1–7, where the Sanhedrin accuses Jesus before Pilate. The accusations are clearly designed to impress the Roman prefect. Jesus is accused of 'misleading' (διαστρέφω) the people, obstructing the payment of taxes to the Emperor (κωλύοντα φόρους Καίσαρι διδόναι) and claiming to be a messiah and a king (λέγοντα ἑαυτὸν χριστὸν βασιλέα εἶναι, 23:2). When Pilate doubts these accusations, they insist by stating that "he stirs up the people by teaching

---

[87] Darr further discusses what the background of 13,31–33 could be, and restates Dibellius' idea of the pericope being formed like a typical Greek *chreia* aimed at verifying the interdependence (αὐτάρκεια) and freedom of speech (παρρησία) of the philosopher even with his life at stake. At the same time, Darr also points to a background in the prophet-versus-king tradition of the LXX as already touched upon (cf. Darr 1998, 183–188).

throughout all of Judea, from Galilee, where he started, to this place" (ἀνασείει τὸν λαὸν διδάσκων καθ᾽ ὅλης τῆς Ἰουδαίας, καὶ ἀρξάμενος ἀπὸ τῆς Γαλιλαίας ἕως ὧδε, 23:5). Upon hearing that Jesus comes from "the jurisdiction of Herod" (ἐκ τῆς ἐξουσίας Ἡρῴδου, 23:7), Pilate sends him to Herod, who is present in Jerusalem.[88]

Second, when Antipas thus finally meets Jesus a long-standing tension is released. Since 9:9 this meeting has been anticipated, and at least since 13:31 with unease. It turns out that Antipas becomes exceedingly glad (ἐχάρη λίαν), since he has wanted to see Jesus (ἐξ ἱκανῶν χρόνων θέλων ἰδεῖν αὐτόν) for a long time, because of what he had heard about him (διὰ τὸ ἀκούειν περὶ αὐτοῦ), and he hoped to see him perform a sign (ἤλπιζέν τι σημεῖον ἰδεῖν ὑπ᾽ αὐτοῦ γινόμενον, 23:8). As Darr points out, when Jesus had previously been told to present a sign he always refused to give anything but "the sign of Jonah" (τὸ σημεῖον Ἰωνᾶ, 11:29, cf. 11:16–17, Darr 1998, 195). The next verse fulfils these bad expectations. Even though Antipas "asked him with many words" (ἐπηρώτα δὲ αὐτὸν ἐν λόγοις ἱκανοῖς),[89] Jesus did not answer him (αὐτὸς δὲ οὐδὲν ἀπεκρίνατο αὐτῷ, 23:9).

Third, why is Jesus silent? Several answers have been suggested (cf. the overview in Soards 1985a; Soards 1985b, 360–363). M. Soards suggests that the background can be found in Isaiah 53:7, where the servant of *Jahveh* is a silent (ἄφωνος) sheep who did not open his mouth (οὐκ ἀνοίγει τὸ στόμα αὐτου) when oppressed. This connection is warranted by the gospel itself, since Jesus has just applied Isaiah 53:12 to himself before his imprisonment (22:37).[90] Darr, for his part, refers to the places in Luke talking about seeing and hearing without being able to understand. Again, just before this passage, Jesus reproaches the Sanhedrin for not being willing to

---

[88] It has been discussed whether Pilate had to send Jesus to Antipas, or whether he did so by his own choice. T. Mommsen argued that at the time of Jesus the accused was put on trial in his home province (*forum domicilii*), whereas Sherwin-White has later established what is accepted today: this custom was only introduced later, and at this time people who had been accused of anything were tried in the province in which the misdeeds had been performed (*forum delicti*, cf. Hoehner 1972, 235–236).

[89] The proposal of Harlow that 'ἐν λόγοις ἱκανοῖς' should not be translated merely 'in many words' but rather 'with violent words' is not justifiable. ἱκανός does not mean "strong, powerful, vigorous, violent" (Harlow 1954, 233). In the New Testament the word is solely used in its two basic meanings of 'sufficient/competent/worthy' when referring to a person, or 'considerable/large' when referring to things, amounts, time etc. Thus, the text does not paint a picture of a violent interrogation by Antipas (cf. Müller 1979, 115 and Hoehner 1972, 240, note 3).

[90] Soards also points to Josephus' description of the trial of Mariamme, in which her silence is interpreted by Josephus as a sign of nobility (*Ant.* 15.234–35, Soards 1985a, 43).

believe even if he answers their questions (22:67), just as those outside "shall see, but not see, and hear but not understand" (βλέποντες μὴ βλέπωσιν καὶ ἀκούοντες μὴ συνιῶσιν, 8:10, cf. Darr 1998, 197–198). In any case, Antipas is clearly depicted as an opponent of Jesus whose evil deeds render him unworthy of hearing or seeing, and who plays a role in the fulfilment of the prophecy of Isaiah 53.

Fourth, the most important issue concerns what role Antipas played in the conviction of Jesus and what position he adopted with regard to the question of whether Jesus was guilty or not. This has been debated very widely, and scholars are divided between those who argue that Antipas played an active role in having Jesus condemned (cf. Harlow 1954; Parker 1987, for instance), and those who argue that he had an insignificant impact on the final verdict passed on Jesus since Antipas found him not guilty (cf. Blinzler 1947; Jervell 1960; Hoehner 1972, 239–249; Soards 1985b, for instance). The text itself is open to discussion. The chief priests and the scribes were present, and accused Jesus before Antipas (κατηγορέω, 23:10). The next verse describes Antipas' reaction, and the grammatical construction can be understood in two ways (contra Darr 1998, 200). ὁ Ἡρῴδης is the single subject for the one finite verb, ἀνέπεμψεν (aorist), and the three participles all in aorist, masculine, singular (ἐξουθενήσας... ἐμπαίξας περιβαλὼν). The question is whether the last participle, the dressing (περιβαλὼν) of Jesus in a white/clear/splendid (λαμπρός) dress (ἐσθής), should be connected to the first two participles describing Antipas' treatment of Jesus with contempt (ἐξουθενήσας) and his ridicule and mocking of him (ἐμπαίξας); or whether it should be connected to the finite verb describing how Antipas sent Jesus back to Pilate (ἀνέπεμψεν). In other words, is the dressing of Jesus part of the despising, mocking ridiculing of Jesus, or is it a separate act connected to Antipas' returning of Jesus to Pilate, implying a statement of his verdict on Jesus? Grammatically the following two translations are both defensible. The first interprets the dressing as part of the ridiculing of Jesus, whereas the second connects the dressing with the sending back: (a) "But also (δε... καὶ) Herod treated him with contempt together with his soldiers and mocked him, dressed him in a white dress after which he sent him to Pilate." (b) "But also Herod treated him with contempt together with his soldiers and mocked him. Dressing him in a white dress, he sent him back to Pilate".[91]

---

[91] For further discussion of the grammatical structure, see Delbrueck 1942, 135–136, who accepts both translations as valid. Delbrueck points to the translation of Vulgate which (like the first option) regards the sending back as a separate action from the dressing in a splendid dress (*sprevit autem illum Herodes cum exercitu suo et inlusit indutum veste alba et remisit ad Pilatum*). K. Müller, on the other hand, argues that περιβαλὼν

Consequently, at least three interpretations of 23:11 have been advanced based on how to understand the grammatical construction and the symbolic meaning of the 'λαμπρὰ ἐσθής.' One option is that Antipas is proclaiming Jesus as guilty. Harlow sees the 'λαμπρὰ ἐσθής' as a royal dress sending the message that Jesus was convicted by Antipas of stirring up the people with messianic expectations (Harlow 1954, 177). Another is that Antipas is holding Jesus in contempt and making fun of him rather than convicting him, and as a part of that he dresses him in an outfit meant to proclaim his ridiculousness. Hoehner suggests it could be the white toga that a candidate for an office would wear (*toga candidata*, cf. Hoehner 1972, 243, note 1 with reference to Polybius); while Blinzler sees in this the proclamation of a "Spottkönig." Antipas "deutet damit sein Urteil über Jesus an: Der Mann ist mehr lächerlich als gefärlich" (Blinzler 1947, 23). Finally, it has been suggested in opting for the second translation that Antipas first shows his contempt for this ridiculous person, but afterwards admits his innocence in the double act of dressing him in a white dress and sending him back. The dress is then understood as a dress of innocence and righteousness, indicated by the consistent use of 'λαμπρός' in the New Testament: "Nirgends im Neuen Testament hat das Adjektiv λαμπρός eine despektierliche Bedeutung" (Müller 1979, 135, cf. also Darr 1998, 198–201).

Luke is not specific about how Antipas judged Jesus, but he is specific about how Pilate perceived Antipas' judgment. In 23:15 Pilate backs his verdict of Jesus as innocent (cf. 23:14) by referring to Antipas: "But also not Herod, for he sent him back to us." (ἀλλ᾽ οὐδὲ Ἡρῴδης, ἀνέπεμψεν γὰρ αὐτὸν πρὸς ἡμᾶς). It is further noted in 23:12 that Antipas and Pilate that day became friends (ἐγένοντο δὲ φίλοι ὅ τε Ἡρῴδης καὶ ὁ Πιλᾶτος), whereas hostility/hatred had prevailed between them previously (ἔχθρα).[92] Once again, the precise interpretation of this has been debated. Those arguing for an active role of Antipas downplay the importance of 23:15. J.B. Tyson simply omits this passage in his article on the relationship between Antipas and Jesus, arriving at the conclusion that Antipas was an active pursuer of Jesus (Tyson 1960). P. Parker argues that it was Antipas who set the process against Jesus in motion and pressed first the Sanhedrin and later Pilate to condemn and convict Jesus to death. Based on Acts 4:27, which says that "Herod and Pontius Pilate together with the gentiles and the peoples of Israel" (Ἡρῴδης τε καὶ Πόντιος Πιλᾶτος σὺν ἔθνεσιν καὶ

---

grammatically only can be subordinated ἀνέπεμψεν and not the preceding and equivalent ἐμπαίξας as interpreted in the Latin Vulgate (Müller 1979, 133).

[92] We are not told what Pilate and Antipas disagreed about. The massacre mentioned in Luke 13:1 is one possibility, as is the dispute over the votive shields mentioned by Philo, if that did not take place after the execution of Jesus (cf. Hoehner 1972, 180–183).

λαοῖς Ἰσραήλ) rose against Jesus, Parker states that it thus "would be appropriate if Antipas himself instigated the conspiracy" (Parker 1987, 201–202). After presenting several arguments for this thesis, Luke 23:15 is downplayed as "not accurate" and meant to 'whitewash' Antipas (Parker 1987, 207). The most vivid argumentation for an active role of Antipas is presented by V.E. Harlow, who argues that the 'ἀλλ᾽ οὐδὲ' of 23:15 should be translated very differently as "but not (indeed)", or read as 'ἀλλ᾽ οὐ δὲ' and also translated "but not" thereby contrasting Pilate's and Antipas' verdicts (Harlow 1936, 75–100; Harlow 1954, 236–237). These suggestions have not been accepted for both philological and textual reasons. In the text of Luke 23:13–16 itself it is hard to explain away the fact that Pilate uses Antipas in his argumentation for the innocence of Jesus (cf. also Hoehner 1972, 244–245), just as the double adversative 'ἀλλ᾽ οὐδὲ' has a positive connotation (indicating 'so also Herod', cf. Müller 1979, 134, "ja sogar") and cannot be translated as suggested by Harlow. Likewise Harlow's suggested correction of 'ἀλλ᾽ οὐδὲ' to 'ἀλλ᾽ οὐ δὲ' is not credible, since it implies an otherwise unknown duplication of the adversative particle.[93]

Thus, judging from the text of Luke itself,[94] those arguing for a passive role of Antipas in the final conviction of Jesus have the better case. Hoehner finds that Luke does not provide any "indication of the verdict reached by Antipas except from the mockery and his sending Jesus back to Pilate" (Hoehner 1972, 243). Darr's reader-oriented investigation delivers a fresh solution. The reader's expectation up until this point is clearly that Antipas will make use of his chance to eliminate the threat of Jesus, as he did with John. But what happens is that even the enemy of Jesus is not able to convict him on the charges of stirring up and misleading the people, and thus returns him to Pilate (Darr 1998, 198–201). The friendship of 23:12 and Pilate's remarks in 23:15 clearly tell the reader that Antipas sided with Pilate: Jesus is innocent.

Fifth and finally, the historical value of the entire Lukan account of Jesus before Herod has been doubted. M. Dibellius argued that the trial was a Lukan invention meant to reinforce Acts 4:25–28's interpretation of Psalms 2:1–2's vision of the gathering against the anointed (cf. Dibelius 1915, 113–126 and also Müller 1979, 111–114). Recent discussions, in-

---

[93] Cf. Blinzler: "Diese Deutung ist schon sprachlich nicht zu rechtfertigen, da sie mit dem unwahrscheinlichen Fall einer Doppelung der Adversativpartikel rechnet" (Blinzler 1947, 24).

[94] In later extra-canonical literature, the picture has changed and Antipas is often presented together with the Jews as one of the indictors of Jesus (cf. Hoehner 1972, 245–249).

cluding those of J. Nolland, J. Fitzmyer and R. E. Brown, find this position problematic and argue for a historical nucleus reused by Luke. Brown concludes:

In my judgment we must settle for a Lucan author of 23:6–12 who is neither a simple recorder of historical fact nor totally a creative, imaginative novelist. He transmits early tradition about Herod Antipas – tradition that had a historical nucleus but had already developed beyond simple history by the time it reached Luke. (Brown 1994, 785, cf. also Fitzmyer 1985, 1478–1480 and Nolland 1993, 1122)

Acts 4:27

The question of the historicity of Luke's description of Jesus before Antipas is thus connected to the notion in Acts 4:27 ranking Antipas among the conspirators against Jesus. In my view, Dibelius' idea that the trial in Luke is an invention intended to explain how Antipas was involved in the fulfilment of the prophecy of Psalms 2 is not convincing. If that was the case, Antipas should have played a far more active role (cf. also Darr 1998, 207, note 87 and Hoehner 1972, 228). Instead, Acts 4:27 should be understood within its context. The communal prayer is a response to what happens in 4:21, where Peter and John are released by the Sanhedrin because they did not know how to convict them. In spite of this and in retrospect, the Sanhedrin remained an enemy of the Jesus community in Jerusalem, just as Pilate and Antipas both eventually were part of the process against Jesus led by "the hand of God" (Acts 4:28, cf. Darr 1998, 207).

4.3.4 Partial Conclusion

Antipas is mentioned in the Gospels of Mark, Matthew and Luke as well as in Acts. His role is very sporadic in Mark and Matthew, but more elaborate in Luke. The New Testament writers were clearly not interested in him for biographical or historical purposes, but focus narrowly on his impact on and relationship to the Jesus movement. Consequently, several interpretations of Antipas and his relationship to Jesus have been advanced. Some argue that Antipas was a sworn enemy of Jesus with a decisive influence on the trial of Jesus. J.B. Tyson favours Luke 9:9 above Mark 6:14 as a reliable description of Antipas' reaction to Jesus, and assumes that Antipas was "an active enemy from whom Jesus was compelled to flee", who "had some part to play in the execution of Jesus" (Tyson 1960, 239). Emphasis is placed upon the withdrawals of Jesus, the direct warnings against Antipas (Mark 8:15; Luke 13:31–33), and Acts 4:27 is seen as the hermeneutic key to understanding Luke 23:6–16, though the crucial verses, 23:11 and 23:15, are not analysed. As noted above, P. Parker also presents Antipas as a crucial part of "the three-way conspiracy, Antipas-Pilate-Sanhedrin" against Jesus (Parker 1987, 199). Again, Acts 4:27 is placed at the centre of the argument, and since Antipas is mentioned first in the list of plotters against Jesus, it is argued that it "would be appropriate if Antipas himself instigated the conspiracy" (Parker 1987, 201–202). Similarly, the texts speak directly of enmity between Jesus and Antipas, as emphasized by Parker (Mark 3:6; 8:15; Luke 13:31–33), as are the withdrawals. Luke 23:11 is also interpreted as a conviction of Jesus downplaying the statement of Pilate in 23:15. In this way, Parker is able to conclude that "Herod Antipas played a far greater role than is sometimes realized" (Parker 1987, 208).

The opposite evaluation of the available material is presented by J. Jervell, among others. Antipas is perceived as a "jødevennlig og god regent, menneskelig svak og lett påvirkelig og romervennlig bare I den grad han som vasallfyrste var nødt til å være det" (Jervell 1960, 28).[95] The withdrawal in Matthew 14:13, for instance, is explained as a literary device used to connect two passages (Jervell 1960, 36); and even though Luke has preserved a tradition according to which Antipas was evil (3:19) and partly responsible for the conviction of Jesus (23:11; Acts 4:27), Luke also ascribes to Antipas a positive attitude towards Jesus (9:7–9; 23:8, 15). Hoehner, for his part, finds that the New Testament describes Antipas as ambivalent and indecisive in a similar way to Josephus (cf. Hoehner 1972, 169). Hoehner argues that Antipas' hesitation and indecisiveness when pestered by Herodias to ask Gaius for kingship (*Ant.* 18.245–246) fits well with Mark's and Matthew's description of the events surrounding the execution of John. The same thing is also true in the description of his relationship to Jesus. Antipas plans to kill Jesus, and the remarks in Mark 6:14–16 and Matt 14:1–2 should be read as irony. But when Antipas finally gets the chance in Jerusalem, he backs out and only plays a very limited role in the trial (Hoehner 1972, 245). Darr, basing his arguments on Luke, finds no reason to describe Antipas as weak and indecisive. Following the pattern of the 'prophet-versus-(evil) king' of the LXX, Antipas is described as "thoroughly wicked (Lk. 3.19)" (Darr 1998, 210). In this way "Herod serves as the conventional foil to idealize the charismatic's virtues" (Darr 1998, 211). Against this background, a true surprise awaits the reader in Luke 23 when Antipas releases Jesus. Even the wicked king could do nothing but declare Jesus innocent.

When assessing these different pictures of Antipas, it is important to realize from the outset what a perilous task it is to argue for a general picture of the psychological personality of Antipas based on single events. This

---

[95] Translation: Antipas "must be characterized as a Jewish friendly and good ruler, weak and impressionable and friendly towards the Romans only to the degree needed of a puppet ruler."

point will be discussed at greater length in Part III. The New Testament not only describes Antipas sporadically – it also does so from a specific point of view. For example, when Antipas is described as 'perplexed' in Mark 6:20, the point is not, even within the text itself, to argue that he was an indecisive ruler in general, but rather that it was when confronted with *Jesus* that he became perplexed, lacking the outlook necessary to perceive and understand what he experienced. On this basis, the next question is what basic picture of Antipas the different Gospels present. First, while there is a different perspective on Antipas in Mark and Matthew on the one hand and Luke on the other, with Luke being more settled in his description of the wicked king (cf. Darr), all three accounts preserve a tradition of Antipas being in a vexed situation when confronted with John and Jesus. Both Mark and Matthew have Antipas stating that Jesus is John resurrected, and while Matthew describes how Antipas was saddened (λυπέω, 14:9) when asked for the head of John, Mark goes on further to say that he was very saddened (περίλυπος, 6:26) just as he became perplexed (ἀπορέω, 6:20) when listening to John. Luke also depicts Antipas as perplexed when confronted with the news of Jesus (διαπορέω, 9:7), and though it is Antipas' stated intention to kill him (ἀποκτείνω, 13:31), he acts almost absurdly when he gets the chance in Jerusalem. First, he is exceedingly glad (ἐχάρη λίαν, 23:8) to see him. Then he treats him with contempt (ἐξουθενέω) and ridicules him (ἐμπαίζω, 23:11) before finally sending him back to Pilate in a way that is understood (at least by Pilate) as an act of acquittal (23:15). Thus, within the different perspectives on Antipas, a consistent element in the description of him in New Testament concerns his ambivalence and indecisiveness toward John and Jesus. Second, and connected to this, it is also consistent that Antipas is described as an enemy of Jesus, despite his hesistation. Matthew links the killing of John to at least one of the withdrawals of Jesus (14:13); Mark directly speaks of this enmity (3:6; 8:15); and so does Luke (3:19; 13:31).

4.4 Chapter Conclusions

This short survey of other literary sources on the life of Antipas besides Josephus has revealed a number of interesting points. First, according to Nicolaos, the Jewish people viewed the possibility of having Antipas as a ruler as preferable to the prospect of having Archelaos (*FGrH* 90, frag. 136 § 9). This corresponds to remarks by Justin, Philo, Luke and Josephus, who also inform us of a positive relationship between Antipas and Jerusalem. Philo describes the way in which Antipas was part of a delegation demanding that Pilate should remove his votive shields from the palace in

Jerusalem; a delegation that was chosen by the Jewish people and included members of the Sanhedrin as well (ἐν τέλει, *Legat.* 300). Justin asserts that Antipas took over the 'ἐξουσία' of Archelaos in Jerusalem (*Dial.* 103.4). Luke narrates how the Jewish leaders came to Antipas, who was in Jerusalem to celebrate the Passover, to accuse Jesus (23:10). Josephus includes a notion of Antipas taking part in the offerings in Jerusalem (*Ant.* 18.122– 123). This is naturally a weak basis upon which to say anything decisive. It is, however, noteworthy that while Pilate, Archelaos and Herod the Great, according to the sources, became involved in violent confrontations with the leaders of Jerusalem as well as the common people (cf. section 3.3), Antipas seemed to have been able to avoid such confrontations with two minor exceptions: the foundation of Tiberias on graves (*Ant.* 18.38), and the execution of the popular righteous man, John (*Ant.* 18.116–119), neither of which provoked any violent confrontation.[96] Thus, a number of written sources indicate that Antipas was mild and modest in his approach to the Jews, and that he therefore succeeded where his father and his brother Archelaos failed, namely in obtaining a constructive relationship with the Jewish leaders in Jerusalem and avoiding popular uprisings and violent confrontations. However, this was not enough to persuade the Romans to transfer the right to appoint high priests to him as they did with Archelaos. According to Strabo, Antipas and Philip had only just returned to their tetrarchies when Archelaos was banished.

Second, it is interesting that one of the dominant elements in the New Testament portrayal of Antipas corresponds well with the portrayal in Josephus, namely the ambivalence and indecisiveness of Antipas in a stressful situation (Mark 6:20; Matt 14:9; Luke 9:7; *Ant.* 18.245–246).

Third, the written sources further depict a glimpse of the internal struggle for power that went on within the Herodian house in connection with the trial (Nicolaos, *FGrH* 90, frag. 136 §§ 8–11) and in the events leading to the banishment of Archelaos (Strabo *Geogr.* 16.2.46 and Dio Cassius LV.27.6), between Pilate and the Jews including Antipas (Philo *Legat.* 299–305; Luke 23,1–25 and possibly Justin *Dial.* 103.4). This will be discussed further in Part III.

---

[96] Strabo's notion in *Geogr.* 16.2.46 represents the one possible exception to this picture. Though it is not stated directly, it is a plausible interpretation that Antipas was accused along with Archelaos in Rome (supposedly by their subjects); and according to Strabo he only just made it back to his tetrarchy. Dio Cassius, on the other hand, specifically states that Antipas was the accuser of Archelaos (LV.27.6).

Chapter 5

Herod Antipas and the Archaeology of Galilee

5.1 Introduction

Apart from Josephus, our main source of information on Herod Antipas comes from the archaeological material, including the numismatic material which is the main topic of this and the next chapter. As in the case of Josephus, a broad contextual approach is utilized. Strictly speaking, the archaeological remains that can be connected to Antipas are to be found in the cities of Sepphoris and Tiberias, and the excavations conducted at these sites will also be treated in detail below. However, in order to obtain a broad contextual perspective, two additional investigations will be conducted. First 'a regional perspective' will be established by looking at three of the villages of Lower Galilee. These will be Yodefat, Cana and Capernaum. Gamla, close by in the Golan, will also be examined. This will provide an important reference point for what went on in the rural parts of Galilee while Antipas' urbanization programme unfolded in the two cities within his area. Next 'an inter-regional perspective' will be added through a short survey of the three neighbouring cities of the Decapolis: Hippos, Gadara and Scythopolis, to which also the city of Caesarea Maritima will be appended. This survey will provide a useful background for understanding the cities of Antipas. The overall objective is to establish a position from which to enter into the historical debate on the socio-economic conditions of first-century Galilee as described in chapter one and discussed at greater length in chapter seven.

First, before embarking on the archaeological material, general archaeological theory and methodology will be introduced and discussed. In a similar way as in the Josephus research, the question of the relationship between sources and history is disputed. When dealing with archaeology it is important to understand how archaeological material is excavated and dated, and how descriptions of historical reality are derived from material artefacts. Archaeological methodology concerns the way in which archaeology is performed in practice and how an artefact is dated, and it is essential to understand the strengths and weaknesses inherent in archaeological method itself. Archaeological theory concerns the way in which archaeologists approach digs and artefacts. While the most basic way of performing a stratified dig is common to all theoretical approaches, the archaeological theory adopted will influence the way a dig is performed in practice, as well as determining what an archaeologist makes of the material uncovered.

5.2 Archaeological Theory and Methodology

5.2.1 Archaeological Methodology[97]

Archaeology is a highly developed discipline using diverse methods, techniques and specially trained experts. The archaeological procedure is divided into three parts. First, the actual dig is performed. Next, the material uncovered is dated. Finally, the dig and the findings are presented in a written report – often accompanied by a wider historical interpretation of their implications. The straightforwardness of archaeology is both its strength and its limitation, as will be seen in the following brief review of the basics of archaeological methodology.

Regarding the digging methods, the basic tool in the modern archaeological dig is the 'Wheeler-Kenyon' method, which was developed to obtain a strictly stratified excavation grid and replace a previous approach that focussed narrowly on uncovering major architectural features and thus discarding a lot of material in order to expose the large structures.[98] The new stratified approach includes a system of carefully recorded areas, loci and baskets. Each site is divided into areas, which are excavated using a grid of squares, usually measuring 5 x 5 m divided by balks. These vertical sections are preserved in their full height throughout the excavation period, providing a constant opportunity for refining the relative chronology.[99] The

---

[97] A handful of fine introductions to Syro-Palestinian archaeology and archaeological method exists. On archaeological methodology, see Drinkard, Mattingly and Miller 1988 (part two); Richard 2003 (part I); McRay 1997, 17–34; Currid 1999; Aitken 1997; Hayes 1997; Laughlin 2000, 17–32; Rast 1992, 33–45; Fritz 1994, 52–67. On the different archaeological periods in the Levant/Palestine, see Richard 2003 (part II); Rast 1992, 47–205. On the archaeological history of digs in modern times, see Moorey 1991; Fritz 1994, 34–51; Biran and Aviram 1993; Drinkard, Mattingly and Miller 1988 (part one); Currid 1999, 23–36.

[98] One result of this approach can be experienced at Tell Megiddo, where G.A. Reisner and C.S. Fisher in the 1920s and 1930s dug out a major portion of the large tell in order to expose individual standing architectural features. This method is sometimes known as the Reisner-Fisher method (cf. Currid 1999, 67–70).

[99] It must be noted, though, that in reality it is often not possible to observe a 5 x 5 m grid, since architectural features demand otherwise. This is especially true of the low-level sites which flourished in the Roman period, when the stable political situation allowed city expansion in unwalled areas. As a result, the stratification does not go very

basic unit within the squares is the locus, which functions as a three-
dimensional 'box' in which all artefacts are dated to the same period. Once
a new and distinguishable feature is uncovered, a new locus is opened.
Within each locus, baskets will be used to collect potsherds, glass and
bones carefully tagged with locus and area numbers.[100]

Once found and properly tagged, the archaeological material has to be
dated. Although new techniques have been developed, the basic way of
dating is still through pottery, which uniquely combines low cost, change-
ability and durability. It was cheap to manufacture, used extensively on a
daily basis, subjected to rapid changes in fashion, and once broken preserved in the fill.[101] Pottery can be dated through a number of observations
such as the method of fabrication (by hand or by wheel, for instance); the
contents of the clay (straw, crushed stone etc.); the temperature of burning;
and most importantly the style and fashion of the pottery revealed by
sherds from the bases, rims, handles and spouts (Borowski 1988, 224).
Sherds of pottery are not the only way to date material. Other ways include
coins, radio-carbon analysis, dendrochronology, epigraphy, and recent scientific measurement methods such as archaeomagnetism and thermolumi-
nescence (Aitken 1997; Drinkard, Mattingly and Miller 1988, 235–278;
McRay 1997, 30–34). Especially important is C14 analysis, since it has the
ability to measure the age of a carbon-bearing material in absolute terms.
When this technique was developed in the 1940s it was welcomed with
great expectations – but these expectations have not entirely been fulfilled,
because it turned out that the content of C14 in the atmosphere has not
been stable over the centuries. Therefore, the determination of age typi-
cally has a margin of uncertainty of plus or minus 100 years (cf. Weinstein
1988, 241). When the remains of a specific locus or stratum are analyzed,
the entire unit is dated through the simple principle that the latest item establishes the *terminus post quem,* i.e. the time after which the locus, stratum, wall etc. must be dated (cf. Borowski 1988, 224). If possible, a *terminus ante quem* will also be established, i.e. the time before which the unit
must be dated. Often this is more difficult, but if a new sealed layer is

---

deep. In addition, when extensive and large building projects were conducted, they often
uprooted earlier material completely instead of flattening it out and building on top of it,
thereby preserving the earlier layers (cf. Currid 1999, 70 and McRay 1988).

[100] An overview of the different technical terms can be found in Dever and Lance
1978, 74–80; Fritz 1994, 52–67 and Laughlin 2000, 17–32.

[101] V.M. Flinders Petrie was the first to discover this when digging at Tell el-Hesi in
1890 (cf. Borowski 1988; Rast 1992, 38). His basic chronology was refined by W.F. Albright in the 1920s and 1930s as well as later by his student G. Ernest Wright. The basic
chronology worked out by Albright is more or less still valid.

found above the layer already dated, this new layer's *post quem* will naturally be the lower layer's *ante quem*.

The third and final task is to present the excavated material in written reports. This part includes making a synthesis on how to read the material. All archaeological material is fragmented. The archaeologist rarely finds more than the base of a structure, and artefacts hardly ever bear an inscription revealing their ancient use or builder. The only way the archaeologist can make assumptions about this is through comparisons. Although imagination is a vital aspect as well, identifications are based on references involving comparisons with structures found elsewhere that have certain similarities. Still, this task is the most widely discussed, and the one most affected by the theoretical approach utilized.

This brief summary of archaeological methodology has illuminated both some of its strong and some of its weak sides. One of the strong sides is the straightforward nature of the methods used when digging, dating and documenting. There are, on the other hand, several limitations. First, due to the laborious and meticulous method employed, only a small percentage of a site is normally excavated. Consequently, any conclusion is by its very nature preliminary, based on what material is available at the moment. Second, generally the archaeological methodology does not allow dating within less than a one-hundred-year span. For this reason the Roman period in Palestine is only subdivided into three parts: the Early Roman Period from 63 BCE to 135 CE, the Middle Roman Period from 135 BCE to 250 CE, and the Late Roman Period from 250 CE to 325 CE.[102] From a historical perspective, this is a long time-span. Especially in the case of Galilee, which experienced radical changes in the Early Roman period in the wake of the war of 66–70 CE and the later Bar Kochba war of 132–135. Finally, the stratification of a site is never straightforward, smooth or complete. This is not least the case for Sepphoris and Tiberias, which both experienced heavy building activity during the Middle and Late Roman periods.

5.2.2 Archaeological Theory

Generally speaking, three different theoretical approaches to archaeology have been propounded labelled "classical archaeology," "New Archaeology" (or "processual archaeology"), and "post-processual archaeology".[103]

---

[102] See e.g. the article on periodization in *The Oxford Encyclopedia of Archaeology in the Near East* (Herr 1997, cf. also Rast 1992, 45). Another division with periods from 63 BCE to 70 CE, 60–180 CE, 180–325 CE is found in McRay 1997, 411. Sometimes the *Herodian period* is also used for the time from c. 40 BCE to 70 CE.

[103] Cf. the overviews in Dever 1980; Dever 1988; Dyson 1993; Sawicki 1994.

A classical archaeological approach[104] still has its advocates, although its heyday was in the 1960s.[105] It focuses on *the big dig* followed by "the cataloguing and ordering of decontextualized material" (Dyson 1993, 195). The scope is narrowly set on *what* was in antiquity, and not *why* it was, and *how* it functioned in society in a broad socio-economic perspective (Longstaff and Hussey 1997, 151). On the other hand, classical archaeologists tend not to make generalisations or wider statements, but are happy to keep things separate. As the classical archaeologist Stephan L. Dyson puts it: "the way most digs publish finds is symptomatic of this. Glass in one volume, pottery in another, coins in another, etc." (Dyson 1981, 10). For this reason, archaeologists with this approach are skilled in ancient languages, architectural features, pottery etc. (Dyson 1981, 8–9).

"New Archaeology" is described as a methodological breakthrough both by its defenders and by its critics (cf. e.g. Dyson 1993, 197 and Shanks and Tilley 1987, 30). As stated by William G. Dever,[106] it implied a shift from a "'classificatory historical' or descriptive phase" to an "explanatory phase" (Dever 1981, 15). Dever describes it as a true shift in paradigms (Dever 1988, 377ff.). Archaeology became a part of anthropology. A new set of questions is voiced in "New Archaeology." Not just, *what* was, but *why* was it*,* and *how* did it function? With this approach, the scope of archaeological enterprise was dramatically widened, and a variety of disciplines were brought into action with the aim of extracting much more information from the same amount of material. Consequently, the archaeological training needed to be widened, bringing in sociology, anthropology and a variety of "hard" sciences. In practice, an archaeological team contains a variety of specialists such as geologists, anthropologists, botanists and zoologists, as well as historians, linguists, stratigraphers, and ceramic typologists (cf. the list in Dever 1980, 46 and Longstaff and Hussey 1997, 152). As stated by Longstaff and Hussey: "A much wider range of materials including soils and minerals, flora and fauna, is now understood to provide valuable information about past human activity" (Longstaff and

---

[104] Normally the term "Classical Archaeology" is used as a reference to the archaeology of Ancient Greece and Rome. However, in the discussion between Dever and Dyson, it is used as well as a reference to a particular theoretical approach prevailing within classical archaeology of the 20th century also utilized within Syro-Palestinian archaeology.

[105] Cf. the informative and personal essay by Stephen L. Dyson, Dyson 1981, and again, Dyson 1993.

[106] While Dever more than anyone else has introduced "New Archaeology" within Syro-Palestinian archaeology (cf. the references in note 103), it is generally speaking connected primarily with L. Binford and later Colin Renfrew (cf. Renfrew 1984; Renfrew and Bahn 1991).

Hussey 1997, 152). The broad socio-economical perspective further influences which sites are chosen for excavation. Using the approach of "New Archaeology," large urban sites are not the only point of interest: rural village sites contribute on an equal footing. Finally, with the ultimate aim of establishing a "scientifically" based picture of the area and time investigated, "New Archaeology" is in close dialogue with text-based historians. *Text and Spade* is a phrase often used, at least within Galilean archaeology.

In the 1980s, "New Archaeology" was criticized heavily for not having a theoretical stand updated with the latest philosophical development. Headed by Ian Hodder, a group of archaeologists based mainly in Cambridge (cf. Dyson 1993, 198) claimed that processual archaeology should be replaced by *post-processual* archaeology.[107] Michael Shanks and Christopher Tilley thoroughly criticise "New Archaeology" in their book, *Re-Constructing Archaeology: Theory and Practice*. Although "New Archaeology" was admittedly a methodological breakthrough, it is based on an erroneous theoretical and philosophical stand derived from the positivism of Hempel.

New Archaeology has embraced explicitly and implicitly a positivist model of how to explain the past and we examine the treatment of the social world as an extension of the natural, the reduction of practice to behaviour, the separation of 'reality', the facts, from concepts and theories. (Shanks and Tilley 1987, 29)

But archaeology cannot be equated with natural science, and it cannot predict anything objective about the past. At best, archaeology is "an active relationship between past and present" (Shanks and Tilley 1987, 2). It is politics! "We attempt to emphasize archaeology as event and experience in the present, as social practice which cannot escape the present" (Shanks and Tilley 1987, 7). With reference to Gadamer, Shanks and Tilley state that interpretation cannot be escaped in any way. Things only exist if they are conceptualized. Even an artefact only exists if it is conceptualized. It is the "I" that opens a gate to the past. "Fore-having, fore-sight and fore-conception or presuppositions provide the foundations for any understanding, truth, or knowledge-claims" (Shanks and Tilley 1987, 106). "Understanding both *reproduces* and *produces*. It is not a recovery confined to original meaning. The meaning comes into being through understanding" (Shanks and Tilley 1987, 107). Hodder takes this to extremes: "It is no

---

[107] Of the many books by Hodder, a good introduction can be found in Hodder 1986 and Hodder 1999. Other instructive introductions are found in Shanks and Tilley 1987 and Whitley 1998.

longer even clear that consensus exists on what an archaeological object (artifact) is" (Hodder 1999, 17).[108]

This critique has not passed unnoticed in the later works by Renfrew, Dever and others. Although some of the statements are accepted as legitimate, the seemingly inevitable final consequence of post-processual archaeology, i.e. radical scepticism, is rejected. Renfrew and Bahn reject the overtly political background for Hodder's, Shanks' and Tilley's critique (Renfrew and Bahn 1991, 430), and instead propose what they call *cognitive-processual archaeology*, which also could be termed a *pragmatic* approach:

> This new synthesis, while willingly learning from any suitable developments in "post-processual" archaeology, remains in the mainstream of processual archaeology. It still wishes to explain rather than merely describe. It still emphasizes the role of generalization within its theoretical structure, and stresses the importance not only of formulating hypotheses but of testing them against the data. It rejects the total relativism that seems to be the end point of Critical Theory... (Renfrew and Bahn 1991, 431)

Dever presents a similar view in his book from 2001, *What did the Biblical Writers Know & When Did They Know It?* Instead of talking about New Archaeology or post-processual archaeology, he talks about *newer archaeology*, which is also described as a pragmatic approach (Dever 2001, 64). On the one hand, Dever is critical of his own background and states that the word "proof" should not be part of an archaeologist's vocabulary (Dever 2001, 71); but on the other, he still believes that newer archaeology provides valid information, simply because it works (Dever 2001, 64)! The key is to learn to ask the right questions. Archaeology should not aim to find the objective truth about the past. Instead, it should aim to ask heuristic questions that enlarge our knowledge.

Generally speaking, theoretical discussions are not often conducted within Galilean archaeology. James F. Strange is an exception, and in two minor articles he presents a theoretical framework for his archaeological enterprise, which is clearly influenced by New Archaeology (Strange 1992c; Strange 1997b).[109] Referring to Renfrew's work on socio-

---

[108] Perhaps feeling the accusation of nihilism and subjectivism approaching, Shanks and Tilley do say as a counterbalance: "Interpretation is an act that cannot be reduced to the merely subjective... The archaeological record itself may challenge what we say as being inadequate in one manner or another. In other words, data represents a network of resistances to theoretical appropriation. We are involved in a discourse mediating past and present and this is a two-way affair" (Shanks and Tilley 1987, 103–104). However, this counterbalance does not seem important in the overall picture.

[109] Another exception is found in the recent publication *Zeichen aus Text und Stein: Studien auf dem Weg zu einer Archäologie des Neuen Testaments* (Alkier and Zangenberg 2003b) containing two articles on archaeological theory and its relevance and impli-

archaeology, Strange describes the task of archaeology as one comprising patterns that reveal "the worlds of social structure and social relations" (Strange 1997b, 294). In this way archaeology produces a 'text', because "such patterns comprise the *logos*" (Strange 1997b, 295). Furthermore, 'written-text' and 'archaeological-text' should be related to one another using "a 'dialogical method'", where text and archaeological material are related to one another in a three-part process going from simple accordance (a "cup" in a written text, a "cup" in archaeological data) to comparing reconstructions of the social world on the most sophisticated level.[110] Through such an approach, a valid picture of antiquity is obtainable (Strange 1997b, 296–297).[111] Actually, within Galilean research, the most cautious statements come from non-archaeologists like Sean Freyne. Although he celebrates the contributions of archaeology, he also asserts that "it would of course be a false supposition to claim that whereas archaeology can provide us with hard data, the literary material is shaped by ideological concerns and must therefore be regarded as secondary or unreliable. Both archaeological data and texts call for interpretation, and the challenge is to discern how each may or may not confirm the picture which the other suggests" (Freyne 2000c, 16, cf. also Freyne 1992, 75; Freyne 1995, 598; Freyne 1997b, 51 and Horsley 1999, 59).[112]

5.2.3 Partial Conclusion

This short introduction has served to clarify the fact that the archaeological enterprise is a highly complex matter, which, just like text-based scholarship, experiences profound theoretical difficulties. As a tentative conclusion, the following may be noted. First, the methodological character of archaeology itself has strong sides as well as built-in limitations. Its strong sides concern the straightforward way of arguing from stratification, and a highly sophisticated and meticulous protocol of procedure. In this way, material can be dated when a *terminus post quem* and (at best) a *terminus ante quem* can be reached. Its limitations concern the precision of the dates

---

cations for New Testament archaeology (Bernbeck 2003 and Alkier and Zangenberg 2003a).

[110] This is presented in diagrammatical form in Strange 1992c, 29.

[111] In a similar way, Strange's co-workers Longstaff and Hussey also directly dismiss the critique from post-processual archaeology and reinforce NA's ability to construct the past (Longstaff and Hussey 1997, with reference to Renfrew and Bahn 1991).

[112] M. Sawicki also makes some critical remarks on the way Galilean archaeology works. She proposes an archaeological approach marked by "chastened realism", which could also be described as pragmatism using the processual paradigm when digging, and the post-processual paradigm when interpreting in order to take seriously the interpreter's own influence on the results (Sawicki 1994).

obtained in this way, and the fact that it is impossible to recover more than a small percentage of an archaeological site. As discussed further below (cf. section 7.3.2), this constitutes a special problem in the case of Roman Galilee since a radical change took place between and after the two wars of 66–70 and 132–135 CE.

Second, it must be emphasized that the development from a classical archaeological approach to New Archaeology was a groundbreaking step. The new and broader focus when digging promises that more data is likely to be recovered from an archaeological excavation, and much less material discarded due to a narrow focus of interest. The broader horizon of questioning, the focus on *why* things were and *how* society worked, and the integrating of insights from anthropology and sociology are all steps in the right direction.

Third, the challenge from post-processual archaeology needs to be taken into account, as done by Renfrew & Bahn, Dever and others. Their response shows that a new *pragmatic* consensus seems to have been reached, preventing archaeology from ending up in mere subjectivism. With a phrase from Dever, this matured version of New Archaeology could be called *newer archaeology*.

Fourth, in line with this, it must be stated that the new and broader perspectives in archaeology have both prosperous prospects and marring problems. It must be admitted, when dealing with human history, thoughts and culture, that certainty and validity are problematic conceptions. "Proof" is not a part of the vocabulary, as Dever has pointed out. Archaeology will deliver insights from constantly fresh sources, but its conclusions will always be open to discussion, refinement and even contradiction.[113]

Taken together, these four points lead to an approach involving a continuously dual reflection. On the one hand, constant awareness is needed of what is *argued* on the basis of the material sources. We do not have direct access to the past. Not even in a theoretical perspective (since the past is *not* the present), or from a practical perspective (since archaeology will only process a certain percentage of the material buried in the ground). Therefore, our approach is always destined to be biased and influenced by our own point of departure. On the other hand, this approach and the conclusions it reaches are not merely subjective. They are based on explicitly argued premises derived from a scholarly discussion and consensus on how to work and deduce, which – though not flawless – is *by definition non-*

---

[113] It is worth noting that such a cautious approach is *also* called for in the book entitled *Benchmarks in Time and Culture*, written by archaeologists influenced by New Archaeology (Drinkard, Mattingly and Miller 1988, 166, 219, 332, 409, for instance).

subjective. The arguments and conclusions are open to inspection, and anyone interested can test the results and proposed implications.

5.3 Tiberias

The sources describing the founding of Tiberias and its further development in the first century are limited to the writings of Josephus and the archaeological material. Josephus' description is found in *Ant.* 18.36–38, just
as *Life* records several events framed in Tiberias such as the burning of
Antipas' palace in sections 64–69. The archaeological material has been
gathered through a number of mainly salvage excavations, five of which
lasted more than one season (cf. Hirschfeld 1993, 1465–1466). The first,
led by B. Rabbani in 1954–56, uncovered the area around the bathhouse.
The next, led by A. Druks in 1964–68, uncovered the remains of a Roman
basilica close to the sea shore. The third, led by Gideon Foerster in 1973–
74, excavated the southern gate and its vicinity. The fourth, led by Y.
Hirschfeld in 1989–94, uncovered the church and its surroundings on top
of Mt. Berenice as well as re-excavating the Roman basilica found by
Druks (cf. Hirschfeld 2004 and Hirschfeld 1997b). Finally, Hirschfeld
launched a new expedition in 2004 scheduled to run for ten years and aiming at re-excavating the areas already touched upon as well as new areas.[114]

5.3.1 The History of Tiberias

According to Josephus, Antipas founded Tiberias after he had rebuilt and
walled Sepphoris and Betharamphtha in Perea (*Ant.* 18.27). As already discussed (section 3.4.3), Josephus explains that Antipas' building project included a mixture of blessings for the people brought to live there, such as
building houses and allotting them plots of land on the one hand, and making the city impure by transgressing the tradition of the fathers by building
it on graves on the other (*Ant.* 18.38). Although it is sometimes assumed
that Tiberias had a partly Gentile population from the outset (cf. Avi-
Yonah 1950–1951, 163; Hirschfeld and Galor Forthcoming, for instance),
Josephus does not actually say that this was the case, and this assumption
might stem from Whiston's translation of σύγκλυδες by "strangers" (*Ant.*

---

[114] There is a list of small and large excavations in Tiberias in Hirschfeld 1992, 55.
The expedition just launched can be followed on the website: http://www.tiberiasexcava-
tion.com. A general description of the history of Tiberias and the results of the digs can
be found in: Hirschfeld 1991b; Hirschfeld 1992; Hirschfeld 1993; Hirschfeld 1997a;
Fortner 2003. The first preliminary report on the present excavations will be released in
Hirschfeld and Galor Forthcoming.

18.37). However, σύγκλυδες is more accurately translated by "mob", and does not imply a certain ethnicity. Actually, there are no indications of a pagan population in either Josephus or the archaeological record. Rather, judging from the events during the war described in *Life,* Tiberias was a Jewish city organized according to a Hellenistic pattern (cf. below section 5.3.2). A different story, however, is that according to *Ant.* 18.37 the town had a *mixed* population in terms of socio-economic status, including not only the 'mob' or 'promiscuous rabble', but also people from Galilee (τὸ Γαλιλαῖον), drafted people from the land subjected to Antipas (ἐκ τῆς ὑπ' αὐτῷ γῆς), magistrates or principal men (ἐν τέλει), fellow citizens (συνοίκους), poor people assembled from all over (τοὺς πανταχόθεν ἐπισυναγομένους ἄνδρας ἀπόρους), and former slaves hardly made free (μηδὲ σαφῶς ἐλευθέρους, 18.38). Nevertheless, there are no indications in any of the sources describing first-century Tiberias of a Gentile section of the population.

The exact year of foundation is not provided by Josephus, and dates between 18 and 26 CE have been proposed (cf. Levine 1974, 143, note 1). However, new numismatic evidence now makes it possible to date Antipas' first series of 'Tiberias coins' to his 24th regnal year, i.e. 19/20 CE (cf. the legend L ΚΔ). There is good reason to believe that this series of coins was issued to commemorate the founding of Tiberias (cf. section 6.4.1). At least the coin confirms that the city could not have been founded later than 20 CE. A later coin issued under Trajan further limits the possible years of foundation. It commemorates the year 100 of Tiberias. Since Trajan acceded to the throne in 117 CE, the city could not have been founded before the year 17 CE (according to Avi-Yonah 1950–1951, p. 168) or 18 CE (according to Hoehner, who counts the founding year as year one, Hoehner 1972, 94). Consequently, the city must have been founded or inaugurated in 18–20 CE and most likely in Antipas' 24th regnal year, i.e. 19–20 CE, as proclaimed by Antipas' first coin series.

When Antipas was banished to Gaul in 39 CE, his nephew and brother-in-law, Agrippa I, was granted his tetrarchy by Gaius (*War* 2.181–183; *Ant.* 18.240–255). Upon Agrippa's sudden death in 44 CE, Tiberias was placed under the auspices of the Roman procurators of Judea together with the rest of Galilee (*Ant.* 19.363). In this period, Tiberias ostensibly received some kind of benefactions from Emperor Cladius, since its city coins from the time of Trajan (98–117 CE) and throughout the rest of the Roman period always entitle the city as 'Tiberias Cladio(polis)' (e.g. TIBEPIEWN ΚΛΑΥΔΙΟ, cf. Kindler 1961, 46; Meshorer 1985, 34). However, one coin issued in Tiberias during the reign of Cladius only features the regular name of Tiberias (cf. no. 2a-b Kindler 1961, 79–80 and 45) as do the coins of Agrippa II minted in Tiberias. For this reason, Chancey suggests that the city first took this new name during the time of Hadrian (Chancey 2005, 102).

During the reign of Nero (54–68 CE), Tiberias was presented as a gift to Agrippa II, who at this time ruled from Caesarea Philippi (*Ant.* 20.159; *War* 2.252; *Life* 37–38). The date of this event is disputed. According to *War* 2.252 it happened while Felix was procurator in Judea, i.e. in 54–60. Following the coins of Agrippa II, a new era of counting his regnal years began either in 55/56 or 60/61 CE which could coincide with his new allocations, and thus 55 or 60 are the most likely years (cf. the discussions in Mason 2001, 44, note 230; Schürer 1979, 473; Bernett 2003 and others). Later, during the war of 66–70 CE, Agrippa II lost control over the city, which witnessed many internal wars between the Jewish rebels, according to Josephus. It was fortified at the outbreak of the war, but later three different factions fought to control it.[115]

After the war, Tiberias was once again placed under the auspices of Agrippa II. When he died, it was placed under direct Roman authority, and reached its maximum size during the following Roman and Byzantine periods. In the early part of the second century, Hadrian possibly erected a temple in Tiberias. It is certainly true that a tetrastyle temple is depicted on coins from Tiberias in his period (119 CE, cf. Meshorer 1985, 34, coin 81 and figure 1). According to Epiphanius, however, the so-called "*Hadrianeion*" was never completed, and was later turned into a church (*Adv. Haer.* 30.12.1, cf. Belayche 2001, 93). Later in the second century, the city seems to have been formally cleansed from the impurity derived from the old graves in the area by Rabbi Simeon Bar Yohai (cf. note 59). In 235, the Jewish leadership of Sepphoris moved to Tiberias. A great study house (*Midrash ha-Gadol*) was established, and much of the Palestinian Talmud was written there (cf. Hirschfeld 1993, 1465).

Tiberias continued to flourish after the Arab conquest, but finally met its fate with the earthquake of 1033. Slightly north of the old city, a much smaller city was erected by the crusaders in 1099, which was also eventually abandoned.

5.3.2 First-Century Tiberias According to Josephus

According to Josephus, first-century Tiberias housed several large or public buildings. Antipas built himself a palace with splendid golden ceilings and figurative art in the interiors (*Life* 64–69, cf. the discussion in section 3.3.8), and moved the royal archive from Sepphoris, where it had been housed since the reorganisation of Judea by Gabinius in 57 BCE (*Ant.*

---

[115] For a detailed presentation of this period, see the well-written article by Tessa Rajak, "Justus of Tiberias" (in particular Rajak 1973, 346–354).

14.91), to Tiberias in order to make it the principal city of Galilee (*Life* 37–38). Josephus also mentions, in the context of events during the war, a stadium (*War* 2.618; 3.539; *Life* 92, 331), a huge synagogue (*Life* 277), and hot baths (*Life* 85). However, none of these buildings are explicitly attributed to Antipas.

Most of the Hellenistic institutions and offices attributed to Tiberias by Josephus are also mentioned in connection with events during the war. This is true of the city council of six hundred members (βουλή, *War* 2.641; *Life* 64, 169, 284, 300, 313, 381), a council president, a mayor (ἄρχων, *Life* 134, 278, 294; *War* 2.599), ten principal men (δέκα πρῶτοι, *Life* 69, 269; cf. also 64 and *War* 2.639), and the governors of Tiberias (ὑπάρχοι, *War* 2.615). While it is possible that such a Hellenistic city constitution was inaugurated by Antipas, in fact only the office of *agoranomos* is explicitly mentioned in connection with events during his reign (*Ant.* 18.149, cf. section 3.4.2).[116]

In several discussions of first-century Tiberias, all of these buildings and institutions are attributed to Antipas without hesitation (cf. Schürer 1973, 342–343; Lämmer 1976; Bernett Forthcoming and others). However, the outline of Tiberias' history presented highlights the need for a rigid distinction between what Josephus does and does not explicitly attribute to Antipas, since the city was ruled by four different groups from its foundation and up until the war. After the first 19 years or so under Antipas, there were five years under Agrippa I followed by 12–17 years under direct Roman rule until the city was transferred to Agrippa II, under whose control it remained for 6–11 years before the outbreak of the war. Antipas thus ruled for only one-third of this period, which is why buildings mentioned by Josephus in connection with the war cannot automatically be connected to his reign, just as the internal turmoil described in *Life* could be based on many later events.

5.3.3 Archaeological Material from the First Century

Since Tiberias remained a flourishing city for one millennium after its foundation, the archaeological material concerns many centuries. Actually, first-century material is rarely found, since the city peaked in the period between Hadrian and well into the Byzantine period, with large construction projects uprooting earlier buildings. A list of early-first-century material comes down to:[117] (a) The southern gate. (b) Portions of a cardo. (c)

---

[116] For further discussion of the various Greek institutions, see Schürer 1979, 178–180; Mason 2001, 58, 61.

[117] Cf. the general map of ancient Tiberias, figure 2, and the map of the present excavation, figure 3. Only three areas are marked as first century.

Some remnants of wall structures and water channels. (d) Portions of a magnificent marble floor and wall structures. (e) Possible remnants of the stadium. (f) Two inscribed lead weights. (g) Coins of Antipas with the legend "TIBEPIAC."[118]

The Southern Gate and the Cardo

Most spectacular of the first-century material is the southern gate excavated by G. Foerster in 1973–74. Two monumental round towers were uncovered along with adjoining walls, rooms and a road running northwards. The round towers measured 7 m in diameter and encompassed a 4–5 m wide entrance to the city. Both of them had a niche inside the entrance as well as a nicely decorated pedestal supporting a column. All of this was masterfully crafted black basalt stone (cf. figure 4, 5 and Segal 1997, 87). It seems that the gate complex was a freestanding monumental structure, since the adjoining walls and rooms did not reveal remains earlier than the sixth or seventh centuries.

When was this complex built? To determine this, probes were dug under the pavement between the towers in order to establish its *terminus post quem*. Potsherds found beneath the heavy basalt stones all dated to the first century, thus pointing to a first-century dating even though no *terminus ante quem* could be established close enough in time to be of any help. This date is further strengthened by the layout of the tower and the ornamentation used. In his entry in NEAEHL, Foerster narrows down the date of foundation even further and concludes: "Judging from the stratigraphy and the architectural evidence, the gate was probably built when the city was founded" (Foerster 1993b, 1471). Unfortunately, Foerster has not published a final report on this excavation yet, and his dating has been questioned. Monika Bernett refers to Josephus, who states that Vespasian was unable to enter the city from the south with his heavy military equipment and had to tear down parts of the wall erected by Josephus (*War* 3.460). This would not have been necessary with a gate which had 4–5 metres of clearance. Based on "ein Vergleich mit den formal und stilistisch ähnlichen Ehrenmonumenten in Gerasa (130 n.Chr. für Hadrian)" (Bernett 2002, cf. also Chancey 2005, 87), Bernett proposes that the gate in Tiberias was also erected in the second century. T. Weber, the excavator of the 'Tiberias gate' in Gadara (cf. section 5.6.1), also questions Foerster's dating. Weber dates the gate in Gadara to the Flavian period, and suggests that the gate in Tiberias was erected also after the war celebrating the Flavian victory: "It is very probable that both gates had been constructed

---

[118] These coins will be treated in the next chapter. It can be noted already that most of the Tiberias coins of Antipas have been found outside Tiberias (cf. 6.4).

as counterparts on a mutual initiative of the citizens of both the Galilean and the Gadarene urban community" (Weber Forthcoming, cf. also Weber 2002, 107; Weber 1991a, 21–22; Hoffmann 1999, 235). According to Weber, the similar layout of the two gates implies interaction (cf. figure 6). For historical reasons, such an interaction was not likely until after the war, since long-term tensions prevailed between Gadara and the Jewish-Herodian kingdom. It is difficult to pursue this discussion any further until the final report is available – or unless the gate complex is re-excavated during Hirschfeld's campaign. According to David Stacey, who has recently published the early Islamic material from Foerster's dig (Stacey 2004), only two probes were made under the pavement and the ceramic material uncovered is too slim to date any closer than 'first century' (personal communication). From a historical viewpoint, Bernett and Weber's argument from Josephus and the strikingly similar gate in Gadara is compelling, though it must be noted that round towers were erected before Antipas in Sebaste and Caesarea Maritima (cf. Segal 1997, 83–86, 88–89).

Foerster also dug under the large stone slabs between the towers and dated this part of the north-south *cardo* to the first century. While other parts of the first-century-cardo have not been attested anywhere else yet, remains of the cardo from the late Roman or Byzantine period have been found just west of a bathhouse complex. It is about 12 m wide with flanking colonnades and shops, making it altogether about 33 m in width (Hirschfeld 1993, 1467). More digs are likely to uncover more remains of the early-first-century cardo.

Wall 302, Possibly an Early-First-Century Wall

A couple of wall structures were found in the spring 2004 season of the Hirschfeld expedition, which could be dated by stratigraphy to the first century. The most interesting structure was uncovered in square O-16 located in area C. This square provides a telling example of how we can expect to find remnants of Antipas' Tiberias. The square contains three walls (cf. figure 7). Wall 300 is a nine-Roman-foot-wide wall dating to the second century, with impressive well-dressed basalt blocks on its outer side. It runs east-west, and is presumed to be part of the temple of Hadrian, the *Hadrianeion*. Abutted to it we find a later wall, no. 301, running north-south. Finally, a wall was exposed on a lower plateau, no. 302, running north-south as well. The *terminus post quem* for this wall was found beneath a stone slab floor which was built into the wall and which is therefore of the same age. Beneath the floor (locus 3016) were found a couple of rims from the early first century along with a handful of body sherds from the late Hellenistic period. The *terminus ante quem* could be established from the pottery found just above the wall, which all dated to the second century. Consequently, the wall must be dated to the first century, perhaps to the foundation of the city. A water installation was uncovered above it (perhaps a fish pond). It is interesting, however, how little of this wall and the water installation has been preserved (cf. figure 7). The later constructions in the area sealed a small part, but destroyed most of it. This might be the case in many other loci as well.

However, first-century material was attested in one other way in this area. The later construction work in the second century used fill containing large amounts of destruction material going back to first-century buildings on the same spot. The fill material just beneath the slab stone floor covering wall no. 302 in locus 3018 contained three highly interesting elements of importance for understanding the architectural layout of the first-century city: a huge amount of white plaster, some painted plaster, and some pieces of a beautiful broken marble panel, coloured red and white (cf. figure 8). This suggests an architectural style of the first-century city using white plastered buildings, some with a coloured fresco-style interior, and perhaps even some imported marble. But caution is needed. The material uncovered is very sparse and was destroyed by later building activity, only to be left in the ancient fill. As we shall see below, the use of similar coloured frescoes are attested in Yodefat and Gamla as well (cf. section 5.5).

Portions of a Magnificent Marble Floor and Wall Structures

In the fifth season of Hirschfeld's Mt. Berenice expedition, excavation was resumed in the structure close to the seashore termed a basilica (cf. figure 9). Beneath the first phase of the basilica (stratum IV), a stratum V with architectural remains from the first and second centuries was exposed including pebble floors, floors with well-smoothed limestone slabs (0.5 x 0.9 m) and most notably floors with coloured marble tiles designed in an *opus sectile* style (cf. the plan in Hirschfeld 1997b, 39). On top of the floors, pottery and coins from the first and second centuries were found, providing an idea of the *terminus ante quem*. At this stage, no probe was dug under the floors to establish a firm *terminus post quem*. In the spring season 2005 of Hirschfeld's ongoing expedition, this stratum was excavated further. Locus 525 (cf. figure 9) was completely excavated down to its foundation level, where an extraordinarily beautiful marble floor surfaced. Though badly preserved, enough was found *in situ* to suggest the pattern of the original floor, which was obviously also designed in the *opus sectile* style (cf. figure 10). Portions of the broken marble were washed, and it turned out that the dust had concealed the most beautiful colours of every kind (cf. figure 11). Marble like this was imported.

The architectural layout of this area is interesting. Locus 525 with the marble floor is enclosed by three large walls (walls 1, 2 and 3), which were built on top of it in connection with the basilica, destroying the original layout of the room where the marble served as a floor. The c. 3 x 3 m portion found in locus 525 seems to have been the south-eastern corner of a larger floor. The corner is demarcated to the south by two bases of tetra-style pillars, which were probably covered with marble slabs since pieces of marble were still attached in a vertical position. On the southern side of locus 525 as well as outside the small wall 105, in locus 526, no marble was excavated of the kind found in the northern part of locus 525. Instead, this area was covered by a pebble stone floor probably used as a foundation for the large well-smoothed limestone slabs already found in Hirschfeld's first expedition in the southern part of locus 526. It thus seems that the marble floor was part of a roofed hall surrounded by tetra-style pillars with a scenic view of the lake front and a nice open pavement area in front. Finally, an interesting element was attested in both locus 525 and also in the northern part of locus 526. In a level just above the pebble floor and the marble floor, a thin line of dark/black earth was found (cf. figure 12). Initial analyses indicated that this was a layer of ash.

The crucial question, naturally, is how this floor should be dated. In the 2005 spring season, Hirschfeld dug a probe beneath the pebble floor in the southern part of locus 525. Only large boulders were found, which served as a solid base for the entire structure. Unfortunately, no *terminus post quem* could be established from the pottery obtained from this probe. The pottery found above the floor indicated a *terminus ante quem* in the first or second century. Hirschfeld himself believes that this is part of a magnificent early-first-century villa and most likely identical with the palace of Antipas, and concludes: "...we have enough evidence that allows us to propose its identification as the palace of Herod Antipas mentioned by Josephus" (Hirschfeld and Galor Forthcoming).

The interesting thing is that with a single exception, similar *opus sectile* marble floors from this period have only been found in the palaces of Herod the Great.[119] Marble was expensive to import, and was generally not used extensively before the Middle Roman period in Palestine.[120] But

---

[119] According to the list in Hachlili 1988, 67 (cf. plates p. 68), *opus sectile* floors have been found in Herod's palace in Jericho, in the bathhouse in the Western Palace of Masada, and in Cypros in Jericho. Finally, traces of such a floor have been found in one of the Upper City houses in Jerusalem. A mosaic floor imitating the coloured patterns of *opus sectile* has likewise been found in Herod's palace in Caesarea Maritima, cf. the discussion below 5.6.2.

[120] In an article on the marble of Caesarea Maritima and the general use of marble in the Roman period, Moshe Fischer notes that while it was Augustus who was the first to employ marble extensively, it was used at "a comparatively low level" (Fischer 1996, 261) throughout the Roman period in Palestine. Although it was used most intensively in

Herod the Great was not averse to spending the means necessary to stay ahead of the architectural fashions of his day. In his winter palace in Jericho, for example, a large hall was built in the western side of the northern wing with an *opus sectile* marble floor of which only the imprints are preserved (cf. figure 11 in Netzer 1977, 10, fig. 63 in Netzer 2001, 54 and the reconstruction in Singer 1977, 14). Actually, the hall, measuring 29 m x 19 m, is "the largest one from the Roman period that has ever been exposed in the Land of Israel" (Netzer 2001, 53) and "in order to cover this large hall, gigantic beams were needed to span the 13 m space between the two rows of columns" (Netzer 1977, 9). The entire palace complex was magnificently built, bridging the Wadi Qelt and making use of its seasonal flowing water (cf. the reconstruction of the palace in Netzer 1975, 98 and Netzer 2001, 62–63). Netzer further believes that a hall similar to the one in Jericho was part of Herod's palace in Jerusalem as it is described by Josephus, and that it might be a type of hall "common in Herod's buildings" (Netzer 1977, 9). As we shall see below, Netzer has also uncovered a floor in a similar style in Herod's palace in Caesarea, only this was produced with *tesserae* stones instead of marble tiles (cf. section 5.6.2).

Thus, since such floors from this period are a common feature of Herodian buildings, the possibility is heightened that the floor of locus 525 in Tiberias could indeed be part of a building constructed by Antipas. If so, it is interesting that the floor was covered with ash, since according to Josephus the palace of Antipas was burned down by rebels during the war (*Life* 64–69).

The excavations in the autumn of 2005 and spring of 2006 further uncovered some wall structures in the same area that can also be connected to the same first-century building. At the same level in the north-east corner of the basilical building, two walls were found (W165 and 166) that were cut and partially destroyed when the basilical building was erected. Unlike the basilical building, the walls of this former building were constructed with limestone and not basalt using the header-stretcher technique of tightly fitting Herodian bossed masonry. In locus 729 between the basilical building and the two limestone walls, a number of interesting discoveries

---

Caesarea, which served as a port for the import of marble, "no architectural complex using marble from the Roman period has thus far been unearthed, except for the theater" (Fischer 1996, 260–261). A considerable amount of marble has been found at Caesarea but much of it in secondary use. The expenses connected to marble were a consequence of it not being a native material of Palestine that had to be imported, and of the skill of employing it requiring hired workmen and architects from abroad as well (cf. Fischer 1996). It must be noted, however, that the amount of marble necessary to construct a floor was lower than the cost of using marble drums or covering entire façades with marble, for instance.

were made. In the fills, several fragments of painted plaster surfaced, decorated in the Second Pompeian style. Fortunately, some of the plaster had survived *in situ*, protected for almost two millenniums by downfallen limestones (cf. figure 13). One boulder of a pillar was also found indicating the use of plastered pillars painted to look like marble using the same technique as in the north palace at Masada.

Remnants of the Stadium

During two rescue excavations in 2002 and 2005, Moshe Hartal discovered some structures that he believes were part of the first-century stadium mentioned by Josephus in which he spoke to a multitude of Tiberians several times during the war (*War* 2.618; *Life* 92, 331), and where Vespasian conducted a cruel slaughter of the prisoners who were too weak to be sold as slaves (*War* 3.539–360, Josephus numbers a total of 37,600 prisoners being present in the stadium). In the 2002 excavations, Moshe Hartal uncovered a huge 9 m thick wall structure on the property of the Galy Kinnereth hotel, preserved to a height of 2 m (cf. figure 14). First-century pottery was found outside the structure but in close connection to it, indicating a first-century foundation. It was not possible to say precisely when in the first century. As can be seen from figure 14, the wall curves beautifully, and according to Hartal, the layout of the wall and the fact that it was built on the beach and not inside the lake indicate that it was part of a large public structure rather than a harbour. The structure was eventually covered with mud as a result of flooding by the Sea of Galilee. In the mud, pottery from the third century was found, indicating that the structure was abandoned in this period.

The excavations in May 2005 were conducted 120 m north of the Galy Kinnereth hotel in the area adjoining to the Ottoman city wall. Close to the waters of the Sea of Galilee, another massive wall was exposed, which according to Hartal should be related architecturally to the wall found in 2002, serving as part of the stadium's western wall, while the curved wall found in 2002 was part of its southern side. It was found in the bottom of the area and exposed only in a length of 1.20 m. It was ca. 1 m wide and preserved in a height of 0.9 m (three courses), and was built with smoothed ashlars of 0.4 x 0.3 m glued together with hydraulic plaster. This second find heightens the possibility that the structure was indeed part of the stadium of Tiberias. It was placed outside the city to the north on the shore in front of the lake.[121] Its exact dimensions have not been clarified yet, but

---

[121] Based on analysis of the passages on the stadium in Josephus and in the Jerusalem Talmud (*Erub* 5.22b), M. Lämmer actually suggested exactly this location (Lämmer 1976, 47–49).

Moshe Hartal hopes that future excavations will uncover more of the structure in its entire length (personal communication).

The question remains which purposes such a stadium would have served (cf. also note 171 below). As already discussed in section 3.3.2, Josephus has an ambivalent relationship to the Herodian rulers' sponsorship of Greco-Roman games and festivities. In *Ant.* 15.267–277 Herod is condemned for building a theatre and an amphitheatre in Jerusalem decorated with inscriptions concerning the Roman emperor, in which splendid games were to be held in honour of him every fifth year attracting combatants from foreign nations for various kinds of athletics games, music contests, horse races, and execution of prisoners by casting them before wild animals. Herod's games in Caesarea, on the other hand, are not condemned by Josephus (*War* 1.415; *Ant.* 16.137–141), nor is Agrippa's sponsorship of games in Berytus (*Ant.* 19.335–337). It has been suggested by M. Lämmer that the stadium in Tiberias was used for various kinds of agonistic contests from which only the specific imperial cultic elements had been removed. According to Lämmer, Antipas deliberately built not only the stadium in Tiberias, but also the hippodrome in Taricheae (*War* 2.599; *Life* 132) and possibly also a theatre not mentioned in the sources as an attempt to establish games in honour of the emperor that he could control and adapt to Jewish practices in the hope that he "der Verpflichtung entgehen konnte, einen echten Kaiserkult mit allen gefährlichen Konsequenzen einzurichten" (Lämmer 1976, 53 followed by Fortner 2003, 88 and Bernett Forthcoming). Lämmer argues mainly from the silence in the sources regarding protests against Antipas but also from the notion in *y. ʿErub* 5.22b, where Rabbi Simeon ben Lachish freely refers to the stadium without condemning it. However, as discussed in section 5.3.2, while it is possible that the stadium was built by Antipas, just as it is possible that he sponsored games purified of the most offensive cultic elements, the material data currently available does not justify a date any more precise than the first century in general. It is at least possible that the stadium was erected during the period of Roman administration after the death of Agrippa I, when the city possibly changed its name to *Tiberias-Cladiopolis.*

Lead Weights and Coins

Also connected to first-century Tiberias are Antipas' Tiberias coins as well as two inscribed lead weights. Although the coins will be treated in the next chapter, it can briefly be mentioned that none of the coins of Antipas show any public buildings of Tiberias as do the city coins minted later during the reign of Hadrian, Antonius Pius and Commodus depicting a tetrastyle temple with Zeus seated in the middle (cf. Kindler 1961, 39). Instead, the reverse features the legend TIBEPIAC encircled by a wreath, and the obverse displays the date, the name 'Herod the Tetrarch' in the genitive (HPWΔOY TETPAPXOY) and a floral decoration which on Antipas' first issue from his 24th regnal year is probably a reed, the *canna communis*, and which on his next three series from his 33rd, 34th and 37th regnal years is replaced by a palm branch (cf. section 6.4.1 and figures 22–23).

The two lead weights are held in a private collection, and were not discovered in a stratified dig. But it is believed that they were found at surface level in or close to Tiberias. One of the weights has an inscription specifically mentioning Antipas: EΠΙ HPWΔOY/ TETPAXOY/LΔΛ ΑΓΟΡΑ/ΝΟΜΟΥ ΓΑΙ/ΟΥ ΙΟΥΛΙΟΥ/ΕΤΑΛΕΝΤΟ ("In the 34th year of Herod the Tetrarch, (in the term of office as) *agoranomos* of Gaius Julius…").[122] Though Tiberias is not mentioned in the legend, it is most likely that the weight derives from Tiberias, and thereby bears witness to the city's use of a market inspector. The same office is mentioned on the second lead weight from the time of Agrippa II. Thus, these two lead weights attest the existence of a marketplace in Tiberias with an attached market inspector, just as Josephus reports (*Ant.* 18.149).[123]

Future Excavations

Some of the buildings attributed to Tiberias by Josephus still remain to be found. Though the marble floor described above might be part of Antipas' palace, we still do not know whether it is possible to recover a larger portion of it. The synagogue mentioned by Josephus has not been found at all. It is also going to be interesting to follow the present Hirschfeld expedition when it begins to excavate the theatre. In a previous dig, Hirschfeld was able to discover the eastern outer wall of this structure, but no date based on potsherds could be determined. On the basis of the architecture, it was dated to the second or third century (Hirschfeld 1991a; Hirschfeld 1992, 23–24; Hirschfeld 1990).

5.3.4 Archaeological Material from Later Periods

Thus far, the archaeological digs at Tiberias have revealed far more material from later periods. The large wall structure from the second century has already been mentioned. It is located in area C of the present excavation, and measures nine Roman feet in width (almost 3 m). Its outer side is made up of very beautifully dressed basalt stone put together without the use of mortar. Furthermore, each line bends a little inwards giving the im-

---

[122] Translation by Shraga Qedar. Both weights have been presented and evaluated by him, and drawings of the weights are provided (Qedar 1986–1987).

[123] It can even be mentioned that Alle Stein has suggested that the Gaius Julius mentioned on the oldest weight is none other than Agrippa I, cf. Stein 1992.

pression of a very tall and solid wall (cf. figure 7). It has a very solid base, and is powerfully designed using mortar and large boulders. Only the discovery of an inscription would justify with certainty the connection to the unfinished temple of Hadrian depicted on one of his coins (cf. figure 1), but it was certainly part of the huge public structure.

In area F-east, near the modern road leading into Tiberias from the south, a large basilical complex was excavated by Rabbanni in the 1950s and again by Hirschfeld in 1993 and from 2004 and onwards in the ongoing expedition (Hirschfeld 1992, 15–16; Hirschfeld 1993, 1467; Hirschfeld 1997b, 38–40; Hirschfeld 1997a, 206). Hirschfeld initially suggested, based on Rabbanni's excavation, that the building's first phase dated to the early second century, serving administrative and juridical purposes as a secular building, whereas in later periods it was redesigned into a Christian church (Hirschfeld 1992, 15–16 and Hirschfeld 1993, 1467). His re-excavation in 1993 led him to re-date the first phase of the actual basilical building to the mid-fourth century with later phases from the sixth century and onwards (Hirschfeld 1997b, 38). Presently, he believes that the complex was not a church, but suggests that it might have served as the house of the Tiberian rabbinic council that eventually compiled the Palestinian Talmud, the *Beth ha-Midrash ha-Gadol*, the Great Study House established by Rabbi Yohanan after he moved the Sanhedrin to Tiberias in c. 235 CE (cf. Hirschfeld 1993, 1464–1465; Hirschfeld and Galor Forthcoming). It is in the stratum (V) beneath the first phase of the basilica (stratum IV) that architectural remains from the first and second centuries were exposed, including pebble floors, floors with well-smoothed limestone slabs (0.5 x 0.9 m) and most notably floors with coloured marble tiles designed in *opus sectile* style as described above.

Another huge public structure was uncovered by Rabbanni just north of the bathhouse. Some very large bases of pillars were found. He believed they were from the sixth century, built to support a roof over a large marketplace covering roughly 800 m^2 (Hirschfeld 1992, 16; Hirschfeld 1993, 1467). Rabbanni also uncovered a bathhouse. It is fairly large, and was equipped with beautiful mosaic floors, coloured plaster on the walls and even marble. It is dated to the Byzantine era and might be the bathhouse referred to in the Palestinian Talmud (Hirschfeld 1991b; Hirschfeld 1997a).

Finally, it is worth mentioning that in a salvage excavation in 1989 Hirschfeld uncovered a large public Roman building dating from the second century (Hirschfeld 1989–1990; Hirschfeld 1993, 1467–1468), just as he in excavations conducted between 1989–1994 uncovered a large monastery complex on the top of Mt. Berenice (Hirschfeld 2004; Hirschfeld 1990; Hirschfeld 1994; Ben-Arieh 1994).

5.3.5 Partial Conclusion

This examination of the reports from the various excavations has clarified a number of issues. First, it has become clear just how little material we have from the time of Antipas, or even the first century as such. The vast majority of what is seen today dates to later periods. This applies to the bathhouse, the theatre, the basilical building, the nine-foot-wide wall, the buildings on top of Mt. Berenice and more. In this way, Tiberias has the same history as Sepphoris with an intensified degree of urbanisation and building activity between and after the wars against Rome.

Second, three important finds qualify first-century Tiberias. (a) Most interesting is the marble floor discovered in the spring season 2005. Though still lacking a date based on stratigraphy, it is likely that the floor was part of a first-century hall built with a scenic view of the lake. The imported marble bears witness to some amount of trade. However, the small portion preserved does not justify a full comparison with the glamorous halls built by Herod the Great. The date of the pottery found above the floor, the quality of the marble, the design in *opus sectile,* the scenic position of the hall, the tetra-style pillars, and the ash layer just above the floor all indicate that this floor could be part of the otherwise unidentified palace of Antipas so vividly described by Josephus in *Life* 64–69. This impression was further strengthened in the two succeeding seasons, during which a wall structure was found that can be connected to the same first-century building. (b) The freestanding monumental gate with its grand round towers, monumental size and beautiful ornamentation must have made a strong impression on anyone entering the city, and bears witness to a well-designed city in the style and size of a minor Greco-Roman *polis.* However, its precise dating is contested, and based on the presently available archaeological material it does not seem possible to date the towers more precisely than to the first century in general. (c) M. Hartal's new discovery of what might be the stadium of Tiberias also qualifies the city's Greco-Roman character. Again, however, its precise dating is uncertain and judging from our knowledge of Tiberias' later first-century history it might be just as plausible that it was added during the period of Roman administration in 44–55/60 CE as during Antipas' reign.

Thus it is fair to conclude that our present archaeological knowledge of first-century Tiberias in general – and early-first-century Tiberias in particular – is rather limited. There is every reason to believe that Antipas' Tiberias contrasted strongly with rural villages and towns due to its use of a typical Roman city layout, houses with white-plastered walls, a palace and a number of monumental buildings and entertainment facilities. However, great care must be taken not to conflate the picture using evidence from several centuries, and inter-regional comparison with nearby cities is needed to put Tiberias into perspective (cf. section 5.6).

For this reason, it must finally be noted that the full-colour drawing found in Crossan and Reed's *Excavating Jesus* (inserted plates) exaggerates the appearance of first-century Tiberias. Although it is a free rendition from an artist's hand, the drawing nevertheless depicts a palace in the mountains, a theatre on the slope, a large open marketplace, a basilical type building next to it, fortification walls next to the southern gate, a harbour with eight sections and a cardo with shops going all the way through the city. In this rendition, Tiberias pairs well with Caesarea Maritima as depicted on the plate right next to it, which is far better validated (cf. section 5.6.2). The problem is that the drawing of Tiberias conflates the entire Roman and Byzantine periods, dating all the evidence back into the first century much in the same way as the drawings in Richard A. Batey's book, *Jesus & the Forgotten City* (Batey 1991), did in the case of Sepphoris – for which reason they were rightly criticized for their lack of a stratified approach (cf. Schiffman 1992; Meyers 1992b; Meyers 1992a; Oster 1993).

5.4 Sepphoris

The largest and most influential archaeological enterprise in Galilee began in 1983, when the first team of many to follow reopened the excavation of Sepphoris. Back in 1931, Leroy Waterman from the University of Michigan conducted one season of excavation but did not follow up with successive seasons (Waterman 1937). A team from the University of South Florida (USF) began digging in 1983 with James F. Strange as director. In 1985, Duke University and the Hebrew University of Jerusalem formed a Joint Sepphoris Project (JSP) under the leadership of Eric Meyers, Ehud Netzer and Zeev Weiss (Meyers 1992c, 322). Eventually, the cooperation dissolved. Netzer and Weiss continued on their own with a team from the Hebrew University (HU), and in 1993, Meyers launched a campaign named The Sepphoris Regional Project (SRP, cf. Meyers and Chancey 2000, 20 and Meyers and Meyers 1997, 527–529). Furthermore, Tsvika Tsuk has conducted surveys and excavations of the aqueducts of Sepphoris. Taken together, this massive archaeological activity has provided extensive information on Roman Sepphoris, and although most of the material is from the second century or later, Sepphoris plays a vital role in any proposed reconstruction of Galilee in the early first century. As Jonathan Reed phrases it: "Sepphoris has become a kind of test case for scholarly characterizations of the historical Jesus and the Gospel traditions" (Reed 2000, 102). Unfortunately, the excavation team's final reports have been somewhat delayed.[124] Even L. Waterman's report on the digs in 1931 is entitled "preliminary" (Waterman 1937). Still, many small updates and briefings have been published in both *Excavation and Surveys in Israel* and in *Israel Exploration Journal*, and in addition a couple of guide books (Meyers, Netzer and Meyers 1992; Netzer and Weiss 1994), a book in connection with an exhibition on Sepphoris (Nagy 1996), and a considerable number of articles on different topics have also been published.

5.4.1 The History of Sepphoris[125]

Sepphoris was a city of importance from the Hellenistic period and onwards, and became a part of the Judean state through its expansions in Galilee in the late second century BCE. After the Roman conquest by Pompey, it was made a regional capital by Gabinius in 57 BCE (*Ant.* 14.82–97). During the reign of Herod the Great, we do not have much information about Sepphoris. Probably Herod did not invest much in Galilee. Drastic events, however, took place after the death of Herod the Great when serious upheavals broke out in Jerusalem and spread all over the country. According to Josephus, violent confrontations erupted in Jerusalem ending in Archelaos' massacre in the temple (*War* 2.4–13; *Ant.* 17.213–218). The disturbances continued while Herod's wills were tried before Augustus in Rome, forcing the Syrian legate, Varus, to intervene leaving one army in the command of Sabinus in Jerusalem to counter the eager Jews (*War* 2.39–40; *Ant.* 17.250–251). Still the violence continued, razing part of the temple (*War* 2.45–54; *Ant.* 17.252–268), and from there the anarchy spread all over Judea (*War* 2.55–65; *Ant.* 17.269–270, 273–285) to a degree that leads Josephus to say: "Judea was full of brigandage" (Ληστηρίων δὲ ἡ Ἰουδαία πλέως ἦν, *Ant.* 17.285). Eventually the upheavals reached Galilee, and Josephus records one event during which Judas, son of Ezekias the ἀρχιληστής, razed Sepphoris and seized the royal arms together with a band of "desperate men" (πλῆθος ἀνδρῶν ἀπονενοημένων, *Ant.* 17.271), after which he was feared by all men (*War* 2.56; *Ant.* 17.271–272). This forced Varus to reoccupy the country by bringing down a large army from Syria heading for Jerusalem (*War* 2.66–79; *Ant.* 17.286–298). In the course of these events, Sepphoris was burned

---

[124] Regrettably, the first final report to be published from the USF excavations (Strange, Longstaff and Groh 2006) was not released until after the present manuscript was completed.

[125] The most thorough study on the history of Sepphoris is found in Miller 1984, cf. also his articles Miller 1992 and Miller 1996. Shorter outlines can be found in Hoehner 1972, 84ff.; Batey 1984, 252ff.; Chancey 2001, 129–130; Chancey 2002b, 70–73; Meyers and Meyers 1997 and elsewhere.

down and its inhabitants sold as slaves by a faction of the army headed by either Varus' friend Gaius (*War* 2.68) or his son (*Ant.* 17.289).

A new era dawned for Sepphoris, according to Josephus, when Antipas enclosed the city with a wall after his takeover in 4 BCE (Ἡρώδης Σέπφωριν τειχίσας), made it the "ornament of all Galilee" (πρόσχημα τοῦ Γαλιλαίου παντὸς), and named it Autocratoris (ἠγόρευεν αὐτὴν Αὐτοκρατορίδα, *Ant.* 18.27).[126] This probably happened at the beginning of his reign.

Like Tiberias, Sepphoris reached its peak after the Early Roman period. In the early second century an increasing number of Roman troops were stationed in Galilee, and after the Bar Kochba rebellion many Jews settled in Galilee (cf. Safrai 1992 and Chancey 2002a). The city expanded right up until the earthquake of 363 CE, which struck it hard. It was rebuilt and continued to flourish in the rest of the Byzantine era.

5.4.2 *Roman Sepphoris According to Archaeological Material*

First-century Sepphoris is a hotly debated issue, and the significance of the question is related to the short distance of 5.6 km between the small hamlet of Nazareth and Sepphoris. Even back in 1926, before any excavation had been conducted, Shirley Jackson Case argued on the basis of the close proximity that it was not possible that Jesus "could have remained completely immune from urban influences" (Case 1926, 15). This argument has been reintroduced by James F. Strange. Sepphoris is depicted as a "test case" (Strange 1992c, 35, 40) that will determine what kind of Galilee Antipas constructed. For Strange, Richard L. Batey, Andrew Overman and others, Sepphoris is the proof of how urbanised first-century Galilee was. Others, like Eric M. Meyers, Mark Chancey and Jonathan L. Reed, are much more cautious in their description, paying more attention to Galilee before and after c. 120 CE, when the Roman presence in Galilee started to increase (cf. most recently Chancey 2005, 61–70).

In what follows, this issue will be approached through a thorough analysis of the material with close consideration of stratification. What can be attributed to the first century, what is doubtful, and what cannot? However, as with Tiberias, several considerations have to be taken into account. First, much of the first-century strata were destroyed by later building activities. Second, there is a long-standing dispute about one of the most central public buildings, the theatre. Should it be dated to the first century, as suggested by Waterman and followed by Strange, or should it be dated later, as initially argued by W.F. Albright and now followed by

---

[126] For a discussion of the possible consequences of this renaming of the city, see note 53.

Netzer, Weiss and Meyers? Third, there is, as mentioned above, a problem with documentation, since most of the excavated material still awaits publication in final reports.

The most important units of excavation are the western unit, the theatre, the Roman villa with the Dionysos mosaic, the cardo and decumanus, the large basilica building next to the cardo and decumanus, the Nile festival building, the bath houses, the synagogue, and finally the water system (cf. figure 15).[127]

The Water System

Tsvika Tsuk was the first to excavate in Sepphoris in recent times. From 1975 to 1990 he conducted a thorough survey and excavation of the ancient water system of Sepphoris, as described in Tsuk 1996, Tsuk 1999 and Tsuk 2000. Tsuk concluded that ancient Sepphoris had two aqueducts, one built in the first century bringing water from the Amitai and Genona springs, and one from the second century bringing water from the El-Qanah spring (a map is provided in Tsuk 2000, 36). The first brought only limited amounts of water to Sepphoris. Due to heavier demands from a growing population in the second century, a new one was constructed with nine times the capacity of the old. The huge reservoirs visible to visitors of Sepphoris today are connected to this last aqueduct.

The Western Summit

The Joint Sepphoris Project (JSP), which was later reorganized as the Sepphoris Regional Project (SRP), focused its expeditions on the western summit.[128] This area consists of large residential houses between 100 and 250 m^2, an east-west road from Roman times 2.2 m wide, as well as many storage rooms, pools and *mikvaot* (cf. figure 16). It is noteworthy that no public building in this area has been attested from the time of Antipas

---

[127] Unfortunately, no good map is provided anywhere describing the excavation areas in detail and including the area numbers. Several small maps are provided here and there, to which reference will be made below. A general map without area numbers is provided in Nagy 1996 and Meyers and Chancey 2000 (cf. figure 15).

[128] It is possible to follow the excavations almost year by year in the two series, *Israel Exploration Journal* (in the Notes and News section) and *Excavations and Surveys in Israel*. The western summit is treated in: Meyers, Netzer and Meyers 1986; Meyers, Netzer and Meyers 1987–1988; Meyers, Netzer and Meyers 1988–1989; Meyers, Meyers and Hoglund 1997; Meyers, Meyers and Netzer 1985; Meyers, Meyers and Netzer 1987; Meyers, Meyers and Netzer 1990; Meyers, Meyers and Hoglund 1994; Meyers, Meyers and Hoglund 1995. In the following articles, the digs in the western summit are evaluated more generally: Netzer and Weiss 1994, 2025; Hoglund and Meyers 1996; Meyers and Meyers 1997; Rutgers 1998; Meyers 1998. So far, the last article is the most conclusive discussion of all the material.

(Meyers 1998, 347). However, evidence of lavishly decorated walls using frescoes with geometrical designs and marble revetment plaques were found in the fills in area 84.1 on top of the hill, indicating a sophisticated urban house design (Rutgers 1998, 183–184). A particular early-first-century private house in this area labelled 'Unit II' is described by Reed as reflecting "the first-century inhabitants' relative wealth" (Reed 2000, 126). It was a 150–m^2 house constructed by skilled craftsmen with an inner courtyard and walls solid enough to bear a second story. However, no columns were used just as the rooms were decorated with frescoes imitating marble panelling. Besides that only a few fine wares were found and among them none of the fashionable *terra sigilatta* ware. Thus, on the one hand, the house attested "awareness of Roman architectural styles", but on the other "implements of the social elite were not adopted in full or were not affordable" (Reed 2000, 126).

The main question is whether a chronology of the settlement in this area can be established. As with anywhere else in Sepphoris, later building activity destroyed earlier phases. In broad terms, therefore, no clear stratified areas from Hellenistic or even Hasmonean times can be attested, though finds in the fills suggest that the area was occupied at least from the Hasmonean era and onwards if not earlier (Meyers and Meyers 1997, 531). Thus, this area constitutes the "old city" going back to the time before Antipas. However, its maximum size was reached in a later period:

The cumulative data of the Joint Sepphoris Project (1985–1989) and the Sepphoris Regional Project (1993–1994) suggests that the heyday of the western summit was in the second and third centuries, with some areas, especially Unit II, providing especially fine Early Roman materials. (Meyers, Meyers and Hoglund 1995, 71)[129]

Meyers further reconsiders in his important article from 1998, "The Early Roman Period at Sepphoris: Chronological, Archaeological, Literary, and Social Considerations," the entire excavation efforts in order to present a refined picture of Sepphoris in the Early Roman period aiming at answering the most important question of what kind of city it was under Antipas (Meyers 1998, 345). For this purpose, Meyers divides the Early Roman (ER) period into ER A (c. 50 BCE–0), ER B (c. 0–68 CE) and ER C (68–135), though he admits that every division is artificial and that it perhaps would be sufficient with only two periods (50 BCE–50 CE and 50–135 CE,

---

[129] Originally, the areas of excavation were named by numbers as 84.1, 84.2, 84.4, 85.1 etc. Later, they were renamed with unit numbers instead, Unit I and onwards. The earliest published map with the original numbers is found in Meyers, Netzer and Meyers 1986. The conversion of numbers began with the Sepphoris Regional Project and its second season in 1994. Maps are provided in Meyers, Meyers and Hoglund 1994 and Meyers, Meyers and Hoglund 1995, see also Meyers, Meyers and Hoglund 1997.

cf. Meyers 1998, 347). Meyers estimates that in ER A Sepphoris occupied roughly 2.5 hectares (Meyers 1998, 345). In the period of Antipas, ER B, the excavations uncovered "significant alterations and renovations around the time of Varus or slightly later (0–70 or 40–70 C.E.)" (Meyers 1998, 346). But, as already mentioned, "no clear evidence of a large public building of the first century has been found on the acropolis" (Meyers 1998, 347), though remains in the fill associated with the Dionysos mansion, such as ER frescoes, "theoretically might be associated with some public building or even marketplace that once existed in the first century C.E." (Meyers 1998, 348–349). Nevertheless, the ER B findings are rather few and according to Meyers it was not until the succeeding ER C period that dramatic expansions took place:

It is during the interwar period, from 68–135 C.E., or at the end of the ER period, that the character of Sepphoris as a great oriental city became a reality. In this third or last stage of ER (ER C) the city expanded in all directions: to the east, to the south, and to the north; and possibly to the west. (Meyers 1998, 349)

This new area added roughly five more hectares to the city. As we shall see below, this picture presented by Meyers corresponds well with the results presented by Weiss and Netzer, whereas Reed and the USF team argue for a larger reorganisation of Sepphoris right back in the period of Antipas.[130]

The Theatre

The theatre (cf. figure 17) was first excavated by the team of L. Waterman in 1931 and dated to the time of Antipas (Yeivin 1937, 29; Manasseh 1937, 6–12). This date was opposed back in 1938 by W.F. Albright, who preferred a second-century dating based on the architectural layout (Albright 1938). The four teams that have dug in Sepphoris in modern times, JSP, USF, HU and SRP, have all excavated portions of the theatre in order to establish a precise dating. So far, no agreement has been reached.[131]

---

[130] Finally it should be mentioned that in their first season of 1985, the JSP team discovered a lead weight in their digs on the western summit. In the initial report, this was dated to the second century CE (Meyers, Meyers and Netzer 1985, 296, cf. also Chancey 2002b, 77–78; Chancey 2005, 104). The weight bears inscriptions on both sides mentioning two Jewish names, Simon and Justus, as market inspectors (ΑΓΟΡΑΝΟΜΟ, for presentation, see Meshorer 1996). The interesting thing is that the weight depicts two rows of columns referring to the layout of the colonnaded cardo. Without providing the reasons, Reed dates the weight to the first century (Reed 2000, 121).

[131] Things became somewhat complicated when the site was turned into a national park and important stratified material was removed to provide access, cf. Strange and Longstaff 1987.

James Strange and the USF team dated the foundation of the theatre to the time of Antipas after their first seasons of digs,[132] and have upheld this conclusion ever since.[133] Ehud Netzer and Eric and Carol Meyers also dug a trench in the theatre in their first season of excavation (86.2). Based on the results this season, they originally proposed a Herodian foundation date.[134] Subsequent digs led them to change the foundation date to the late first century on the basis of new soundings under the floor.[135]

To progress further in this matter, the final reports from each team providing detailed analysis are needed. Presently, Tom McCollough is preparing the final report of the USF team's excavation in this area, in which he adopts the suggestion by Richard L. Batey that the enigma is based on confusion of two distinct phases of the theatre. In the period of Antipas, a small theatre was constructed seating roughly 3,000 spectators. Later, a third storey was erected adding the outer wall, a building technique which Albright correctly dated to the second century.[136]

---

[132] "A tentative hypothesis based on the 1983 and 1985 excavations would suggest that the theater was built in the first century, most likely in the Herodian period. At least twice in the theater's history substantial destruction led to major reconstructions in the Middle Roman and early Byzantine periods. By the end of the Byzantine period, the theater seems to have been abandoned and the area used for agriculture" (Strange and Longstaff 1985b, 102, cf. Strange and Longstaff 1985a, 299). Evidence includes: (a) Stones cut in Herodian style with drafted margins. (b) Accumulated debris against the wall contained late-first-century CE pottery.

[133] See Strange 1984; Strange and Longstaff 1987, 280; Strange and Longstaff 1987–1988; Strange, Groh and Longstaff 1988. It seems that after the 1987 season Strange left his Field II (the theatre) to concentrate on Field V, the basilical building in the eastern plateau, see note 145 below.

[134] "In one section dug into the foundational substructure of the theater, only Late Hellenistic and Early Roman pottery was identified, suggesting that Herod Antipas may have been the builder of the theater" (Meyers, Netzer and Meyers 1986, 103). However, a note of caution was given in the IEJ note: "No definitive results were possible because of the destruction of the theater down to bedrock" (Meyers, Meyers and Netzer 1985, 297). Still, the early date was accepted in the article by Zeev Weiss in NEAEHL from 1993: "The theater apparently was built in the early first century CE, possibly in the reign of Antipas" (Weiss 1993).

[135] "Although it was first assumed that the theater was constructed early in the first century by Herod Antipas, extensive soundings under its foundations indicate a late date perhaps as late as the early to mid-second century, when the city underwent extensive rebuilding after the First Jewish Revolt" (Meyers and Meyers 1997, 533, cf. also Meyers, Netzer and Meyers 1992, 33; Meyers and Weiss 1994, 18–19; Weiss and Netzer 1996a, 32; Netzer and Weiss 1997, 121–122).

[136] McCollough's report will be published as volume 2 of the USF team's final report series, and Batey's suggestion will be presented in Charlesworth 2006. I wish to thank T. McCollough and R.L. Batey for providing me with this information.

It will be interesting to discuss this matter when the final reports are made available. What can be said on the basis of the material published so far is that Sepphoris had a theatre built sometime in the Early Roman period, whether in the Herodian part or in the latter part. It was reconstructed a couple of times, until it finally went out of use some time in the Byzantine period, turning into a limestone quarry.

In its final layout, the theatre could contain roughly 4,500 spectators. It was constructed in the normal Roman fashion, although it was not free-standing. Instead, it was built into the slope. It had a diameter of about 74 m, a strict semicircular *cavea* (semicircular auditorium), three barrel-vaulted *vomitoriae* (entrances) measuring 2.2 m, two *paradoi* (side entrances with direct access to the *orchestra*), and a *scaena* measuring 31x 6 m with a *scaenae frons* (the wall behind the stage) behind (cf. Netzer and Weiss 1994, 16–19; Meyers and Meyers 1997, 533).[137]

The Roman Mansion with the Dionysos Mosaic

In just their second season,[138] the JSP team discovered what turned out to be the most beautiful mosaic complex ever found in Israel: the Dionysos mosaic located in a large Roman mansion just south of the theatre on top of the western summit.[139] The complex consisted of a peristyle courtyard, a dining hall with a triclinium and the Dionysos mosaic as a floor (cf. figure 18), private chambers, and a toilet.[140] It was destroyed in the earthquake of 363 CE, never rebuilt in its old form, and thereby partly preserved. When was this magnificent villa built? A clear *terminus post quem* in the early third century could be established from the material under the floors (Meyers, Netzer and Meyers 1988–1989, 172; Meyers and Meyers 1997, 533).

---

[137] On theatres in the Roman Empire in general, see Boatwright 1990. A special focus on theatres in Roman Palestine can be found in McRay 1997, 51ff.; Sperber 1998, 77ff. and Segal 1995.

[138] Again, much can be gained through careful study of the brief annual reports in ESI and IEJ. The first report of the Roman villa (area 86.1 and 85.2) is given in Meyers, Netzer and Meyers 1987–1988 and Meyers, Meyers and Netzer 1987. It turns out that the JSP team only excavated part of the mansion in the 1986 season. The toilet with the Greek inscription "health" (ΥΓΕΙ) was uncovered, but the great surprise was not found until the 1987 season, namely the fantastic mosaic in the triclinium hall as reported in Meyers, Netzer and Meyers 1988–1989 and Meyers, Meyers and Netzer 1990.

[139] A general description of the Roman villa can be found in Netzer and Weiss 1994, 30–39; Weiss 1993, 1326–1327; Meyers and Meyers 1997, 533–534; Meyers, Netzer and Meyers 1987; Meyers et al. 1996.

[140] A plan of the Roman villa can be found in Weiss and Netzer 1993 and Netzer and Weiss 1994, 31, 33.

The Eastern Lower Plateau

Both the USF and the JSP team spent their first seasons digging on the western summit as well as in and around the theatre. The USF team was the first to open up an area east of the summit on the lower plateau (Field V, cf. Strange, Longstaff and Groh 1989–1990). When the JSP team was dissolved after the 1989 season, Ehud Netzer and Zeev Weiss continued on their own from 1990 with a team from the Hebrew University (HU). They focused on the eastern lower plateau right from the beginning (Weiss and Netzer 1993; Netzer and Weiss 1993). Both teams immediately found large structures and a well-planned city layout.[141] In outline, the HU team uncovered a large area and revealed an orthogonal road grid system. A prominent 13.7 m wide cardo ran north-south. It was constructed with large hard limestone slabs worn by many years of use but still in perfect line and colonnaded *stoai* (sidewalks) paved with mosaics (cf. figure 19). Perpendicular to it ran a decumanus, also with a *stoa* on both sides. Other smaller roads ran parallel and perpendicular, forming three large rectangular *insulae*: a western, a central and an eastern *insula*.[142] Inside these the remains of two public bathhouses were found, as well as a building with a beautiful mosaic known as the "Nile festival",[143] two churches, a synagogue (north of the three *insulae*), a marketplace and a large basilical building.[144]

From the 1987 season and onwards, the USF team focused on the large basilical building and its adjoining courtyard.[145] In the third century, it measured around 40 x 60 m, covering an entire block with an entrance from the cardo right next to the intersection between the cardo and the de-

---

[141] A general description of the eastern lower city can be found in Netzer and Weiss 1994, 40–58; Weiss and Netzer 1996a; Meyers and Meyers 1997, 534–535 and Netzer and Weiss 1997.

[142] Cf. the map in Netzer and Weiss 1993, 191, and the detailed description in Weiss and Netzer 1994, 41–42.

[143] For more details, see Weiss and Netzer 1996b.

[144] The excavations of the HU team led by Netzer and Weiss, and from 1995 Weiss alone, can be followed in Weiss and Netzer 1993; Netzer and Weiss 1993; Weiss and Netzer 1994; Weiss and Netzer 1998; Weiss 1999b; Weiss 1999c; Weiss 2000; Weiss 2002; Weiss 2003.

[145] A suggested reconstruction of the appearance of the building can be found in Strange 1996a, 118. A general description of the basilical building can be found in Strange 1996a and Strange 1992b. The excavation of Field V can be followed in Strange, Longstaff and Groh 1989–1990; Strange, Longstaff and Groh 1993; Strange 1993; Strange 1994b; Strange 1995; Strange 1996b; Strange 1997c; Strange 1998; Strange 1999; Strange 2000b; Strange 2000c; Strange, Groh and Longstaff 1999a; Strange, Groh and Longstaff 1999b; Strange, Groh and Longstaff 1999c (the last three provide the most details, including maps).

cumanus. It went out of use in the second half of the third century, either after the Gallus revolt of 351 CE or after the earthquake of 363 CE (Strange 1996a, 117). However, its entire history has been difficult to reconstruct for the excavators due to later construction in the area, which will be discussed below (cf. Strange, Groh and Longstaff 1999a). According to the excavators, the building was used either as a market, since many coins were found within it and since we know of a lower market in Sepphoris from rabbinic sources, and/or as a public meeting place for the high classes of Sepphoris (Strange 1996a, 119–120).

The combined efforts of the two excavation teams have thus uncovered evidence of a large and flourishing metropolis, and the crucial question is: when was this part of the city founded, and when did it achieve the extent and appearance apparent today? The excavators have addressed this question in several publications, and the disagreements are obvious. Netzer and Weiss have presented their perception of the chronological sequence of the lower city in three articles: Weiss and Netzer 1996a; Weiss and Netzer 1996c and Netzer and Weiss 1997. Their excavations indicate rather unambiguously that two periods of major development can be observed in this area. The first major period of building activity took place in the first half of the second century CE. Before this time, Sepphoris was confined mainly or even only to the western summit, the acropolis, and its slopes covering an area of about ten acres or four hectares (Netzer and Weiss 1997, 118). Weiss and Netzer admit that it is not yet certain whether some buildings stood on the lower plateau, or whether the area was solely used for agriculture (Weiss and Netzer 1996a, 31). But, "the first half of the second century C.E. witnessed a dramatic change in the urban layout" (Netzer and Weiss 1997, 118). The city was expanded to the lower eastern plateau with the development of an area with a perfect orthogonal road grid and large public buildings, covering a total area of about 12 acres (4.9 hectares). During this phase of building activity, the cardo and decumanus were constructed. The basilical building excavated by Strange also experienced its fullest extent in this period, possibly serving as the lower market, although an earlier phase is suggested which will be discussed in a moment. Netzer and Weiss also date the theatre to this period of expansion around and after the turn of the second century CE. A *terminus post quem* was found in a cistern predating the construction of the theatre, which contained ceramic vessels from the second half of the first century. They conclude: "We are therefore of the opinion that the theater was built at the end of the first century C.E." (Netzer and Weiss 1997, 121–122, cf also Weiss and Netzer 1996a, 32). A new aqueduct was erected to meet the needs of a growing and more demanding population. Two public bathhouses as well as the Roman mansion with the Dionysos mosaic were also constructed in this period, which is historically connected to the enlarged Roman presence in Galilee between and after the wars, and the radical increase of Jewish presence in Galilee after the Bar Kochba rebellion. This first phase of intensive construction on the eastern plateau came to an end with the major earthquake of 363, which is attested in the archaeological record on the eastern plateau as well, though mainly on the summit, where it struck the hardest (Weiss and Netzer 1996c, 81). Many buildings were partly or totally destroyed. In the wake of this earthquake, the eastern plateau witnessed a second period of intensive construction. Some of the old buildings were restored, while other areas were cleared to make space for new buildings (Netzer and Weiss 1997, 123). The house with the Nile festival mosaic is the most notable of the new buildings. In addition, two churches were constructed on the eastern lower plateau when the Christian population grew during the Byzantine period. A synagogue with a beautiful mosaic floor was also built in this period. As discussed above, this picture of a rather confined city during the time of Antipas, which only experienced noteworthy enlargements in the post-war era, coincides with Meyers' presentation.

Another view allowing for more expansion of the city in the time of Antipas is presented by the USF team as well as Jonathan Reed, who served as an area supervisor in the JSP team headed by Meyers. The USF team argues that expansion of Sepphoris on the eastern lower plateau has been validated in two instances. First, C. Thomas McCollough and Douglas R. Edwards report the finding of an earlier phase of the present visible limestone slab cardo. Paving stones were removed in two spots, and evidence was found of hard-packed soil and a lime cobblestone road. This earlier road could be dated to the early first century by coins and pottery. The excavators conclude that this road "was part of a planned systematic expansion of the city to the east on previously unoccupied territory, probably during the reign of Herod Antipas" (Edwards and McCollough 1997b, 140). Second, the basilical building uncovered by the USF team (Field V) is presumed to have a first-century foundation date. Unfortunately, the evidence given in the short reports is not conclusive. In an article from 1992 that summarizes the first six USF seasons, Strange outlines the history of the building by saying that it had an Early Roman period foundation date, though evidence of this was only found in one spot. We are not supplied with any information of this evidence. The mosaic floor seen today dates to around 300 CE (Strange 1992b, 351). In later seasons, more Early Roman pottery was found in probes under the floors, walls and robbers' trenches. Still, the excavators are reluctant to give an Early Roman dating with certainty, instead allowing for either an Early Roman or a Middle Roman period (Strange, Longstaff and Groh 1993). The fact that even an Early Roman date gives a span between 63 BCE and 135 CE underlines the uncertainty in identifying Antipas as the builder. Nevertheless, in his article in Nagy 1996, Strange suddenly writes: "The building was founded early in the first century C.E., perhaps as early as the turn of the century" (Strange 1996a, 117). The only evidence given for this suggestion is stones in the walls dressed with the typical Herodian bossed masonry (figure 20). No further evidence is given in later reports.

Jonathan Reed emphasizes that major construction activity took place on the western summit at the beginning of the Early Roman period. Before this period, the city served as a Hasmonean stronghold with less than 1,000 inhabitants on a small 2–3 hectare area, but "dating to the beginning of Antipas's rule in Galilee, considerable building activity is discernible across the site, when the city grew to a population of between 8,000 to 12,000" (Reed 2000, 117, cf. Reed 2000, 77–80). Reed backs this presentation by referring to the new domestic houses on the acropolis, to the USF team's probes beneath the cardo pointing at an earlier road from the time of Antipas, as well as to the basilica excavated by the USF team. Reed even argues that the present 13.5 m wide cardo was in existence in the time of Antipas in its first phase (Reed 2000, 118). At the same time, Reed points out that Antipas only made use of local material in his constructions and eschewed imported material, which is why his Sepphoris ranked "in the second tier of urban parlance" (Reed 2000, 118).

5.4.3 Partial Conclusion

From the many years of excavations, an interesting picture appears of a Sepphoris that experienced several periods of unusual building activity in the Roman era. The first period goes back to before the Hasmonean conquest. The buildings from this period are mainly large residential houses on the western summit. No well-planned city layout is attested, though a 2 m wide road ran east-west on the summit. Sepphoris probably served as a stronghold and was inhabited according to Reed by less than 1,000 residents.

The next period of notable building activity occurred in the first part of the first century. Houses on the acropolis were reorganised, and the city began to spread down the slopes. However, the key question is how much it spread in this early period. According to Meyers, Weiss and Netzer, Sepphoris remained a small entity on the acropolis covering perhaps only up to 4 hectares. According to Reed and the USF team, on the other hand, the first phase of building activity on the eastern lower plateau was begun by Antipas including a hippodamian grid system, at least one public basilical building, and perhaps also the first phase of the theatre.

Nevertheless, despite the two different pictures of Antipas' Sepphoris, the combined results of all teams attest that it was only after the war of 66–70 CE that Sepphoris gained the size and layout visible today, which corresponds to what we know from written sources of an intensified settlement activity of both Roman troops and Jews resettling from Judea. New quarters were erected on the flat eastern slope with a paved state-of-the-art Greco-Roman style road grid system, shopping areas, bathhouses, a large basilical building possibly serving as a market etc. The expensive and difficult task of building an aqueduct was undertaken, increasing the amount of incoming water by about nine times. The theatre possibly dates to this period too. Just before this period came to an end with the earthquake of 363, the splendid Roman villa with the Dionysos mosaic was constructed, now providing a glimpse of the rich and fashionable Sepphoris of Middle and Late Roman times.[146]

Thus, at the time of writing, just before the final reports are to be published, the picture of Roman Sepphoris is somewhat disputed. On the one hand, it is agreed that Sepphoris was definitely a city of importance both prior to the time of Antipas and in the time of Antipas. It was built as a stronghold on a summit overlooking and controlling the surrounding fertile valleys and inland trade routes. It is also certain that much of what can be seen today when visiting the site definitely dates to the post-war periods: the cardo and decumanus, the eastern lower plateau with the three insulae, the mansion with the Dionysos mosaic, the Nile festival building, the large basilical building in its final shape, the theatre in its final layout, the northern synagogue and the huge cisterns just outside the city limits. All of this is dated later than the first century CE. On the other hand, the central question of Antipas' Sepphoris is more complicated. When speaking strictly of material indisputably dating from his period, the city is limited to the acropolis and its slopes covering up to 4 hectares. The only feature found outside this area, besides the early rather small aqueduct, is the hard-packed limestone road, not to be confused with the presently visible cardo of tight-packed limestone slabs. No extravagant or expensive building activity has been detected in the strata. However, when taking into account the disputed material, two more features come to light, namely the theatre and the building below the basilical building in Field V of the USF dig. Historically, it is definitely a possibility that Antipas could have constructed a theatre, as his father did in several other places (cf. Richardson 1999, 186–188). The construction of a large building possibly serving as a

---

[146] It can finally be noted that in the Byzantine period, new buildings were erected on top of the destroyed ones, and the city kept its status as the metropolis of the interior of Galilee.

market is also within the parameters of what can be expected of a local prince. Both features would add to the picture of a city of a certain level.

To further this discussion, the final reports are needed. However, to my mind, a picture of Antipas' Sepphoris must try to balance certain observations. First of all, building activity on the western summit can be attested in his period. Second, early-first-century material is rarely found in Sepphoris or Tiberias and anywhere else due to later building activity. In addition, the entire area south of the acropolis has been left untouched by the excavation efforts. For both reasons, Antipas' Sepphoris could have encompassed a larger area than presently demonstrated. Third, even if the first phase of the eastern lower plateau relates to Antipas, it is still crucial to put its style into perspective and observe with Reed that Antipas seemingly only made use of local material in what could be termed a 'second tier' of urban style and quality.

To conclude, it is historically plausible and archaeologically possible that Antipas sponsored a certain amount of building activity in Sepphoris. How much is presently an open question. Nevertheless, even if the theatre, the cardo and the basilical building are included, Antipas' Sepphoris was in its 'urban infancy', only just deserving the term *polis* in comparison with the surrounding urban areas (cf. below section 5.6).

5.5 A Regional Perspective – Villages of Lower Galilee

As discussed in chapter one, the impact of the Galilean urbanization process is widely disputed and the approach taken to the urban-rural relationship is often filtered through a specific sociological model. Since the methodology of the present investigation is focused on interpreting the sources on the reign of Antipas through a contextual approach, it is necessary to examine the context of Antipas' urbanisation programme. This includes, first, an examination of selected rural areas in Galilee. It is to be expected that any influence, positive or negative, from the urbanization program of Antipas would be felt first in the surrounding rural areas. It is therefore essential to survey the villages (or towns)[147] of Lower Galilee such as Yodefat/Jotapata, Cana, and Capernaum to see whether any significant development can be traced in the early-first-century material. What does the material culture from *this* particular area show? Or just as

---

[147] It is difficult, if not impossible, to distinguish between towns and villages. Gamla, Yodefat, Capernaum and even Cana could be termed towns as well as villages. My aim here is not work out a clear definition of farmsteads, hamlets, villages and towns, but rather to describe the rural area as such in contrast to the cities.

importantly; is enough material available to draw any conclusion? In addition to sites in Lower Galilee, Gamla of the Golan will also be treated. Taken together this will provide a *regional perspective* on the influence of the urbanisation programme of Antipas, which is necessary in order to engage with the various models proposed in the recent research (cf. section 1.2.4 and 7.3.3). Second, an investigation of selected surrounding cities is also called for in order to establish an *inter-regional perspective* to which the cities of Antipas can be compared.

5.5.1 Yodefat

The site of Yodefat (or Iotapata in Greek) was first identified by E.G. Schultz in 1847 as the walled town of Yodefat known from Josephus. This identification was, however, contested for a long time, and the first non-salvage excavation did not take place until 1992 (cf. Edwards 1997, 251). Under the direction of Douglas Edwards, Mordechai Aviam and David Adan-Bayewitz, seven seasons were conducted (Aviam 2002, 121). The site consists of two areas. On the crest of the hill, a walled Hellenistic settlement covered around 14 acres or 5.7 hectares (Aviam 2002, 121). In the Early Roman period, the settlement spread to the large southern slope (Richardson 2000, 67). According to pottery and coins, an unequivocal *terminus post quem* for the destruction of the site could be established to the sixties CE, since "the latest securely identifiable object found throughout these areas is a coin found on one of the floors from the reign of the Roman emperor Nero" (Aviam 2002, 121). Likewise, numerous ballista stones and arrow heads indicate an identification of the destruction of the site with the one described in Josephus (*War* 3.141–339).

Overall, the excavations uncovered five residential areas consisting mostly of private dwellings with "cisterns, ritual baths (*miqva'ot*), storage areas, cooking ovens, pressing installations, loom weights, spindle whorls, clay and stone vessels, and coins" (Aviam 2002, 121). An oil press in a cave was also excavated, as well as pottery kilns, and one private house described as "a luxurious mansion with frescoed walls and floors" (Aviam 2002, 121). Two phases of the fortification system of the city could be observed. The first system consists of a huge tower and walls enclosing the crest of the hills, which goes back to the Hellenistic period. The second system was constructed in Early Roman time, enclosing a much larger area to the south. In some areas it was constructed as a strong casemate wall, while in other areas it consisted solely of a solid wall. Aviam concludes that "these changes are likely the result of the short time and the stressful situation under which construction occurred" (Aviam 2002, 126–127).

Of special interest are the remains indicating industrial activity, differentiated houses and inhabitants of Jewish ethnicity. First, several things

indicate that Yodefat housed industrial activities such as olive oil production, pottery fabrication and textile production (cf. table 4.1 in Richardson
2004, 64). The first area to be properly excavated was an Early Roman oil
press situated in a large cave just outside and below the eastern wall. In
1989 M. Aviam conducted a salvage excavation of the cave and was able
to date the time it went out of operational use to the second half of the first
century CE. It is a large oil press with "a large crushing basin" with a diameter of 1.6 m (Aviam 2004b, 89, cf. Aviam 1990).[148] During the seven-
season expedition another oil press was uncovered as well (Aviam 2004a,
17). Aviam describes olive oil production as one of the local industries of
Yodefat. Another industry was attested in the southern part of the city in
what Aviam names the "potters' quarter" (Aviam 2004a, 18). Three kilns
were found, one of which went out of use when a wall was built right
through it in the desperate last year of the city. A new kiln was constructed
right beside it, and judging from the low wear of the stones normally
caused by long periods of extensive heat, this happened just before the destruction of the site (personal communication with M. Aviam, cf. Aviam
2002, 125). Finally, hundreds of clay loom-weights used for wool weaving
were found, indicating intensive production of textiles (Aviam 2004a, 17;
Adan-Bayewitz and Aviam 1997, 162, note 42).

Second, as at Cana and Gamla (cf. below), evidence of differentiated
neighbourhoods was uncovered. While most of the houses at Yodefat were
of the simple Palestinian dwelling-house style with floors of packed soil
and walls of unhewn stone (Richardson 2000, 68), the 1997 season made
one spectacular discovery. On the higher eastern slope, an elite area was
found including a large mansion with walls still having beautiful frescoes
intact in the geometric First Pompeian style preserved up to 1.6 m above
the floor (cf. Aviam 2005, ii),[149] and floors covered with frescoes designed

---

[148] Interestingly, a ritual bath was found close to the large olive oil press, perhaps indicating concern for ritual purity in connection with its production (Richardson 2000, 70;
Edwards 1997, 252). At Gamla, the olive oil production area also included a ritual bath
(cf. sections 5.5.4).

[149] Since the work of A. Mau in the 19th century, Roman wall painting has generally
been distinguished in four Pompeian styles. The First style ('incrustation'), originating in
the second century BCE, imitates marble tiles by painting different coloured marble slabs
with the typical veneering of marble. The Second style ('architectonic'), also known
from Israel in this period and originating in the early first century BCE in Rome, incorporated architectural elements such as windows, porticos, columns and horizontal archi-
traves imitating an open view. The Third style ('ornamental') was marked by elaborate
scenery and did not become very popular in Israel in the Second Temple period, possibly
due the ban against images (cf. Fittschen 1996, 150). For a general introduction, see
Liversidge 1983, 98–107, for instance. For an overview of the wall decorations of Herod
the Great, see Fittschen 1996; Rozenberg 1996.

as *opus sectile* (Aviam 2004a, 17). As Richardson notes, this was an unexpected find in a Jewish village of Galilee, since such interior designs are normally only known from the rich mansions in Jerusalem and Herod's palaces. He even asserts that "the fresco is the most vividly painted intact first-century wall in Israel; the painted plastered floor is unique in Galilee. Was this a peristyle house?" (Richardson 2000, 69). When related to the large expansion of the village on the southern slope in the late first century BCE and first century CE, this neighbourhood witnessed a relatively thriving economy possibly upheld by a combination of regular farming and small-scale industrial activity. One question in this connection is whether evidence of public buildings was found as in Cana and Gamla (cf. below). While no actual evidence of such buildings was found, indirect evidence is attested through finds of several column drums, capitals, a monumental doorpost and a piece of architrave (cf. Richardson 2000, 68; Richardson 2004, 67).

Third and finally, the excavators note how the sum of the material indicated that Yodefat was probably inhabited by a distinct Jewish community with trade connections with Jerusalem and Judea from the first century BCE and onwards. A five-fold argument is advanced: (a) Two stepped-pools were found in the south-eastern residential area clearly distinguishable from the underground reservoirs found in almost every house. While reservoirs were large (up to 36 m3), and constructed with a small opening and notstairs, the stepped pools were small (2–3 m3), with a stairway limiting the practical usefulness in terms of water storage (Adan-Bayewitz and Aviam 1997, 163–164). (b) A huge number of sherds from broken soft limestone vessels were found. Such vessels were generally used due to halachic concerns (cf. section 1.1.2).[150] (c) There is a noteworthy lack of imported fine tableware such as Eastern *terra sigillata*, which otherwise appears widely in other excavations in sites outside the Jewish area proper, such as Qeren Naftali, Tel Anafa and Samaria-Sebaste (Adan-Bayewitz and Aviam 1997, 165; Aviam 2004a, 19). (d) No evidence of figurative art was uncovered, which also indicates the presence of a Jewish community (cf. Adan-Bayewitz and Aviam 1997, 165). (e) Finally, a dramatic change in the coin circulation is attested to have occurred around the last decade of the second century BCE. From this time and onwards "there is virtually no numismatic evidence of contact between Yodefat and the cities of the Phoenician coast. From this period there are abundant Hasmonean coins" (Adan-Bayewitz and Aviam 1997, 160). In the earliest strata in the crest of the hill, many Seleucid and Phoenician coins were found (constituting

---

[150] In the seasons from 1992–1994 alone, about 120 fragments were found (Adan-Bayewitz and Aviam 1997, 164).

roughly 41 percent of the total number of coins).[151] In the later strata, Hasmonean coins are abundant (constituting 36.7 percent of the total coinage) with a minor percentage of Herodian coinage (4.1 percent, cf. table 1 in Adan-Bayewitz and Aviam 1997, 157). In comparison, at Tel Anafa, inhabited by a non-Jewish population, only three Hasmonean coins were uncovered, while 67.9 percent of the coins found in Gamla, inhabited by a Jewish population, were Hasmonean (cf. Adan-Bayewitz and Aviam 1997, 160). On this basis, the excavators conclude that the site of Yodefat went through a dramatic development going from "inhabitants tied to the Phoenician coastal cities in the second c. to those who avoided contact with those cities", that is, a change to "a Jewish population aligned with the Hasmonean kingdom and not in contact with the Phoenician coastal cities" (Adan-Bayewitz and Aviam 1997, 161).

To sum up, the excavations of Yodefat provide important, sealed, undisturbed, early-first-century material to which only Gamla is comparable. The village seems to have thrived right up until its destruction, with small-scale industries supporting a local upper class. The south-eastern residential area bears witness to the dramatic events described by Josephus. At a certain point in the mid-first century, the area was fortified rapidly, destroying the original kiln and forcing the inhabitants to construct another which was not used extensively until the entire area was destroyed. But until the war, the excavations at Yodefat paint a picture of a flourishing Galilean village. Aviam asserts that "Galilee developed into a small, prosperous Jewish kingdom under Herod Antipas. Those were almost 40 years of growing and flourishing, probably with almost no domestic turmoil. The development and expansion of the town of Yodefat to the southern plateau probably dates to the years of Antipas' reign" (Aviam 2004a, 21–23). Likewise, Richardson and Edwards conclude that Yodefat:

...began as a small late Hellenistic fortified farmstead and was taken over by the Hasmoneans as a hilltop town. In the late first century B.C.E. or early first century C.E. it expanded substantially southward. Other small towns such as Cana seem similar. Rural village life expanded and improved at the same time that urbanization was proceeding at Sepphoris and Tiberias (perhaps prompted by the increased opportunities of trade, commerce, and agriculture; Richardson 2000). Decline of village life, abandonment of houses, and reduction of opportunities does not seem apparent. (Richardson and Edwards 2002, 255)

---

[151] Data from the only published preliminary report, which unfortunately only covers the seasons 1992–1994.

5.5.2 Khirbet Cana

The site of Khirbet Cana is located approximately two kilometres south of Yodefat. Since the surveys conducted by G. Dalman, it has generally been identified as the town of Cana known from the gospels (John 2:1–11; 4:46–54, cf. Strange 1992a and Mackowski 1979). Under the direction of Douglas R. Edwards, the site was surveyed and excavated from 1997 to 2001.[152] It consists of three areas: an upper area (the acropolis), a lower area on the southern slope, and a surrounding necropolis (for a map, see Edwards 2002, 106). Edwards differs slightly in his estimation of the size of the site. In one place, the acropolis is estimated to cover 12.5 acres (5 hectares) and the lower area 10 acres (4 hectares), while the total area in-cluding the necropolis measured 115 acres or 47 hectares (Edwards 2001, 109). In his latest and most thorough article on Cana, the estimation of the lower southern area is reduced to 4.8 acres (2 hectares), while the total size of the village excluding the necropolis is reduced to 12–16.8 acres (5–7 hectares), making it a "modest-sized village" (Edwards 2002, 106, cf. also table 1 p.107).

Unlike Yodefat, Khirbet Cana was occupied continuously even after the Jewish war, reaching its "peaks of settlement in Early Roman and Byzan-tine periods" (Richardson 2000, 73).[153] The finds from the Early Roman period reveal a village life similar to that found at Yodefat, with Jewish identity markers and ongoing building activity. Cana expanded in the Late Hellenistic and Early Roman periods. 35% of the identifiable sherds date to this period (cf. Edwards 2002, 110), Hasmonean coins were introduced (cf. Syon and Yavor 2002; Richardson 2002, 329; Edwards 2001, 110) and stoneware became common (cf. Richardson 2000, 73), as did stepped pools identifiable as *mikvaoth* (cf. Richardson 2000, 73; Edwards 2001, 110). The Hasmonean coins, the stoneware and the stepped pools all confirm a Jewish observation of the inhabitants in the Early Roman period. Edwards states that "Hasmonean coins and pottery from this period are indicative of the shift of power towards the south" (Edwards 2001, 110). The necropolis also bears witness to a Judean connection featuring 13 tombs with around 100 *loculi* or *kokhim*. Although some differences can be observed,

---

[152] While the final reports are being processed, the most detailed preliminary report can be found in Edwards 2002. The website for the dig, www.nexfind.com, also contains several otherwise unpublished field reports. Another detailed discussion can be found in Richardson 2004, 55–71. Shorter discussions include Edwards 2001; Richardson 2000 and Richardson 2002.

[153] In the Byzantine period, the site developed into a place of pilgrimage featuring a "pilgrimage cave" full of Christian inscriptions in Greek and places for six stone vessels (Edwards 2001, 110).

Richardson concludes that "the tombs show that this is a Jewish village" (Richardson 2002, 328). Finally, adding to this conclusion was the discovery of an ostracon with a three-letter Jewish script (cf. Edwards 2002, 116).

The architect of the excavation, P. Richardson, has conducted a study of the domestic architecture in Cana revealing that the houses of the domestic areas can be divided into three different types placed in different quarters. Terrace houses were located on the steep east and west slopes of a simple two-floor construction without courtyards and densely packed down the hill. Side courtyard houses, also with a relatively simple design, were found on less steep ground. Finally, a central courtyard house was found on the hilltop ('field 1', cf. the map in Edwards 2002, 108) and more are expected to be located on lower north slopes (Richardson 2004, 65, cf. Richardson 2002, 328–329). The remains of field 1 attract attention in particular. In the north-east corner of the seventh-century trapezoidal wall on the crest of the hill, a rectangular building was uncovered with "fine wall plaster with a well-constructed plaster floor" (Edwards 2001, 109) including a well-dressed pilaster (cf. plate 20 in Richardson 2004 and Edwards 2002, 111). The largest room in this field measures ca. 12 x 8 m, and Edwards and Richardson disagree on whether it was a public building (Edwards 2002, 111) or an "elite house" (Richardson 2002, 328; Richardson 2004, 67). Though the complex was in use in later periods as well, "much of the structure is Early Roman" (Richardson 2002, 328).

The most remarkable building from the Early Roman period was discovered in the south-west corner of the trapezoidal wall (field 2). The size of the largest room in the field was 10 x 15 m according to Richardson 2004, 66 (cf. plate 16), but 20 x 15 m according to Edwards 2002, 111. The floor was well-plastered, the walls about 1.5 m thick, and footings for columns or pilasters were found 5 m apart and 2.5 m from the side walls indicating that the roof was supported by two rows of columns. Actually, an Ionic capital was found *in situ* although it was secondary use (cf. plate 15, 17 in Richardson 2004 and Edwards 2002, 111–113). In addition, a bench was found in one place along the outer wall of the large room, and a smaller room (3 x 4 m) was found to the north-east – also with benches. Finally, "in the vicinity was found an abundance of fine roof tiles" (Edwards 2002, 113). Pottery analyses combined with carbon 14 analyses of organic material point to a founding of the complex in the Early Roman period (Edwards 2002, 113. The initial identification of both Edwards and Richardson is that this complex was a synagogue with an attached *Beth ha-Midrash*. So Edwards: "The fine rooftiles, plastered benches, columns and Ionic capital all point to a public structure. Its form is similar to that of the

Gamla synagogue, and this is our working hypothesis for its identification" (Edwards 2002, 114).

How could such a small village support one or perhaps two public facilities? The answer might come from industrial complexes which were also found in the Early Roman strata. A *columbarium* was found on the eastern slope, which according to Edwards was used for the raising of pigeons (Edwards 2002, 116). Glass wasters found on the hilltop are interpreted as indicators of "a small glass-blowing activity" (Richardson 2004, 62), and four plastered complexes on the south-eastern side of the site, also dated to the Early Roman period, are interpreted as having "had an industrial purpose such as dyeing, tanning or as fullery" (Edwards 2002, 117). Finally, an oil press was found east of the site indicating olive oil production (Edwards 2002, 117).

Thus it seems that Khirbet Cana provides another example of a thriving rural community in the Early Roman period. As in the case of Yodefat, the most notable shift took place in the time of the Hasmonean takeover. In the early first century, no dramatic changes seem to have occurred. The rural village, supported by agriculture and small-scale industry, continued its business, and the economic activities were apparently able to support local village elite. Though no Pompeian style fresco wall paintings were found, two large buildings were excavated, one of which may have been the town convention centre (the synagogue) and the other possibly a large central courtyard house. Both of them differed from other houses in the village due to their white-plastered walls and floors, and the 'synagogue' further by its fine roof tiles.

5.5.3 Capernaum

The ancient town of Capernaum was discovered and identified in the nineteenth century, and most of the site was successively acquired by the Franciscan Custodians of the Holy Land, while the eastern part was acquired by the Greek Orthodox Patriarchate of Jerusalem. The synagogue in the Franciscan part was examined and partly restored in the early twentieth century. Large-scale excavations of the entire area were carried out in the Franciscan part between 1968–85 by V. Corbo and S. Loffreda (altogether 18 seasons). On the Greek Orthodox side, four seasons of excavations were carried out by V. Tzaferis in the period 1978–82.[154] The discussion of

---

[154] A general description of the modern archaeological work in Capernaum can be found in Loffreda 1997, 417. The Franciscan excavations are well presented by the excavators in Loffreda 1985; Corbo 1992; Loffreda 1993; Loffreda 1997. A review of the original reports can be found in Strange 1977. The excavations on the Greek orthodox side are presented in e.g. Tzaferis 1983; Tzaferis 1993; Laughlin 1993. Since the struc-

these extensive excavations has predominantly concentrated on the complex believed to be the house of Peter and the synagogue in an effort to determine their foundation dates and general history. However, in the following the focus will be held narrowly on the first-century strata, including a discussion of the fishing industry on the Sea of Galilee.

Corbo's and Loffreda's excavations uncovered evidence of uninterrupted habitation from the Hellenistic period up until the Arab invasions of the 7th century, after which some of the buildings were abandoned (Loffreda 1993, 292). The town experienced its peak in the Byzantine era as a centre of Christian pilgrimage (cf. Laughlin 1993, 54). The two excavators seem to differ on how to understand its appearance; was it a village or a (minor) city? Loffreda describes the site as an unfortified and "relatively small village" that extended some 300 m along the lake, occupying a total of 10–12 acres or 4–5 hectares (Loffreda 1993, 292), which was later revised to 13 acres (6 hectares), with around 1,500 inhabitants (Loffreda 1997, 418). Corbo, on the other hand, states: "The city was laid out according to the orthogonal, or Hippodamian, urban plan, which consisted of a *cardo maximus* or *via principalis* (e.g., main N-S thoroughfare) and numerous decumani (e.g., E-W intersecting streets)" (Corbo 1992). Apart from this, the excavations uncovered several dwelling areas containing what are believed to be large "clan" dwellings, characterized by a closed appearance to the life outside its walls with just one entrance, and an open community inside organized around internal courts where the business of daily life took place (cf. Corbo 1992). One of the most intriguing questions concerns how to date the various phases of the synagogue. As noted by Donald D. Binder, Loffreda and Corbo did not initially date any of its phases to the first century. M. Avi-Yonah was the first to suggest that the basalt floor beneath the white synagogue belonged to an earlier synagogue (cf. Binder 1987, 189, note 61; Magness 2001, 19–20). Later excavations convinced them, however, that the first stratum of the synagogue should be dated to the first century (cf. Loffreda 1985, 46–49). While this dating is rejected by some (cf. Magness 2001, 19–20), it seems to be accepted by most. Binder, for instance, writes:

The combined force of the archaeological evidence and the literary attestation makes it probable that the basalt stone walls and the stone floor constitute the remains of a synagogue constructed in the first century C.E. If this identification is accepted, then the Capernaum synagogue represents the largest synagogue discovered thus far from the Second Temple period. Measuring 24.5 by 18.7 meters on the outside (22 x 16.5 m. on

---

tures from this part of the site were dated to the 7th to 10th century, these excavations will not be dealt with in this connection.

the inside), it is slightly larger than the synagogue at Gamla. (Binder 1987, 192, cf. also Runesson 2001, 182ff.; Runesson 2002, 136–139)

Jonathan L. Reed has also thoroughly investigated the uncovered evidence from first-century Capernaum, focusing among other things on the location of the village in a regional and interregional perspective, on the population size, and on the internal layout of the village. First, it has been argued that Capernaum was placed next to one of the arms of the international road *Via Maris*, implying "traffic, commerce, and the flow of ideas and information, including gossip" (Strange 1992c, 42). Reed rejects this scenario for two reasons. On the one hand, Roman milestones are not found in the area from the Early Roman period, but only from constructions related to Hadrian's projects in the east. On the other, the international bi-sections between the Kings Highway and the *Via Maris* did not take the route north of the lake, but rather south on the plain via Scythopolis or north through Caesarea Philippi (cf. the map in Reed 2000, 147). On an international scale, then, Capernaum was not a dot on the map. Regionally, however, Capernaum was better placed than most Galilean villages due to two reasons: it was placed on the border between the tetrarchies of Philip and Antipas, and it had one of the anchorages around the lake connecting it by boat to the major cities of Tiberias, Hippos and Gadara. Thus Reed concludes that while Capernaum "was not on a major international trade route... It would have witnessed considerable regional and some interregional traffic, which would become a prominent feature of its character during the first half of the first century C.E." (Reed 2000, 148).

Second, Reed discusses the population size of Capernaum, which has been estimated quite differently with numbers as high as 12–15,000 by Meyers and Strange (cf. Meyers and Strange 1981), and even 25,000 by H. Clark Kee (cf. Reed 2000, 65). Reed demonstrates how these numbers are reached by accepting an estimation of the inhabited area reported by Captain Wilson in 1871 to 30 hectares, and by using the same density as Ostia in Rome (cf. Reed 1992, 9–10; Reed 1994b, 208). For his part, Reed estimates the inhabited area to have covered between 15 and 25 acres (6 and 10 hectares) accommodating around 1,700 inhabitants (Reed 1994b, 212) or 600–1,500 (Reed 2000, 152) if not 1,000 (Crossan and Reed 2001, 81).

Third and most importantly, Reed evaluates what kind of site first-century Capernaum was, describing it as an unplanned organic growing village in contrast to the picture given by Corbo, Strange and others. For one thing, the public layout of the site does not earn the designation 'polis,' lacking centralized planning, an orthogonal grid with perpendicularly intersecting thoroughfares, streets paved with stone slabs adorned with columns and porticoes, channels for running water, or any public buildings ordered around an agora (cf. Reed 2000, 152ff.; Crossan and Reed 2001,

82). For another, "Capernaum's houses were constructed without the benefit of a skilled craftsman' techniques or tools" (Reed 2000, 159) instead
having roughly made doors, jambs and walls "in contrast to the tightly fitting Herodian bossed masonry, well-planned *opus quadratum* technique, or
header-stretcher ashlar construction" (Crossan and Reed 2001, 83). Likewise, no plaster, frescoes, patches, granite, marble, *tesserae* stones or red
roof tiles associated with city life have been found (Reed 2000, 157). Thus,
unlike Yodefat and Cana, no proof of a local elite was uncovered:

> There is no evidence in the archaeological record suggesting that any individuals lived
> affluent lives in Capernaum, nor is there any evidence of social elites displaying their
> civic responsibility at Capernaum by sponsoring public buildings, as the wealthy did at
> Scythopolis, Caesarea, Sepphoris, and Tiberias. (Reed 2000, 165).

Still, some families seem to have been in possession of rather large house
complexes, probably combined with boats for fishing on the lake. Thus, to
sum up, Capernaum was certainly one of the larger villages of Galilee, but
not a *polis* in any sense of the word comparable to Tiberias or other cities.

The important question remains whether it is possible to trace how
Capernaum fared from a socio-economic perspective during the reign of
Antipas. While probably having an early-first-century phase, the splendid
white synagogue we see today belongs to the later Byzantine period, as
does the octagonal church, during which time it seems that external funds
were injected into the town due to widespread pilgrimage. In the first century, the socio-economic condition of the city was determined by three factors: fishing on the lake, agriculture on the surrounding hills and valleys,
and the central location on a regional road close to the border attracting
some regional trade and commerce. Reed evaluates this combination in
two ways. On the one hand, "some of the peasants at Capernaum may have
been better off than others; some fishers may have owned their boats", and
"one suspects that Capernaum was a slight step up from Nazareth on the
socio-economic ladder... Travelers passing through Capernaum on the regional trade network included affluent merchants, Herodian officials, or
ostentatious elites" (Reed 2000, 164–165). On the other, fishing was, according to Reed, heavily taxed, and the evidence of hired workmanship in
Mark (μισθωτοί, Mark 1:20) indicates displaced peasants. Reed concludes
that "the people of Capernaum would have had greater exposure to the
visible signs of wealth than those at Nazareth, but at the same time, these
conditions likely also attracted beggars, cripples, and prostitutes, who find
their homes in the stories of the Gospels" (Reed 2000, 165).

Two archaeological investigations deepen our understanding of the
socio-economic character of Capernaum and the region around the lake.
First, in 1986 a boat from around the first century was discovered by
chance in the mud at the lake front, south of Kibbutz Ginosar at the west-

ern shore of the Sea of Galilee (cf. Wachsmann 1997; Rousseau and Arav 1995, 25–30. It measures about 8.8 m in length, 2.5 m in breadth and 1.25 m in depth, and is probably a specimen of the largest boat type in operation on the lake, used specifically for the large seine net (Wachsmann 1997, 378). According to a first-century mosaic found at Magdala displaying such a boat, at least five people were needed to operate it: four oarsmen and one captain.[155] Josephus and the Gospels indicate that ships sailed with anything from five to a dozen people (*Life* 164; *War* 2.239; Mark 1:20; John 21:2–3, cf. Wachsmann 1997, 378–379). All in all, this incidental find confirms what we know from literary sources, which is that relatively large boats travelled on the lake in the first century for at least two purposes: transport and an intensive skilled fishing industry using effective nets such as the large seine net.

Second, thanks to the highly valuable research conducted by Mendel Nun, a fisherman for more than 50 years living in Kibbutz Ein Gev, a detailed understanding of ancient fishing on the lake has been obtained. Nun demonstrates how the remains of approximately 17 ancient harbours and anchorages have been found around the lake (cf. the map in Nun 1993a, 7). When the water level in the lake is low breakwaters can still be seen, and combined with underwater research, impressive stone bases have been located four to six metres wide and two to three metres high. It is naturally difficult to establish an exact founding date for such a harbour. Broadly speaking, however, they can be dated to the Roman period, since the Romans facilitated maritime transport, whereas the Arabs neglected it (Nun 1988). Furthermore, as already mentioned, there is written evidence available from Josephus and the New Testament to confirm the existence of extensive sailing on the lake. In addition, Strabo notes that Taricheae was famous for its salted fish (*Geogr.* 16.2.45). Nun has also found many stone anchors and net sinkers from ancient times (cf. Nun 1993a). From 1989 to 1991 the water level was unusually low in the lake, revealing many ancient artefacts from the fishing industry ranging from large anchor stones with drilled holes to small lead or pebble stone sinkers used in connection with the larger drag or seine nets (cf. the photos in Nun 1993a, 39–53).

In addition to his survey of anchorages, Nun has investigated the specific fishing techniques and fishing nets utilized in antiquity (cf. Nun 1989; Nun 1993b; Nun 2001). The largest net used was the seine net, measuring 250+ m in length and 3–8 m in height. It was cast about 100 m from the shore and dragged ashore by as many as 16 men (Nun 1989, 16). This fishing method is mentioned in both the Old Testament (Hab 1:14–15, Ezek

---

[155] For a discussion of the various symbols on the mosaic, see Zangenberg 2001, 50–56.

26:5, 14; 47:10) and the New Testament (Matt 13:47–48, terming the net σαγήνη) as well as in the Talmud (*b. B. Qam.* 81a-b, cf. Nun 1989, 20ff.). Another large net was the trammel net, consisting of five separate nets combining to form a long wall used to encircle large shoals of the musht fish. Again, references in the Old Testament (Job 19:6–8, Eccl 9:12) and the New Testament (Matt 4:21–22; Mark 1:19–20) can be found. Finally, a small cast-net was used. It was round, with a diameter of six to eight metres and sinkers attached. The fisherman would stand in the water and throw this net over a shoal of fish. This net is mentioned directly in Mark 1:16–18. Nun does not extract socio-economic consequences from his analyses, but he does note that "the wealth of stone implements found during the last few years shows us how well-developed and diversified the technology used by early fishermen was on the Sea of Galilee, especially during the Roman-Byzantine period, and to what extent the various techniques were used to complement each other" (Nun 1993a, 63–64).

In an essay from 1997, K. C. Hanson investigates the fishing traditions in the New Testament and the socio-economic importance of fishing for the region around the lake. On the one hand, Hanson underlines how important fishing was for the Galilean economy in the first century, (Hanson 1997, 100) by going through the methods implied and the wealth of resonance found in the Gospels pointing to the predominant position of fishing for the local communities around the lake. On the other, Hanson stresses that it would be anachronistic to perceive the economic situation of boat-owning fishermen as being any better than landowning peasants. They were also heavily taxed in a complex Roman system of channelling money to the top which was particularly severe in the early first century:

> Josephus calls Herod Antipas a "lover of luxury" (ANT. 18.245). This luxurious lifestyle is only comprehensible in view of his extraction of Galilean resources. Since Josephus himself ranked among the urban elite, I take this as quite a cutting comment, intimating that Herod Antipas was 'way over the top.' (Hanson 1997, 103)

In this connection, the translation of "ἀγαπῶν τὴν ἡσυχίαν" as "lover of luxury" is absolutely not defensible. The basic meaning of "ἡσυχία" is stillness, rest, quiet or alternative solitude (cf. the entry in LS).[156] In the context of *Ant.* 18.245, it would also make no sense whatsoever, since the paragraph concerns Antipas' rejection of Herodias, when she wanted to set sail for Rome to ask for his kingship, since he was not a lover of luxury, but a lover of quietness. Thus, while there is every reason to believe that the fishermen were taxed like everyone else, the conclusions of Hanson do

---

[156] Whiston translates "out of the love of ease" (Whiston 1995, 492) while Feldman translates more freely "for he was content with his tranquility" (Feldman 1965, 147).

not come from particular sources but rather from an overall conception of how the socio-economic system of the Roman world worked. He may be right that the term "middle class" or "entrepreneurs" is anachronistic when speaking of first-century fishermen, but what he primarily demonstrates in his essay is how complex and skilled the fishing enterprise that took place by the Sea of Galilee in the first century really was.

In conclusion, first-century Capernaum was one of the larger villages around the lake. While no evidence of a local upper class has been demonstrated, large dwelling units with multiple rooms were found. It is also credible that the earliest phase of the synagogue dates back to this time. Capernaum probably benefited from some regional trade passing by on the road leading around the lake, just as its inhabitants could participate in the large-scale fishing opportunities on the lake.

5.5.4 Gamla

Finally, the town of Gamla is interesting in this connection as well. Though located in the Golan, in Philip's tetrarchy, and outside the immediate boundaries of Antipas, two things connect Gamla to Galilee. First, coin finds indicate trade connections between the two areas. Actually, Gamla is the area where most coins of Antipas have been found.[157] Second, Gamla was clearly a Jewish town, featuring a synagogue and ritual baths.

Gamla covered around 37 acres or 15 hectares (Syon and Nemlich 2001, 11), and like Yodefat it was never rebuilt after the Roman destruction in 67, for which reason it provides an otherwise unparalleled amount of undisturbed first-century material (cf. Gutman 1993, 459).[158] The extensive excavations directed by S. Gutman from 1976–89 uncovered a wall complex, a synagogue, a residential quarter labelled 'the Hasmonean quarter', and a residential quarter labelled 'the wealthy quarter' with an olive-oil extraction plant (cf. Gutman 1993). In addition, in 1997–2000 four seasons of excavation were carried out directed by D. Syon and Z. Yavor (Syon and Yavor 2002; Syon and Yavor 2005), which among other things exposed a large mansion in the new area K, and an extensive public building in area S tentatively identified as a basilica. From a socio-economic perspective, three of the discoveries are of special interest. First, an unusual number of coins were uncovered, altogether 6,314 (cf. Syon 2004, 27). Most of them

---

[157] Altogether 61 coins of Antipas were uncovered, while only 36 coins of Philip were found (cf. Syon 2004, 49). In comparison, only 14 coins of Antipas were found in Yodefat, and so far only one in Tiberias. The coins of Antipas will be treated in detail in chapter six.

[158] For a general description of the history of Gamla with emphasis on the siege and destruction, see Syon 1992 and Syon and Yavor 2002.

were bronze or copper coinage, but a hoard of 27 silver coins surfaced as well (Gutman et al. 1990, 9; Syon and Nemlich 2001, 18). Roughly 3,900 of these were Hasmonean coins, which were virtually the only ones in circulation after the Hasmonean takeover, when the amount of Seleucid coinage decreased dramatically (cf. Syon 2004, 14).[159] In other words, Gamla was clearly financially attached to the Hasmonean and later Herodian kingdom.

Second, like Yodefat and Cana, Gamla seems to have hosted a well-to-do segment, whose abilities were grounded in small-scale business and trade. In the western quarter (area S and R) remains of coloured and white plaster were found in every room in the same high quality as that found in the palaces of Masada (Gutman 1993, 462). Beautiful jewellery was also found in this area (Syon and Nemlich 2001, 22). East of the wealthy residential quarter, an area of commercial and manufacturing activities was discovered including a street of shops, a flour mill and an olive-oil extraction plant (Gutman and Wagner 1986; Gutman et al. 1990). It was "paved throughout with basalt slabs fitted to perfection" and "laid out around a 'plaza', where goods were probably displayed and traded" (Syon and Nemlich 2001, 17). The excavators also found several Doric capitals and large well-cut ashlars indicating an "impressive" building technique (Gutman et al. 1990, 11). The olive plant attracts attention. It was comprised of a crushing apparatus and two press-beds. Stoves were found in the room, implying operation even in the winter-time (cf. the plan in Gutman 1993, 461). Most interestingly, a *mikveh* was cut in the bed-rock with an adjoining storage basin (Syon and Nemlich 2001, 19). According to Gutman, this proves the care taken in this period "to ensure that oil would be produced by individuals who were in a state of ritual purity" (Gutman 1993, 463). The large houses of this quarter with plastered walls attest the possible revenue of ritual pure olive oil: "It was clearly a business whose profits were sufficient to provide owners handsome mansions and a high-quality lifestyle" (cf. Syon and Nemlich 2001, 19). Another building complex supporting this conclusion was found during the excavations in 1997–2000. In the new area K, situated in between the synagogue and the western quarter, a multi-roomed house was uncovered with a façade "of the highest quality stonemasonry uncovered until now at Gamla" (Syon and Yavor 2005, 10), and the excavators suggest that "better economic conditions (due to income generated from the sale of olive oil?), enabled the erection of new, more opulent homes in the vacant spaces of this quarter, instead of in the crowded eastern parts" (Syon and Yavor 2005, 10).

---

[159] D. Syon's dissertation treats all the coins found at Gamla, cf. the discussion in sections 6.4.3.

Third, two public buildings were discovered that indicate the relatively good economic infrastructure of the town. Most notable is the synagogue near the town wall, which is a 20 x 16 m complex including tiers of stone seating, a niche probably intended for the Torah scroll, at least four rows of columns with beautiful heart-shaped double columns in the corners, an adjoining large *mikveh*, and an adjoining room most likely used as a 'study room' (Gutman 1984; Gutman 1979). Thus, "the synagogue, adjoined by a study room, a ritual bath, and a courtyard, thereby constituted a community center of sorts for study and prayer" (Gutman 1993, 461–462). The foundation date is not certain, but finds beneath the floor point to a date early in the reign of Philip (Gutman 1984, 26; Syon and Nemlich 2001, 15). The other public building was found recently in the wealthy western quarter and labelled by 'a basilica' by its excavators and assumed to have "served some administrative function" (Syon and Nemlich 2001, 18). It comprises three aisles with a raised platform in the central aisle (a *bema*), and dimensions of 16 x 15 m make it almost as spacious as the synagogue. Most of the walls were plastered, and a decorated lintel found in the area was possibly set above the main entrance (Syon and Yavor 2005, 10). According to the excavators, "it is an entirely new type of religious and/or secular Jewish public building of the Second Temple period" (Syon and Yavor 2005, 10), which in its architectural layout closely resembles the Roman basilica designed for judiciary purposes.

Despite the fact that Gamla was outside Antipas' immediate economic sphere, it is highly noteworthy that this town provides a very similar picture of financial, industrial and trade levels as that indicated in Yodefat, Cana, and to some extent Capernaum. For one thing, the town was clearly attached to the rest of the Hasmonean and later Herodian kingdoms through religion, culture and trade. In addition, no sign of economic decline is witnessed in the first century CE. On the contrary, Gamla flourished and its inhabitants were able to erect and sustain a least two public buildings.

5.5.5 Partial Conclusion

This survey of Yodefat, Cana, Capernaum and Gamla has aimed to establish a regional perspective on the urbanization process of Antipas in order to gain a contextual view on the urban-rural relationship. Although the number of villages or towns investigated is small[160], it is nevertheless in-

---

[160] Of other sites that could have been included, Magdala/Tarichaea is particularly relevant – as is also et-Tell. The excavations at Magdala/Tarichaea are thoroughly described in Zangenberg 2001. To summarise briefly, the town had a certain urban character in the first century including a cardo, large villas with mosaic floors and not least a

teresting that this survey unequivocally paints a picture of a thriving first-century Galilee when evaluated on general signs of decline or village enlargement, the presence of public buildings, industrial activities and local upper-class quarters, as illustrated in table 1 below. Yodefat expanded southwards on the hill, local industries operated, and some families were able to afford rather fine houses with frescoes in the geometric First Pompeian style and floors designed in the *opus sectile* style. Cana also hosted local industries and a village community that was able to uphold one if not two public buildings, one of which had fine plastered walls and a floor besides fine roof tiles. In Capernaum no major changes are attested in the Early Roman strata. Its inhabitants fished on the lake and lived in rather large living units with several families living together. Although this is disputed, it seems likely that the earliest stage of the synagogue stretches back to this period. The village of Gamla presents important material. Local industry flourished, providing an economic base for a wealthy quarter and two public buildings including the large synagogue. In general, it seems that the most notable changes in the rural village life of Galilee happened before this period (the Hasmonean takeover) and after this period (in the Middle Roman period). In the first part of the first century CE, the villages surveyed all appear to have flourished.

	Yodefat	Cana	Capernaum	Gamla
No signs of decline	x	x	x	x
Public buildings		x	x	x
Industrial activities	x	x	x	x
Upper-class houses	x	x		x

Table 1: Indicators of the welfare of the villages of Galilee in the first century.

public building that has been variously interpreted as a synagogue, a *nympheum* or latest by Zangenberg as a latrine (Zangenberg 2001, 29–44). In conclusion, Zangenberg states: "Magdala war kein verschlafenes Landstädtchen, sondern verfügte über beträchtlichen Reichtum und zeigte ein beachtlich „urbanes" Gesicht" (Zangenberg 2001, 74). Thus Magdala adds to the picture of thriving milieu in Galilee outside the urban centres of Tiberias and Sepphoris. The excavations in et-Tell, located in Philip's tetrarchy and identified as Bethsaida by its excavators, paint a picture of a modest first-century town with several large courtyard houses and perhaps a small temple. The settlement seems to have experienced a certain decline in the first century (cf. Savage Forthcoming). In this respect, et-Tell differs from the other sites surveyed in this section (for more, see the three excavation volumes, Arav and Freund 1995; Arav and Freund 1999; Arav and Freund 2004).

5.6 An Inter-Regional Perspective – Nearby Cities

Finally, 'an inter-regional perspective' is needed as a way of putting the level of urbanization in Galilee into perspective. Several cities are of interest, such as Hippos, Gadara, Scythopolis, Caesarea Maritima, Sebaste and Bethsaida. Each of these sites has been excavated to the same extent or even more than Sepphoris and Tiberias. However, a thorough treatment of each site will exceed the limits of the present investigation. What follows will focus on Scythopolis, Hippos and Gadara, since the *chora* of these cities bordered on Galilee from the side of Decapolis, as well as Caesarea Maritima, since it was the main urbanization project of Antipas' father, Herod the Great.[161]

5.6.1 Bordering Cities of Decapolis: Hippos, Gadara and Scythopolis

As in the case of many other cities in this region, the first-century strata of the cities of Decapolis,[162] Hippos, Gadara and Scythopolis near Tiberias have been almost completely removed by the intense building activity in the second and third centuries, which took the cities to their peak. Still, the material data firmly datable to the first century paints a consistent picture of Greek cities equipped with various public institutions such as theatres, monumental gates, temples etc.

The city of Hippos was located just opposite Tiberias on the eastern side of the Sea of Galilee. At night it would literally have been possible to see the city lights across the lake, and direct interaction between the two regions is described by Josephus (*Life* 42, 153, 349). While small-scale excavations were carried out in 1950–55 (Epstein 1993), a large-scale campaign is being conducted at present under the directorship of A. Segal from the University of Haifa.[163] The history of Hippos goes back to the Hellenistic era, when it was recognized as a *polis*. The campaigns of Alexander Jannaeus placed it under Jewish rule (*Ant.* 14.75), but Pompey reestablished its sovereignty as one the cities in the Decapolis. During most of the reign of Herod the Great, it was once again ruled from Jerusalem, only to be placed under the legate of Syria upon Herod's death (cf. Epstein 1993 and Tzaferis 1990). Most of the public buildings found in excava-

---

[161] More comprehensive research into these and other cities can be found in Chancey 2002b, 120–166.

[162] For an in-depth survey of all the cities of Decapolis, see Lichtenberger 2003.

[163] In an exemplary manner, the 'Hippos (Sussita) – Excavation Project' has released most of its detailed preliminary reports, photos and maps on the project's website: http://hippos.haifa.ac.il. The first five seasons of excavation are summarised in Segal 2004.

tions belong to the Middle Roman and Byzantine periods: a Roman grid system with a colonnaded cardo ending in an elaborate forum area, a water system, and three churces.[164] However, the excavators have identified the base of what they believe to have been a temple encircled by a *temenos* founded in the second century BCE in the area labelled 'The Hellenistic Compound' (Segal 2004, 19–35; Segal 2002, 7; Segal 2003, 15). This corresponds with coins minted in 37 BCE with the image of Tyche (cf. Chancey 2002b, 133). Similarly, the eastern gate with a round and square tower is dated to the first century CE on the basis of the partly architectural similarity with the southern gate in Tiberias and the 'Tibereriade Gate' in Gadara. Thus, while the exact layout of Hippos in the first century CE is unclear, the city was undoubtedly a well-established *polis* in possession of a temple and minting authority, and had a *chora* of small villages attached to it (cf. *Life* 42).

Gadara was another of the cities of Decapolis sharing borders with Galilee (cf. *Life* 42, 349). Written sources reveal a proud history going back to the Hellenistic era, including famous philosophers and poets (cf. Weber 1990, 4) and a prominent political role in the region in both Hellenistic and Roman times (cf. Weber 1990, 6–9 and Chancey 2002b, 137). Excavations show that at its peak in Roman times, Gadara contained two theatres, monumental gates, elaborate tomb complexes, a basilica, a long colonnaded cardo, public baths and a stadium, as well as controlling the hot springs of Emmatha (Hammath Gader).[165] As in the case of Hippos, much of this was built in the second and third centuries. However, a temple complex going back to the second century BCE was uncovered. It was destroyed by fire in the mid-first century CE, and the excavators suggest that this could have been caused by the Jews, who according to Josephus raided Gadara among other cities during the war (cf. *War* 2.459 and Weber Forthcoming). Josephus also attests that there were temples in Gadara (*Ant.* 15.357), and city coins bear witness to regular Greco-Roman cultic practices. As already discussed, Gadara also featured a monumental freestanding gate at the western entrance to the city from the direction of Tiberias, with a layout very similar to that of the southern entrance gate to Tiberias (cf. section 5.3.3). Unfortunately, stratigraphy of the gate foundations is not conclusive, and it has been debated whether it was built in the Julian or

---

[164] Detailed city plans can be found at http://hippos.haifa.ac.il/excavationReport/-2003/FinalDrawings2003/index.html. Cf. also fig. 1 in Segal 2004 and Tzaferis 1990, 54 for an artist's rendition of the city layout.

[165] Preliminary excavation reports have been published successively, cf. Weber 1991b and Wagner-Lux et al. 1993 and the reports cited there. The most thorough survey is provided in Weber 2002.

Flavian period (Hoffmann 2002, 114). As noted above, the excavator, T. Weber, dates it for typological and historical reasons to the Flavian period.

Finally, from the side of the Decapolis, the *chora* of Scythopolis also bordered on Galilee, and the city itself is said to be "a neighbour of Tiberias" (*War* 3.446, cf. *Life* 42, 340–349). Intense excavation campaigns since 1986 have uncovered extensive remains from the Roman and Byzantine city below the mound, most of which (if not all) also date to the Middle Roman period and onwards.[166] At its prime, the city featured a large theatre, large bathhouses, a least five temples, wide colonnaded streets with an abundance of shops, a main street (the 'Palladius Street') featuring a semi-circular plaza in the middle, a *nymphaeum*, and an amphitheatre (cf. the plans in Foerster 1993a, 224 and Tsafrir 1998, 210). However, according to Josephus, Scythopolis was already the largest city of the Decapolis in the first century CE (*War* 3.446), and the gigantic low-site tell also features first-century remains. Evidence has been found of an earlier theatre than the one presently visible dating to this period (Foerster 1993a, 226). The monumental temple on the mound was in use in the first century (Applebaum 1989, 5), and one of the temples in the low-site area also originates in the first century (Tsafrir 1998, 210). The temple activity in this period is further emphasized by first-century CE coins displaying Tyche and Nike (Chancey 2002b, 141). Remains from the Hellenistic city have also been found, including parts of a third-century BCE amphitheatre (Chancey 2002b, 140). So in the first century Scythopolis was already a regular Greek polis, including several of the institutions connected with this status.

5.6.2 Herod the Great's Caesarea Maritima

Caesarea Maritima is unusual in several respects: It was founded by Herod the Great in the late first century BCE (22–10 BCE), constituting his largest single building project. It is thoroughly described by Josephus (*War* 1.408–415; *Ant.* 15.331–341). Although building activity was conducted in successive periods, the city was not profoundly rebuilt or reorganized in the Middle Roman period, which is why so many of the original Herodian structures remained in place (cf. Holum and Raban 1993, 283). Finally, the area has been intensively excavated since the 1950s, including advanced under-water excavations of the harbour.[167] In general, most of the material

---

[166] The most detailed overview is provided in Foerster 1993b. A list of the preliminary reports can be found in Tsafrir 1998, 208 note 28. Chancey's concise exposition is also helpful (Chancey 2002b, 140–143).

[167] A detailed description of the history of these excavations can be found in Holum 1997.

data from the Early Roman period found in Palestine derives from the building projects of Herod the Great (cf. the list in Richardson 1999, 197–202), and of these Caesarea has rightly been described as his most prestigious project.[168] Caesarea also presents an interesting parallel to the city of Tiberias. Both were built in honour of the emperor, and both were virtually built from scratch. Thus, Caesarea provides a suitable comparison when judging the building abilities of Antipas.

Structures from the time of Herod the Great include: the harbour, the temple platform of the Augusteum, the theatre, the palace known as the Promontory Palace, the city plan including defences, the amphitheatre, and possibly also the eastern part of the upper aqueduct. No wonder Josephus describes the splendours of Caesarea in detail, and in fact his description "by and large corresponds with the archaeological facts" (Holum and Raban 1993, 283).

The harbour of Caesarea is possibly Herod's most impressive architectural achievement. Its architectural splendour and its functional ability to harbour large ships at a spot where there was no natural protection seem to have impressed Josephus the most (cf. *War* 1.409–413; *Ant.* 15.332–340). Its construction was made possible by the recent invention of hydraulic concrete, which could harden under water using volcanic sand, and the Roman engineer Vitruvius' publication from 25 BCE, *De Architectura*, in which a chapter describes harbour construction (cf. Vann 1983; Raban 1993, 287; Brandon 1996). It was designed with three basins, one inside the other, the largest of which was built out into the sea using the new technique of hydraulic concrete being poured into the water in boxes made of wood-beams – some of which have been found in situ (cf. Vann 1983; Brandon 1996). Among other things, Josephus notes the economic advantage of the harbour, which was able to dock even the largest ships in a safe and convenient way which had not previously been possible along the entire coastal line of the Judean kingdom (*War* 1.409; *Ant.* 15.333–334).

The city itself was equipped with most of the public buildings known to be part of a Greco-Roman *polis*. It was protected by a city wall enclosing a vast area of 164 acres or 66 hectares (cf. Bull 1982). Its centre was occupied by an acropolis raised 13 m above sea level using twelve huge barrel vaults each 8.5 m high (Holum and Raban 1993, 283) On top of it stood a temple dedicated to Augustus. The *temenos* itself measured 90 m x 105 m.

---

[168] Cf. Josephus, who describes the city using words as "magnificently" (μεγαλοπρεπῶς, *Ant.* 15.331) with palaces designed to show his "great-minded nature" (τὸ φύσει μεγαλόνουν ἐπεδείξατο, *War* 1.408), a harbour constructed of expensive imported materials (*Ant.* 15.332) besides other large-scale public buildings (cf. *War* 1.408–415; *Ant.* 15.331–341).

The design was performed so "the temple platform and the Sebastos harbor formed a single grandiose architectural conception that bears the earmarks of Herodian design and engineering" (Holum and Raban 1993, 283). 'The promontory palace' was located further to the south, constituting another edifice breaking with the natural limits of architecture. Extending into the sea on a natural cliff, the palace's main entrance could only be accessed by ship. A semi-circular peristyle courtyard provided a panoramic view of the setting sun on the Mediterranean Sea (cf. the plan in Burrell, Gleason and Netzer 1993, 52; Netzer 1996b, 199). Numerous rooms were organized around a large pool measuring 18 m x 35 m, of which a large dining room stood out in particular with a multicoloured mosaic floor designed in the *opus sectile* style also known from Jericho and now Tiberias (cf. photo in Netzer and Levine 1993, 282). The central pool is believed by the excavators to have been a fresh water pool for swimming in its original design. Only later, when the palace was destroyed, was it reused as a fish pond (Netzer and Levine 1993, 281; Netzer 1996b, 197–198, contra Holum and Raban 1993, 283). They also believe that the palace is identical with one of the palaces of Herod mentioned by Josephus and described as "the most costly palace" (βασιλείοις πολυτελεστάτοις, *Ant.* 15.331). Its foundation could be dated through finds of unbroken lamps and fine red-ware pottery from this period (Burrell, Gleason and Netzer 1993, 54).[169]

Two facilities for public entertainment could also be dated to the Herodian phase. First, a theatre was located at the southernmost tip of the city. Excavations revealed that its first phase indeed goes back to the foundation of the city as mentioned by Josephus (*War* 1.415). It could seat around 4,000 persons (Bull 1982; Negev, Frova and Avi-Yonah 1993, 273–274). Second, when visiting Caesarea today, the structure occupying the most space is the hippodrome located right next to sea between the theatre and the harbour. Nevertheless, it was discovered rather recently in 1992 (cf. Porath 1995, 15), and older reports only operate with the oval imprint of a structure visible in the fields east of the later Byzantine city wall as a possible candidate for the amphitheatre mentioned by Josephus.[170] He describes the ἀμφιθέατρον as capable of receiving a large multitude (πολὺν ὄχλον ἀνθρώπων δέχεσθαι δυνάμενον) and as "care-

---

[169] A general introduction to the palaces of Herod can be found in Netzer 1996aa.

[170] Actually, at its peak Caesarea had four different entertainment facilities: Herod's theatre, Herod's 'amphitheatre' (or stadium), an oval amphitheatre located outside the city walls to the north-east, and finally a large hippodrome (or *circus* in latin) outside the city walls to the south-east (cf. the map in Porath 1995, 16). For a general introduction to the excavation of Herod's amphitheatre-stadium, see Porath 1995; Porath 1996; Patrich 2002. For a discussion with a focus on relationship of the Jews to the games, see Weiss 1998; Weiss 1999a; Weiss 1996.

fully placed with a view of the sea" (κείμενον ἐπιτηδείως ἀποπτεύειν εἰς τὴν θάλασσαν, *Ant.* 15.341). In other texts, it is termed a "stadium" (στάδιον, *War* 2.172; *Ant.* 18.57). The structure is U-shaped and not oval as in a regular Roman amphitheatre.[171] The arena was 300 m x 50.5 m with seats *(caveae)* in 12 rows on the three sides providing capacity for about 10,000 spectators (Patrich 2002, 30). The starting gates were located in the northern end. According to Josephus, the amphitheatre-stadium was used for music and athletic contests, gladiatorial fights, the hunting of wild beasts and horse-races for which Herod inaugurated quinquennial festivals in honour of the emperor at his own great expense (*War* 1.415; *Ant.* 16.137–41, cf. Patrich 2002, 36).[172] Thus, Caesarea provides a vivid example of a large, well-planned and well-equipped *polis* of full pagan nature constructed almost from scratch by Herod the Great. However, the incredible investment required was counterbalanced by the income the port was able to produce for Herod in trade and taxes (cf. Blakely 1996).

5.6.3 Partial Conclusion

Two important points can be learned through 'an inter-regional perspective'. First, the urbanization programme of Antipas was not an isolated phenomenon. Instead, it brought to Galilee what was already present in other parts of the Jewish area and in the Decapolis. Scythopolis, Gadara and (in particular) Hippos were placed in such close proximity to Tiberias that the city of Antipas did not represent an isolated phenomenon. Second, the ancient *poleis* existed in different sizes with different numbers of public buildings. From the investigation above, it seems that both Sepphoris

---

[171] In the first century CE, the various terms for the different entertainment facilities were not completely fixed. The Greek tradition originally included the *theatron* for theatrical performances and the *stadion* for athletic contests and horse-races. The Roman tradition added the *amphiteatron* as a term for the oval-shaped construction (amphi: 'around') for gladiatorial fights and animal baiting, and the *hippodromos* or *circus* (Latin) as a term for the large-scale stadium for horse-races. However, in the east the *stadion* served as a multi-purpose facility to be used both for horse-races, gladiatorial combats and animal baiting. For this reason the terms *amphiteatron* and *hippodromos* were also applied, and thus only *theatron* was used distinctively in the first century CE, while the three other terms were used synonymously (cf. Welch 1998; Humphrey 1996). Although the eastern 'hippodrome-stadium' was often shaped like the Roman hippodrome, it lacked the central physical barrier because it was also used for athletic contests. It did not need to be U-shaped, but could be rectangular as in Samaria and Jericho.

[172] For a detailed description of the different contests, see Patrich 2002, 33–61. It is interesting to note that Josephus does not condemn Herod for adopting the Roman gladiatorial games in connection with the festivities of Caesarea (*War* 1.415; *Ant.* 16.137–41), as he does in the description of the games conducted in Jerusalem (*Ant.* 15.267–277, cf. the discussion above sections 3.3.2).

and Tiberias were *minor* cities with only a few public facilities. In comparison, Caesarea Maritima and possibly Scythopolis were larger and better equipped with various Greco-Roman entertaining facilities. Herod the Great's Caesarea featured a theatre, an amphitheatre, a monumental palace, a magnificent harbour and a temple. Scythopolis also possessed an amphitheatre, a theatre and at least two temples in the first century. Less is known of early-first-century Gadara and Hippos, but both featured temples in this period. This picture corresponds with what is concluded by J. Reed:

It must be noted that neither Sepphoris nor Tiberias shows the same kind of appetite for materials, buildings, and particularly decorative elements that symbolized Greco-Roman culture, compared to Caesarea Maritima or Scythopolis, the major cities in Palestine. Nor did they belong in the same category as these metropolises, in terms of site size, population, or agricultural demand. (Reed 2000, 93–94)[173]

5.7 Chapter Conclusions

This examination has adopted a three-stage approach. First the nature of archaeology was investigated with regard to its methodological and theoretical approaches. It was concluded that factors of uncertainty prevail in both regards. It is in general difficult to date material data more precisely than within a hundred years, and in addition the path leading from artefacts to reconstructed history involves a leap of interpretation and perhaps of the imagination as well. Therefore, any historical reconstruction needs to observe a strict stratified approach, keeping the uncertainties down to a minimum, as well as keeping the assumptions behind the various proposals explicitly stated in order to allow a subsequent evaluation.

Second, Antipas' own programme of urbanization in Tiberias and Sepphoris was investigated. To sum up, the picture emerging is one of modest urbanization. In both places, intensive periods of building activity were experienced in the Middle and Late Roman periods. In contrast, no public building has been found in Sepphoris that is indisputably dated to Antipas' era, which naturally does not exclude the existence of any such building – after all, the theatre, the cardo and the basilical building are dated by some to his period. In Tiberias a beautiful mosaic floor and some wall structures

---

[173] Reed further states: "Imported marble columns are ubiquitous at Caesarea and Scythopolis, an index of their wealth and ability to import massive items – 30 yoke of oxen are needed to transport a single drum. They are virtually absent at Sepphoris and Tiberias" (Reed 2000, 123–124). While the latter is true, the first statement needs to be corrected. Although many marble columns have been discovered at Caesarea, none has been found in an original first century strata but always in secondary use (cf. note 120).

have been unearthed that might be part of an elaborate first-century palace, and the southern gate complex was dated to the period of Antipas by its excavator – although this dating has been disputed. Recently, Tiberias' first-century stadium has probably also been identified by Moshe Hartal, although without clarifying its foundation date any more precisely than the first century. However, even if disputed features are accepted as being from Antipas, no temples or other Greco-Roman cultic emblems have been found in either Sepphoris or Tiberias, and the use of local building material qualifies the cities as only 'second-tier' urban areas as phrased by Reed.

Third, the urbanization programme of Antipas was elucidated through a regional and an inter-regional perspective. As discussed in chapter one, it is accepted without exception that urban and rural areas were connected through socio-economic ties – whether parasitic or reciprocal in nature. For this reason it is highly interesting to see whether Antipas' activities left any traceable marks in the rural areas. Based on the villages and towns that have been investigated, it seems clear that the first century until the war of 66 CE was a period that provided the stable conditions needed for expansion and growth. No dramatic impact has been verified. Similarly, the modesty of Antipas' achievements is highlighted by comparison with the building activities of Herod the Great in Caesarea Maritima, for instance. In addition, the inter-regional view from the eastern neighbour cities of Decapolis highlights the fact that Antipas, rather than imposing real novelties, brought Galilee up to date with some of the infrastructure already known in the area. The wider historical consequences of these investigations will be discussed in Part III.

Chapter 6

Message and Minting – The Coins of Herod Antipas

6.1 Introduction[174]

The importance of coinage as a source material cannot easily be overestimated. Apart from a limited amount of monumental inscriptions, coinage provides the only surviving epigraphic material from the hands of the Jewish rulers of the Second Temple period. It communicates in two ways. First, coinage was potentially, on a religious/political level, a propaganda tool through its use of iconography and palaeography. In a society of illiteracy, coins were an effective way of circulating certain messages.[175] In particular, the Jewish coins were potentially loaded with political and religious significance due to the ban against images in the Decalogue. Second, coins are, on a socio-economic level, important for understanding the economic conditions at work and the level of monetization of an ancient agrarian society such as that of Galilee.

In consequence, the coins of Antipas are used as evidence on two levels in the ongoing discussion of how to picture his Galilee. First, the *message* of the coins is interpreted by Horsley, Silberman and others as provocative propaganda meant to reinforce Antipas' political ambitions and messianic dreams:

The small bronze coins minted by King Herod's son Antipas… reveal a powerful juxtaposition of political symbols that earliest Christianity arose to contest. With a palm branch stamped on one side (calling to mind biblical descriptions of the fertility of the Land of Israel) and a Roman laurel wreath on the other (symbolizing the *auctoritas* and *dignitas* of the world-conquering Emperor Tiberius), the coins issued by Herod Antipas gave symbolic expression to his own political ambitions and messianic dreams. (Horsley and Silberman 1997, 22)

Second, it is argued that the *minting* of the coins was done with the intention of monetizing the economy of Galilee in order to incorporate inland

---

[174] This chapter will be published in a slightly revised form in Jensen Forthcoming.

[175] For a general discussion of coins as a means of propaganda, see Evans 1992, 17–32.

Galilee in the wider Roman world and facilitate cheap and effective tax collection. As an example, Arnal argues:

The Galilean economy was not especially monetized by the time of Antipas came to power but became increasingly so from that point onward, and did so as a result of, or at least with the encouragement of, deliberate political policy. The simultaneous foundation of Tiberias and of a Galilean mint is no coincidence: an effort to urbanize corresponded to an effort to monetize. Monetization was unquestionably in the interests of the wealthy and ruling classes, as well as the Romans: it allowed value to be removed from Galilee without the burdensome requirement of transporting bulky items overland... as a result, the wealth of this very productive region could be tapped effectively and relatively cheaply. (Arnal 2000, 138)[176]

The purpose of this chapter is to provide a comprehensive examination of the coins of Antipas by taking into account both message and minting; i.e. the iconography and the circulation of the coins. As a consequence of the contextual method approach utilized in this investigation, the coins of Antipas will be examined in their wider Second Temple context, resulting in the following outline. First, the importance of coinage as a source is introduced; second, the Hasmonean and other Herodian and Roman coins of Judea are discussed, providing the necessary context; and third, the coins of Antipas are discussed in terms of both iconography and circulation. The objective of this threefold investigation is finally to assess the picture of Antipas' reign that emerges from his coins.

6.2 Coinage on a Religio-Political and Socio-Economic Level

6.2.1 The Message; The Ban On Images

The ban on images derives from the Decalogue's second commandment, which forbids the making of an image (פֶּסֶל/εἴδωλον, LXX) or a representation (תְּמוּנָה/ὁμοίωμα, LXX) of anything in heaven, on earth or in the waters below (Exod 20:4; Deut 5:8). In Exodus 20:23 and Leviticus 26:1 the ban is qualified as a ban against various types of idols for worshipping such as silver gods (אֱלֹהֵי כֶסֶף/ θεοὺς ἀργυροῦς, LXX, Exod 20:23), gold gods (אלהי זָהָב/θεοὺς χρυσοῦς, LXX, Exod 20:23), idols (אֱלִילִם/χειρο-ποίητα, LXX, Lev 26:1), an image (פֶּסֶל/γλυπτὰ, LXX Lev 26:1), a masseba (מַצֵּבָה/στήλην, LXX, Lev 26:1), or a stone with a carved image (אֶבֶן מַשְׂכִּית/λίθον σκοπὸν, LXX Lev 26:1).

---

[176] The same argumentation can be found in Freyne 2000b, 108 and Crossan and Reed 2001, 70. Chancey also notes the problematic aspect of Arnal's approach, Chancey 2005, 181.

The way in which the ban against images in the Decalogue's second commandment was interpreted differently in different time periods forms an interesting study in its own right. From the textual and archaeological evidence, it turns out that the period from the rise of the Hasmonean dynasty and until after the Bar Kochba revolt was marked by a strict interpretation generally prohibiting images with the exceptions of floral motifs and geometric designs (cf. Levine 2000, 209; Hachlili 1988, 83). Holy utensils from the temple, living creatures and pagan motifs are remarkably absent in the material culture of the first centuries BCE and CE, whereas various symbols, including owls and deities, appear on the *Yehud* coins from the period of the Persian satrapy of Judah (cf. e.g. Meshorer 2001, 2), and human representation as well as religious symbols from Greek mythology, such as zodiacs, flourished in the later Rabbinic period on mosaic floors in synagogues, in the ornamentation on sarcophagi and elsewhere (cf. Levine 2000, 206–224, for instance). In contrast, the figurative art on mosaic floors, frescoes, lamps and other objects from the intervening period consists almost exclusively of geometric patterns.[177] In the words of Lee I. Levine:

For a period of three hundred years or so, down to the mid-second century C.E., the Jews appear to have studiously avoided any kind of figural representation, as is attested on their coins, mosaic floors, frescoes, lamps, and other small finds. The Jews selectively borrowed motifs from the world around, but eschewed any kind of figural or pagan image. (Levine 1997, 117–118)[178]

Textual evidence reveals that this change was not motivated by a mere shift in fashion, but encouraged by religious concerns. Josephus is the prime source in this connection, since throughout his narrative he shows great concern for abiding by this law, although it is qualified as a ban not

---

[177] Hachlili provides a helpful overview of the most common motifs in this period grouped into floral patterns, geometric patterns, architectural motifs, varia, faunal motifs, temple vessels and motifs on Jewish coins. Art depicting temple vessels has only been found in a few instances (cf. Hachlili 1988, 81–82), and she concludes in concordance with Levine that in this period there "evolved a local Jewish art, strictly aniconic, using neither figures nor symbols" (Hachlili 1988, 83). It is also interesting to note that Herod the Great also refrained in his palaces from using the complete decorative systems of the contemporary Third Pompeian style (the 'ornamental') of wall paintings, preferring the Second 'architectonic' style if not adjusting the Third style (cf. Fittschen 1996, 150 and note 149).

[178] Since Jewish art in this period thus did not eschew images totally, Steven Fine has a point when arguing that it is improper to term it 'aniconic.' Fine argues that it rather was anti-idolatrous (Fine 2005, 80, followed by Chancey 2005, 195). Nevertheless, the term 'aniconic' is still used in what follows, but should, as discussed above, not be understood as a categorical ban against all types of imagery.

against any image but against living creatures (εἰκόνα ζῴου, *Apion* 2.75, cf. Vogel 1999, 76, note 29 and Roth 1956). Thus, he assures the reader that the decorations of the curtains in front of the Holy of Holies did not include living creatures (πλὴν ζῴων μορφῆς, *Ant.* 3.126), and that the two cherubim of the atonement were not like any other living animal known (*Ant.* 3.137). Likewise, King Solomon is said to have sinned (ἁμαρτάνω, *Ant.* 8.195) when he placed images of oxen and lions in the temple and in his palace. In *Apion* 2.74–75 Josephus directly contrasts Greek and Jewish customs. While the Greeks paint pictures of their families as well as of themselves, the Jewish lawgiver has forbidden images (*interdixit imagines fabricari*, 2.75), since they were neither necessary nor useful (cf. also *Apion* 2.12, 191). In several passages, Josephus refers to this law as an explanation of Jewish resistance against the authorities' use of various images.[179]

6.2.2 The Minting; Coinage Circulation, Monetization and Urbanization

The second reason for the importance of coinage as a source material is related to its level of circulation and what this reveals about the economic situation in antiquity. In what way can coin circulation be connected to trade, and what does it reveal about the level of monetization and urbanization? Unfortunately, it is exceedingly difficult to determine not only the number of coins minted in each series, but also where and for how long the coins circulated. There are few studies that undertake the burdensome task of counting the number of known coins of a given area and time period. A noteworthy exception in this regard is Danny Syon's dissertation, *Tyre and Gamla: A Study of the Monetary Influence of Southern Phoenicia on Galilee and the Golan in the Hellenistic and Roman Periods*, which will be discussed below in connection with the coins of Antipas.[180]

Initially, the following four points may be noted. First, a clear distinction between silver and copper coinage should be made. Heavy transactions in connection with building projects, acquisition of land and so forth would have been conducted in silver (or gold), while copper coinage was designed for daily market transactions. The consequence of this is two-

---

[179] Examples are: the trophies of Herod (*Ant.* 15.277–279), the eagle in the temple (*War* 1.650; *Ant.* 17.151), the trophies of Pilate (*War* 2.169–174; *Ant.* 18.55–59), the statue of Gaius Caligula in the temple (*War* 2.184–203.; *Ant.* 18.261–309), and the palace of Antipas (*Life* 64–69). In a comment to *Life* 65, S. Mason explains that the Jewish ban against images was well-known in the ancient world, and that it actually corresponded with several Greco-Roman philosophers' critique of anthropomorphism. For references, see Mason 2001, 59, note 349.

[180] I am grateful to Danny Syon for providing me with a pre-published version of his dissertation and a copy of his database of the more than 6,000 coins found at Gamla.

fold. On the one hand, an autarkic society characterised by barter economy and self-sufficiency could still make use of silver coinage for the occasional larger transactions. On the other, the low value of copper coinage implies that an ancient ruler would not be able to fund his regime through large-scale production of copper coinage, even though the metal used was cheap compared to silver. It is remarkable that neither the Hasmoneans nor the Herodians seem to have minted any silver coinage.[181] They ostensibly confined themselves to silver coinage primarily of Tyre. Second, since silver was a precious metal, it was seldom accidentally lost but rather remelted. Most of the silver coins found today turn up in stored hoards. For this reason, our knowledge of the circulation of silver coins is more elusive. The behaviour of copper coinage was completely different. It was an object to be lost, dropped and discarded, and therefore turns up everywhere in excavations, providing relatively good information on its circulation (cf. Syon 2004, 158–159). Third, it follows that since the Hasmonean and Herodian rulers issued only copper coinage and imported silver coinage for major transactions, the relationship between foreign coins and interregional trade is more complicated than it would have been had they produced silver coinage.[182] Finally, and most importantly, the question is what we can deduce from the circulation of copper coinage with respect to the level of monetization and urbanization of the ancient economy. Syon refers to an interesting macro period study by Morgan Kelly, who argues that the level of small change in use reveals the degree of urbanization. It is to be expected that in societies with specialization and intense division of labour, self-sufficiency will decrease and the level of daily transactions performed in small change will increase, which results in a heavy demand for fractional coinage (Kelly, 1–2). On a macro scale, the amount of copper coinage should be much higher in industrialized Europe than in medieval times, and possibly also high in Roman times. Kelly is able to validate this expectation: "Roman output of copper was several times higher than medieval levels, and was not equalled again in Europe until the early nineteenth century" (Kelly, 2, cf. figure 2 p.10). It thus follows that a sudden demand for copper coinage, resulting in heavy minting, is likely to be an indicator of a rise in urbanization, implying specialized labour, a decline of self-sufficiency and heavier monetization.[183]

---

[181] The proposal of Meshorer (cf. Meshorer 2001, 73–78) that Herod the Great moved the mint of Tyre to Jerusalem is not widely recognized (cf. Syon 2004, 164, note 104).

[182] For this reason, Horsley has argued against a linear deduction from the circulation of Tyrian silver in Upper Galilee to trade in the region and Tyre (Horsley 1994, 105; Horsley 1996, 69).

[183] It must be noted, though, that this proposal implies an assumption not universally agreed on, namely that coins were minted to meet market needs. The question of 'why'

6.3 The Context: Second Temple Coinage

In the following section, a broad framework for the coins of Antipas will be established by looking at the iconographic and palaeographic profile of the other Hasmonean, Herodian and Roman coins in circulation at the time of Antipas. This will establish a context through which his emissions can be interpreted. The question about circulation will be treated in connection with the coinage of Antipas itself.

6.3.1 The Hasmonean Coinage

Hasmonean coinage plays a prominent role in the coinage of the Second Temple period, being the first coinage issued by independent Jewish rulers, and it forms the background for understanding the succeeding Herodian coinage. The central question is how the Hasmonean rulers took advantage of their independent rights to mint coins. The earliest known coins, the *Yehohanan* coins of Hyrcanus I (134–104 BCE), are interpreted differently with regard to the extent to which they embodied nationalistic or religious propaganda. They are rather poorly made, and borrow symbols from Seleucid coinage such as the helmet, the wreath and, most prominently, the double *cornucopiae,* which became the hallmark of Jewish coinage in the Second Temple period, although it was connected to cults of fertility such as the Demeter cult in its original Seleucid setting (cf. the discussion in Meshorer 1982a, 67–68). The inscriptions are all in Hebrew using the old Paleo-Hebrew script, which by that time was in the process of being replaced by the Aramaic script (cf. Hendin 1976, 13 and Meshorer 2001, 40–41). Consequently, Rappaport concludes that "the Hasmoneans did not see their coinage as a vehicle for propaganda or as a major advantage to their regime and were quite indifferent to its production, fulfilling the role of minters only out of necessity" (Rappaport 1984, 32, cf. also Kindler 1958, 12). Still, according to Hendin, it is worth noting that images of living creatures are specifically avoided, which is why "Hyrcanus's small bronze

---

coins were minted is, as discussed by C. Howgego, difficult to answer. Possibly multiple factors were implied, of which state expenditure was more important than meeting market demands (Howgego 1995, 33–35). Naturally, the Herodian state expenditure could not be met with fractional coinage. Nevertheless it is argued by D. Ariel that Herod the Great and others minted copper coins to reduce expenses when paying expenditure in amounts smaller than the smallest silver coin could cover (personal communication). But still, in this case, the soldier or construction builder would only accept payments in coins if the economy was monetized in a way that would make this beneficial. It may thus be advanced as a working hypothesis that a highly monetized economy would demand a high level of coin circulation, which would support the assumption that the coin circulation indicates the level of monetization.

coins were unlike most other coins in use at the time", and for this reason embodied strong nationalistic propaganda. Similarly, the use of the old paleo-Hebrew script could be loaded with nationalistic connotations (Hendin 2000, 8).

In any case, the successive coins of Alexander Jannaeus (103–76 BCE) and later Mattathias Antigonus (40–37 BCE) show a striking level of innovation which reveals the potential of coins as vehicles for propaganda. Under Jannaeus' rule, Judea became a naval regional power controlling the coast from Egypt to the Carmel ridge. To celebrate, coins were issued which had, on the obverse, a Greek legend reading ΒΑΣΙΛΕΩΣ ΑΛΕΞΑΝΔΡΟΥ surrounding an anchor in the middle and, on the reverse, an Aramaic inscription reading מלכא אלכסנדרוס (King Alexander) enclosing an eight-pointed star itself enclosed by a diadem (TJC L1[184]) or, on another very similar issue, a legend in Hebrew reading יהונתן המלך (King Yehonathan) also surrounding an eight-pointed star (TJC K1, cf. Meshorer 2001, 209–210). Though 'the star' has been interpreted in various ways (cf. Hendin 2000, 11), the proposal of B. Kanael seems to be accepted seeing it as a reference to the old Israelite tradition in Numbers 24:17 of the kingship as a rising star (Kanael 1963, 44–45, cf. Meshorer 2001, 37–38; Hendin 2000, 11). While Jannaeus thus refrained from minting his self-portrait with a diadem on his head, as was the custom of the Seleucid kings, he found an alternative way of communicating his royal status using three different languages and symbols of naval and royal power.

The coins of Antigonus (40–37 BCE) represent real innovation in Jewish coinage. First, Antigonus introduced non-identical bilingual legends on his coins, 'king' in Greek, and 'High Priest' in Hebrew (TJC 36), proudly presenting both his double offices, which Herod could not rival. Second, and more importantly in this connection, is the coin decorated with the menorah and the shewbread table. Though this coin is rare, with only 40 known specimens, it is highly remarkable as "the only Jewish coin from antiquity that features the *menorah* and the shewbread table" (Meshorer 2001, 54). While oil lamps and ossuaries in this period were occasionally decorated with a menorah, it was kept in a simple form, often with either more or less than seven candlesticks (cf. Sussman 1973). Likewise, the later coins from the Bar Kochba rebellion, which otherwise display many items from the temple like trumpets, harps, lyres, and even the façade, do not display the menorah or the shewbread table (cf. Meshorer 2001, 55). This specific coin is therefore quite extraordinary, and according to Kanael, "the implication was clear: Antigonus, the High Priest, defends the

---

[184] All references to coins are to Meshorer's newest presentation, *A Treasury of Jewish Coins* (TJC).

temple against Herod and the Romans, just as his ancestors Mattathiah and Judas Maccabeus had fought for the temple against the Hellenizers and Antiochus Epiphanes" (Kanael 1963, 47).[185]

6.3.2 The Coins of Herod the Great

All rulers of the Herodian house issued coins, which can firmly be attributed to each ruler through the legend's combination of name, title and date.[186] The coins of Herod can be divided into an early dated series and several later undated series. The single dated series is marked "year 3" (LΓ, TJC 44–47). Although other options have been suggested, this is generally taken to be the third year after Herod's enthronement in Rome, i.e. from April 38 to March 37 BCE.[187] The place of minting was most likely Samaria. Not only did Antigonus control Jerusalem until 37 BCE, but this rather rare coin, constituting less than two percent of all the known coins of Herod, is found in much larger percentages in Samaria than in Jerusalem or anywhere else (cf. Meshorer 2001, 62). Herod's undated series was probably issued in Jerusalem, and forms the bulk of his coinage. Compared with the dated series, this coinage is crudely designed and not as well executed as one would have expected (cf. Ariel 2000–2002, 101).

In the dated "year 3" series, the largest denomination displays a helmet between two palm branches on the obverse and, on the reverse, a tripod on a base with a bowl on top, enclosed by an inscription reading HPΩΔOΥ ΒΑΣΙΛΕΩΣ (TJC 44). One-half of the denomination also displays a helmet on the obverse, but a decorated shield on the reverse (TJC 45). One-quarter of the denomination displays a winged *caduceus* on the obverse and, on the reverse, a plant interpreted either as a poppy head or a pomegranate (TJC 46). Finally, one-eighth of the denomination displays an *aphlaston* on the obverse (a decorative element on the stern of ships) and a palm branch on the reverse (TJC 47). Three interpretations of this issue's iconography have been suggested: (a) J. Meyshan and A. Reifenberg argue for a Jewish flavour of the images, explaining the cap as a temple vessel,

---

[185] For a detailed description of the coin and the history of the Menorah, see Meshorer 2001, 54–57.

[186] For an overview, see Meyshan 1958, 30–31.

[187] Cf. Rappaport 1984, 41; Meyshan 1958, 31–32; Kanael 1963, 48; Jacobson 2001, 100, and Brenner 2001, 213. Meshorer dates the coin to the year 40 BCE based on an alternative reading of the peculiar monogram found on the obverse, also compounding the Greek letters TP, which he does not take as another "year 3" marker (TPITOΣ), but as a shortening of TETPAPXHΣ, which could have been the title he officially bore before his inauguration as king in Rome (cf. Meshorer 2001, 61ff.). However, it remains an open question why Herod on the same coin would title himself king while refering to a tetrarchy.

the tripod as a temple table or the incense altar, and the plant head as a pomegranate, which unlike the poppy head was a recognized Jewish symbol (Meyshan 1958, 34–35 and Reifenberg 1969, 18–19). (b) Restating the proposal of Narkiss (cf. Meyshan 1958, 34, note 9), David M. Jacobson, on the other hand, argues that the symbols of these coins show Herod's true colours as a worshipper of Apollo. The three-legged table on the large denomination is interpreted as the tripod of Apollo, for whom Josephus says Herod had a temple rebuilt at Rhodes after a fire (*War* 1.424; *Ant.* 16.147). The helmet on the obverse is seen as a Dioscuri cap of the Greek mythological heroes, Castor and Pollux. Jacobson suggests a reference to Herod himself as "an allegorical portrait of the monarch with a reverential theme" (Jacobson 2001, 101). Thus, Jacobson concludes that Herod "was an 'unrepentant' pagan, who paid mere lip service to his adopted Jewish faith" (Jacobson 2001, 103).[188] (c) Finally, Meshorer argues that the dated coins represent Herod's way of showing gratitude and obedience to his Roman masters since "all the symbols – with one exception – were taken from contemporaneous Roman coins" (Meshorer 2001, 63). The cap of the large denomination is explained as an *apex*, the ceremonial cap of the Roman priests, the augurs, and the tripod as a regular object used by Roman priests. Both the apex and the tripod appear on Roman coins from the years 43–2 BCE (cf. Meshorer 2001, 64). So does the winged *caduceus* of one-quarter of the denomination coin, being a popular symbol of the god of health, Hermes, and the *aphlaston* on the small *prutot*. The one exception is the plant head on the reverse of one-quarter of the denomination (TJC 46). Meshorer identifies it as a poppy head and not a pomegranate, and defines it as a symbol of Samaria itself, where the cult of Demeter and her daughter Persephone was popular (Meshorer 1982b, 20–22; Meshorer 2001, 64). The plant was used as a drug in the festivities and functioned as universal symbol of the Demeter cult. Later, Herod had a temple built in Sebaste, dedicated to Demeter (cf. Meshorer 2001, 64). In conclusion, Meshorer states that "the Herodian coins minted in Samaria bear certain symbols copied from contemporaneous Roman coins to express Herod's esteem of and gratitude to the Romans" (Meshorer 2001, 65). Thus, Herod's dated series probably contained images connected to Greco-Roman culture, although it is debated whether they referred in an unambiguous manner to the cult of Apollo, the Demeter cult and hero cults, or

---

[188] Jacobson's proposals have been contested in a direct response by C. Brenner, who argues that the cap is better interpreted as a regular Roman military helmet, since the caps of the Dioscuri are normally represented in pairs, and that the item above the cap is better interpreted as a crest than as the star of the Dioscuri caps (Brenner 2001).

whether the symbols were meant to honour Herod's political patronage in his insecure first years of reign in a less specific manner.

How do the later undated coins from his reign in Jerusalem compare? On the one hand, much of the imagery used in this period was taken from Hasmonean coinage, and the careless execution raises the question of how profoundly propaganda was part of their intention.[189] On the other, certain coins contain images which have prompted diverse interpretations (cf. the overview in Ariel 2000–2002, 103–106). Three of the most controversial coins are: (a) Coins showing a three-legged table (TJC 48–58). Kanael argues that Herod intended to be ambiguous in his design: "Heathens might have recognized in it the tripod of Apollo, and Jews might have argued for the table of showbread viewed obliquely" (Kanael 1963, 49). In contrast, Meshorer interprets the image as one of the tables used in the temple in connection with sacrifice. *M. Shekalim* 6.4 describes how the service vessels were placed on two silver tables. Some of the three-legged coins clearly show vessels on top, and according to Meshorer Herod thus communicated his connection to the temple and the re-furnishing of its interior (cf. Meshorer 1982b, 23–24; Meshorer 2001, 66–67). (b) The same discussion unfolds around the coin displaying an eagle (TJC 66), which seems to be a clear transgression of the ban against images of living creatures. In the Jewish tradition, however, the eagle is viewed as holy (cf. Deut 32:31; Ezek 1:10; 17:7), and thus Meshorer argues that "the Jewish masses possibly saw the golden eagle in the Temple as a symbol of the might of their God who resided therein" (Meshorer 2001, 68). (c) The most interesting of Herod's later coins is the common *prutah*, which is also the one minted in the greatest number (TJC 59). The symbols on both sides are known from Hasmonean coins: an anchor on the obverse and a double *cornucopiae* on the reverse. There is an interesting difference, however: while the *cornucopiae* on the Hasmonean coins are displayed with pomegranates or ears of wheat between the two horns, on Herod's coins they are displayed with a *caduceus* in the centre; i.e. the sceptre of Hermes, the messenger of the gods, which was formed as a staff with two curled snakes at the end and also used as a symbol of Asclepios' healing skills (cf. Meshorer 1982b, 27; Meshorer 2001, 67, note 23). Again the ambiguity is striking. It could be argued that since the winged staff was not detailed, the ordinary person might have seen just the old Hasmonean pomegranate (Kanael 1963, 50), or that the two snakes in a Jewish context could be understood as the

---

[189] Cf. also D. Ariel: "In general the types on the undated coins are unrevealing: unlike mythological figures on many contemporary coins from outside of Judea, whose messages are clearer, one cannot easily determine how profoundly the symbolism of an inanimate object was intended" (Ariel 2000–2002, 101).

bronze serpents of Moses (Meshorer 1982b, 27). According to Meshorer, however, this slight alteration captures the double-sided nature of Herod:

This is a wonderful example of the planning of a significant design that served as an instrument for advancing the political interests of the ruler who minted these coins. At one and the same time, Herod aspired to bolster the legitimacy of his regime by marrying Mariamme the Hasmonean and to take on the appearance of a ruler who differed from his predecessors – and these aspirations found expression on his coins. (Meshorer 2001, 67)

This double-sided message is bolstered further by the fact that Anthony had issued coins featuring the double *cornucopiae* with a *caduceus* between them. "Herod thus alluded to a link and continuity with the Hasmoneans and at a connection with his Roman patron" (Meshorer 2001, 67).

In conclusion, the coins of Herod the Great have attracted considerable debate. Herod did not only use well-established Hasmonean symbols, such as the double cornucopia, the wreath, the Greek title "king," the anchor, and other maritime symbols. He also introduced some innovations, such as new symbols including the eagle, the *caduceus*, the three-legged table, the poppy head, and the helmet if it is indeed a Dioscuri cap. Yet, as we have seen, all of these symbols can be interpreted as having a Jewish flavour and are therefore probably (at best) only ambiguous and not directly pagan. Likewise, as Richardson has pointed out, it is noteworthy what Herod did not include on his coins, for example names of emperors, images of emperors, or indisputably pagan symbols (Richardson 1999, 214–215). In this way Herod possibly tried to design his coins to convey messages pleasing both his Jewish subjects and his Roman masters at the same time.

6.3.3 The Coins of Archelaos

Although Archelaos only ruled for ten years, he issued far more coins than his brothers Antipas and Philip. In style they are similar to those of Herod the Great, though special emphasis is given to maritime symbols, which appear on five out of six coins (cf. Meshorer 1967, 69). Only the last issue differs in this respect by featuring, on the obverse, a bunch of grapes on a vine and, on the reverse, a crested helmet with a *caduceus* below (TJC 73–74).

Two of the maritime coins feature an anchor on the obverse and on the reverse either a double *cornucopia* or an inscription within a wreath resembling earlier coins issued by Herod the Great, distinguished only by the legend minted on both sides reading "Herod" on the obverse and "ethnarch" on the reverse (TJC 67–69). All of Archelaos' coins entitle him Herod and ethnarch. The next three series display either a full war galley or the prow of a war galley on the one side (the war galley on the reverse and the prow on the obverse), and a double *cornucopia* or a wreath on the other side (TJC 70–72). The intense use of maritime symbols is generally

regarded as Archelaos' way of communicating his superiority in both political and economic respects. In contrast to his brothers, he ruled over the
only part of their father's kingdom that had substantial international connections through Mediterranean harbours, controlling the international
trade routes. Though perhaps not a true *basileus,* Archelaos issued coins so
closely connected to the coins of his father that his status as *the* true royal
heir was emphasized (cf. Meshorer 1967, 69; Rappaport 1984, 42).[190]

The most interesting of Archelaos' coins is the last issue, displaying a
bunch of grapes on a vine with the legend HPWΔOY above on the obverse and a crested helmet with a *caduceus* and a legend reading
EΘNAPXOY on the reverse (TJC 73–74). While one of Herod's coins
might display a vine (TJC 58), the image on the coin of Archelaos is a
fresh design which has been very beautifully crafted. The implication
seems clear. Both Josephus and later the Mishnah tell us that a golden vine
was part of the ornamentation on the doors in the temple (*Ant.* 15.394–395,
M. Middot 3.8, cf. Meshorer 2001, 69–70). His father before him had also
minted coins with images referring to the temple (the vine, the silver table,
the eagle, and perhaps the monogram, cf. Meshorer 2001, 65–66), and Archelaos uses the same method to display his sovereignty over and protection of Jerusalem and its temple (cf. Meshorer 1982b, 32–33; Meshorer
2001, 79–80). Furthermore, the crested helmet might refer back to the coin
of John Hyrcanus I with a helmet on the reverse (TJC H), or to the coins of
Herod with a helmet (TJC 45). Also, as Meshorer points out, the legend
EΘNAPXOY imprinted below the helmet can be translated back into Hebrew as "head of the nation", calling to mind the legend on Hyrcanus'
helmet coin, ראש חבר היהודים (Meshorer 2001, 80). Thus, the coins of Archelaos bore a powerful message within their specific context. By contrast
with the coins that Philip and Antipas were able to mint, Archelaos established himself as the true heir of their father's kingdom by proudly displaying his international political and financial relations as well as his responsibility as protector of Jerusalem and its temple. In many ways he ad-
vertised himself as *the head of the nation.*

6.3.4 The Coins of Philip

In comparison with the coins of Herod the Great and Archelaos, the coins
of Philip come as a surprise. They are truly innovative examples of Jewish

---

[190] Meshorer further speculates that the coins with the war galleys were minted to
commemorate Archelaos' successful voyage to Rome after the death of Herod. Not only
were the Romans known to issue coins in connection with important sea voyages, but
perhaps Archelaos likewise sought a way to enforce his authority by reminding his subjects of his legal right as ruler (cf. Meshorer 1982b, 31–32; Meshorer 2001, 79).

coinage that are very different from earlier coins – a fact which is most often explained as a consequence of Philip's rather remote tetrarchy, mostly populated by non-Jews.[191] All of them depict a human image, and most of them also a tetrastyle façade of a temple, likely to be the Augusteum at Caesarea Philippi. In total, eight series of Philip's coins are known, beginning with the fifth year of his reign and proceeding to his thirty-seventh year (cf. the table in Meshorer 1982b, 50). The coins were not minted in great quantities, and mainly circulated in Philip's own area (Meshorer 1982b, 49).

Philip's first issue features his own portrait on the reverse, bareheaded without a crown or diadem, encircled with the legend ΦΙΛΙΠΠΟΥ ΤΕΤΡΑΡΧΟΥ. The obverse features the head of Augustus with the legend ΚΑΙCΑΡ CΕΒΑCΤΟΥ (TJC 95). This coin is rather rare, and in the same year, Philip exchanged his own portrait for the façade of the Augusteum (TJC 96). In an interesting analysis, Fred Strickert points out that this first series of temple façade coins is the only one to feature a lily on the temple pediment. Later issues generally have a dot in its place. Strickert suggests that Philip could argue, if reproached by complaining Jews, that it was the façade of the temple and not the Augusteum, since the lily was a well established Jewish symbol (Strickert 1995, 167–168). Philip's later coins do not show much variation but mostly feature the image of the emperor and the Augusteum. However, by comparing the chronology of the coins minted in Jerusalem by the procurators with the chronology of the coins of Philip and Antipas, Strickert is able to trace a certain meaningful development in the scenery of the coins, which he relates to an ongoing fight for authority (cf. the table Strickert 1995, 169). In general, an issue was released in the year a new procurator was placed in office, and thus "it would seem that issuing coins served to publicize the legitimacy of one's own authority in the face of foreign domination" (Strickert 1995, 170).

In particular, Strickert emphasizes a connection to the coins of Pilate. In the year 29 CE, Pilate issued the first of two series depicting a Roman cult symbol which may have been offensive to Jewish feelings, namely the *simpulum*, a ladle used by the Roman priests to pour wine over sacrifices. The inscription on the reverse reads ΙΟΥΛΙΑ ΚΑΙCΑΡΟC (TJC 331). Strickert argues that the coin was issued to commemorate the death of Julia Livia, the wife of Augustus and mother of Tiberius. Livia was often depicted as a priestess of Augustus, and hence the cultic symbol on the obverse was appropriate. Livia was associated with Abundantia, the goddess of agricultural plenty (cf. Strickert 1995, 172). Strickert argues that Philip deliberately tried to rival this coin. In the year 30 he issued a coin with the

---

[191] As already noted by Madden, cf. Madden 1864, 102.

image of Livia surrounded by the legend: ΙΟΥΛΙΑ ΣΕΒΑΣΤΗ. The reverse features three ears of grain, but this time none of them are bowing their heads. Rather, they are held forward by a hand and the inscription reads ΚΑΡΠΟΦΟΡΟΣ (TJC 107). Thus it would seem that Julia Livia "is fulfilling her role as goddess of abundance" and as Strickert further notices, "ironically, Philip was able to do something that Pilate could not do: use the image of Julia" (Strickert 1995, 172). In essence, Philip thus deifies Livia even against the will of her son, Tiberius, who had ordered public mourning emphasizing her mortality. Livia was eventually deified by Claudius in 41 CE (cf. Strickert 1995, 183–184).

The second offensive cult symbol on Pilate's coin, the *lituus,* is featured on coins from 30 and 31 (TJC 337–339). According to Strickert, "this augural staff represented the authority of the Roman state". The reverse features the date enclosed in a wreath. In the year 30, Philip reintroduces his own image on the obverse of a coin which, on the reverse, closely resembles the coin of Pilate from the same year. Strickert interprets this as the intention of Philip to claim his own authority over Pilate.

Finally, Strickert argues that the single undated coin of Philip with a puzzling round symbol between the pillars of the Augusteum is also connected to his ongoing rivalry with Pilate (TJC 100). Meshorer, for his part, dates this coin to the year 14, since the obverse depicts the heads of both Augustus and Livia entitled ΣΕΒΑΣΤΩΗ, a title which Livia received after the death of Augustus in the year 14. Thus, the coin could have commemorated the death of Augustus (Meshorer 2001, 87). Strickert, on the other hand, argues that the reverse inscription reading ΕΠΙ in front of Philip's name indicates that the coins must have been issued later than 26 CE, from which time all of Philip's coins used this legend. Why would Philip substitute the date with a round-shaped symbol on this coin? Strickert interprets the symbol as a shield referring to the dispute over Pilate's attempt to set up golden votive shields in Herod's palace in Jerusalem. According to Philo, four of Herod the Great's sons, surely including both Antipas and Philip, played an instrumental role in having them removed (*Legat.* 299–305). Though perhaps too speculative, Strickert is thus able to suggest: "Would not a symbolic depiction of a shield in a Temple of Augustus on Philip's coin serve to remind people of Pilate's fiasco and Philip's triumph?"

In all instances, the coins of Philip are highly remarkable in their "international and pagan character" (Meshorer 2001, 85). For the first time we have: (a) the head of the ruler himself, (b) the head of an emperor, (c) the name of the emperor, (d) a façade of a temple, (e) and a perhaps even a reference to the imperial cult with the coin deifying Livia.

6.3.5 The Coins of Agrippa I

The coinage of Agrippa I can be divided naturally into the *prutah* dated to the sixth regnal year and minted in great quantities probably in Jerusalem, and the coins minted elsewhere, dated from the second to the eighth regnal year and only issued in small quantities. While the Jerusalem *prutah* remains within the conformities of Jewish coinage, the other coins continue the pagan practice and style of Philip – even adding new elements.

Agrippa's first series is dated to his second regnal year, i.e. 38/39 CE. At this point of time, Agrippa was king only in the old territory of Philip and contested by Antipas, who also sought to be king. Perhaps this is the reason why the largest denomination of this series boldly honours his patron in Rome, Gaius Caligula. The obverse features the image of the emperor, while the reverse displays his three sisters, Julia, Drusilla and Agrippina. The accompanying legends contain their names (TJC 112). The second largest denomination depicts Agrippa's own portrait with the mark of royalty, the diadem. This was only the second time a Jewish ruler depicted his own image on a coin.[192] The reverse depicts his son Agrippa II on a galloping horse (TJC 113). The second smallest denomination features the portrait of his wife, Queen Cypros (TJC 114), and the smallest denomination displays the Augsteum in Caeserea Philippi (TJC 115, cf. Meshorer 2001, 92–93).

Three coins of the later series represent true innovation, featuring images connected to Greco-Roman religious practices not seen on Jewish coins before: (a) On the reverse of a coin from Agrippa's fifth regnal year, a *quadriga* (four span) is depicted, displaying the goddess of victory, Nike, on the side (TJC 116, cf. Meshorer 2001, 93–94).[193] (b) An extraordinary image is found on an issue from Agrippa's seventh regnal year (43/44), depicting an event in a temple with two supporting pillars between which four figures can be seen. Following Sukenik, Meyshan argues that the coin was minted to commemorate Claudius' victory over the Britons, pointing to the similarity with the *Judea Capta* coins (Meyshan 1954, 189–190). Meshorer, on the other hand, follows A. Burnett, who suggests that the scene depicts Agrippa's treaty with Claudius in the Temple of Jupiter on the Capitol (Meshorer 2001, 98, cf. *War* 2.216; *Ant.* 19.274). Whatever the

---

[192] Again in his seventh regnal year a coin was issued with his portrait and the accompanying legend, ΒΑΣΙΛΕΥΣ ΜΕΓΑΣ ΑΓΡΙΠΠΑΣ ΦΙΛΟΚΑΙΣΑΡ, "the great king Agrippa, friend of the emperor" (TJC 122).

[193] This identification of the ornamentation of the chariot is proposed only in Meshorer 2001, whereas it does not feature in earlier studies (cf. Meyshan 1954, 188 and Meshorer 1982b, 52–53). It is based on a comparison with a coin issued by Gaius Caligula, cf. Meshorer 2001, 94.

truth of the matter, this is the first Jewish coin to portray a specific event in a Roman temple. (c) In his 7th regnal year, and for the second time, Agrippa issued a coin featuring his own image on the obverse. The reverse depicts Tyche holding a palm branch in one hand and a ship's rudder in the other. The legend reads ΚΑΙCΑΡΙΑ Η ΠΡΟC ΤΩ CΕΒΑCΤΩ ΛΙΜΗΝ[Ι], "Caesarea near the harbour called Sebastos" (TJC 122). Thus, the coin honours the city goddess of Caesarea.

In contrast to these coins stands the *prutah* minted in Jerusalem dated to the sixth regnal year. The obverse depicts a canopy, which is actually also an innovation in Jewish coinage. The legend reads ΑΓΡΙΠΑ BACIΛEWC.[194] The reverse displays three ears of grain placed in a kind of bowl with ears (TJC 120). The canopy may be explained as a symbol of royalty. The people of Jerusalem would have seen Agrippa on parade in their city protected against the sun under a canopy. In this way, Agrippa managed to express his royalty without depicting his own image. The ears of grain are not held by a hand, and there is no reason to see them as anything other than a reference to the Seven Species symbolizing the fertility of the land of Israel (cf. Meshorer 2001, 96–97). As already mentioned, this coin is by far the most common of Agrippa's coins (cf. Meshorer 2001, 97–98).

All in all, the coins of Agrippa demonstrate the great significance connected to Jewish coins from this period. While his Jerusalem *prutah* observed the ban against images, his coins minted outside Jerusalem continue Philip's practice of issuing coins in a full non-Jewish style. Particularly interesting is the largest denomination in Agrippa's first issue, which boldly honours Gaius Caligula at the same time as his kingship is contested by Antipas.

6.3.6 The Coins of the Roman Administration

Finally, the coins minted by the first Roman administration are of interest because they circulated in Galilee as well. Four of the seven prefects before 41 CE minted coins: Coponius (6–9 CE), Marcus Ambibulus (9–12 CE), Valerius Gratus (15–26 CE), and Pontius Pilate (26–36 CE). None included the name of the issuer, but through a combination of the names of the emperors and the date of issue the coins can be securely attributed.[195] It is important to note that the symbols are different from any other Roman

---

[194] All the other coins of Agrippa spell his name using two 'Π', while some of Agrippa II's use only one. For this and other reasons, it has been suggested that this coin should be attributed to Agrippa II (cf. Hendin 2001, 188–189). This suggestion has not been widely accepted.

[195] A complete chart of the legends can be found in Meshorer 1982b, 173–174.

issues known from the period. Coponius, Ambibulus and Gratus ostensibly took care not to offend Jewish religious feelings. Though the name of the emperor featured on their coins, which at the time was a novelty for coins meant for circulation in Judea, the symbols on both sides closely corresponded to the Jewish tradition by using ears of corn, palm trees, lilies, the *cornucopia* with a *caduceus*, ceremonial vessels (on the coins of Gratus), palm branches and branches of a vine (cf. TJC 311–330).

Pilate's coinage broke with this tradition. Although it did not depict the image of the emperor, as did the contemporary coins of Philip, it did, as already discussed, display images deriving from Roman cult practices in a way unprecedented on 'Jewish' coins, namely the *simpulum* (a ladle) on the first issue from the year 29 CE (TJC 331), and the *lituus* (Roman augural staff) on his next issue from the year 30 CE, which was re-issued in the year 31 CE (TJC 333–336). Although it has been argued that these two symbols would have been unknown to most Jews (Fontanille and Gosline 2001, 34–38), the innovations of Pilate are generally interpreted as another proof of his "intentional injury of Jewish feelings" (Rappaport 1984, 42). To this may be added the proposal of Strickert that Pilate's second and third series with the augural staff were minted to reinforce his authority in competition with the two Herodian tetrarchs in the north. Certainly, whether offensive or not to the common Jew, Pilate did change the style of Roman administration coinage in a way which might very well have been challenging for Jewish authorities and rulers.

6.4 The Coins of Herod Antipas

Turning now to the coinage of Herod Antipas, the question is how his emissions compare to the other coins in circulation at his time in terms of legends, imagery and scale of minting. His coinage can be divided into four groups: (a) Coins dated 'year 24' with the inscription TIBEPIAC on the reverse, (b) coins from the three series dated to the years 33, 34 or 37 also with the inscription TIBEPIAC on the reverse, (c) coins dated 'year 43' with a new inscription on the reverse, ΓΑΙΩ ΚΑΙCΑΡΙ ΓΕΡΜΑΝΙΚΩ and, finally, (d) a newly found coin identified by D. Hendin. This coin was minted before the founding of Tiberias, and so far only this one specimen exists (Hendin Forthcoming). It is dated to the year four and the legend reads TET PA_ _HC Δ, HP W. Thus, five series are known plus the new coin. In general it may be noted that all of them adhere to the Jewish aniconic tradition, featuring only floral decoration, and that three out of the four images used are innovations of Antipas in Jewish coinage, namely the reed on the 'year 24' coin, the palm tree with clusters of dates on the 'year

43' coin and the single cluster of dates also on the year '43 coin.'[196] Furthermore, as in the case of Herod the Great, Archelaos, Philip and later
Agrippa, all the legends are in Greek. In contrast to Herod the Great and
Archelaos, but like Philip before and Agrippa later, the 'year 43' coin features a legend with the name of the emperor. Finally, Antipas' coins are
rare and generally only found in the area around Galilee and in the Golan,
just as they represent rather poor workmanship and are generally not very
well preserved.

The coins of Antipas will be discussed below. First their use of images
and legends, and second their circulation and numbers. In both cases, it is
crucial to understand their relationship with the other Hasmonean,
Herodian and Roman coins in circulation at the time.

6.4.1 Images and Legends on the Coins of Antipas

Regarding the four groups of the coins of Antipas, the following may be
noted:

(1) Hendin's single coin was discovered in a large lot said to have be-
en found in the Jordan valley. It is a rather small coin, 1.58 grams, much
like the *prutot* of Archelaos. The obverse features a grain of barley or
wheat surrounded by the legend TET PA_ _HC Δ. The reverse shows a
palm tree with seven branches and the legend HP W (cf. figure 21).[197] The
two images are common for Jewish coinage. The legend can safely be interpreted as reading *Tetrarch, Herod* (in the nominative). The question is
what the delta signifies. All the dated coins of Herod the Great, and all the
coins of Antipas, signify dates with the prefix 'L' indicating that the following letters are to be read as numerals. This, however, is omitted on
coins from Tyre. Hendin admits that there is one other possible identification of this coin, namely to ascribe it to Herod the Great, who as a young
man, from about the year 41 BCE, served as tetrarch of Galilee appointed
by Anthony (*Ant.* 14.325–326). However, Hendin also advances three arguments against such an identification. First, Ariel's work on the chronology of the coins of Herod the Great has demonstrated that the early coins
consistently use the 'Ω' form, while the later coins all use the 'W' form
(cf. Ariel 2000–2002). The 'W' form of this coin thus contradicts its early
date if it was a coin issued by Herod the Great. Second, Hendin argues that
it is unlikely that Herod would have been allowed to issue coins as a tetrarch under the jurisdiction of Hyrcan II in Jerusalem. Finally, if 'Δ' refers

---

[196] The palm tree with dates, though, features on coins minted by Coponius and Ambibulus from 6 to 12 CE (TJC 311–315).

[197] I wish to express my gratitude to D. Hendin for allowing me to use his unpublished
material.

to year 4, then Herod would already be king. It thus seems most likely that this coin is the earliest known coin issued by Antipas, probably minted in Sepphoris and possibly in extremely small numbers – or perhaps as a trial issue.[198]

(2) The first series of coins is dated to Antipas' 24th regnal year (L KΔ, 19/20 CE, TJC 75–78, cf. figure 22). The date on this rare and badly preserved series was discovered by Father A. Spijkerman and attested by Meshorer (cf. Meshorer 1967, 74). It is not clear why Antipas did not issue a full series before his 24th regnal year, or why he ceased to mint again until his 33rd regnal year. Meshorer suggests that Antipas "was particularly unambitious (according to Josephus), and that the minting of coins was not one of his primary concerns. It seems that Antipas saw no remarkable economic or political advantage in continuous coin minting" (Meshorer 2001, 84). Thus, if Antipas did not mint coins from fiscal or economic necessity, this first series must have had a particular political purpose probably connected with the foundation of Tiberias, as the legend on the reverse reveals: TIBEPIAC.

The series was minted in four denominations,[199] which, unlike Agrippa's coins, have similar imagery. The reverse features the legend TIBEPIAC encircled by a wreath. The obverse features the date, the name 'Herod the Tetrarch' in the genitive (HPWΔOY TETPAPXOY), and a stalk with its leaves bowing downwards. How is this floral image to be identified? It is clearly different from the three other floral images on Antipas' coins: a palm tree, a palm branch, and a palm tree with dates. Even so, Madden and Hill speak of it as a palm branch (Madden 1864, 97; Hill 1965, 229). C. Cavedoni was the first to identify it as a reed, the *canna communis* (cf. Wirgin 1968, 248). W. Wirgin, on the other hand, identifies it as a laurel and argues for a connection with the laurel wreath on the reverse, seeing in it an allusion to the triumphal procession of the emperors, which at this time would have the emperor resembling Nike holding a laurel in his hand and bearing a laurel wreath on his head (Wirgin 1968, 249). Even the unskilled eye, however, can detect a difference in the shape of the leaves of laurel wreath on the reverse and the leaves of the plant on the ob-

---

[198] One of the historical consequences of such an identification would be that the name 'Herod' was obviously used by Antipas throughout his reign, and not solely after the downfall of Archelaos, as suggested by H. Hoehner and N. Kokkinos (Hoehner 1972, 109; Kokkinos 1998, 233). Interestingly, W. Otto asserted long ago that Antipas changed his named to Herod at the outset of his reign: "Antipas hat im Anschluß an seine Einsetzung als Tetrarch seinen Namen geändert" (Otto 1913, 170, cf. section 1.3.1).

[199] The largest denomination weighs between 12 and 17.5 grams. The half denomination weighs 7 grams on average, the quarter weighs 3.5 grams on average, and finally the eighth of the denomination (the *prutah*) weighs 1.8 grams on average.

verse. Moreover, there is no compelling reason to read any deeper symbolic meaning into the wreath, which at this time was one of the most common images on Jewish coins.

There is, however, good reason to identify the plant as a reed. Meshorer notes how the reed was a common plant in the area of Tiberias, often connected in Talmudic literature with fertility and durability, wisdom, and the founding of cities. Thus the motif of a reed may be one way of "expressing good wishes for the success and stability of the new city" (Meshorer 2001, 82, cf. Meshorer 1967, 73–74; Meshorer 1982b, 36–37). Furthermore, in an investigation of the quotation in Matthew 11:7 on "a reed shaken by the wind," G. Theißen has added several arguments for such an identification. First, one might expect Antipas to look for a special symbol to emphasize the importance of his new city, just as the coins of Archelaos proudly depict maritime symbols and the coins of Philip also proudly depict the Augusteum (cf. Theißen 1985, 47–48). The reed could serve this purpose, as a positive symbol not previously displayed on any Jewish coin. Second, the reed was a common symbol for cities lying close to rivers (cf. Theißen 1985, 47). Third, the reed could be a uniting symbol between Antipas' two geographically divided areas, Galilee and Perea, which were connected only through the River Jordan (Theißen 1985, 48). Unlike both Samaria and Judea, the reed would be a common plant of these two territories. Fourth, both Strabo (*Geogr.* 16.2.16) and Pliny the Elder (*Nat. Hist.* 24.85) attribute the reed (κάλαμον/*harundo*) to the land of Palestine in general (cf. Theißen 1985, 48).[200] Thus, by displaying a reed on his new series of coins commemorating the foundation of Tiberias, Antipas simultaneously communicated his foundation of Tiberias, labelled the preferences of his tetrarchy in competition with his brothers and the Roman administration, united his divided tetrarchy, and adhered to the Jewish aniconic ban.

(3)   After a nine-year break, Antipas again issued coins in his 33rd regnal year (L ΛΓ, 28/29 CE, TJC 79–82, cf. figure 23), 34th regnal year (L ΛΔ, 29/30 CE, TJC 83–86) and 37th regnal year (L ΛZ, 32/33 CE, TJC 87–90). Since Antipas did not find it necessary to issue a full series up until the celebration of his new city, it is to be expected that the renewed minting of coins was also connected to a political event. As in the case of Philip, there is good reason to connect Antipas' renewed minting to the

---

[200] Theißen concludes: "Die Wahl des Pflanzenmotivs „Schilfroh" auf den ersten Münzen des Antipas wäre nach all dem verständlich: Es handelt sich um ein bekanntes Attribut Palästinas – insbesondere aber des Jordantals. Es verbindet die beiden getrennten Landesteile und wächst am Ufer des galiläischen Sees, an dem Herodes Antipas seine Hauptstadt gründete – jene Stadt, deren Gründung Anstoß und Anlaß seiner ersten Münzprägung war" (Theißen 1985, 49). Theißen has also presented his analysis in Theißen 1992, 26–39.

aggressive policy of Pilate, who issued his first series in 29 CE.[201] The three series of Antipas are virtually identical, except for the dating, and were struck in four denominations. The reverse side of the coins is identical with the first series from 'year 24' featuring the name TIBEPIAC (or just the abbreviation T-C on the smallest denomination). The obverse also bears the legend, HPWΔOY TETPAPXOY 'of Herod the Tetrarch' (in the genitive), but the floral decoration has changed into what is probably a palm branch.

It is worth considering whether the new symbol was part of a deliberate attempt by Antipas to outdo the coins of Pilate. Three possible explanations of the connotations of the palm branch are possible. (a) The most obvious solution would be to interpret the palm branch as a common Jewish symbol. Although not nearly as common as the double *cornucopia* with a pomegranate in the middle on the Hasmonean coinage, the palm branch does feature on the obverse side of some of John Hyrcanus I's coins (TJC J) and on some of Jannaeus' coins (TJC O). The palm branch appears on several dated and undated coins of Herod the Great (TJC 48–57). In all cases, the palm branch appears as a single item, as it does on Antipas' coins. Therefore, the identification with the *lulav* of the feast of Tabernacles is uncertain. On some of the coins from the two Jewish wars against Rome, it appears both as a part of the four species and as a separate design (e.g. TJC 210–214, 218–219).[202] (b) Meshorer goes further and argues for a distinct communicative element in the shift from the reed to palm branches as a way of marking the city's consolidation, changing "from an uninhabited locality, abounding with reeds and wild vegetation, to a settled and cultivated site in which date palms had been planted instead of reeds" (Meshorer 2001, 82). (c) Finally, in this coin Wirgin also sees an association to Nike and the winning hero through the combination of the laurel wreath and the palm branch: "Antipas, in placing the double symbol on his coins, wanted to emulate Roman custom and to flatter his overlord" (Wirgin 1968, 248). If this is the case, one might extend the argument of Strickert that while Pilate tried to reinforce Roman authority by displaying the *lituus* on his first series, and Philip tried to honour his patron by displaying the head of Tiberius, Antipas entered the competition by displaying a common symbol of the Roman goddess of victory. Wirgin's proposal is weakened, however, as he himself notes, by the fact that up until then,

---

[201] Meshorer agrees, arguing that the series struck by Philip and Antipas in the same period "served to emphasize their legitimate rights as Jewish rulers" (Meshorer 1982b, 38, cf. Strickert 1995, 168ff.).

[202] For further discussion of the palm branch as a symbol, see Klimowsky 1958, 89–90; Fine 1989; Meshorer 2001, 35 and others.

Nero the emperor held a laurel in his hand during parades and thereafter a palm branch. So no direct link can be established between Tiberius and a palm branch. Similarly, the wreath is a common symbol featured on the obverse of most Hasmonean coins, and not necessarily an honorific emblem. Thus, even accepting the weak proposal of Wirgin that the combination of a wreath with a palm branch in a *Roman* context would be understood as honorific, it would be understood in a *Jewish* context as a continuation of common symbols on the preceding Hasmonean and Herodian coinage. The proposal of Horsley and Silberman that this coin is an expression of Antipas' supposed messianic dreams is absolutely unwarranted.

To sum up, the symbol of the palm branch in the context of Antipas' coins might have served several purposes, as the reed did previously. First, it adhered to the Jewish aniconic ban. Second, it might bear religious connotations as the *lulav*. Third, it recalled a tradition going back to the Hasmoneans. Fourth, it might have communicated the transition of Tiberias into a mature and well-established *polis*. Finally, in a discrete manner compared with Philip's practice, the series honoured Tiberius through its main legend reading: TIBEPIAC.

(4)   Antipas struck his final series in his last year as tetrarch, 38/39 CE, dated 'year 43' (ETOC MΓ or L MΓ, TJC 91–94, cf. figure 24). Like the former four series, it came in four denominations (according to Meshorer 2001, 82–83 contra Meshorer 1982b, 39–40), but it differed in three other respects. First, different images are displayed on the obverse. The whole and half denomination display a date palm with hanging dates, the quarter displays a palm branch, and the eighth of the whole denomination displays either a palm branch or a cluster of dates. Second, the image of a full date palm with hanging dates is an innovation by Antipas in Jewish coinage. As Steven Fine has pointed out, it conveys a message of prosperity. Throughout antiquity, the date palm was a source of trade and wealth and this product of Palestine was renowned for its superior quality (Fine 1989, 107–110). Third, the most surprising element in this series is the new legends. On the obverse the name of Herod is changed into the nominative form, HPΩΔHC TETPAPXHC. The marker for 'year' is also changed on the whole denomination from L to ETOC (or ETOY on some coins). Most important, on the reverse the name 'Tiberias' is replaced with a legend reading, ΓAIΩ KAICAPI ΓEPMANIKΩ, the name of Emperor Gaius Germanicus in the dative. As Meshorer notes, the genitive form of a name emphasizes possession, while the nominative is more suppressed and open. The dative, on the other hand, "suggests that the coins were symbolically struck *for and in honor of* the emperor" (Meshorer 1982b, 41). The two sides read together would translate according to Meshorer: "Herod the Tetrarch to Gaius Caesar Germanicus". At this time, the only Jewish ruler to

mint the name of the emperor on his coins was Philip, while it was done routinely on the coins of the Roman administration. Schürer describes this as a way of straddling the fence between the full-blown version of Philip with both the name of the emperor and his portrait on the obverse, and Herod's and Archelaos' total avoidance of both the name and the portrait (cf. Schürer 1973, 343, note 16). Thus, we are again compelled to look for a political motivation behind the release of the coins of Antipas. Why did he resume the minting of coins after a six-year break, and why did he change the legends dramatically? It is reasonable to connect this series to the story in Josephus on Antipas' pledge for kingship brought before Gaius when Agrippa was awarded Philip's old territory (*Ant.* 18.240–255). It might even be a demonstration of the notion in Josephus saying that Antipas "prepared himself lavishly not escaping anything demanded" (παρασκευασάμενός τε ὡς ἐνῆν πολυτελῶς καὶ φειδοῖ μηδενὸς χρώμενος, 18.246) before setting sail for Rome. However, in the fight for the favour of Gaius by using coins, Antipas might eventually have found himself defeated by Agrippa, who the same year issued his first series displaying the portrait of Gaius on the obverse and his three sisters, Julia, Drusilla and Agrippina, on the reverse (TJC 112)! So Antipas' last series was also politically motivated and designed to convey a message. Though one could argue with Schürer that Antipas crossed a line when including the name of the emperor, what he refrained from doing in comparison with Agrippa's coins from the same year is equally noteworthy.

6.4.2 Excursus: Two Monumental Inscriptions

Antipas' worries about adhering to the ban against images are put in perspective by two monumental inscriptions found at Cos and Delos, respectively (Dittenberger 1903, no. 416, 417), revealing how Antipas took part in the regular Greco-Roman cult practice outside Galilee. Both inscriptions are dedicated to "Herod the Tetrarch, son of King Herod." It is not likely that this designation could refer to Philip as well, since the name 'Herod' is never used in connection with Philip, who always included his own name on his coins, unlike Antipas, who always referred to himself as 'Herod' on his coins.[203]

A literal translation of the inscription from Cos reads: "Herod, the son of Herod the King, tetrarch, Philo, son of Aglaos, but by birth son of Nikonos, his guest and friend" (Ἡρῴδην, Ἡρῴδου τοῦ βασιλέως υἱόν, τετράρχην, Φιλίων Ἀγλαοῦ, φύσει δὲ Νίκωνος, τὸν αὐτοῦ ξένον καὶ φίλον, following Dittenberger 1903). The accusative, Ἡρῴδην, indicates

---

[203] Cf. also the discussion by Dittenberger in the note to inscription no. 416 (Dittenberger 1903, 628).

that the accompanying statue was erected in honour of Herod. A 'πρός τόν' or a form of ἀνατίθημι is implied with Philon as the subject. In this context, αvατίθημι would have the sacral meaning of 'set up, dedicate.' What is actually erected is not told, probably because it was obvious in its original setting, since the inscription possibly accompanied a monumental statue. The object, i.e. the receiver of the honour in question, is Herod – which is why the accusative is used. A freer translation following this would then be: "Philon, son of Aglaos, but by birth son of Nikonos, erected this (statue) in honour of Herod, son of Herod the King, tetrarch, his guest and friend". This inscription thus attests that Antipas had international connections just like his father before him, and that he occasionally visited the family of Nikonos on the island of Cos. Furthermore, it attests that in a non-Jewish context Antipas adapted to regular Greco-Roman practices.

This becomes more evident with the inscription from Delos. It was discovered by T. Homolle in 1878 in the *propylon* (a monumental roofed gateway) of the temple of Apollo, indicating "recognition of some sort of improvement" undertaken by Antipas (Noy, Panayotov and Bloedhorn 2004, 235). It is not known from other sources that Antipas provided funds for temples outside Palestine, though it would not be unprecedented since his father rebuilt the temple of Apollo at Rhodes (*War* 1.424). Unfortunately, the inscription was only preserved in a broken condition. It has also apparently been lost, making it difficult to assess the various reconstructions of its full text. As can be seen from table 2 below, a number of different texts have been proposed.

The major disagreements concern whether Ἀπόλλωνι should be inserted in line five, and whether the original inscription included the last lines following Ἀπόλλωνι. The last issue concerns the dating of the inscription. Noy et al. follow the restoration of M. Holleaux, while Dittenberger is closer to the original restoration of Homolle (cf. Noy, Panayotov and Bloedhorn 2004, 234). Schürer discards the lines altogether. For our purposes, the most interesting issue is the reading of line five. Since Ἀπόλλωνι is only a restoration, caution is warranted. What is certain is that the inscription accompanied a statue, which was erected in honour of Herod. It is also certain, given the location, that a connection existed to Apollo. The question is, however, whom the statue depicted. According to Kokkinos, it was a statue of Antipas himself (Kokkinos 1998, 137). The dative in Ἀπόλλωνι would then designate to whom the statue was dedicated. Another possibility would be to interpret the dative as an *instrumentalis*. Then it would designate by which means Antipas' was honoured, i.e. by a statue of Apollo. The third possibility, in accordance with Schürer, would be to discard the restoration completely. In this case it is still possible to follow the proposal of Kokkinos that the inscription accompanied a statue of Antipas himself placed in the temple of Apollo to be looked after by the god. In any case, the connection between Antipas and Apollo is certain, just as it is certain that Antipas was honoured as a benefactor (εὐεργέτης) for his activities in the temple.

Taken together, the two inscriptions point to some kind of international relations of Antipas, though possibly on a smaller scale than his father, for whom many more honorific inscriptions have been found (cf. the discussion in Richardson 1999, 203–211). As a natural part of these international connections, Antipas contributed to and took part in the activities connected to the Greco-Roman temples.

Dittenberger 1903, no. 417	Schürer 1901, 432	Noy et al. 2004, 234–235
Ὁ δῆμος ὁ Ἀ[θηναίων καὶ οἱ]	Ὁ δῆμος ὁ Ἀ[θηναίων καὶ οἱ]	Ὁ δῆμος ὁ Ἀθ[η]ν[αίων καὶ οἱ]
κατοι[κ]ο[ῦντες τὴν νῆσον]	κατοικο[ῦντες τὴν νῆσον]	κατοικοῦ[ντ]ε[ς] τὴ [ν νῆσον]
Ἡρῴδην βασιλέ[ως Ἡρῴδου υἱὸν]	Ἡρῴδην βασιλέ[ως Ἡρῴδου υἱὸν]	Ἡρῴδην βασιλέω[ς Ἡ]ρ[ῴδου υἱὸν]
τετράρχην ἀρετῆ[ς ἕνεκεν καὶ εὐνοί-]	τετράρχην ἀρετῆ[ς ἕνεκεν καὶ εὐνοί-]	τετράρχην ἀρετῆς [ἕνεκεν καὶ εὐνοί-]
ας τῆς εἰς ἑαυτοὺ[ς Ἀπόλλωνι	ας τῆς εἰς ἑαυτοὺ[ς... ἀνέθηκαν]	ας τῆς εἰς ἑαυτοὺ[ς Ἀπόλλωνι
ἀνέθηκαν]		ἀνέθηκαν?]
ἐπὶ ἐπιμ[ελητοῦ τῆς νήσου Ἀπολ]		ΣΤΗΣΕΙ[– – – – – – – – – – – – – –]
λωνίου		νῦν δὲ Κ[– – – – – – – – – – – – – –]
		ἐπὶ ἐπιμ[ελητοῦ τῆς νήσου
		Ἀπολλωνίου τοῦ Ἀπολ-]
		λωνίου Ῥα[μνουσίου – – – – – – – –]

Richardson 1999, 209	The Author's Translation	Noy et al. 2004, 234–235
The Athenian people and those living on the island, for Herod, son of Herod the King, Tetrarch on account of piety and good will shown to them when Apollonios, son of Apollonios of Rhamnous was *epimeletes*.	The A[thenian] people and those who live [on the island], [erected (the statue of) Apollo] for Herod, King [Herod's son,] tetrarch, because of piety and goodwill towards them, when Apollonios served as pro[curator of the island]	The Athenian people and those living on the island (honoured) Herod the tetrarch, son of King Herod, for his kindness and goodwill towards them, (and) dedicated to Apollo(?) ... now... in the time of the *epimeletes* of the island Apollonius (son) of Apollonius from Rhamnous

Table 2: The Delos inscription in various restorations and translations.

6.4.3 The Circulation of the Coins of Antipas

Obviously, Antipas did not issue many series, but how heavily did he mint each series, and how did it circulate? As already mentioned, Danny Syon's recent investigation provides a field study of all known coins from 186 places in Galilee and Golan from the Persian period to the Middle Roman, with special emphasis on the coins found in the Gamla excavations. Likewise, the coins of ten non-Galilean sites are investigated by way of comparison. Taken together, Syon is able to detect changes in the circulation patterns with important historical implications.

At the excavations in Gamla, 6,314 coins were found, of which 5,895 are identifiable. The most noticeable impact in the material culture was made by the Hasmoneans. 3,964 or 62.8% of the coins were Hasmonean. Only 304 or 4.8% are Herodian or from the Roman administration, whereas 610 or 9.7% are Seleucid, and 928 or 14.7% are Phoenician or autonomous (cf. figure 1 in Syon 2004, 27). Moreover, many of the non-Jewish coins were found in strata predating the Hasmonean period, in which a dramatic fall in the number of coins from Tyre is witnessed. As Syon notes, "during the years 126–98 BCE over 600 Tyrian coins arrive at the site, following 98 until 40 BCE only 14 coins from that city arrive!" (Syon 2004, 14). In the Early Roman period, the Hasmonean coinage continued to constitute the main part of the coins in circulation and the latest coins of Alexander Jannaeus continued to be "in heavy use for many decades after his death" (Syon 2004, 14). Altogether, Syon assesses that "compared to the enormous quantities of Hasmonean coins, the number of coins of *all* the coins of the house of Herod found at Gamla is very modest" (Syon 2004, 47). Regarding the coins of Antipas specifically, Gamla has actually yielded more specimens than anywhere else to date (altogether 61), representing all five series (cf. figure 19 in Syon 2004, 48). Since only 36 coins of Philip's were discovered, Syon asserts that the Jewish inhabitants of Gamla conducted more business with the Jewish Tiberias than with the pagan Paneas (Syon 2004, 246).

Syon's broad investigation of 186 excavated sites and kibbutz collections of coins offers an account of the coin distribution and circulation patterns in Galilee and the Golan divided into the following five subsequent periods: Ptolemaic (301–200 BCE), Seleucid (200–125 BCE), Hasmonean (125–63 BCE), Early Roman (63 BCE-70 CE), and Middle Roman (70–256 CE). Syon builds on the proposal of Kelly that the amount of minted copper coinage in a certain period reflects the scale of urbanization and level of monetization (Syon 2004, 162). It is therefore Syon's aim to determine what kinds of coins were in circulation, and to what extent. In general, Syon's investigation detects important changes in circulation only in the Hasmonean and Middle Roman periods and not in the Early Roman.

With the advent of the Hasmoneans "a dramatic change takes place" in the coin circulation (Syon 2004, 224). Map 19 (Syon 2004, 230, cf. figure 25) shows how the percentage of Hasmonean coinage is very high throughout the central Galilee and western Golan. Thus, "the creation of the Hasmonean state considerably reduced the demand for the bronze coinage of Akko-Ptolemais and that of Tyre" (Syon 2004, 233). In comparison with the Hasmonean period, "the changes in the Early Roman period are not great" (Syon 2004, 237). The fall in the circulation of non-Jewish coins continues due to the "tighter control of currency in the domains of Herod and Philip" (Syon 2004, 237). However, it is most interesting, as illustrated by figure 62 (Syon 2004, 191, 248, cf. figure 26), that only 723 coins were found from the entire Herodian dynasty, the Roman administration and the Great Revolt, compared with the 5,632 coins from the Hasmonean dynasty. Of these 723 coins, only 128 were from the Tiberian mint, including Antipas' coins (the majority) and coins from the later Roman administration (cf. figure 71 in Syon 2004, 248, cf. figure 27 below). The numbers indicate that Antipas' coinage was not the most common in circulation in early-first-century Galilee. Still, as map 28 and 29 show (cf. figure 28 and 29), it was widely distributed in both Upper and Lower Galilee as well as in the Golan (Syon 2004, 249).

Next to the change in the coin profile in the Hasmonean period, another major change in the coin circulation occurred in the Middle Roman period witnessing a

…quite dramatic rebounding in the share of the Phoenician mints in the coin circulation in Galilee, and especially that of Tyre. Coins of Sidon are now found at 25 sites as opposed to ten in the preceding period, though numerically it is still only 81 coins. Tyre is up from 31 to 64 sites and from 186 to 764 coins! (Syon 2004, 253)

Moreover, there was a dramatic rise in the total number of coins in circulation. This point is interpreted by Syon as evidence of an increased monetization of the economy: "Thus, in this period more than in any other, the coin distribution pattern is evidence of trade and commerce, or in other words, of the increased monetization of the economy" (Syon 2004, 256). And furthermore:

For period 5 (70–256 CE) the observable increase in both the quantity and the number of mints of bronze coinage can also be taken to confirm the argument for greater urbanization, reflected in greater division of labor, hence a greater need for 'small change'. This is in accord with what we know of the great urbanization undertaken in the East under the Severan dynasty. (Syon 2004, 263)

Syon's analyses have important bearings for the understanding of the mint of Antipas. First, the number issued was very modest. Antipas obviously did not mint out of market needs for small change, or if so, the need of the market was very small. Even after the foundation of Tiberias, the Hasmonean coinage supplemented with other Jewish as well as Roman coinage could supply the market with most of what was needed. Second, the distribution of the coins of Antipas indicates that they were widely used in both Upper and eastern Lower Galilee as well as in the lower Golan. In fact, in the Jewish village of Gamla, the coins of Antipas were preferred over the coins of Philip. Third, in general, the number of coins in circulation did not increase in Galilee in the Early Roman period. According to Syon, dramatic changes in circulation were instead experienced before, during the Hasmonean period,[204] and after, during the Middle Roman period, in which a dramatic rise in circulation was attestable. Thus, the proposal of Arnal that Antipas' new mint in Tiberias radically changed the circulation of coins in Galilee cannot be attested.[205] This is not to say that the economy was not monetized to a certain degree, but rather to point out that the specific impact of Antipas' minting efforts was modest.

6.5 Chapter Conclusions

The coinage of Herod Antipas takes its place within the late Second Temple period coinage, and analyzed within this context, the following may be concluded:

First, as far as we know at present, Herod Antipas minted five series of coins in three groups, to which must be added the single specimen detected by Hendin from Antipas' fourth regnal year. The first group consists of a single series released in his 24th regnal year connected to the foundation of Tiberias and featuring the name of the city on the reverse and a reed plant on the obverse. After a break of nine years, Antipas issued identical series in his 33rd, 34th and 37th regnal years distinguished only by the date. Compared to the first series, the sole change is a new image on the obverse now showing palm branches instead of reeds. The last series was issued in Antipas' 43rd regnal year, and was innovative in several ways: (a) A new honorific legend on the reverse featured Gaius' name in the dative. (b) Antipas' name on the obverse was changed from the genitive to the nomina-

---

[204] The radical rise in the circulation of Hasmonean coins in this period is also attested in the archaeological excavations at Yodefat and Cana, cf. Adan-Bayewitz and Aviam 1997, 160; Richardson 2002, 329; Edwards 2001, 110.

[205] The entire idea of Arnal that Antipas' fractional coinage could be used as a cheap way to collect taxes for Rome misconstrues the market value and intention of copper coinage, which was intended for daily transactions and not tax payment. For instance, it took 64 *prutot* to equal just one Roman silver *denarius* (cf. Hendin 2001, 32–37).

tive. (c) The different denominations were given different images on the obverse. While the palm branch still features on one-half and one-eighth of the denomination, the whole denomination displays a date palm with clusters, and one-quarter of the denomination displays a cluster of dates.

Second, the modest number of series issued was not counterbalanced by heavy minting. The most thorough study to date by Danny Syon discovered less than 128 provenanced coins of Antipas' mint in Tiberias. While the number of coins from Philip's mint in Paneas was also low (90), 511 coins of Herod the Great, Archelaos and the Roman administrators were counted in the area of Galilee and the Golan, and 5,632 coins from the Hasmonean dynasty. The paucity of Antipas' coins was noticed by Meshorer as well (cf. Meshorer 1982b, 41; Meshorer 2001, 85). At the same time, only 39 Roman imperial coins are recorded from the Early Roman period (Syon 2004, 249) restricting the coins in circulation in Galilee in this period, to mainly Hasmonean and thereafter Herodian and Roman coins. Although exact numbers are combined with great uncertainty such as the 'change factor' when excavating (not all coins are detected), the general picture in Syon's study is consistent: the reign of Herod Antipas did not lead to a rise in the amount of small change in circulation. Business was conducted as usual with Hasmonean coinage, and only in the following Middle Roman period did Galilee experience an intensified coin circulation including many Roman imperial coins (cf. Syon 2004, 255). According to Kelly, a process of intense urbanization would imply intensified circulation of small change. Following this thesis, the urbanization programme of Antipas did not demand more from the monetary situation than it was able to provide with the coins already in circulation, helped by the series minted by Antipas infrequently and in low numbers. Apparently, Antipas did not mint out of market needs – or if he did, it took only a modest number of coins to satisfy the need.

Third, the five series can be attributed to political reasons instead. As already noted, the first and the last series are probably connected to two events known from Josephus, i.e. the founding of Tiberias in honour of Tiberius, and Antipas' pledge of kingship from Gaius. The three mid-series might be connected to a political event too, namely Pilate's series of coins from the same years, underlining his provocative style and tendency to demonstrate his power.

Fourth, this being the case, it is worth noting which measures Antipas took to get a message across, and which he refrained from using. (a) Regarding the legends, Antipas continued the practice introduced by his father of only using Greek legends. In the first four series, he also followed his father's and Archelaos' examples of avoiding the emperor's name, while the reverse of his last series issued in 38/39 CE honours Gaius Germanicus. At that time, this practice was a well-established tradition on the coins of Philip, and Agrippa's first series released in 38 CE also features both the name and portrait of Gaius. While this new legend comes as a surprise and may be described as "a middle position" (cf. Schürer 1973, 343, note 16), it is equally surprising in view of the political situation that Antipas did not mint the image of the emperor as well, but confined himself to the obviously less flattering symbol of a palm tree. My suggestion is that Antipas' last series must be interpreted in connection with Agrippa's first series and the political circumstances described by Josephus (*War* 2.181–183; *Ant.* 18.240–255). (b) Regarding the images, Antipas clearly and unambiguously adhered to the aniconic tradition of the Jews by only using floral decoration. The symbols were chosen carefully. The reed of the first series was a clever move by Antipas. Staying within the aniconic ban, he managed to find a symbol that was a novelty in Jewish coinage, full of positive connotations of streams of water, durability and wisdom, uniting the two areas of his tetrarchy. Again, it is worth remembering what Antipas might have done in this situation. Taking into account that Tiberias was a tribute to his Roman patron, he could have included a portrait of Tiberius or a least his name on the commemorating series of coins. The second to fourth series feature a palm branch. As suggested by Strickert, these series could be connected to an ongoing contest for authority with Pilate, as witnessed in Philo (*Legat.* 299–305) and the New Testament (Luk 23:12). Both Pilate and Philip released series in the same years as Antipas struck his second and third series (28/29 and 29/30 CE). While Pilate depicted Roman religious symbols and Philip routinely depicted the image of the emperor, Antipas adhered to the aniconic ban and displayed a palm branch. According to Meshorer, this was probably done to convey a message of prosperity. The last series elaborated further on this theme by replacing the palm branch by a full-figure palm tree with dates on the largest denomination and a cluster of dates on one-quarter of the denomination. As already mentioned, considering the difficult political situation Antipas was placed in and how the first series of Agrippa boldly displayed the image of Gaius on the obverse and his three sister's on the reverse, it is all the more astonishing how anxious Antipas was to uphold the aniconic ban on his coins. Although the palm tree was beautifully crafted, it did not seem to serve its purpose well, if that indeed was to flatter Gaius. Antipas' wish to adhere to the aniconic ban is even more highlighted by the two known inscriptions from Cos and Delos testifying how he participated in the regular Greco-Roman cult practices in non-Jewish areas.

In conclusion, measured by the two main parameters of circulation and iconography/palaeography, the coins of Antipas are best described as modest, carefully adapted, and slightly insignificant. Before him, his father had issued a coin in Samaria with, at best, dubious pagan symbols. His brother Archelaos flooded the market with coins with maritime symbols not especially common in Jewish coinage up until then. His brother Philip launched several series of coins profoundly breaking with the tradition. Pilate issued coins displaying innovative symbols connected to Roman religion. Agrippa I launched a series of coins in his second regnal year that, although not widely circulated, were completely in line with the coins of Philip. Within this diverse situation, Antipas might be described as the leader who adhered most closely to the Jewish aniconic tradition, at least up until his last series, as illustrated in table 3. It is even likely that for the average Galilean user these coins would have entered the circulation fairly unnoticed, as just another edition of regular Jewish coinage with floral images. And even more so, Antipas' coins were minted in fairly low numbers and more probably for political reasons than due to market concerns.

	Hasmoneans	Herod I	Archelaos	Philip	Agrippa I	Pilate	Antipas
Hebrew/Aramaic legends	x						
Greek legends	x	x	x	x	x	x	x
Emperor's name				x	x	x	x
Animals		x			x		
Human images				x	x		
Temple facades				x	x		
Temple scenes					x		
Cultic emblems		(x)		x	x	x	

Table 3: The images and legends of the coins of Antipas in context.

Part III

Assessment

Chapter 7

Discussion and Synthesis

7.1 The Problem of Investigation in Perspective

What was the relationship between the reign of Herod Antipas and the socio-economic conditions of early-first-century Galilee? As announced in Part I, the present investigation attempts to answer this question through a source-oriented contextual approach in two stages. Part II has dealt with the first stage by analyzing the sources in their own context. Part III will focus on the second stage, the broad historical discussion and synthesis bringing together the different groups of sources that have been investigated. A dual approach will be implemented. First, the perspectives on Antipas present in the sources themselves will be discussed in accordance with the contextual approach. Thereafter, the specific problem under investigation concerning the socio-economic impact of Antipas' reign will be discussed. On this basis, the next and final chapter will evaluate the impact of the reign of Antipas, against the background of the approach taken throughout the study.

7.2 Descriptions of Herod Antipas in Perspective

The various written sources on the reign of Herod Antipas are largely concerned with two main issues: Antipas' outer relations to Rome, and Antipas' inner relations to his subjects and his character as a ruler. They will be dealt with in this order below.

7.2.1 The Outer Perspective – Herod Antipas as a Roman Client Ruler

Herod Antipas was a Jewish-Herodian client ruler of the Roman Empire. In an excellent analysis of the use of client rulers, or as he prefers to call them, *friendly* rulers, David Braund provides a number of interesting observations which are useful in trying to gain 'an outer perspective' on Antipas, in order to understand his abilities as a ruler from a Roman viewpoint. First, Braund's survey concludes that the preferred term was not "client" (*cliens*) but rather "friend" *(amicus)* or "ally/partner" (*socius*) if not simply "king" (*rex*, cf. Braund 1984, 7, 23–37). These titles reflected the fact that the most important element in the relationship between Rome (the Senate or the Emperor) and the friendly client ruler involved personal relations (patronage). For this reason, the children of the kings were sent to Rome to be raised in the circles of the ruling elite with the intention of continuing the personal relationships into the next generation (Braund 1984, 11). Throughout the reign it was of crucial importance for the king or ruler to uphold the personal relationship and the status of *amicus* or φίλος with the Emperor or the Senate. The ruler took great care to constantly renew his loyalty by providing signs of honour. Actually, according to Suetonius each of the kings under Augustus founded *Caesareas urbes* (Suet. Aug. 60, cf. Braund 1984, 107). In many cases, the imperial cult was connected to the city in the form of temples dedicated to Augustus or Rome, or in the form of festivals dedicated to the emperor, and the connection to Rome also generally implied a religious dimension (Braund 1984, 110–116).

Second, such a relationship to Rome mediated by friendship and deepseated reliance could save the king in times of crisis. There are several examples of incidents in which a king's enemies accused him before the emperor but were turned down for no other reason than the emperor's trust in the king (Braund 1984, 83). Likewise, it could have fatal consequences if the reliance was compromised, which could happen as a result of something the king had done (or not done), or as a consequence of the constantly changing policies in Rome bringing new people to power.

Third, an interesting point of Braund's is that tithes and taxes were not the primary interest of Rome, as often assumed. Rather, the friendly king was important for a large array of reasons: He provided a buffer against outer hostile kingdoms; he was capable of dealing with internal low-intensity threats such as bandits; he provided a reservoir of soldiers, weapons and money to be used in times of need; and from time to time he served as a bridgehead for further Roman expansion (Braund 1984, 91–99).

Herod Antipas and Augustus

When evaluating the rule of Antipas, it is important to recognize his Roman connection and obligation – after all, he was a son of Herod the Great who was sent to Rome for his education (*Ant.* 17.20). Antipas ruled under three emperors, and most of the literary sources we have on his reign are specifically interested in his relationship to these emperors, with the New Testament as the only exception. Under the reign of Augustus, the following is reported: first, Antipas was entrusted with the title of tetrarch and made ruler of Galilee and Perea. As testified by Josephus (*War* 2.20–32; *Ant.* 17.224–227) and Nicolaos (*FGrH* 90, frag. 136 §§ 8–11), this was less than he had hoped for, and judging from the sources available, it seems rather remarkable that Antipas did not win his case before Augustus: (a) He was designated as the sole heir in Herod the Great's last will before he became seriously ill and wrote his final will favouring Archelaos (*Ant.* 17.188). (b) He had a strong group of Herodian supporters led by Salome and Nicolaos' brother Ptolemy besides the advocate Irenaeus (*Ant.* 17.224– 227). (c) The Roman procurator of Syria, Sabinus also wrote a letter of support to Augustus (*War* 2.23). (d) Antipas may not have been actively supported by the Jewish delegation, but according to Nicolaos they preferred him instead of Archelaos as king (*FGrH* 90, frag. 136 § 9). (e) Most importantly, Antipas seemed to have had a good case, helped by Archelaos' brutal slaughter of the pilgrims in the temple. Nevertheless, as amply discussed by Hoehner (Hoehner 1972, 21–31), while there were several reasons why Augustus chose Archelaos as the main heir with the prospect of being king, the most obvious issue seems to have been that Augustus did not have faith in Antipas as the main heir and king of Herod the Great's old territory. Seemingly, Archelaos made a stronger impression on Augustus, since according to Josephus he had shown himself most worthy to have the kingdom in the eyes of the Emperor (ἀξιώτατον εἶναι τῆς βασιλείας, *Ant.* 17.248, cf. *War* 2.37).

Second, probably shortly after his inauguration as tetrarch in 4 BCE, Antipas made Sepphoris his capital and renamed it αὐτοκρατορίς, which was probably intended as a gesture of honour towards Augustus implying a reference to his Latin title, *Imperator* (*Ant.* 18.27). As noted by Josephus, Antipas also walled a city called Betharamptha and "renamed it Julias after the wife of the emperor" (Ἰουλιάδα ἀπὸ τοῦ αὐτοκράτορος προσαγορεύει τῆς γυναικός, *Ant.* 18.27). As discussed in note 53, it is not likely that Antipas' renaming of Sepphoris also implied an imposition of the cult of Augustus, as suggested by Feldman (Feldman 1981–1982, 51). There are no traces of this in the archaeological record, the numismatic evidence or the literary sources. Furthermore, if Antipas had done this in Sepphoris, he would probably have done it in Tiberias as well. Had that been the case, Josephus would probably have included it in the line of Antipas' other transgressions of the law.

Third, no full series of coins was issued by Antipas in this period. A recent discovery by D. Hendin suggests that Antipas minted a trial coin, which features his own name but not the emperor's (cf. section 6.4.1). In comparison, Archelaos continued the mint of his father in Judea, and Philip issued coins with emblems never seen before in Jewish coinage, including the facial portrait of Augustus (cf. section 6.3).

Fourth, no internal disturbance in Galilee proper is recorded from this period. The disturbances in Galilee that took place after the death of Herod the Great, seemingly coordinated by Judas son of Ezechias (*War* 2.56; *Ant.* 17.271–272), can naturally not be blamed on Antipas – although they struck a significant blow against Galilee, including the recapturing and razing of Sepphoris by the Romans (*War* 2.68; *Ant.* 17. 288). Nothing indicates that the disturbances orchestrated by Judas of Gamala or Judas the Galilean following the disposal of Archelaos took place outside Judea (*War* 2.117–118; *Ant.* 18.1–10).

Fifth and finally, there are indications in the sources that Antipas was part of the events surrounding the downfall of Archelaos. Perhaps he was accused along with Archelaos and Philip and had to bribe his way back to his tetrarchy (Strabo, *Geogr.* 16.2.44–45); or perhaps he took part in the delegation of Jews and Samaritans charging Archelaos (Dio LV.27.6, cf. section 4.2.2). Josephus briefly states in both *War* and *Antiquities* that Antipas and Philip kept their tetrarchies when Archelaos was deposed (*War* 2.167; *Ant.* 18.26–28).

Herod Antipas and Tiberius

Most of the events known from the reign of Antipas took place under Tiberius, and it is evident that Antipas managed to cultivate a good relationship to his new emperor. First, according to Josephus, Antipas was able to obtain the title of friend of the emperor, since he "advanced much before Tiberius in regard to friendship" (φιλία, *Ant.* 18.36, cf. section 3.4.2).

Second, Antipas showed his gratitude in at least two ways. For one thing, he founded a new city and named it Tiberias after his emperor. It is specifically mentioned how "he founded it in the best region of Galilee" (τοῖς κρατίστοις ἐπικτίσας αὐτὴν τῆς Γαλιλαίας, *Ant.* 18.36) by the Sea of Galilee, not far from the hot springs of Ammathus. Nevertheless, when assessing the city of Tiberias as 'a gift of honour,' an important perspective can be gained from cities founded by Herod the Great in honour of Augustus. In contrast to Herod's cities of Caesarea, Sebaste and Paneas, there is no reason to believe that Tiberias contained a temple for the emperor. Nor are there any indications of spectacles, though at the time of the war the city contained a stadium which might have been built by Antipas (*War* 2.618; *Life* 92, 331). In addition, Antipas issued four series of coins between 19 and 34 CE with the inscription TIBEPIAC on the reverse (cf. section 6.4.1). Once again, an important perspective can be gained through a comparison with the other Herodian rulers. Possibly out of concern for his Jewish subjects, Antipas refrained from minting the image of the emperor on his coins as was the normal custom throughout the Roman Empire. All the coins of Philip and most of the coins of Agrippa I featured the image of the emperor (cf. section 6.3.4 and 6.3.5).

Third, the good relationship proved itself beneficial for both Antipas and Tiberius. When Agrippa accused Antipas before Tiberius, he was turned down without any further investigation (*War* 2.178), and Tiberius immediately ordered Vitellius to declare war on Aretas and kill him if necessary after being informed by Antipas of Aretas' attack on the border (*Ant.* 18.113–115). In return, when Tiberius later succeeded in establishing peace negotiations with Parthia, Antipas played an instrumental role as the host of the meeting held on a bridge crossing the Euphrates (*Ant.* 18.96–105, cf. section 3.4.2).

Fourth, in the two cases where 'low-threat' internal disturbances are reported to have taken place, Antipas obviously managed the situation before it got out of hand, though reluctantly so, according to the New Testament. In the case of John the Baptist, it is clear from the analysis in section 3.4.3 that Josephus intends to present Antipas as an unlawful transgressor. Nevertheless, in the light of the obligations of a friendly client ruler it becomes evident that Josephus instead manages to paint a picture of a cautious ruler who took preventive steps to neutralize a possible uprising in its infancy. John had caused a gathering of a mob over which he had such a strong influence that it seemed willing to do whatever he said (*Ant.* 18.118). The accounts in the Gospels provide a different perspective, and explain Antipas' execution of John as a result of John's censure of his marriage to Herodias (Matt 14:3–5; Mark 6:17–19; Luke 3:19). Only Matthew mentions the crowd in this connection, stating that Antipas was actually reluctant to execute John out of fear of the crowd (θέλων αὐτὸν ἀποκτεῖναι ἐφοβήθη τὸν ὄχλον, 14:5). Nevertheless, despite his hesitation, from a Roman point of view Antipas was apparently able to solve the problem of John, since no further riots are reported. The same is true from one point of view in the case of Jesus. Though most of Jesus' activities took place in Galilee, and although the Gospels in numerous places describe how multitudes assembled around Jesus, Antipas was able for whatever reason (luck, cleverness or perhaps passiveness) to avoid a violent confrontation in his area. As discussed above, according to Matthew, Mark and Luke, Jesus perceived Antipas as a threat and took cautious steps to avoid a direct confrontation (cf. section 4.3.1). When the confrontation finally happened, the scene had changed to Jerusalem and the problem conveniently transferred to Pilate, who according to Luke 23 was unsuccessful in having the responsibility for the fate of Jesus re-transferred to Antipas.

Fifth and finally, in one instance the events got out of hand for Antipas and he had to ask his patron in Rome for help. His new marriage to Herodias became the excuse for his former father-in-law, Aretas, to declare war because of a border issue. On this occasion, the army of Antipas was destroyed (*Ant.* 18.113–115). As already mentioned, Tiberius dispatched

Vitellius to punish Aretas, but due to his sudden death the order was never carried out (*Ant.* 18.120–125).

Herod Antipas and Gaius Caligula

Under Gaius Caligula, two things are reported in the sources concerning Antipas' outer relations to Rome. First, Antipas issued his final series of coins in 38/39 CE. These coins differed remarkably from the preceding series in featuring the name of the emperor as a way to gain favour with Gaius (cf. section 6.4.1). The death of Tiberius had left Antipas in a fragile situation. Nevertheless, despite the attempt to impress Gaius with this new legend, Antipas must have found himself outperformed by Agrippa I, who issued his first series in the same year, in which the largest denomination features the name of Gaius Caligula and his portrait on the obverse, as well as honouring Gaius' three sisters, Julia, Drusilla and Agrippina on the reverse (cf. section 6.3.5).

Second, the final act of Antipas occurred when he sailed to Rome to ask Gaius for kingship. The event is a telling example of the importance of personal friendly relations between the emperor and the ruler, as described by Braund. Antipas lost his patron with the death of Tiberius, and was unable to gain the favour of the new emperor. Antipas obviously overstepped his capability in this fatal event. Even though Agrippa was not present in Rome himself, his letter of allegations presented by an envoy carried more weight than Antipas' personal attendance. Confidence in Antipas had evaporated, and he was unable to refute the charges, which according to Josephus included an old allegation for conspiracy with Sejanus against the government of Tiberius and a new one for conspiracy with the Parthian Artabanus against Gaius (*Ant.* 18.250, cf. section 3.4.2). Antipas' possession of armour for 70,000 soldiers was presented as evidence. It is not possible to determine whether these allegations were true or not. However, judging from Josephus himself it seems unlikely. Undoubtedly, Antipas cultivated relations to Sejanus as did anyone in the years of his supreme power until his execution by Tiberius in 31 CE, but Josephus himself does not report any troubles for Antipas when Sejanus fell. On the contrary, Tiberius had enough confidence in Antipas to use him in the peace negotiations with Parthia, and to trust his report in a way that rendered Vitellius' report superfluous – to his great irritation (*Ant.* 18.104–105). Moreover, it does not seem credible, judging from Josephus, that Antipas would have undertaken such a high-risk affair to ask Gaius for kingship if he was conspiring with Parthia at the same time. The armour could easily have been stored for the benefit of the Roman army at a time of need. It seems most likely from Josephus' description that Antipas simply lost his base of friendship in Rome. While this friendship had previously safeguarded Antipas against possible allegations, its loss was now fatal, and thus dubious statements were used against him.

Herod Antipas: A Minor Roman Client Ruler

To sum up, when assessing the life and reign of Herod Antipas, it is important to remember that the sources focus to a large extent on his relationship to the Roman emperors. As discussed above, the success of a ruler or king under Roman patronage was determined first and foremost by his ability to cultivate a strong friendship with the emperor and the powerful people in the circles around the emperor. This dependency was not fostered primarily (if at all) by taxes and tithes, but by signs of honour such as dedicated cities, temples, coins and festivals, by the ability to keep 'low-threat' up-risings in check, by keeping the outer borders calm, by providing assistance of various kinds when the need arose, ranging from armour to logistics and diplomacy. Although the sources are either scant and to some extent accidental (archaeological sources), or by their nature biased (textual sources), the present investigation warrants the conclusion that from a Roman point of view, Antipas was a minor client ruler, unremarkable in both greatness and cruelty (in contrast to his father), without obvious qualities or capabilities deserving promotion. This is not to say that Antipas was an incompetent or bad ruler. In contrast to his brother Archelaos, for instance, he ruled his area for the lengthy period of 43 years – in which time no serious upheavals are reported but rather internal investments were conducted. Similarly, on at least one occasion, according to Josephus, he played a role in a major international peace negotiation between Rome and Parthia. However, due to the following four considerations, Antipas was obviously viewed as, and treated like, a less important ruler.

First, Antipas was never promoted, and in no less than four instances he was bypassed for an obvious opportunity: (a) In the year 4 BCE, when Augustus decided which will of Herod's to follow, Antipas was not made sole heir and king. (b) In the year 6 CE, when Archelaos was removed, Antipas was not promoted to rule over his area as well. Instead a whole new institution of Roman prefects was inaugurated. Although the evidence concerning this event leaves many questions unanswered, it seems likely that both Antipas and Philip were involved. According to Strabo they almost even lost their realms. Antipas was not even given the right to appoint high priests, which had been in the hands of the Herodians since Herod the Great (cf. *Ant.* 18.92). From 6 CE the Romans controlled the high priesthood until Agrippa I took over (*Ant.* 19.292–298). Upon his death, the right was transferred to Herod of Chalcis and successively to Agrippa II (*Ant.* 20.15–16, 104, 138, 179, 196–197, 203) who both reigned outside Jerusalem – as did Antipas. (c) In the year 34 CE, when Philip died, Antipas did not receive his realm even though Antipas was ostensibly on good terms with Tiberius. Instead, Tiberius arranged that the legate of Syria should govern the area while the tribute was kept stored until a permanent solution could be found (*Ant.* 18.108). (d) Finally, when Antipas daringly asked for kingship himself, he was turned down by Gaius, deprived of his status and property, and exiled.

Second, from a Roman point of view Antipas showed himself to be a mediocre if not directly bad politician in at least three instances: (a) In the case of his marriage to Herodias, Antipas had obviously not calculated the risks beforehand, and the event resulted in a regional conflict that Antipas was unable to resolve without Roman assistance from the Syrian legate Vitellius (*Ant.* 18.109–115). (b) In connection with the peace treaty with Parthia, Antipas was incautious enough to jeopardize the relationship to his nearest superior and protector, Vitellius (*Ant.* 18.101–105). (c) Finally, Antipas had once again not calculated the risks when he travelled to Rome to ask for kingship. This time he lost not only his army, but his entire realm (*War* 2.181–183; *Ant.* 18.240–255).

Third, in the one instance when Antipas is reported to have conducted a war, he proved to be a less than mediocre strategist of warfare, and his entire army was destroyed due to an internal mutiny by some refugees from the territory of Philip, who had been enrolled in the army of Antipas (*Ant.* 18.114).

Fourth and finally, the question is whether Antipas could have done *less* to cultivate friendships with the three emperors during his rule. Neither Sepphoris nor Tiberias were equipped with temples dedicated to the emperor cult, and no reports of regular festivals to the honour of the emperor are given. Both customs were regularly observed in the new cities built by Herod the Great. Likewise, the iconography on the coins of Antipas was rather subdued compared to the coins of Philip and Agrippa, at least, but possibly to the dated series of Herod the Great as well. In a non-Jewish context, however, at least the inscription at Delos testifies that Antipas took part in the regular Greco-Roman cult (cf. section 6.4.2), which he ostensibly avoided in a Jewish context.

Thus, judging from the sources available the only possible conclusion seems to be that the Romans viewed Antipas as a ruler of minor importance. On the positive side, Antipas was able to keep his area relatively calm for 43 years, and in one instance he was granted a certain role in the peace negotiations with Parthia. But on the negative side, he was a mediocre politician, war strategist and builder to whom Rome was not prepared to entrust a larger realm.

7.2.2 The Inner Perspective – Herod Antipas and His Jewish Subjects

The second obvious inherent perspective in the sources on Antipas concerns his 'inner relationship' to his Galilean subjects and to Jerusalem. This issue is clearly on the agenda for Josephus and the New Testament, just as the iconography of Antipas' coins is significant in this respect. There are also a few other written sources that describe Antipas' relations to Jerusalem. Finally, it is relevant in this connection to consider whether the material sources give evidence of a subtle covert resistance.

Josephus

As discussed in chapter three, Josephus has an interest in presenting the relationship between the rulers of the Herodian house and the Jews as negative. This is especially true in the case of Herod the Great, who functions in *Antiquities* as Josephus' prime example of how kingship leads to corruption, cruelty and impiety. In several editorial remarks (cf. 14.274; 15.266–267, 328; 16.150–159; 17.180–181, 191–192; 18.127–129 and elsewhere), Josephus explicitly censures Herod as a cruel tyrant who profoundly violated the Jewish laws by the introduction of new ideas and practices. According to Josephus, Herod was eventually one of the causes of the destruction of the temple (*Ant.* 15.267, 281). It is also interesting to note that in the eyes of Josephus, the fourth philosophy represented a similar negative position. In the important paragraphs of *Ant.* 18.1–10, Judas and his followers are accused of the introduction of new ideas otherwise unknown in Judaism (18.9, cf. *War* 2.118), and of unprecedented cruelty (*Ant.* 18.18.6–8) which eventually led to the destruction of the temple (18.8, cf. 20.166). In contrast, Josephus emphasizes that Agrippa I was no innovator or violator of Jewish practices and beliefs. Instead, his pious and just life represents the hope of the Jews that God is able to raise what has fallen if the utmost respect is paid to the old Jewish way of life (19.293–296, 331, cf. section 3.3.7).

It is within this broader framework that Josephus presents his stories of Antipas, focusing largely on Antipas' relationship to the Jewish nation and religion as discussed in detail above (cf. section 3.4.3). The interesting thing is that Josephus, especially in *Antiquities,* judges Antipas negatively while revealing enough details to soften the negative picture of Antipas by explaining his acts as sound. On the one hand, the founding of Tiberias is judged as being against the law because it was built on graves (*Ant.* 18.36). The same applies to Antipas' marriage to Herodias (18.136) and his execution of John the Baptist, at least in the eyes of the Jews (18.116–119). The most explicit verdict of Antipas is given in connection with his downfall, which is interpreted as an infliction by God for his and Herodias' impious acts (18.255). Finally, it is important to note that Josephus' only series of events with Antipas as the subject (*Ant.* 18.101–129) deliberately contrasts him to Philip (18.106–108) and Agrippa I (18.129), who are both described as moderate, pious and just rulers.

On the other hand, there are a couple of open ends in this picture of Antipas. Josephus' story about the foundation of Tiberias seems ambivalent. The people dragged to live there are described as former slaves or tenants subjected to Antipas who actually received plots of land and fully furnished houses in Tiberias as compensation, granting Antipas the role of benefactor (18.38). Similarly, the problem of the graves did not prevent Josephus from entering the city during the war as described on several occasioins in *Life*. Furthermore, the text on John the Baptist is not entirely coherent when it comes to the role of Antipas. As discussed above, Josephus actually manages to present a rather clear-cut picture of an event in which the friendly client ruler had to intervene. Josephus also informs us that on one occasion at least Antipas took part in the celebrations in Jerusalem (18.122). Most importantly, it seems that although Antipas is presented as another bad ruler from the Herodian house, Josephus is unable to present any truly indisputable examples of tyranny and cruelty as he does in the cases of Herod the Great and Archelaos. Finally, no riots are caused by bad government or introduction of new ideas ascribed to the reign of Antipas as in the case of Pilate (cf. section 3.3.5) except for the riot long after the death of Antipas during the war of 66–70 CE caused by the images of living animals in his palace (*Life* 64–69).

The New Testament

Of the other written sources on Antipas, only the New Testament has preserved traditions that include specific descriptions of Antipas. However, as discussed in chapter four, the Gospels are not interested in Antipas in general – they only intend to describe how he related to two specific subjects. Rome is not mentioned. To sum up, the picture of Antipas is one of an ambiguous and perplexed ruler who on the one hand is fascinated by John and Jesus, but on the other perceives them as threats. First, the fascination bordering on perplexity is expressed in several places: (a) The rumours of the activities of Jesus make Antipas wonder if he could be John resurrected. While Luke maintains Antipas' astounded reaction as a question (9:7–9), Mark (6:14–16) and Matthew (14:1–2) present it as a statement. Although it could be interpreted as a sarcastic statement, as Hoehner does (Hoehner 1972, 190), it is more likely that the Gospels in this way deliberately portray Antipas as perplexed when confronted with the message of Jesus (cf. 4.3.1). (b) The report in Mark 6:20 of Antipas' interrogation of John also emphasizes that Antipas was fascinated by John, saying that Antipas gladly listened to John although he became greatly perplexed (πολλὰ ἠπόρει). (c) Furthermore, both Mark and Matthew state that Antipas was saddened by the request for John's head (Matt 14:9; Mark 6:26). (d) While the Gospel of Luke does not mention any fascination for John, it does say that Antipas was fascinated by Jesus. In 9:7 Antipas is said to be perplexed (διηπόρει) about the reports he had received on Jesus, for which reason he wanted to meet him (9:9). When that eventually happens in 23:8, we are told that Antipas became exceedingly glad (ἐχάρη λίαν). Finally, it has been argued in accordance with Darr and Hoehner (cf. section 4.3.3) that the role allotted to Antipas by Luke 23 in the conviction of Jesus is very modest (cf. Pilate's reaction in 23:15). Antipas could not find any proper reasons for convicting Jesus. He was perplexed by what he saw, and therefore returned Jesus to Pilate.

Second, the Gospels also share the description of Antipas as a threat to John and Jesus: (a) Unlike Mark, Matthew directly states that it was not only Herodias but also Antipas who wanted to kill John (14:5). (b) Mark states that the Herodians and the Pharisees wanted to kill Jesus (3:6), just as Jesus warns against "the yeast of Herod" (8:15). (c) In both Mark and Matthew it seems that the execution of John forced Jesus to alter his public appearance. Matthew 14:13 explicitly states that Jesus departed to a place of solitude upon being informed of the execution of John. Likewise, both Mark and Matthew have Jesus on a constant journey after this event without any public preaching of the Kingdom of God. (d) Antipas' enmity to John and Jesus is more pronounced in Luke. Following the analysis of Darr, Luke presents Antipas as an evil ruler who persecutes the prophet. Unfortunately, no examples are given of the asserted evilness of Antipas in 3:19, except for the imprisonment of John and later on the stated wish of Antipas to kill Jesus (13:31). Although his role in the final conviction of Jesus seems to have been limited, the picture of Antipas is genuinely negative as a despotic ruler who became one of those outside the Kingdom of God who both saw and heard but did not perceive (8:10). (e) Finally, the enmity between Antipas and the young Jesus movement might be further emphasized by the fact that none of the Gospels mention any contact between the two cities of Sepphoris and Tiberias and Jesus and his followers. Freyne argues that this lack of references cannot be incidental. According to him, the most obvious solution is not lack of success in these areas or avoidance of gentile areas, since the latter is attested in several places in the Gospels, and since a lack of success would likely have been followed by a series of woes as in the case of Chorazin, Bethsaida and Capernaum. Rather, the key is to be found in Matthew 11:7–8 and Luke 7:24–25, where not only the negative connotation of the reed is referenced to Antipas (Matt 11:7, cf. 6.4.1), but also the chastisement of those dressed in luxurious dresses (μαλακοῖς ἠμφιεσμένον, Matt 11:8) and living in the palaces of the kings (τοῖς οἴκοις τῶν βασιλέων, Matt 11:8, cf. τοῖς βασιλείοις, Luke 7:25, cf. Freyne 1994, 84; Freyne 1995, 610–620; Freyne 2004, 144–145 and others). However, as noted above, Reed argues on the other hand that the use of urban metaphors on several occasions in the Gospels makes it implausible that the cities were loci of animosity (cf. section 1.2.2).

Nevertheless, it seems that the main tendency in the Gospels is to paint a deliberately ambiguous picture of Antipas. He was not as decisive as his father (Matt 2:3–18). Instead, he was fascinated and perplexed by John and Jesus, while simultaneously posing a threat to them as an unpredictable ruler – a "fox" who strikes in a more unanticipated way than the lion. In Luke, this perspective on Antipas is used to emphasize both the innocence and the greatness of John and Jesus. Not even this unpredictable ruler, who had already killed John, and who apparently wanted to kill Jesus as well, could find him guilty of the religio-political charges brought against him by the Jewish leaders (cf. section 4.3.4).

The Internal Power Balance of Jerusalem

Another interesting issue in the written sources concerns Antipas' relations to Jerusalem and his part in the internal power struggle between Pilate and the Sanhedrin. Throughout the late Second Temple period, it is possible to observe continued tensions if not direct violent clashes between the different rulers, backed by the military power and the religious groups of Jerusalem. While the Hasmoneans were able to checkmate some of this tension by seizing both the office of the High Priesthood and the royal throne, this was not an option for the Herodian family, who were forced to find a new mode of co-existence and co-operation. For this reason Herod the Great took control over the appointment of high priests, which immediately brought him into confrontation with his Hasmonean family in-laws and led to his killing of the young high priest Alexander (*Ant.* 15.23ff.). Josephus also relates that Herod safeguarded the vestments of high priests in order to control possible uprisings (*Ant.* 18.91–92). The internal power balance in Jerusalem was also an important element behind the violent protests against Herod's introduction of standards in the theatre of Jerusalem and a golden eagle in the temple (cf. section 3.3.2). Who has the right to control the correct Jewish way of life? Judging from Josephus and Nicolaos, it was precisely this power struggle that Archelaos got caught up in. He was unable to gain the confidence of all the factions involved, and eventually caused a massacre in the temple itself. For this reason, a delegation of Jewish leaders rejected him as king after Herod (Nicolaos, *FGrH* frag. 136 § 9; *War* 2.80–92; *Ant.* 17.299–314), and was eventually successful (*War* 2.111; *Ant.* 17.342–344). From the first period of Roman administration (6–41 CE), detailed traditions are preserved solely regarding Pilate. The reason is precisely this: Pilate touched upon the power balance in Jerusalem by introducing standards in Jerusalem, by placing votive shields in his palace in Jerusalem, and by financing the construction of an aqueduct with money from the temple treasury (cf. section 3.3.5). As mentioned above, in this period the appointment of high priests was in the hands of the Romans (cf. *Ant.* 18.26, 34–36, 95, 123 and elsewhere), as were the vestments until Vitellius restored them to the high priest (*Ant.* 18.93–95). Furthermore, according to Josephus the "greatness" of Agrippa I was also connected to his relationship to Jerusalem. Agrippa is praised for his deep-felt loyalty to the temple, and eventually he gained control over the high priesthood (*Ant.* 19.292–298). When Agrippa died, the right to appoint high priests was transferred by Claudius to his brother King Herod of Chalcis (*Ant.* 20.15–16), and upon his death it passed on to Agrippa II, first when he received his uncle Herod's realm (20.104), and later when he was transferred to Philip's old realm (20.138). It is thus interesting to note that during the second period of Roman administration of Judea (44–66 CE), the mandate to appoint high priests was not in the hands of the Roman procurators. For this reason Felix at one time had a high priest poisoned to death because he did not have the authority to remove him (20.162–166) as Agrippa II could (cf. 20.179, 196–197, 203 and elsewhere). Josephus also includes several stories about Agrippa II in which the central core is the power balance between him and the various leading groups of Jerusalem, such as the story of the wall built by the priests to block Agrippa's view of the temple platform from his palace (*Ant.* 20.189–196), and the story of Ananus' stoning of James, the brother of Jesus (20.197–203, cf. Bilde 2005).

As discussed above (cf. section 4.4), it is highly interesting to see how the written sources in several places touch upon Antipas' relation to Jerusalem, and on how he played a role in the fight for power between the various groups. According to Nicolaos, Philo, Luke and Josephus, Antipas managed to gain a positive relationship to the leading Jews of Jerusalem, who wanted him as their king if they could not be ruled directly from Rome (Nicolaos, *FGrH* 90, frag. 136 § 9). They also later included him as a member of the delegation sent to Pilate to complain over his introduction of votive shields in his palace in Jerusalem (Philo, *Legat.* 300). Antipas himself visited Jerusalem for at least two feasts, during which (according to Josephus) he took part in the offerings in the temple (*Ant.* 18.122–123), and (according to Luke) he received accusations from the leading Jews against Jesus (23:10). Thus, on the one hand, Antipas played a certain role in the power balance of Jerusalem, and was able to cultivate a constructive relationship to the Jewish leaders and to avoid religiously based upheavals of the scale witnessed during Herod the Great's and Archelaos' rule. However, on the other hand, it seems to confirm what was discussed above that

Antipas was only successful to a certain degree. Justin's statement that An-
tipas took over the ἐξουσία of Archelaos can only be confirmed partially
(*Dial.* 103.4). Antipas did not receive the right to appoint the high priests
or the custody of the vestments as did the later Herod of Chalcis and
Agrippa II, who like Antipas did not have the actual political primacy in
Jerusalem (*Ant.* 20.15–16, 104, 138, 179, 196–197, 203).

The Coinage

Coins are important for the two reasons of iconography and circulation.
While their circulation reveals information on the monetization of a society, which will be discussed in the next paragraph, their iconography reveals information about which messages the minter wanted to send. In a
Jewish context, and especially in the late Second Temple period, this issue
was connected with concerns for the second commandment against images.
As discussed above, evidence from both archaeological material and
Josephus confirms that this ban was observed as a ban against three things:
living creatures, symbols of idolatry and holy objects from the temple (cf.
section 6.2.1). As a consequence the iconography used on coins was a sensitive matter in a Jewish context, and although both the Hasmonean and the
Herodian rulers only minted fractional copper coinage which was often of
poor workmanship, the coins were nevertheless used, at times even to a
wide extent, as tools of propaganda by both the Hasmoneans and the
Herodians.

Besides the still valuable Hasmonean coinage, the coins in circulation at
the time of Antipas included Herod the Great's coins, some of which had a
dubious pagan character (cf. section 6.3.2); Archelaos' coins with maritime symbols intended to communicate his superiority (cf. section 6.3.3);
and Philip's coins introducing legends and symbols not seen on Jewish
coins before, including the facial portrait of himself besides the emperors
Augustus and Tiberius, and the façade of the temple in Paneas (cf. section
6.3.4). The coins of Pilate also introduced symbols not seen before in this
area, namely the *simpulum*, a ladle used in the temples by the Roman
priests, and the *lituus,* an augural staff functioning as an emblem of the
Roman priests (cf. section 6.3.6). Finally, the same year as Antipas issued
his last series, Agrippa issued his first series, on which he proudly presented his patron in Rome, Gaius, on the obverse, and the portrait of
Gaius' three sisters on the reverse (cf. section 6.3.5). Thus, as illustrated in
table 3, the ban against images was apparently violated by several emissions in circulation in this period. The interesting thing is that it is possible
to connect the iconographic innovations to specific historical circumstances. In the period before Jerusalem and his throne was secured, Herod
the Great needed to issue coins with a strong connection to his Roman pa-

trons, just as Antigonus in Jerusalem issued equally innovative coins featuring holy utensils from the temple, such as the menorah (cf. section
6.3.1). Archelaos needed to substantiate his authority as the main heir controlling the international naval trade routes. In connection with Strickert's
analysis, it is also possible to see the coins of Philip and Pilate issued the
same years as part of an internal stuggle for authority and the favour of Tiberius. Finally, it seems obvious to connect Agrippa's first series with his
ongoing successful attempt to cultivate a strong relationship to Gaius.

How did Antipas enter into this competition on propaganda? Two things
are important in this connection. On the one hand, Antipas did not issue
more than five series in his 43 years of reign, the first of which was not issued until his 24th regnal year (19/20 CE), and in total he only issued a
small number of coins. On the other, the investigation above revealed that
Antipas' coins were also well designed to send specific messages even
though they strictly observed the ban against prohibited images. His first
series was issued to commemorate the founding of Tiberias, and following
the analyses of Meshorer and Theißen it was a brilliant move to display the
reed on the obverse of these coins. As a novelty in Jewish coinage, the
reed could send a strong message of water, fertility and durability, while at
the same time observing the ban against images. Antipas' next three series
are identical except for the date. It is interesting to note that they were issued in the same period as Pilate and Philip minted series. It is possible
that Antipas was also trying to reinforce his authority in the struggle for
power and favour. However, unlike Pilate and Philip, Antipas still did not
display forbidden images but confined himself to replace the reed by a
palm branch, which was a well-known symbol on both Hasmonean and
Herodian coinage. According to Meshorer, the change from the reed to the
palm branch might have been a way to communicate the prosperous development of Tiberias with cultivated farm land. Antipas' anxiety to observe
the ban against images is best illustrated in his last series. This emission
was probably one of the initial attempts made by Antipas to gain favour
with Gaius before asking for kingship (*Ant.* 18.246). For this reason, Antipas changed the legends. His own name on the obverse is changed from a
genitive modus to a nominative, while the reverse for the first time features
the name of the emperor kept in the dative tantamount to the translation:
"Herod the Tetrarch to Gaius Caesar Germanicus." However, as mentioned, this honorific legend paled in comparison with Agrippa I's coin
from the same year featuring the image of Gaius himself. Antipas' worries
concerning the ban against images on his coins are put in perspective by
the fact that he broke the ban on at least two other occasions. His palace in
Tiberias was graced with figures of living creatures (*Life* 65), and at Delos
he was honoured for his benefactions bestowed on the temple of Apollo

(cf. section 6.4.2). Thus, Antipas' adherence to the ban against images was not grounded in personal preferences, but in concerns for his Jewish subjects.

Therefore, the coins of Antipas seem to describe a ruler who was sensitive about not offending his subjects with forbidden iconographic material even in a politically extremely stressed situation. At the same time, they also describe a ruler who was only able to (or only cared to) issue a very modest number of coins in an average to low quality of workmanship. It follows that it is out of context and a gross exaggeration when Horsley and Silberman interpret Antipas' coins as expressing messianic dreams (cf. section 6.1). On the contrary, Antipas' coins were very much adjusted to the situation, and while the political messages of the iconography were understood by some, most of the Galilean users would probably have seen nothing more than just another edition of regular Jewish coin minting. Antipas did not break any barriers with his coins, which probably entered market circulation almost unnoticed.

Evidence from the Material Culture – A Covert Mode of Resistance?

The archaeological material is also important when assessing the internal relations between Antipas and his subjects. In this connection, it is advantageous to treat the material culture from two perspectives, distinguishing between the private sphere and the public sphere. In this way, it is possible to detect whether a specific culture evolved hidden in the private sphere indicating covert resistance against the system. As discussed in the next paragraph, when summarizing the picture available of Galilee's public sphere, it seems unequivocal that Antipas did not cause a degree of Hellenization similar to that occurring in Caesarea Maritima, for instance. When evaluating the public sphere, it is also interesting that Antipas did not build an extensive system of fortifications and strongholds in Galilee. Presumably, he did not feel the need to build hideaways as did his father (cf. Richardson and Edwards 2002, 254; Aviam 2004b, 103ff.; Moreland 2004, 43).

Regarding the private sphere, several studies have pointed to possible evidence of a covert mode of resistance in the material culture of Galilee. Richardson and Edwards define potential expressions of covert resistance to be: "insistence on using a language different from those in power, dressing in a manner that stresses allegiance to one's own group, using particular forms of pottery or artifacts or textiles, and emphasizing one's religion and tradition" (Richardson and Edwards 2002, 248). They point to the attestation of widespread use of Hasmonean coins, *mikvaoth,* stone vessels, and the absence of pig bones as "indications of efforts to establish a special identity against very powerful outside cultural influences" (Richardson and Edwards 2002, 250). More or less the same list is given by Reed and Crossan, who also emphasize that distinct features in the private sphere are indicators of a covert mode of resistance (Crossan and Reed 2001, 136–172). These are often referred to as identity markers, and as discussed in section 1.1.2, they were not confined to Galilee or to the first century CE for that matter, but were a feature of the late Second Temple period throughout the period from the Hasmoneans to the destruction of the temple. The question is, nevertheless, whether the use of these markers was intensified in the early first century.

In two recent articles (Berlin 2002; Berlin 2004) as well as in a forthcoming book (Berlin forthcoming), Andrea M. Berlin argues for a notable change in the patterns of the household pottery in this period. Her studies are based mainly on a detailed analysis of the pottery of Gamla, which she is in charge of publishing, but she also provides a further comparison of patterns in pottery between the regions of Golan, Galilee, Qumran and upper-class Jerusalem. The two articles are centred on two issues: a factual counting and comparison of the pottery, and a superimposed interpretation of its political and religious implications. Regarding the first, Berlin argues for an abrupt change in some parts of the material culture from first-century BCE to first-century CE, and for a regional difference between on the one hand Gentile cities in the perimeter of Galilee and upper-class Jerusalem, and on the other hand Galilee proper, Golan and rural Judea. In these last three places, the import of mould-made lamps and red-slipped pottery, the *Eastern Terra Sigillata* (ETS), comes to a complete stop. Instead, illumination was provided by plain knife-pared 'Herodian'-style lamps without any decoration, just as dinner was served with plain locally produced tableware (Berlin 2004, 17ff.; Berlin 2002, 59, 67).[206] Table 4.1, 4.2 and 4.3 as well as figure 4.1 in Berlin 2002, 60ff. summarizes how Jewish sites as Yodefat, Capernaum, Bethsaida and Gamla all had ETS tableware and fancy mould-made lamps in the first century BCE, whereas the import of this came to a complete stop in the first century CE. In the pagan and mixed sites investigated, Tel Anafa, Pella, Caesarea Philippi and Sepphoris, both elements continue into the first-century CE:

---

[206] Illustrations of mould-made lamps vs. plain knife-pared lamps are provided in Berlin 2004, 18. Photos of red-slipped plates and bowls vs. plain locally made tableware are provided in Berlin 2004, 27. The knife-pared lamps are especially interesting due to their outspoken lack of decoration: "Compared to just about all other lamps made and used in the eastern Mediterranean (including Italian imports), knife-pared lamps were distinctive and instantly recognizable by virtue of one particular aspect: they carried no decoration save for an occasional line or impressed circles on the nozzle" (Berlin 2004, 19).

Whereas the people living in Gentile and mixed sites continued to import red-slipped table vessels and mold-made lamps (now of early Roman rather than late Hellenistic
styles), Jews stopped. Instead, Galilean Jews set their tables exclusively with locally
manufactured, small, undecorated buff-colored saucers and bowls and white chalk vessels, and lit their homes with wheel-made knife-pared lamps. (Berlin 2004, 63)

However, the more detailed study of 2004 reveals that Gamla is the only
place from which Berlin has exact numbers being part of the team herself.
Judging from the amount of fragments, a first-century BCE household of
Gamla would have owned seven to nine ETS dishes, and though that number is reduced to none in the subsequent period, 4,000 fragments of the
same tableware were found in a single house alone at Tel Anafa in Upper
Galilee indicating the use of a substantially larger amount of tableware
(Berlin 2004, 28). Thus, for the red-slipped ware, the change in pattern is
more like going from almost none to absolutely none in the place where
exact numbers are available, which is not the case for the three other sites
(Berlin 2004, 29). Berlin also compares this data with data available from
upper-class Jerusalem. Here no change in import patterns can be established. The inhabitants of the Upper City continued to display their wealth
through decorated dining rooms with geometric designs and architectural
painting (the 'Pompeian Second Style', cf. Berlin 2004, 33), imported fine
ware, as well as heavily decorated burials. In conclusion:

In the first century C.E., Jerusalem's wealthy residents entertained in formal dining
rooms of Hellenistic style, prepared Roman dishes in Italian-style pans, and used beautifully decorated serving dishes and individual place settings. They also built elaborate,
public display tombs whose large courtyards and impressive façades provided a classiciz-
ing backdrop for opulent funeral ceremonies. Formal dining and elaborate funerals were
practices previously confined to Judean royalty – both the Hasmonean kings and Herod,
in the first century B.C.E. Their adoption by Jerusalem's elites likely accompanied and
fostered a sense of social superiority. At this same time Jews in Galilee and Gaulanitis
chose to live by a very different cultural ethic, in which even a few decorated serving
vessels had no place. (Berlin 2004, 50)

Berlin acknowledges that the difficult part is to explain why these changes
took place, and accordingly she presents more than one scenario. In her article from 2002, Berlin argues for a deliberate element of "anti-
Romanization" in Galilee around the takeover of Philip and Antipas. Up
until then there is evidence of trade with the cities of the Phoenician coast,
although political relations had been negative for a long time. But "the
change, abrupt and consistent, occurs towards the end or just after the rule
of Herod the Great" (Berlin 2002, 67). While some aspects of Roman life
were adopted, such as interior stucco and painting at Gamla and Yodefat
(Berlin 2004, 69), as a covert mode of resistance at least two elements
were left out of the private sphere:

I suggest that these fancy household items, often the only foreign and certainly the most noticeable goods found in a typical household assemblage, performed a convenient communicative role. Those bright, shiny red-slipped table vessels would be immediately visible within the small and simply planned first century B.C.E. and C.E. houses. As a manifestation of foreign and, I suggest, now specifically Roman, control, Galilean Jews rejected them. By this, they made a political statement of solidarity and affiliation with a traditional, simple, unadorned, Jewish lifestyle, as well as demonstrating a unified opposition to the newly looming Roman presence. (Berlin 2002, 69)

However, the more detailed study of 2004 adds a new aspect. In the mid-first century BCE, slightly before the termination of import of foreign tableware, it is already possible to observe that specific items gained popularity forming a distinct 'household Judaism':

From the early-mid first century B.C.E., Jews throughout these regions adopted what I have called 'household Judaism' – using cooking vessels produced by Jewish potters, locally manufactured oil and wine, and, in some places, neighborhood *mikva'ot* (ritual baths) – all of which allowed people to incorporate a religious sensibility into their daily lives. At the end of the first century B.C.E. and in the early first century C.E., they began using stone dishes and plain, knife-pared oil lamps as markers of religious identity. (Berlin 2004, 46)

Finally, her most recent study suggests a different explanation. It was not only the fancy foreign red-slipped serving vessels that disappeared from the household. All other types of serving plates were exchanged for locally made casseroles as well. It seems that a new dining practice was introduced with larger community meals and serving directly from the bowls. The first-century CE residents of Gamla, "unlike their grandparents, rarely held group meals in their homes. Instead they shared prepared food in the larger communal setting of the synagogue. There people dined simply, serving themselves directly from the vessels in which the food had been cooked, and eating from small, plain buff fabric bowls" (Berlin forthcoming, 29). In this way an explanation of the cessation of import of foreign tableware could simply be that it no longer served the preferred dining habits.

Thus, the admirably meticulous studies of Berlin emphasize the prospects of well-performed archaeology as well as the problems involved in drawing historical implications. On the basis of Berlin's own presentations, it seems unwarranted to picture Antipas as a crucial factor behind an intensified expression of covert resistance. Rather, from the Hasmonean period and onwards several identity markers were utilized increasingly, and Antipas himself participated in the evolution of a distinct Jewish culture by minting aniconic coins and by abstaining from building many of the regular Greco-Roman cultic institutions.

Herod Antipas: An Adjusted Local Jewish Ruler

To summarize, the concurrent picture of the 'inner relationship' between Antipas and his Jewish subjects that appears from the sources is one of a modest and adjusted ruler who reigned for a long time, avoided serious upheavals as far as we know, dealt with a couple of instances of 'low-threat' religious leaders, and refrained from imposing provocative imagery on his coins or Greco-Roman cultic buildings in his cities.

7.2.3 Partial Conclusion – The General Description of Herod Antipas

When assessing the picture of Antipas in general, it is interesting to recall the various descriptions in the non-Galilean research on Antipas (cf. section 1.3). According to M. Brann, Antipas was slack, lazy and extremely phlegmatic (Brann 1873, 306), blindfolded by his love of Herodias. He finally fell due to his lust and greediness (Brann 1873, 474). Schürer describes Antipas more positively as a miniature of his father, intelligent, ambitious and a lover of splendour, "nur weniger thatkräftig" than Herod the Great (Schürer 1901, 432). The same is expressed by Otto. Although Antipas was a true Hellenist, he was also a lover of quietness (*Ant.* 18.245) who lacked his father's cruelty. Only his relationship to Herodias was a sign of the prevalent immorality in the Herodian house (Otto 1913, 189–190). The most negative judgment of Antipas is found in the work of Harlow, who describes Antipas as a weak character due to his mixed ancestry (Harlow 1954, 142). F.F. Bruce mainly depicts Antipas as a good ruler who was able to remain in office for a long time and who avoided serious upheavals (Bruce 1963, 8). Hoehner also designates Antipas as a "good ruler" conducting a "wise administration" (Hoehner 1972, 57), while being "much milder than Herod the Great" (Hoehner 1972, 264). However, Hoehner also emphasizes the reluctant and ambivalent side of Antipas as a persistent characteristic throughout his reign, calling him "basically a coward" (Hoehner 1972, 201).

Thus, the descriptions of Antipas are as diverse as in the recent Galilean research. The reason for this is naturally to be found in the sources, which (deliberately or not) paint a two-sided if not multisided picture of Antipas. To my mind, this ambiguity can be explained in terms of contradictions between the four poles of 'good, able, adjusted' vs. 'minor, unremarkable, incompetent' and 'decisive' vs. 'indecisive' as illustrated in table 4 below: (a) The fact that Antipas was a good and able ruler is shown by his long period of reign, the lack of upheavals, his acting as benefactor when founding Tiberias, his dealing with John the Baptist, his relations to Jerusalem including participation in the feasts, and the way he avoided provocative actions such as coins with forbidden imagery. (b) On the other hand, when viewed from Rome, on some occasions Antipas showed himself to be an unremarkable if not directly incompetent ruler. His marriage to Herodias brought him into trouble with the Nabatean kingdom, which he was unable to deal with himself. His war against Aretas was a disaster. So was the way he informed Tiberius on the negotiations with Parthia behind the back of Vitellius, to the great regret of Vitellius. Likewise, it is reasonable to ask whether as a builder Antipas could have done any less to please his Roman patrons. At least the archaeological excavations have not uncovered material that can in any way be compared to the achievements of his father. The most important indicator in this connection is the fact that Antipas was never promoted, even though several obvious occasions occurred. (c) The other pair of contrasts is found primarily in the way Antipas is described as resolute and decisive. During the trial in Rome in 4 BCE he claimed the entire kingdom, just as he participated in the delegation demanding that Pilate should remove the shields from his palace in Jerusalem. Finally, the way in which Antipas participated in the peace negotiations with Parthia and afterwards informed Tiberius can also be seen as an expression of resoluteness. (e) On the other hand, according to both the New Testament and Josephus, Antipas was occasionally indecisive and perplexed, namely when confronted with John and Jesus, and when pestered by Herodias to travel to Rome to ask for kingship.

Good/Able/Adjusted	Minor/Unremarkable/Incompetent
43 years in office.	No promotions.
No major upheavals reported.	Second marriage to Herodias a politi-
Benefactor and builder.	cal failure.
Taking care of messianic threats.	Lost war against Aretas.
Took part in celebrations in Jerusalem.	Mediocre builder.
No provocative imagery on coins.	Infuriated Vitellius.
Decisive	**Indecisive**
Fought for the entire kingdom of	According to Matthew and Mark per-
Herod the Great.	plexed by John.
Part of a delegation against Pilate.	According to Luke perplexed by Jesus.
Informed Tiberius about the negations	Doubts over going to Rome to ask for
with Parthia.	kingship.

Table 4: Contradictory descriptions of Herod Antipas

This obvious ambiguity in the sources is not surprising, since the sources are written from different as well as extremely selective perspectives, and nowhere do they intend to provide an elaborate description of Antipas. This conclusion should warn us against attempts to discern Antipas' psychological nature based on single events. Instead of constructing a picture from events known from single sources only, it is better to accept that only a contour of Antipas' reign can be reached by focusing on its outer parameters and its impact on the region. This endeavour will be pursued further below, but the sum of the investigation up until this point points to one basic conclusion: Herod Antipas was a minor Roman client ruler, unremarkable in both success and failures. On the one hand, to a certain degree Antipas was an able ruler of his tetrarchy, in which he remained for a long period until he failed to gain the trust of the new emperor in Rome, Gaius Caligula. In this period we have no reports of major upheavals. On the other, Antipas was never promoted even though his two brothers' areas were rearranged during his time. Similarly, the excavations of Sepphoris and Tiberias do not provide a picture of Antipas as a builder with nearly the same capabilities as his father.

7.3 The Urbanization Programme of Antipas in Perspective

It follows from the preceding investigation of the inherent perspectives in the sources on the reign of Antipas that the central socio-economic issue in the Galilean research – resulting in the two conflicting descriptions of first-century Galilee as discussed in chapter one – is not on the agenda in the written sources. For this reason sociological models are often utilized to interpret the various sources. In the following, the relationship between the reign of Antipas and the socio-economic conditions will be discussed by focusing on the archaeological and numismatic sources in particular. The aim is to provide an overall presentation of the picture emerging from the material sources by focusing on: (a) The material data that can be connected to Antipas from Sepphoris and Tiberias and from the coin circulation. (b) The 'blind spots' in the discussion in terms of the often overlooked regional and inter-regional perspectives as well as the question of chronology. (c) The question of models by briefly discussing the relationship between the models used by Crossan, Moreland and Freyne and the data provided by the present investigation.

7.3.1 The Material Sources Describing Antipas' First-Century Galilee

While the advocates of a 'picture of harmony' argue that urbanization is not *per se* bad news for rural areas, the advocates of a 'picture of conflict' often assume that the building of two cities within a short period of time and within a relatively small area such as Lower Galilee *must have had* a profound impact on the socio-economic conditions of that region (cf. Horsley and Draper 1999, 58–59; Horsley 2001, 36 and Freyne 2004, 134–139, for instance). However, the preliminary reports are not always scrutinized in order to establish a well-argued perception of what Sepphoris and Tiberias looked like in the time of Antipas. The investigation in chapter five and six aimed to provide such a presentation by paying close attention to stratigraphy, and the results regarding Tiberias and Sepphoris as well as the circulation of Antipas' coins can be summed up as follows:

In the case of Tiberias, the material uncovered by excavations conducted so far mainly dates to later periods. Remains from Antipas' period include (cf. section 5.3.2): (a) During the present excavation campaign, first-century material has been found in fill material of later second-century construction, indicating that earlier buildings were demolished during the sequence of later constructions. Fortunately, three remaining first-century structures have also been found so far. In area C, adjoining the nine-foot-wide wall termed 'the Hadrianeion,' a minor wall with a water installation was uncovered. More interesting is the spectacular find of portions of a magnificent marble floor in area F. The floor was laid in the *opus sectile* style, and was probably part of an elaborate structure with a roof supported by tetrastyle pillars and an outer pavement of large limestone slabs and an open scenic view towards the lake front. It is a feasible suggestion that this floor was part of a Herodian structure, since floors of this kind, from this period, have only been found otherwise in palaces of Herod the Great. This suggestion was underlined even further by the newly found walls in the same area erected in limestone in the well known, tightly fitting Herodian bossed mansory. (b) A lead weight held in a private collection attests the existence of an *agoranomos* during the time of Antipas, just as the four first series of coins minted by Antipas with the inscription, TIBEPIAC on the reverse attest the city's status as a *polis*. (c) It is finally argued by the excavator of the southern free-standing monumental gate that this complex should be dated to the reign of Antipas. However, as discussed above, the case presented seems inconclusive, lacking detailed final publication. It is beyond doubt that future excavations will uncover more first-century material. The most eagerly anticipated of these is a thorough excavation of the theatre, which is presently dated to the third century (a date that naturally could be reconsidered following a full excavation). Likewise, it would be interesting if more material from the suggested stadium north of the city could be found.

In the case of Sepphoris, the picture is fairly similar. There are few buildings dating back to Antipas compared with those found from later periods (cf. section 5.4.2): (a) Tsuk's investigation of the water system revealed that Sepphoris was fed with water from only one aqueduct in the early first century – another being added later bringing in nine times the amount. (b) Most of the remains from Antipas' time have been found on the western summit, consisting of several housing units. Thus far, no large

public building has been attested, though remains in the fill of later buildings suggest that such a building might have existed. (c) The most interesting point is the appearance of the eastern lower plateau in the time of Antipas. According to Meyers, Weiss and Netzer, it was only in the period
following the war of 66–70 CE that extensive construction work began
outside the western summit. The road grid and the buildings uncovered by
Netzer and Weiss have all been dated to later periods. However, the USF
team argues that early-first-century material has been found in two instances. Probes revealed evidence of an earlier hard-packed soil and lime
cobblestone road beneath the cardo visible at present, which could be dated
to the first century. Strange also argues in his latest published discussion
that the basilical building found in Field V dates back to the time of Antipas in its earliest phase. (d) Finally, the founding date of the theatre has
turned into something of a conundrum in the research. At present the final
reports of the USF digs are being prepared for publication, and it would be
wise to await them before a final verdict is issued. However, it is important
to note that even if the first phase is dated back to Antipas as suggested by
McCollough and Batey, the theatre was comparably small, adding to
Reed's general characterization of Antipas' Sepphoris as a 'second tier'
urban site.

The number of coins in circulation has also been discussed above (cf.
section 6.4.3) as an important factor for understanding the level of monetization. It is assumed that the level of fractional coinage in circulation reflects the level of monetization of the daily household transactions. For
this reason, studies that focus not only on the iconography of the coins but
also on their circulation are highly important for understanding the socio-
economic dynamics. In his recent dissertation, Danny Syon has provided a
meticulous overview of the coin profile from 186 places in Galilee and Golan. It turns out that the number of coins minted by Antipas was apparently
very low. Less than 128 coins of his could be attested. In comparison, a total of 5,632 Hasmonean coins were attested. Antipas minted late in his career and at irregular intervals – and he also did so on a modest scale. So
Arnal's suggestion that Antipas caused a dramatic intensification of the
level of monetization for reasons of collecting taxes cannot be substantiated.

7.3.2 Chronological, Regional and Inter-Regional Perspectives

Important perspectives on the urbanization programme of Antipas may be
gained from three considerations that could be termed 'blind spots' because they are often neglected in studies that argue for a picture of conflict.
First, regarding chronology, it seems clear that the major changes that can
be observed in the material culture of Galilee occurred before and after

Antipas, as argued thoroughly in Chancey 2002b and Chancey 2005. Before Antipas, Galilee experienced a radical political tidal shift with the Hasmonean conquest and takeover – just like the period following the war of 66–70 CE that led to a heavier Roman military presence in Galilee (cf. Safrai 1992) only to be followed by an intensified Jewish presence in Galilee after the war of 132–135 CE. In the heyday of the High Empire under the Severan dynasty, Galilee experienced a heavy Roman presence and building activity equal to what was experienced in many other places in the Roman east (cf. Syon 2004, 263). In detail, the tidal shifts before and after Antipas have been demonstrated in the following instances: (a) At Sepphoris (cf. section 5.4.3), the western summit was reorganized under Antipas but even if the initial phase of the eastern plateau is dated to his period as well, it was only in the period after the war of 66–70 CE that extensive building activity took place erecting this area to its current appearance, with a cardo and decumanus besides several magnificent private dwellings as well as several public buildings such as a large basilica probably serving as a marketplace. Similarly, a new aqueduct was built enlarging the water supply by a factor of nine. (b) According to Josephus, Tiberias was Antipas' masterpiece. Nevertheless, material from his period remains elusive in the archaeological record, and the largest buildings unearthed all date to succeeding periods. This is true of the large basilical building of area F, the nine-foot-wide wall that could be part of the Hadrianeion known from Epiphanius, the theatre, the bathhouse, the large marketplace just north of the bathhouse, and the buildings on top of Mt. Berenice. The present excavations have, however, uncovered parts of a large mansion that could be the palace of Antipas, and there is every reason to believe that more will be found as the excavations proceed. (c) Finally, detailed studies of the coin circulation in Galilee also reveal that the major changes took place before and after Antipas. According to Aviam, the Hasmonean conquest was followed by an overall change in the material culture, among which was a new and widespread use of Hasmonean coinage (cf. section 1.2.2). At Gamla, destroyed and sealed in 67 CE, 62.8% of the coinage found was Hasmonean. Likewise, Hasmonean coinage replaced earlier Phoenician coinage in Yodefat (cf. section 5.5.1). In both places the Herodian coinage constitutes a fairly low percentage of the coins excavated, less than five percent (cf. section 6.4.3). At the same time, Syon's major survey demonstrates that in the period from 70–256 CE the total number of coins in circulation increased dramatically, as did the proportion of the Phoenician mints. Thus, while it could be expected that the imposition of a local ruler in Galilee would have left a dramatic impact on the material culture, it does not seem to be the case with regard to Sepphoris, Tiberias and coin circulation. It is true that the marks of Antipas' reign can be traced in the material culture, but from a broader chronological perspective, more dramatic impacts were made on Galilee in the period following the war of 66–70 CE.

Second, a highly important perspective on the impact of the urbanization programme of Antipas can be gained from a survey of the regional villages or towns of Lower Galilee. According to the advocates of a picture of conflict, the impact of Antipas' reign was felt most intensely in the rural areas, striking its peasant population. On the other hand, the advocates of a picture of harmony argue that Antipas' activities were beneficial for the rural community, providing new opportunities for trade and interaction. The examination above of the excavations of Yodefat, Cana and Capernaum, as well as Gamla in the Golan, produced a general picture of the rural areas without signs of decline in the early first century. On the contrary, expansion took place supported by small-scale local industries: (a) In Yodefat (cf. section 5.5.1) evidence of olive oil production, pottery fabrication and textile production has been attested. At the same time, the city expanded on the southern slope throughout the first century up until the war in 66. Most interesting is the discovery of an upper-class area with an elite house featuring walls decorated with the geometric First Pompeian style and floors designed in the *opus sectile* style. No intact public building was found, though the discovery of several large building blocks could indicate that such a building existed. (b) The excavations at Cana (cf. section 5.5.2) also produced material evidence of a small village community in steady progress and expansion. On the crest of the hill, a rectangular building was found with a large room measuring c. 12 x 8 m equipped with plastered walls and a plastered floor. The excavators interpret this as either an elite house or a public building. Evidence of a second public building was found close by, which is cautiously interpreted as a synagogue based on the discovery of roof tiles, plastered benches, columns and an Ionic capital. Evidence of small-scale industrial activity was also uncovered, including oil production, textile production, glass-blowing and the raising of pigeons. (c) The excavations at Capernaum (cf. section 5.5.3) have produced a picture of a medium- to large-sized village in the Early Roman period mainly consisting of large living units. With the possible exception of the earliest phase of the synagogue, no public buildings were attested, just as no evidence of white plastered walls, paved roads or other distinguished architectural elements was found. The location of Capernaum at the north end of the lake gave it a double competitive advantage compared to other villages of the area: a regional road connecting the tetrarchies of Antipas and Philip ran through it, and in addition to farming, income could be generated by fishing on the lake. A network of harbours has been testified, and a boat suitable for intensive fishing was found in 1986. (d) The excavations at Gamla (cf. section 5.5.4) have also produced some highly interest-ing results. In the western quarter an upper-class area was discovered com-prising skilfully constructed houses with plastered walls. To the east of this quarter, a commercial area was found including a large olive-oil extraction plant, a flour mill, and a street of shops with a large open plaza probably serving as a marketplace. The latest excavations produced evidence of an-other area with a large mansion, as well as unearthing a basilical building that the excavators believe was a public building housing administrative functions. Another public building was found not far from the eastern city wall, and is accepted as one of the earliest dated synagogues. Although Gamla was outside the perimeter of Antipas' reign, more coins of his were found than coins of Philip, and there is good reason to believe that there was some interaction between the two areas. Thus, the 'regional perspec-tive' provides a unique perspective on the impact of Sepphoris and Tibe-rias from the period of Antipas up until the war of 66 CE, and it seems in-disputable that the rural area was able to sustain its livelihood and even expand it in this period. Surprisingly, small-scale businesses were con-ducted supporting a local elite. No general economic decline has been at-tested. Naturally, it is not possible to determine the number of poor and landless people from these excavations, just as it is an open question whether the Jewish identity markers, also attested in all four places, should be interpreted as a mode of covert resistance against Antipas and the Ro-man rule.

Third, another important perspective on Antipas' projects in Galilee comes from an inter-regional comparison with the cities of Hippos, Gadara and Scythopolis in the Decapolis, and the hallmark of the building projects of Herod the Great, Caesarea Maritima (cf. section 5.6). In a significant way, they illuminate the scale and type of Antipas' cities: (a) In the Deca-polis, Hippos, Gadara and Scythopolis existed before the founding of Tibe-rias and had the status of *poleis*. (b) Like Tiberias and Sepphoris, these three cities also peaked in the Middle and Late Roman periods, in which they witnessed an intense building activity. (c) In the first century, all three cities could boast of Greco-Roman temples, and Scythopolis also had a theatre and an amphitheatre. (d) Caesarea Maritima is in a category of its own, built almost completely from scratch by Herod the Great and master-fully equipped with a harbour, a Roman temple dedicated to Augustus, a theatre, an amphitheatre, an elaborate city plan including defences, and an aqueduct. Consequently, when Sepphoris and Tiberias are placed in the context of the cities in their immediate vicinity, it becomes evident that on the one hand they did not represent a degree of urbanization that was un-precedented in the neighbouring areas, and that on the other they were small-scale cities in comparison with at least Caesarea Maritima and possibly also Scythopolis.

7.3.3 *Sociological Models Applied*

As discussed in section 1.2.4, the issue of how to combine sociological models and textual and material sources (and indeed whether they should be combined at all) is intriguing. It has been greatly debated by Biblical scholars, leaving, as demonstrated, at least four unsolved problems. Although it is not within the focus of the present investigation to discuss this issue separately, it is nevertheless warranted at the present point to apply some of the models utilized to the results of the source-oriented approach above. As a consequence of the clear fact that advocates of a picture of conflict are almost the only ones to utilize sociological models, the most urgent question concerns how the different reference points of these models relate to the sources. In the following, the models utilized by Freyne, Moreland and Crossan will be briefly summarized and discussed. With different nuances and weight, they argue for a picture of conflict and see the implied parameters or reference points of their models present in the sources on early-first-century Galilee.

Freyne applies the model worked out by T.F. Carney to the literary and archaeological sources on early-first-century Galilee. This model emphasizes that rapid change in a society can be detected through three probe zones. If *specialization* in production, *monetization* of the economy and *attitudinal changes* marginalizing traditional values and belief systems occurred at the same time, rapid changes took place in the society (cf. Freyne 2000b). Moreland examines the way in which the model of James C. Scott illuminates the socio-economic conditions in Antipas' realm. Scott's model describes the peasant ideology and peasant culture as one of the four key elements of *safety-first* principle, *redistributive norms and risk-sharing measures,* vulnerable against a *negative impact of administrative urban centres,* and avoiding *overt modes of resistance* preferring the subtle mode of *covert resistance* since the overall value was stability. In a period of rapid changes, this peasant ideology would be under pressure. Finally, the work of Crossan utilizes particularly the models of G. Lenski and J. Kautsky. According to Lenski, if *urbanization, monetization* and *scribalization* increase in a society at the same time, social inequality increases too. According to Kautsky, such a society is no longer traditional but *commercialized* and marked by a growing class of landless people and accumulated wealth in the cities. In response, *peasant resistance* escalates in its overt mode as another marker of a society in rapid change:

In a traditional agrarian empire, land is a familial inheritance to be retained by the peasantry. In a commercializing agrarian empire, land is an entrepreneurial commodity to be exploited by the aristocracy. Rural commercialization, land expropriation, and peasant dispossession are more or less synonymous. And as they increase, so also do the incidences of peasant resistance, rebellion, or revolt. (Crossan 1999, 159)

Added together, these three models emphasize that if a picture of conflict is to be substantiated, the sources on early-first-century Galilee must reveal traces of several of the key elements necessary for describing the society in rapid change with increasing pressure on the lowest classes, such as specialization, monetization, attitudinal changes, urbanization, scribalization, increasing overt modes of resistance, difficulties in upholding the peasant ideology of safety-first, risk sharing and protection from urban centres.

Without debating whether it is justified to apply this scenario to first-century Galilee in the first place, the question is how the results of the present investigation fit into these parameters. Before answering this question, it must be stressed that the present investigation has not aimed to examine all relevant issues in this connection, focusing instead deliberately on the sources on Antipas' reign. It is interesting, nevertheless, that this perspective does not seem to generate a measurable effect on any of these parameters except for a possible rise in covert modes of resistance. When compared to the periods before and after, the period of Antipas does not yield evidence of intense monetization, urbanization or scribalization.[207] Likewise, negative impacts from the administrational urban centres could not be found in the rural areas. In addition, there are no indications of intensified monocropping or specialization. Rather it seems from Yodefat, Cana, Capernaum and Gamla that several types of small-scale industrial activity were conducted parallel with different kinds of farming.[208] It is worth noting that the analyses of Milton Moreland seem to warrant this conclusion as well. According to Moreland, Galilee experienced a period of stabilization under Antipas in which (a) no major fortresses were built, (b) no natu-

---

[207] Chancey has provided, regarding 'scribalization', an overview over the known epigraphic material from Galilee in the period of Antipas and after, and as in the cases of monetization and urbanization, intensified use of inscriptions cannot be attested until after the period of Antipas: "A clear trajectory is visible when one looks at Galilee's epigraphic corpus through this lens: the later the period, the more numerous the Greek inscriptions" (Chancey 2003, 180).

[208] This corresponds with what was noted by Gary Gilbert in a review of Crossan and Reed's book, *Excavating Jesus*. There are no indications of monocropping or large estates in Galilee in this period, just as there is no evidence of monocropping at all in the Roman Empire. On the contrary, the Roman practice was based on polycropping for the obvious reason of reducing the vulnerability of crop failures and for the economic advantages of spreading the agricultural circle of sowing and harvesting as much as possible (cf. Gilbert 2003, 8–9).

ral disasters were experienced, (c) no signs of extreme wealth were imposed, and (d) no form of extreme exploitation were witnessed (Moreland
2004, 42–43). Moreland actually sees this stable climate as the main reason why the early Jesus movement seemingly did not gain a foothold in the
rural areas of Galilee. For the non-uprooted Galilean peasantry, the statements about leaving one's family behind, turning son against father,
daughter against mother, hatred against one's parents in order to become a
disciple, neglecting of burial practices etc. (Luke 9:60; 12:53; 14:26; Mark
3:35) were clearly too counter-cultural to gain acceptance (Moreland 2004,
45–46). At the same time, the Gospels include sayings of Jesus against exploitation and wealth gained on behalf of the poor, and Moreland certainly
sees the new administrative and colonial centres as representing bad news
for the peasants. However, the truly important point of his analyses is that
at the time of Antipas even a model based on Finley's parasitic urban-rural
description does not produce results that substantiate a picture of conflict
to any notable degree. On the contrary, the model of Scott implies that
"urbanization, at least in the short run, is generally a condition of more
prosperous economic times" (Moreland 2004, 43, cf. Edwards 1992, 62–
65). Thus, when applying these three models on the sources describing the
impact of the reign of Antipas, a picture of conflict is not substantiated.

7.3.4 Partial Conclusion

When Antipas arrived in Galilee after the trial in Rome in 4 BCE, serious
upheavals and battles had just taken place between different factions of
Jews and the Roman army commanded by the legate of Syria, Varus (cf.
the summary in section 5.4.1). While most of the incidents described by
Josephus took place in Judea (cf. *Ant.* 17.285), Galilee was hit as well
when Judas, son of Hezekija, captured the city of Sepphoris and took hold
of its weapon arsenal. The army of Varus recaptured the city in 4 BCE,
burned it to the ground and sold off the inhabitants as slaves, according to
Josephus (*War* 2.56, 68; *Ant.* 17.271–272, 289). In *Antiquities,* Josephus
notes that when Antipas finally took over his tetrarchy he fortified Sepphoris and renamed it Autocratoris. This probably occurred at the beginning of
his reign, although it is listed in Josephus in connection with the downfall
of Archelaos in 6 CE. Later Antipas founded Tiberias, which was built
from scratch as the hallmark of his reign.

　　Thus, it is beyond doubt that through Antipas the people of Galilee felt
the hand of the Roman colonial administration moving closer. It is also beyond doubt that there were plenty of reasons to dislike any Roman puppet
ruler on the grounds of both the demands of taxes and an extravagant lifestyle in general. It has nevertheless been the objective of this section to put
the programme of urbanization imposed by Antipas into perspective, by

discussing it in its chronological, regional and inter-regional context, and in this light the following three points may serve as a conclusion. First, the excavations at Sepphoris and Tiberias concordantly attest that Antipas' urbanization programme was of a rather moderate scale. No large-scale *poleis* were erected, and despite many years of digging Antipas remains elusive in the archaeological record. The picture of Antipas as boldly *remaking* Galilee (Horsley and Silberman 1997, 22) by redesigning "Israel's landscape as little Italy" (Sawicki 2000, 158) in order to attract "wealthy business travelers and their families" (Sawicki 2000, 146, cf. Mack 1993, 55) to Tiberias seems clearly overstated.

Second, in order to understand the impact of Antipas' cities more thoroughly, important perspectives are provided by examining the chronological aspects of the development of Tiberias and Sepphoris and of the coin circulation. Again it is concordantly attested that the most noticeable changes took place in the previous Hasmonean period and succeeding Middle Roman period. Further illumination of the impact of Antipas' efforts is provided through a regional and inter-regional perspective. The sites that have been surveyed show that the rural villages in Galilee were expanding and thriving right up until the war of 66 CE, and from a comparison with the neighbouring cities it becomes evident that Antipas was not imposing a novelty on Galilee – he was raising it to the standard already present nearby.

Third and finally, three studies pointing at a picture of conflict were examined to see whether the reference points of the utilized models were justified by the sources describing the impact of Antipas' reign on first-century Galilee. As indicated in the study of Moreland, it does not seem so to any noticeable extent.

Chapter 8

Conclusions

8.1 Two Pictures – Three Outputs

First-century Galilee has become an issue of intense focus in several fields of scholarly research, and not least studies into the historical background of Jesus and his movement. One of the most, if not *the* most decisive factor for understanding Galilee in this period, is Herod Antipas. However, as stressed in chapter one, the impact of the reign of Antipas is described in highly conflicting ways. Broadly speaking, two pictures of early-first-century Galilee have been put forward, both of which have Antipas as their determining factor.

At one end of the spectrum, Antipas is described as a "buffer for Galilee from the excesses of Roman provincial rule" (Freyne 1997a, 68), and it is stated that "for the ordinary people the advantages of a peaceful reign out-weighed the disadvantages of having to support a hellenistic-style mon-arch" (Freyne 1980b, 192). This way Antipas' "39–year reign was peaceful and probably contributed much to the expansion and strengthening of both structures and society in general" (Aviam 2004b, 315). Thus, "Galilee de-veloped into a small, prosperous Jewish kingdom under Herod Antipas. Those were almost 40 years of growing and flourishing, probably with al-most no domestic turmoil" (Aviam 2004a, 21). In short, Antipas was good news for the rural villages: "They operated fully within a vibrant economic environment under Herod Antipas that witnessed an expansion in popula-tion, agricultural activity and a variety of structures ranging from public buildings, to frescoed private dwellings to olive presses and specialty goods like ceramics, stone vessels or dove production" (Edwards Forth-coming, 13). Thus "Antipas was a good tetrarch" who "undertook large building projects that helped reduce unemployment" (Sanders 1993a, 21, cf. Sanders 1993b, 440).

At the other end of the spectrum, Antipas is described as the "immediate historical context" (Freyne 2000b, 113) for the Jesus movement, and it is claimed that during his reign "the slide from peasant owner to day-labourer, to brigand was rapid, and all the evidence points to the fact that this was increasingly the case in first-century Galilee" (Freyne 2001, 204). In short, "Antipas intensified the structural political-economic conflict in

Galilee" (Horsley 1996, 36), and therefore "the impact of Antipas's direct rule in Galilee, both political-economic and cultural, must have been intense, particularly during the generation of Jesus and his followers" (Horsley and Draper 1999, 58, cf. Horsley 2001, 36). It is asserted that "it cannot be coincidental… that the prophet John the Baptist condemned Antipas (*Ant.* 18.116–119), and that Jesus and his movement emerged in Galilee under Antipas" (Horsley and Draper 1999, 59). Antipas was the provocative factor behind the emergence of the prophet Jesus: "If anyone was seeking the Kingdom of God, Antipas was eager to show that the era of its fulfilment had arrived" (Horsley and Silberman 1997, 35–36). However, in contrast to Antipas, "Jesus did not believe that the Kingdom of God would arrive with fire and brimstone. And he was convinced that he would not need aqueducts, palaces, coins, marble columns, or soldiers to utterly remake Galilee" (Horsley and Silberman 1997, 42). Jesus reacted as the new Amos: "If we think of covenant rather than commerce, would an Amos have said anything very different to Antipas at Tiberias in the first century than he said to Jeroboam II at Samaria in the eighth century long before?" (Crossan and Reed 2001, 114–115).

Thus, the Galilean research is at present caught at an impasse on how to depict the consequences of the reign of Antipas. The presentation in chapter one of the state of the research on Antipas within the Galilean studies further clarified that no thorough study of the sources on his reign had been conducted. Sometimes, swift conclusions are reached by asserting that his building programme *must have* intensified the economic exploitation of the rural areas. On other occasions, sociological models are imported to interpret the results, and scattered evidence is presented as an argument without taking the contextual entirety into account. As such, not only an impasse but also a lacuna exits in the Galilean research on the life, reign and impact of Herod Antipas. This situation consequently produced the following two objectives for the present investigation: (a) To fill out the lacuna by providing a thorough investigation of the sources available on Antipas' reign through a contextual approach aiming at a careful discussion of the different evidence in their own context before bringing them into the perspective of the Galilean studies. (b) An attempt to make progress on the main problem of how the reign of Antipas affected the socio-economic conditions of early-first-century Galilee, or at least clarify the role of Antipas in this relationship. As initially noted, three outputs on this issue are logically possible. Either the picture of conflict is substantiated, or else the picture of harmony is. If not, it must be concluded that the evidence is too limited to warrant a substantiation of either.

8.2 Main Conclusions

8.2.1 Herod Antipas: A Minor Ruler with a Moderate Impact

The methodology utilized in order to approach this situation has stressed the need to read the sources within their broader context. Against this background the present investigation's main conclusion is that Herod Antipas is best described with adjectives such as: minor, moderate, adjusted and unremarkable. Consequently, in all probability the impact of his reign on the socio-economic conditions of early-first-century Galilee was moderate and adjusted too. Thus, Herod Antipas was a minor ruler with a moderate impact.

8.2.2 Argumentation

Four arguments warrant this conclusion: First, as thoroughly discussed above (section 7.2.1), Antipas was a minor ruler with mediocre success from the point of view of the Roman overlords. It counts to his credit that he was able to keep his tetrarchy for 43 years in a relatively stable and calm condition with no known major upheavals apart from a couple of 'low-threat' incidents, and that to some extent he gained the trust of Emperor Tiberius. On the other hand, it has been demonstrated that Antipas failed to receive the promotion he desired on no less than four obvious occasions, that he was a mediocre politician who lost some of his good relations to his nearest allies (Vitellius and Aretas), and that he finally failed to obtain the friendship of Gaius Caligula. It has also been suggested that one important reason behind Rome's treatment of Antipas was his inability to provide persuasive proof of his loyalty and forcefulness. It seems that Antipas confined his flattering gestures to renaming Sepphoris Autocratoris, renaming Betharamphtha Livia, naming his new city Tiberias, and finally issuing a series of coins with the name of Gaius Caligula featured in the legends. The archaeological remains and the literary descriptions of both Sepphoris and Tiberias provide no indication that Antipas imposed the emperor cult with a temple, for instance, as his father did in Caesarea Maritima, Sebaste and Paneas. Similarly, Antipas' handling of his relations to Vitellius and Aretas did not provide the impression of a resolute and forceful ruler.

Second, contrary to the statements of Josephus, Antipas seemingly managed relations to his Jewish subjects well, being sensitive about difficult matters: (a) The analysis of Josephus' narrative on Antipas within its contextual framework revealed that Josephus uses Antipas as yet another example of bad Herodian government. However, Josephus is unable to present real evidence of cruelty, which he amply provides in the cases of Herod the Great, Archelaos, the fourth philosophy and Pilate. As con-

cluded above (section 3.5), read in conjunction with Josephus' own disclosed intentions in his many editorial remarks, for instance, the picture he
presents his readers of Antipas is one of an unremarkable ruler in both
deeds and misdeeds, credits and discredits. It would have served the cause
of Josephus had he been able to present more unambiguous evidence of
Antipas being part of the reason for the ultimate disaster. Instead, the picture cracks and Josephus provides us with enough detail to see that Antipas' actions might have been sounder than judged by Josephus. (b) Several
written sources indicate that Antipas played a certain role in Jerusalem. At
that time, the Romans controlled the right to appoint high priests, keeping
this right until it was transferred to Agrippa I. The fragile power and peace
balance between the Roman authorities and the various Jewish factions in
Jerusalem was disturbed by Pilate, and the evidence indicates that Antipas
was used by the Jewish leaders as a counterweight in this situation. According to Luke, they presented Jesus to Antipas when Pilate refused to
obey their wishes. According to Philo, Antipas was included as a prominent member in the delegation sent to Pilate to complain about the votive
shields, just as Josephus informs us that Antipas took part in the celebrations in Jerusalem. At the same time, Antipas was not entrusted with the
right to appoint high priests, as were other later Jewish rulers living outside Jerusalem. This could be taken as yet another indication of the fact
that Antipas was only successful to a certain degree. (c) The same conclusion appears evident based on the analysis of the coins of Antipas with regard to message and minting; iconography and circulation. Compared with
the coins minted by Pilate, Philip and Agrippa I, the coins of Antipas show
a remarkable anxiety to observe the ban against images. Judging from
Josephus' notion of the ornamentation in Antipas' palace in Tiberias, and
from the inscriptions found at Cos and Delos, it seems clear that this concern was not based on Antipas's personal preferences but guided by considerations for his Galilean subjects. Apparently, not even an upcoming
voyage to Rome to seek the favour of Gaius or coins minted by Agrippa I
featuring Gaius' and his sister's portraits could provoke Antipas to do
more than include the name of Gaius. At the same time, Antipas' series
were minted late in his reign, infrequently and in low numbers. While earlier numismatic studies have noted that Antipas' coins are rare, the new investigation by Danny Syon allows us for the first time to see how many
provenanced coins are known from 186 sites in Galilee and the Golan. Altogether less than 128 coins were registered, which should be compared to
the nearly 5,632 registered Hasmonean coins. Thus, Antipas' coins neither
insulted by their iconography nor made a noticeable impact on the overall
coin circulation. (d) Furthermore, it has been discussed whether there are
indications in the material culture of a growing covert resistance during the

time of Antipas. While several things indicate that certain distinct elements featured in the private sphere, it has not yet been proven that the preference for Jewish identity markers was provoked or catalyzed specifically by Antipas, instead of being part of the general trend in the late Second Temple period. (e) Finally, when assessing the different sources in order to describe Antipas, I believe that it is better to emphasize the external factors of his reign rather than describing his personal character through isolated incidents. The various psychological descriptions of him in the research should warn us against extrapolating a general picture of Antipas based on the New Testament and Josephus. The sources notoriously paint an ambiguous picture of Antipas as demonstrated in table 4, and even if Antipas was perplexed and reluctant when confronted with John, Jesus and the wish-list of his wife, the material available does not justify a general assessment of his character. Instead, when assessing Antipas' inner relations to his subjects, emphasis should be given to the fact that Antipas did not see the need for enclosing Galilee with an extensive net of fortresses, and the fact that no major upheavals are recorded. The fact that Antipas remained in office for more than four decades counts on the plus side, too.

Third, an important element in the description of the reign of Antipas comes from the archaeological excavations of urban and rural Galilee as well as of surrounding areas. The discussion above emphasized the following: (a) When evaluating the excavations at Sepphoris and Tiberias, it is important to observe a strict chronological approach, since both places were radically transformed in the post-war era. Such a chronological approach highlights the fact that at the time of Antipas the two urban centres were modest versions of what they were destined to become in the later Roman periods. The survey of the coin circulation by Syon strongly suggests the same thing: Galilee was not nearly as urbanized or monetized in early first century as it was to become in the second century and after. (b) Furthermore, important perspectives on the urbanization programme of Antipas are found in the welfare of the regional villages and inter-regional neighbouring cities. These perspectives are often neglected, and could be termed 'blind spots' in the present state of the discussion of early-first-century Galilee. From the investigation of selected villages it turns out that rural Galilee was apparently thriving and expanding right up until the war of 66–70 CE. No decline can be attested. Instead, evidence points to an expanding rural village culture including different small-scale industrial activity, support of public buildings and use of differentiated housing units. From the investigation of neighbouring cities it becomes evident that Antipas' cities were modest in terms of the size and equipment of their public buildings, and that to a large extent they only updated the cultural matrix of Galilee to a level known in both the Decapolis and the areas in which his father had invested heavily.

Fourth and finally, when applying some of the models used in Galilean studies to these source analyses, it becomes evident that Antipas did not provoke any sincere swings in the probe zones needed to evaluate a society as being in rapid change or commercialized.

8.2.3 Substantiation

Against this background, the main conclusion on the relationship between the reign of Herod Antipas and the socio-economic conditions of early-first-century Galilee can be substantiated. Before doing so, three qualifications are called for: (a) As stressed above, the present investigation does not seek to describe Antipas' personal character, just as it is not within its objectives to provide a general *Vita* of Antipas. (b) Neither does the present investigation seek to determine how one singular person responded to Antipas' reign. It is perfectly possible that a single person, especially one with a strong religious motivation, would react differently than people in general. Thus it is beyond the perimeters of this investigation to determine whether or not Jesus was provoked by Antipas. This is a question that can only be determined by examining the New Testament accounts. The objective in this regard is solely to evaluate the contextual component in the various scenarios of Antipas' impact on Jesus. (c) Most importantly, it is not the aim of this investigation to analyze the urban-rural relationship *per se*. The question of whether this should be understood as reciprocal or rather parasitic is properly assessed in a separate investigation. The refined focus of this investigation is to establish a well-argued position from which to determine the extent to which Antipas influenced the urban-rural relationship, whether it functioned in one way or the other.

With this in mind, the following points are presented as the investigation's main conclusions: First, it is concluded that the sources present a coherent picture of Antipas in respect to the question of the outer parameters of his reign. In contrast, it is not possible to assess Antipas' personal qualities or to describe his psychological character. But on the question as to whether or not it is possible to assess the impact of the reign of Antipas against the background of the sources available, the investigation above has proved that a concurrent picture of Antipas emerges.

Second, it is concluded that Antipas was a minor Roman client ruler, mediocre in both his successes and failures, and his impact on the archaeological record of Galilee is surprisingly rather elusive. It is thus not warranted to name Antipas a *remaker* of Galilee – instead, the description *modest developer* would be more appropriate. This conclusion is a result of the concurrent picture in the sources: (a) Josephus treats Antipas as one of the minor persons within the Herodian house, and though it would have substantiated his line of thought, he is not able to attribute any real examples of despotic cruelty to Antipas. Instead Josephus actually labels him "a lover of quietness" (*Ant.* 18.245). (b) Antipas is barely mentioned in other written sources apart from the New Testament. (c) Despite extensive excavations at both Sepphoris and Tiberias, Antipas remains elusive in the archaeological record. Although there is no reason to doubt that Antipas built a city of some size at least at Tiberias, there are no signs of extreme wealth, expensive public institutions or intensive use of expensive imported building materials. (d) The coins of Antipas are a striking showcase on his modest and adjusted approach as a ruler. Ostensibly, his coins did not serve as vehicles for extensive monetization or Roman propaganda. Despite the fact that outside Israel Antipas was a modest benefactor of regular Greco-Roman cults, and that he decorated his palace in Tiberias with pictures of living creatures, he also refrained from introducing cult symbols or facial portraits on his coins – even at a time when such an act was most called for in order to gain the favour of Gaius and to outbid the competing coins of Agrippa I. (e) When evaluating Rome's treatment of Antipas, the same conclusion shines through. Antipas did not appear to Rome as a vigorous king, and was never promoted beyond the status of a tetrarch, allotted a larger realm or given the right to appoint high priests.

Third, it is concluded that the 'picture of conflict' cannot be substantiated to any notable degree by referring to the reign of Antipas. To recapitulate, it is not concluded that the urban-rural relationship was symbiotic or reciprocal rather than parasitic. Instead, it is asserted that it is unwarranted to place Antipas in the middle of a deterioration process which *"must have"* taken place under him. There are no indications of such a process either in the archaeological record or in the literary sources. While the latter point may be a result of a different focus in the texts, it is important that future studies on this issue consider chronological factors more carefully when describing Antipas' urbanization programme, as well as realizing the important perspectives retrievable from the archaeological record of the rural villages of Galilee and the neighbouring cities of the Decapolis.

Fourth, it is finally concluded that the picture of the historical Jesus as provoked by and opposed to the reign of Antipas cannot be substantiated by a contextual component. Again, to recapitulate, it is not possible from a contextual analysis to determine what made a single person react. Furthermore, it is beyond any doubt that poverty was a persistent fact of life in this period, and that there were more than enough reasons for a social prophet to be loaded with discontent, irrespective of the presence of Antipas. However, the present investigation arrives at a picture of first-century

Galilee that opposes the attempt to explain Jesus as a result of imminent action-reaction factors. The feeling is that the stakes are too high concerning Herod Antipas because he was contemporaneous with the historical Jesus, and that many of the hypotheses launched serving as 'factors of explanation' are too bold and unwarranted. Too much is explained with too little.

Bibliography

Achtemeier, Paul J. 1970. Toward the Isolation of Pre-Markan Miracle Catenae. *Journal of Biblical Literature* 89:265–91.

Adan-Bayewitz, David. 1993. *Common Pottery in Roman Galilee: A Study of Local Trade*. Israel: Bar-Ilan University Press.

Adan-Bayewitz, David, and Mordechai Aviam. 1997. Iotapata, Josephus, and the Siege of 67: Preliminary Report of the 1992–94 Seasons. *Journal of Roman Archaeology* 10:131–65.

Adan-Bayewitz, David, and I. Perlman. 1990. The Local Trade of Sepphoris in the Roman Period. *Israel Exploration Journal* 40:153–72.

Adan-Bayewitz, David, and Moshe Wieder. 1992. Ceramics From Roman Galilee: A Comparison of Several Techniques for Fabric Characterization. *Journal of Field Archaeology* 19:189–205.

Aitken, Martin J. 1997. Dating Techniques. Pages 113–7 in vol. 2 of *The Oxford Encyclopedia of Archaeology in the Near East*. Edited by Eric M. Meyers. 5 vols. Oxford, New York: Oxford University Press.

Albright, William F. 1938. Review of Waterman's Preliminary Report on the 1931 Excavations. *Classical Weekly* 21:148.

Alkier, Stefan, and Jürgen Zangenberg. 2003a. Zeichen aus Text und Stein. Ein semiotisches Konzept zur Verhältnisbestimmung von Archäologie und Exegese. Pages 21–62 in *Zeichen aus Text und Stein: Studien auf dem Weg zu einer Archäologie des Neuen Testaments*. Edited by Stefan Alkier, and Jürgen Zangenberg. Tübingen, Basel: Francke Verlag.

–, eds. 2003b. *Zeichen aus Text und Stein: Studien auf dem Weg zu einer Archäologie des Neuen Testaments*. Tübingen, Basel: Francke Verlag.

Alt, Albrecht. 1953. Vol. 2. *Kleine Schriften zur Geschichte des Volkes Israel*. München: C.H. Beck'sche Verlagsbuchhandlung.

Applebaum, S. 1989. *Judaea in Hellenistic and Roman Times*. Studies in Judaism in Late Antiquity 40. Leiden: Brill.

Arav, Rami, and Richard A. Freund, eds. 1995. *Bethsaida: A City by the North Shore of the Sea of Galilee*, eds. Rami Arav, and Richard A. Freund. Kirksville, Mo.: Thomas Jefferson University Press.

–, eds. 1999. *Bethsaida: A City by the North Shore of the Sea of Galilee, Vol. 2*, eds. Rami Arav, and Richard A. Freund. Kirksville: Truman State University Press.

–, eds. 2004. *Bethsaida: A City by the North Shore of the Sea of Galilee, Vol. 3*, eds. Rami Arav, and Richard A. Freund. Kirksville: Truman State University Press.

Ariel, Donald T. 2000–2002. The Jerusalem Mint of Herod the Great: A Relative Chronology. *Israel Numismatic Journal* 14:99–124.

Armenti, Joseph R. 1981–1982. On the Use of the Term "Galileans" in the Writings of Josephus Flavius: A Brief Note. *Jewish Quarterly Review* 72:45–9.

Arnal, William E. 2000. *Jesus and the Village Scribes: Galilean Conflicts and the Setting of Q*. Minneapolis: Fortress Press.

Attridge, H. W. 1984. Josephus and His Works. Pages 185–232 in *Jewish Writing of the Second Temple Period*. Edited by Michael E. Stone. Philadelphia: Fortress Press.

Attridge, H.W., Dale B. Martin, and Jürgen Zangenberg, eds. Forthcoming. *Religion, Ethnicity and Identity in Ancient Galilee*. Tübingen: Mohr Siebeck.

Aune, D. E. 1997. Jesus and Cynics in First-Century Palestine: Some Critical Considerations. Pages 176–92 in *Hillel and Jesus: Comparative Studies of Two Major Religious Leaders*. Edited by James H. Charlesworth, and Loren L. Johns. Minneapolis: Fortress Press.

Avi-Yonah, M. 1950–1951. The Foundation of Tiberias. *Israel Exploration Journal* 1:160–9.

Aviam, Mordechai. 1990. Tel Yodefat, Oil Press. *Excavations and Surveys in Israel* 10:106.

–, 1993. Galilee: The Hellenistic to Byzantine Periods. Pages 452–8 in vol. 2 of *The New Encyclopedia of Archaeological Excavations in the Holy Land*. 4 vols. Jerusalem: The Israel Exploration Society & Carta.

–, 2002. Yodefat/Jotapata: The Archaeology of the First Battle. Pages 121–33 in *The First Jewish Revolt: Archaeology, History, and Ideology*. Edited by Andrea M. Berlin, and J. Andrew Overman. London and New York: Routledge.

–, 2004a. First Century Jewish Galilee: An Archaeological Perspective. Pages 7–27 in *Religion and Society in Roman Palestine: Old Questions, New Approaches*. Edited by Douglas R. Edwards. New York and London: Routledge.

–, 2004b. *Jews, Pagans and Christians in the Galilee*. Land of Galilee 1. Rochester NY: University of Rochester Press.

–, 2005. Yodefat: A Case Study in the Development of the Jewish Settlement in the Galilee During the Second Temple Period. Unpublished PhD dissertation presented at the Bar-Ilan University. Ramat-Gan.

Batey, Richard A. 1984. 'Is Not This the Carpenter?' *New Testament Studies* 30:249–58.

–, 1991. *Jesus & the Forgotten City: New Light on Sepphoris and the Urban World of Jesus*. Grand Rapids, Michigan: Baker Book House.

Ben-Arieh, Roni. 1994. A Wall Painting of a Saint's Face in the Church of Mt. Berenice. *Biblical Archaeologist* 57(3):135–7.

Belayche, Nicole. 2001. *Iudaea-Palaestina: The Pagan Cults in Roman Palestine (Second to Fourth Century)*. Religion der römischen Provinzen 1. Tübingen: Mohr Siebeck.

Berlin, Andrea M. 2002. Romanization and Anti-Romanization in Pre-Revolt Galilee. Pages 57–73 in *The First Jewish Revolt: Archaeology, History, and Ideology*. Edited by Andrea M. Berlin, and J. Andrew Overman. London and New York: Routledge.

–, 2004. Jewish Life before the Revolt: The Archaeological Evidence. Paper presented at the Society of Biblical Annual Meeting 2004. [Cited May 2006]. Available from http://pace.cns.yorku.ca/York/york/conference2004–ext.htm.

–, forthcoming. *Gamla 1. The Hellenistic and Roman Pottery*. IAA Reports.

Bernbeck, Reinhard. 2003. Zur Theorie der Archäologie. Einführung in den Stand der Fachdiskussion. Pages 2–20 in *Zeichen aus Text und Stein: Studien auf dem Weg zu einer Archäologie des Neuen Testaments*. Edited by Stefan Alkier, and Jürgen Zangenberg. Tübingen, Basel: Francke Verlag.

Bernett, Monika. 2002. *Der Kaiserkult als teil der politischen Geschichte Iudeas unter den Herodianern und Roemern (30 v. – 66 n. Chr.)*. München: Habilitationsschrift.

–, 2003. Zur politischen Zeitrechnung des Königs Agrippa II. Pages 25–37 in *Saxa Loquentur: Studien zur Archäologie Palästinas/Israels*. Edited by Cornelius G. Den Hertog, Ulrich Hubner, and Stefan Munger. Münster: Ugarit-Verlag.

–, Forthcoming. Roman Imperial Cult in the Galilee: Structures, Functions and Dynamics. In *Religion, Ethnicity and Identity in Ancient Galilee*. Edited by Jürgen Zangenberg, Harold Attridge, and Dale B. Martin. Tübingen: Mohr Siebeck.

Betz, Hans Dieter. 1994. Jesus and the Cynics: Survey and Analysis of a Hypothesis. *Journal of Religion* 74(4):453–75.

Bilde, Per. 1979. The Causes of the Jewish War According to Josephus. *Journal for the Study of Judaism* X(2):179–202.

–, 1980. Galilæa og galilæerne på Jesu tid. *Dansk teologisk tidsskrift* 43:113–35.

–, 1983. *Josefus som historieskriver – En undersøgelse af Josefus' fremstilling af Gaius Caligulas konflikt med jøderne i Palæstina (Bell 2, 184–203 og Ant 18, 261–309) med særligt henblik på forfatterens tendens og historiske pålidelighed*. København: G.E.C. GAD.

–, 1988. *Flavius Josephus Between Jerusalem and Rome: His Life, His Works, and Their Importance*. Journal for the Study of the Pseudepigrapha Supplement Series 2. Sheffield: JSOT Press.

–, 1994. The Geographical Excursuses in Josephus. Pages 247–62 in *Josephus and the History of the Greco-Roman Period: Essays in Memory of Morton Smith*. Edited by Fausto Parente, and Joseph Sievers. Leiden: Brill.

–, 2005. Josefus om henrettelsen af Jakob (Ant 20,197–203). Et bidrag til at drøfte og illustrere problemstillingen "historie og konstruktion". Pages 42–59 in *Historie og konstruktion*. Edited by Mogens Müller, and Thomas L. Thompson. København: Museum Tusculanums forlag.

Binder, Donald D. 1987. *Into the Temple Courts: The Place of the Synagogues in the Second Temple Period*. Society of Biblical Literature Dissertation Series 169. Atlanta, Georgia: Socity of Biblical Literature.

Biran, Avraham, and Joseph Aviram, eds. 1993. *Biblical Archaeology Today, 1990*. Israel: Israel Exploration Society.

Blakely, Jeffrey A. 1996. Toward the Study of Economics At Caesarea Maritima. Pages 327–45 in *Caesarea Maritima: A Retroperspective After Two Millennia*. Edited by Avner Raban, and Kenneth G. Holum. Leiden: Brill.

Blasi, Anthony J. 2002. General Methodological Perspective. Pages 61–79 in *Handbook of Early Christianity: Social Science Approaches*. Edited by Anthony J. Blasi, Jean Duhaime, and Paul-André Turcotte. Walnut Creek - Lanham - New York - Oxford: Altamira Press.

Blinzler, Josef. 1947. *Herodes Antipas und Jesus Christus: Die Stellung des Heilandes zu seinem Landesherrn*. Bibelwissenschaftliche Reihe 2. Stuttgart: Verlag Kath. Bibel-Werk.

Boatwright, Mary T. 1990. Theaters in the Roman Empire. *Biblical Archaeologist* 53:184–92.

Bond, Helen K. 1998. *Pontius Pilate in History and Interpretation*. Society for New Testament Studies Monograph Series 100. Cambridge: Cambridge University Press.

Borowski, Oded. 1988. Ceramic Dating. Pages 223–33 in *Benchmarks in Time and Culture: An Introduction to Palestinian Archaeology*. Edited by Joel F. Drinkard, Gerald L. Mattingly, and Maxwell J. Miller. Atlanta, Georgia: Scholars Press.

Brandon, Christopher. 1996. Cements, Concrete, and Settling Barges At Sebastos: Comparisons with Other Roman Harbor Examples and the Descriptions of Vitruvius. Pages 25–40 in *Caesarea Maritima: A Retroperspective After Two Millennia*. Edited by Avner Raban, and Kenneth G. Holum. Leiden. Brill.

Brann, M. 1873. Die Söhne des Herodes. Eine biographische Skizze. 2. Antipas. *Monats-schrift für Geschichte und Wissenschaft des Judentums* XXII(7):305–44, 407–20, 459–74.

Braund, David. 1984. *Rome and the Friendly King: The Character of the Client King-ship*. London & Canberra: Croom Helm.

Brenner, Charles. 2001. Herod the Great Remains True to Form. *Near Eastern Archae-ology* 64(4):212–4.

Brown, Raymond E. 1994. *A Commentary on the Passion Narratives in the Four Gos-pels*. Vol. 1. *The Death of the Messiah: From Gethsemane to the Grave*. New York: Doubleday.

Bruce, F. F. 1963. Herod Antipas, Tetrarch of Galilee and Peraea. *The Annual of Leeds University Oriental Society* 5:6–23.

Bull, Robert J. 1982. Caesarea Maritima: The Search for Herod's City. *Biblical Archae-ology Review* 8(3):24–40.

Burrell, Barbara, Kathryn Gleason, and Ehud Netzer. 1993. Uncovering Herod's Seaside Palace. *Biblical Archaeology Review* 19(3):50–7, 76.

Carney, T. F. 1975. *The Shape of the Past: Models and Antiquity*. Lawrence, Kansas: Coronado Press.

Case, Shirley Jackson. 1926. Jesus and Sepphoris. *Journal of Biblical Literature* 45:14–22.

Chancey, Mark A. 2001. The Cultural Milieu of Ancient Sepphoris. *New Testament Stud-ies* 47:127–45.

–, 2002a. Jesus, The Centurion, and the Shadow of Rome. Paper presented at the SBL Annual Meeting. Toronto.

–, 2002b. *Myth of Gentile Galilee: The Population of Galilee and New Testament Studies*. Society for New Testament Studies Monograph Series 118. Cambridge: Cambridge University Press.

–, 2003. Galilee and Greco-Roman Culture in the Time of Jesus: The Neglected Signifi-cance of Chronology. *Society of Biblical Literature Seminar Paper Series* 42:173–87.

–, 2005. *Greco-Roman Culture and the Galilee of Jesus*. Society of New Testament Monograph Series 134. Cambridge: Cambridge University Press.

Charlesworth, James H., ed. 2006. *Jesus and Archaeology*. Grand Rapids, Michigan: Eerdmans.

Colson, F.H., Translator. 1962. *Philo: The Embassy to Gaius*. The Loeb Classical Library 379. Cambridge, Massachusetts: Harvard University Press.

Conder, C.R., and H.H. Kitchener. 1881. *Galilee*. Vol. 1 of *The Survey of Western Pal-estine*. Edited by E.H. Palmer, and Walter Besant. London: The Committee of the Pal-estine Exploration Fund.

Corbo, Virgilio C. 1992. Capernaum. Pages 866–9 in vol. 1 of *The Anchor Bible Diction-ary*. Edited by David Noel Freedman. 6 vols. New York: Doubleday.

Cotton, Hannah M., and Werner Eck. 2005. Josephus' Roman Audience: Josephus and the Roman Elites. Pages 37–52 in *Flavius Josephus and Flavian Rome*. Edited by Jonathan Edmonson, Steve Mason, and James Rives. Oxford: Oxford University Press.

Crossan, John Dominic. 1991. *The Historical Jesus: The Life of a Mediterranean Jewish Peasant*. San Francisco: HarperSanFrancisco.

–, 1997. Itinerants and Householders in the Earliest Jesus Movement. Pages 7–24 in *Whose Historical Jesus?* Edited by William E. Arnal, and Michel Desjardins. Canada: Canadian Corporation for Studies in Religion.

–, 1999. *The Birth of Christianity: Discovering What Happened in the Years Immediately After the Execution of Jesus*. Edinburgh: T. & T. Clark Ltd.

–, Forthcoming. The Relationship Between Galilean Archaeology and Historical Jesus Research. Unpublished article.

Crossan, John Dominic, and Jonathan L. Reed. 2001. *Excavating Jesus: Beneath the Stones, Behind the Texts*. New York: HarperSanFrancisco.

Currid, John D. 1999. *Doing Archaeology in the Land of the Bible: A Basic Guide*. Grand Rapids, Mich.: Baker Books.

Darr, John A. 1998. *Herod the Fox: Audience Criticism and Lukan Characterization*. Journal for the Study of the New Testament Supplement Series 163. Sheffield: Sheffield Academic Press.

Delbrueck, Richard. 1942. Antiquarisches zu den Verspottungen Jesu. *Zeitschrift für die neutestamentliche Wissenschaft* 41:124–45.

Derrett, J. Duncan M. 1965. Herod's Oath and the Baptist's Head. *Biblische Zeitschrift* IX:49–59, 233–46.

deSilva, David A. 2004. Embodying the Word: Social-Scientific Interpretation of the New Testament. Pages 118–29 in *The Face of New Testament Studies: A Survey of Recent Research*. Edited by Scot McKnight, and Grant R. Osborne. Grand Rapids, Michigan: BakerAcademic.

Dever, William G. 1980. Archeological Method in Israel: A Continuing Revolution. *Biblical Archaeologist* 43:41–8.

–, 1981. The Impact of the "New Archaeology" on Syro-Palestinian Archaeology. *Bulletin of the American Schools of Oriental Research* 242:15–30.

–, 1988. Impact of the "New Archaeology". Pages 337–52 in *Benchmarks in Time and Culture: An Introduction to Palestinian Archaeology*. Edited by Joel F. Drinkard, Gerald L. Mattingly, and Maxwell J. Miller. Atlanta, Georgia: Scholars Press.

–, 2001. *What Did the Biblical Writers Know and When Did They Know It?: What Archaeology Can Tell Us About the Reality of Ancient Israel*. Grand Rapids, Michigan: William B. Eerdmans Publishing Company.

Dever, William G., and H. Darrell Lance. 1978. *A Manual Of Field Excavation*. Cincinatti: Hebrew Union College.

Dibelius, Martin. 1915. Herodes und Pilatus. *Zeitschrift für die neutestamentliche Wissenschaft* 16:113–26.

DiTommaso, Lorenzo. 1999. Review of *Turbulent Times?* by James McLaren. *Journal for the Study of Judaism in the Persian, Hellenistic and Roman Period* 30(3):359–63.

Dittenberger, Wilhelmus, ed. 1903. Vol. 1. *Orientis Graeci Inscriptiones Selectae: Supplementum Syllogoges Inscriptionum Graecarum*. Lipsiae: S. Hirzel.

Downing, F. Gerald. 1987. The Social Contexts of Jesus the Teacher: Construction or Reconstruction. *New Testament Studies* 33:439–51.

–, 1988. *Christ and the Cynics: Jesus and Other Radical Preachers in First-Century Tradition*. JSOT Manuals 4. Sheffield: Sheffield Academic Press.

–, 1992. *Cynics and Christian Origins*. Edinburgh: T. & T. Clark Ltd.

Drinkard, Joel F., Jr., Gerald L. Mattingly, and Maxwell J. Miller, eds. 1988. *Benchmarks in Time and Culture: An Introduction to Palestinian Archaeology*. Atlanta, Georgia: Scholars Press.

Dyson, Stephan L. 1981. A Classical Archaeologist's Response to the "New Archaeology". *Bulletin of the American Schools of Oriental Research* 242:7–14.

–, 1993. From New to New Age Archaeology: Archaeological Theory and Classical Archaeology – A 1990s Perspective. *American Journal of Archaeology* 97:195–203.

Edwards, Douglas R. 1988. First Century Urban/Rural Relations in Lower Galilee: Exploring the Archaeological and Literary Evidence. Pages 169–82 in *Society of Biblical*

Literature 1988 Seminar Papers. Edited by David J. Lull. Vol. 27 of *Society of Biblical Literature Seminar Paper Series*. Atlanta, Georgia: Scholars Press.

–, 1992. The Socio-Economic and Cultural Ethos of the Lower Galilee in the First Century: Implications for the Nascent Jesus Movement. Pages 53–73 in *The Galilee in Late Antiquity*. Edited by Lee I. Levine. New York: The Jewish Theological Seminary of America.

–, 1997. Jotapata. Pages 251–2 in vol. 2 of *The Oxford Encyclopedia of Archaeology in the Near East*. Edited by Eric M. Meyers. 5 vols. New York, Oxford: Oxford University Press.

–, 2001. Cana (Khirbet). Pages 109–10 in *Archaeological Encyclopaedia of the Holy Land*. Edited by Avraham Negev, and Shimon Gibson. 1 vol. New York – London: Continuum.

–, 2002. Khirbet Qana: From Jewish Village to Christian Pilgrim Site. Pages 101–32. Edited by J.H. Humphrey. Vol. 3 of *The Roman and Byzantine Near East* of *Journal of Roman Archaeology Supplementary Series Number 49*. Portsmouth: JRA.

–, Forthcoming. Identity and Social Location in Roman Galilean Villages. In *Religion, Ethnicity and Identity in Ancient Galilee*. Edited by Harold W. Attridge, Dale B. Martin, and Jürgen Zangenberg. Tübingen: Mohr Siebeck.

Edwards, Douglas R., and C. Thomas McCollough, eds. 1997a. *Archaeology and the Galilee: Texts and Contexts in Graeco-Roman and Byzantine Periods*. Atlanta, Georgia: Scholars Press.

–, 1997b. Transformation of Space: The Roman Road At Sepphoris. Pages 135–42 in *Archaeology and the Galilee: Texts and Contexts in the Graeco-Roman and Byzantine Periods*. Edited by Douglas R Edwards, and C. Thomas McCollough. Vol. 143 of *South Florida Studies in the History of Judaism*. Atlanta, Georgia: Scholars Press.

Elliott, John H. 1993. *What Is Social-Scientific Criticism?* Minneapolis: Fortress Press.

Epstein, Claire. 1993. Hippos (Sussita). Pages 634–6 in vol. 2 of *The New Encyclopedia of Archaeological Excavations in the Holy Land*. Edited by Ephraim Stern. 4 vols. Jerusalem: The Israel Exploration Society & Carta.

Esler, Philip F. 1994. *The First Christians in Their Social Worlds*. London and New York: Routledge.

–, 2000. Models in New Testament Interpretation: A Reply to David Horrell. *Journal for the Study of the New Testament* 78:107–13.

Evans, Jane DeRose. 1992. *The Art of Persuasion: Political Propaganda From Aeneas to Brutus*. Ann Arbor: The University of Michigan Press.

Feldman, Louis H., Translator. 1965. *Josephus: Jewish Antiquities Books XVIII-XIX*. The Loeb Classical Library 433. Cambridge, Massachusetts: Harvard University Press.

–, 1981–1982. The Term "Galileans" in Josephus. *Jewish Quarterly Review* 72:50–2.

–, 1996. *Studies in Hellenistic Judaism*. Leiden. Brill.

Fiensy, David A. 1991. *The Social History of Palestine in the Herodian Period: The Land Is Mine*. Studies in the Bible and Early Christianity 20. Lewiston/Queenston/Lampeter: The Edwin Mellen Press.

Fine, Steven. 1989. On the Development of a Symbol: The Date Palm in Roman Palestine and the Jews. *Journal for the Study of the Pseudepigrapha* 4:105–18.

–, 2005. *Art and Judaism in the Greco-Roman World: Toward a New Jewish Archaeology*. Cambridge: Cambridge University Press.

Fischer, Moshe. 1996. Marble, Urbanism, and Ideology in Roman Palestine: The Caesarea Example. Pages 251–61 in *Caesarea Maritima: A Retroperspective After Two Millennia*. Edited by Avner Raban, and Kenneth G. Holum. Leiden: Brill.

Fittschen, Klaus. 1996. Wall Decorations in Herod's Kingdom: Their Relationship with Wall Decorations in Greece and Italy. Pages 139–61 in *Judaea and the Greco-Roman World in the Time of Herod in the Light of Archaeological Evidence*. Edited by Klaus Fittschen, and Gideon Foerster. Göttingen: Vanderhoeck & Ruprecht.

Fitzmyer, Joseph A. 1985. *The Gospel According to Luke X-XXIV*. The Anchor Bible 28a. Garden City, N.Y.: Doubleday.

Foerster, Gideon. 1993a. Tiberias: Excavations in the South of the City. Pages 1470–3 in vol. 4 of *The New Encyclopedia of Archaeological Excavations in the Holy Land*. Edited by Ephraim Stern. 4 vols. Jerusalem: The Israel Exploration Society & Carta.

–, 1993b. Beth-Shean At the Foot of the Mound. Pages 223–35 in vol. 1 of *The New Encyclopedia of Archaeological Excavations in the Holy Land*. Edited by Ephraim Stern. 4 vols. Jerusalem: The Israel Exploration Society & Carta.

Fontanille, Jean-Philippe, and Sheldon Lee Gosline. 2001. *The Coins of Pontius Pilate*. Marco Polo Monographs 4. Warren Center, Pennsylvania: Shangri-La Publications.

Fortner, Sandra. 2003. Tiberias – Eine Stadt zu Ehren des Kaisers. Pages 86–92 in *Leben am See Gennesaret: Kulturgeschichtliche Entdeckungen in einer biblischen Region*. Edited by Jürgen Zangenberg et al. of *Sonderbände der Antiken Welt*. Mainz am Rhein: Verlag Philipp von Zabern.

Frankel, Rafael et al. 2001. *Settlement Dynamics and Regional Diversity in Ancient Upper Galilee*. IAA Reports 14. Jerusalem: Israel Antiquities Authority.

Freyne, Sean. 1980a. The Galileans in the Light of Josephus' *Vita*. New Testament Studies 26:397–413.

–, 1980b. *Galilee From Alexander the Great to Hadrian 323 B.C.E. To 135 C.E.: A Study of Second Temple Judaism*. University of Notre Dame Center for the Study of Judaism and Christianity in Antiquity 5. Wilmington: Glazier/Notre Dame University Press.

–, 1988a. Bandits in Galilee: A Contribution to the Study of Social Conditions in First Century Palestine. Pages 50–68 in *The Social World of Formative Christianity and Judaism: Essays in Tribute of Howard Clark Kee*. Edited by Jacob Neusner et al. Philadelphia: Fortress Press.

–, 1988b. *Galilee, Jesus and the Gospels: Literary Approaches and Historical Investigations*. Philadelphia: Fortress Press.

–, 1992. Urban-Rural Relations in First-Century Galilee: Some Suggestions From the Literary Sources. Pages 75–91 in *The Galilee in Late Antiquity*. Edited by Lee I. Levine. New York: The Jewish Theological Seminary of America.

–, 1994. The Geography, Politics, and Economics of Galilee and the Quest for the Historical Jesus. Pages 75–122 in *Studying the Historical Jesus: Evaluations of the State of the Current Research*. Edited by Bruce Chilton, and Craig A. Evans. Leiden: Brill.

–, 1995. Jesus and the Urban Culture of Galilee. Pages 597–622 in *Texts and Contexts: Biblical Texts in Their Textual and Situational Contexts*. Edited by D. Hellholm, and T. Fornberg. Oslo, Copenhagen, Stockholm, Boston: Scandinavian University Press.

–, 1997a. Galilean Questions to Crossan's Mediterranean Jesus. Pages 63–91 in *Whose Historical Jesus?* Edited by William E. Arnal, and Michel Desjardins. Canada: Canadian Corporation for Studies in Religion.

–, 1997b. Town and Country Once More: The Case of Roman Galilee. Pages 49–56 in *Archaeology and the Galilee: Texts and Contexts in the Graeco-Roman and Byzantine Periods*. Edited by Douglas R. Edwards, and C. Thomas McCollough. Vol. 143 of *South Florida Studies in the History of Judaism*. Atlanta, Georgia: Scholars Press.

–, 1999. Behind the Names, Galileans, Samaritans, *Ioudaioi*. Pages 39–55 in *Galilee Through the Centuries: Confluence of Cultures*. Edited by Eric M. Meyers. of *Duke Judaic Studies Series Volume 1*. Winona Lake, Indiana: Eisenbrauns.

–, 2000a. Archaeology and the Historical Jesus. Pages 160–82 in *Galilee and Gospel: Collected Essays.* Tübingen: J.C.B. Mohr (Paul Siebeck). Repr. 1997. *Archaeology and Biblical Interpretation.* London: Routledge.

–, 2000a. Herodian Economics in Galilee. Searching for a Suitable Model. Pages 86–113 in *Galilee and Gospel: Collected Essays.* Tübingen: Mohr Siebeck. Repr. 1995. Pages 23–46 in *Modelling Early Christianity: Social-Scientific Studies of the New Testament in Its Context.* London and New York: Routledge.

–, 2000a. Introduction. Galilean Studies: Problems and Prospects. Pages 1–26 in *Galilee and Gospel: Collected Essays.* Tübingen: J.C.B. Mohr (Paul Siebeck).

–, 2001. A Galilean Messiah? *Studia theologica* 55(2):198–218.

–, 2004. *Jesus, A Jewish Galilean: A New Reading of the Jesus-Story.* London – New York: T&T Clark International.

–, Forthcoming. The Galilean Social World: A Josephan Perspective in *Jesus und die Archäologie Galiläas.* Edited by Jörg Frey, and Carsten Claußen. of *Biblische theologische Studien.* Neukirchener: Neukirchen-Vluyn.

Fritz, Volkmar. 1994. *An Introduction to Biblical Archaeology.* Journal for the Study of the Old Testament. Sheffield, England: JSOT Press.

Fuks, Gideon. 2002. Josephus on Herod's Attitude Towards Jewish Religion: The Darker Side. *Journal of Jewish Studies* LIII(2):238–45.

Gal, Zvi. 1992. *Lower Galilee During the Iron Age.* American Schools of Oriental Research Dissertation Series 8, trans. Marcia Reines Josephy. Winona Lake, Indiana: Eisenbrauns.

Garrett, Susan. 1992. Sociology of Early Christianity. Pages 89–99 in vol. 6 of *The Anchor Bible Dictionary.* Edited by David Noel Freedman. 6 vols. New York: Doubleday.

Gilbert, Gary. 2003. Review of *Excavating Jesus: Beneath the Stones, Behind the Texts*, by John Dominic Crossan, and Jonathan L. Reed. *Review of Biblical Literature.* [Cited May 2006]. Available from http://www.bookreviews.org

Gillman, Florence Morgan. 2003. *Herodias: At Home in That Fox's Den.* Interfaces. Collegeville, Minnesota: Liturgical Press.

Gutman, Shmaryahu. 1979. Gamla: The Masada of the North. *Biblical Archaeology Review* 5(1).

–, 1984. Gamla – 1983. *Excavations and Surveys in Israel* 3:26–7.

–, 1993. Gamla. Pages 459–63 in vol. 2 of *The New Encyclopedia of Archaeological Excavations in the Holy Land.* Edited by Ephraim Stern. 4 vols. Jerusalem: The Israel Exploration Society & Carta.

Gutman, Shmaryahu et al. 1990. Gamla – 1987/1988. *Excavations and Surveys in Israel* 9:9–13.

Gutman, Shmaryahu, and D. Wagner. 1986. Gamla – 1984/1985/1986. *Excavations and Surveys in Israel* 5:38–41.

Hachlili, Rachel. 1988. *Ancient Jewish Art and Archaeology in the Land of Israel.* Handbuch Der Orientalistik 7. Leiden: Brill.

Hanson, K.C. 1989a. The Herodians and Mediterranean Kinship Part 2: Marriage and Divorce. *Biblical Theology Bulletin* 19:142–51.

–, 1989b. The Herodians and Mediterranean Kinship Part I: Genealogy and Descent. *Biblical Theology Bulletin* 19:75–84.

–, 1990. The Herodians and Mediterranean Kinship Part III: Economics. *Biblical Theology Bulletin* 20:10–21.

–, 1994. BTB Readers Guide: Kinship. *Biblical Theology Bulletin* 24:183–94.

–, 1997. The Galilean Fishing Economy and the Jesus Tradition. *Biblical Theology Bulletin* 27(3):99–111.

Hanson, K.C., and Douglas E. Oakman. 1998. *Palestine in the Time of Jesus: Social Structures and Social Conflicts*. Minneapolis: Fortress Press.

Hanson, Richard S. 1980. *Tyrian Influence in Upper Galilee*. Meiron Excavation Project 2. Cambridge: ASOR.

Harlow, Victor E. 1936. *Jesus' Jerusalem Expedition*. Oklahoma City: Harlow Publishing Corporation.

–, 1954. *The Destroyer of Jesus: The Story of Herod Antipas Tetrarch of Galilee*. Oklahoma City: Modern Publishers.

Hayes, John W. 1997. Ceramics of the Hellenistic and Roman Periods. Pages 469–71 in vol. 1 of *The Oxford Encyclopedia of Archaeology in the Near East*. Edited by Eric M. Meyers. 5 vols. Oxford, New York: Oxford University Press.

Hendin, David. Forthcoming. A New Coin Type of Herod Antipas. *Israel Numismatic Journal*.

–, 1976. *Guide To Ancient Jewish Coins*. New York: New York Attic Books Ltd.

–, 2000. Numismatic Expressions of Jewish Sovereignty: The Unusual Iconography of Coinage of the Hasmonean Dynasty. [Cited 2005]. Available from http://www.david-hendin.com.

–, 2001. *Guide to Biblical Coins*. 4th ed. New York: Amphora.

Herr, Larry G. 1997. Periodization. Pages 267–73 in vol. 4 of *The Oxford Encyclopedia of Archaeology in the Near East*. Edited by Eric M. Meyers. 5 vols. Oxford, New York: Oxford University Press.

Hill, George Francis. 1965. *Catalogue of the Greek Coins of Palestine: Galilee, Samaria and Judaea*. 1914. Reprint. Bologna: Arnaldo Forni.

Hirschfeld, Yizhar. 1989–1990. Tiberias. *Excavations and Surveys in Israel* 9:107–9.

–, 1990. Tiberias. *Excavations and Surveys in Israel* 10:94–7.

–, 1991a. Excavations At Tiberias Reveal Remains of Church and Possibly Theater. *Biblical Archaeologist* 54:170–1.

–, 1991b. Tiberias: Preview of Coming Attractions. *Biblical Archaeology Review* 17(02):-44–51.

–, 1992. *A Guide to Antiquity Sites in Tiberias*. Jerusalem: Israel Antiquities Authority.

–, 1993. Tiberias. Pages 1464–70 in vol. 4 of *The New Encyclopedia of Archaeological Excavations in the Holy Land*. Edited by Ephraim Stern. 4 vols. Jerusalem: The Israel Exploration Society & Carta.

–, 1994. The Anchor Church At the Summit of Mt. Berenice, Tiberias. *Biblical Archaeologist* 57(3):122–33.

–, 1997a. Tiberias. Pages 203–6 in vol. 5 of *The Oxford Encyclopedia of Archaeology in the Near East*. Edited by Eric M. Meyers. 5 vols. Oxford, New York: Oxford University Press.

–, 1997b. Tiberias. *Excavations and Surveys in Israel* 16:35–42.

–, 2004. *Excavations At Tiberias, 1989–1994*. IAA Reports 22. Jerusalem: Israel Antiquities Authority.

Hirschfeld, Yizhar, and Katharina Galor. Forthcoming. New Excavations in Roman, Byzantine and Early Islamic Tiberias. In *Religion, Ethnicity and Identity in Ancient Galilee*. Edited by Jürgen Zangenberg, Harold Attridge, and Dale B. Martin. Tübingen: Mohr Siebeck.

Hobsbawn, Eric. 1969. *Bandits*. England: George Weidenfeld & Nicolson, Ltd.

Hodder, Ian. 1986. *Reading the Past: Current Approaches to Interpretation in Archaeology*. Cambridge: Cambridge University Press.

–, 1999. *The Archaeological Process: An Introduction*. Oxford: Blackwell Publishers Ltd.

Hoehner, Harold W. 1972. *Herod Antipas*. Society for New Testament Studies Monograph Series 17. London: Cambridge University Press.

Hoffmann, Adolf. 1999. Gadara – Stadt und Umland. Pages 223–36 in *Stadt und Umland: Neue Ergebnisse der archäologischen Bau- und Siedlungsforschung*. Edited by Ernst-Ludwig Schwandner, and Klaus Rheidt. Vol. 7 of *Diskussion zur Archäologischen Bauforschung*. Mainz: Verlag Philipp von Zabern.

–, 2002. Topographie und Stadgeschichte von Gadara/Umm Qais. Pages 98–124 in *Gadara – Gerasa und die Dekapolis*. Edited by Adolf Hoffmann, and Susanne Kerner. Mainz: Verlag Philipp von Zabern.

Hoglund, Kenneth G., and Eric M. Meyers. 1996. The Residential Quarter on the Western Summit. Pages 39–44 in *Sepphoris in Galilee: Crosscurrents of Culture*. Edited by Rebecca Martin Nagy. Raleigh: North Carolina Museum of Art.

Holmberg, Bengt. 1990. *Sociology and the New Testament: An Appraisal*. Minneapolis: Fortress Press.

Holmén, Tom. 1999. Doubts About Double Dissimilarity: Restructuring the Main Criterion of Jesus-of-History Research. Pages 47–80 in *Authenticating the Words of Jesus*. Edited by Bruce Chilton, and Craig A. Evans. Leiden: Brill.

Holum, Kenneth G. 1997. Caesarea. Pages 399–404 in vol. 1 of *The Oxford Encyclopedia of Archaeology in the Near East*. Edited by Eric M. Meyers. 5 vols. New York, Oxford: Oxford University Press.

Holum, Kenneth G., and Avner Raban. 1993. Caesarea: The Joint Expedition's Excavations, Excavations in the 1980s and 1990s, and Summary. Pages 282–6 in vol. 1 of *The New Encyclopedia of Archaeological Excavations in the Holy Land*. Edited by Ephraim Stern. 4 vols. Jerusalem: The Israel Exploration Society & Carta.

Hopkins, Ian W.J. 1980. The City Region in Roman Palestine. *Palestine Exploration Quarterly* 113:19–32.

Horrell, David G. 1999. Social-Scientific Interpretation to the New Testament: Retrospect and Prospect. Pages 3–28 in *Social-Scientific Approaches to New Testament Interpretation*. Edited by David G. Horrell. Edinburgh: T&T Clark.

–, 2000. Models and Methods in Social-Scientific Interpretation: A Response to Philip Esler. *Journal for the Study of the New Testament* 78:83–105.

–, 2002. Social Sciences Studying Formative Christian Phenomena: A Creative Moment. Pages 3–28 in *Handbook of Early Christianity: Social Science Approaches*. Edited by Anthony J. Blasi, Jean Duhaime, and Paul-André Turcotte. Walnut Creek: Altamira Press.

Horsley, Richard A. 1979a. Josephus and the Bandits. *Journal for the Study of Judaism in the Persian, Hellenistic and Roman Period* X(1):37–63.

–, 1979b. The Sicarii: Ancient Jewish "Terrorists". *Journal of Religion* 59:435–58.

–, 1981. Ancient Jewish Banditry and the Revolt Against Rome, A.D. 66–70. *Catholic Biblical Quarterly* 43:409–32.

–, 1984. Popular Messianic Movements Around the Time of Jesus. *Catholic Biblical Quarterly* 46:471–95.

–, 1986. The Zealots: Their Origin, Relationships and Importance in the Jewish Revolt. *Novum Testamentum* 28(2):159–92.

–, 1988. Bandits, Messiahs, and Longshoremen: Popular Unrest in Galilee Around the Time of Jesus. Pages 183–99 in *Society of Biblical Literature 1988 Seminar Papers*. Edited by David J. Lull. Vol. 27 of *Society of Biblical Literature Seminar Paper Series*. Atlanta, Georgia: Scholars Press.

–, 1989. *Sociology and the Jesus Movement*. New York: Crossroad.

–, 1993. *Jesus and the Spiral of Violence: Popular Jewish Resistance in Roman Palestine*. San Francisco: Harper & Row, 1987. Reprint. Minneapolis: Fortress Press.

–, 1994. The Historical Jesus and Archaeology of the Galilee: Questions From Historical Jesus Research to Archaeologists. Pages 91–135 in *Society of Biblical Literature 1994 Seminar Papers*. Edited by Eugene Lovering, H., Jr. Vol. 33 of *Society of Biblical Literature Seminar Paper Series*. Atlanta, Georgia: Scholars Press.

–, 1995a. Archaeology and the Villages of Upper Galilee: A Dialogue with Archaeologists. *Bulletin of the American Schools of Oriental Research* 297:5–16; 27–8.

–, 1995b. Archaeology of Galilee and the Historical Context of Jesus. *Neotestamentica* 29(2):211–29.

–, 1995c. *Galilee: History, Politics, People*. Valley Forge, Pennsylvania: Trinity Press International.

–, 1996. *Archaeology, History, and Society in Galilee: The Social Context of Jesus and the Rabbis*. Valley Forge, Pennsylvania: Trinity Press International.

–, 1999. Jesus and Galilee: The Contingencies of a Renewal Movement. Pages 57–74 in *Galilee Through the Centuries: Confluence of Cultures*. Edited by Eric M. Meyers. Winona Lake, Indiana: Eisenbrauns.

–, 2001. *Hearing the Whole Story: The Politics of Plot in Mark's Gospel*. Louisville: Westminster John Knox Press.

Horsley, Richard A., and Jonathan A. Draper. 1999. *Whoever Hears You Hears Me: Prophets, Performance, and Tradition in Q*. Harrisburg, Pennsylvania: Trinity Press International.

Horsley, Richard A., and John S. Hanson. 1985. *Bandits, Prophets, and Messiahs: Popular Movements in the Time of Jesus*. Minneapolis: Winston Press.

Horsley, Richard A., and Neil Asher Silberman. 1997. *The Message and the Kingdom: How Jesus and Paul Ignited a Revolution and Transformed the Ancient World*. Minneapolis: Fortress Press.

Howgego, Christopher. 1995. *Ancient History From Coins*. Approaching the Ancient World. London: Routledge.

Humphrey, John. H. 1996. "Amphitheatrical" Hippo-Stadia. Pages 121–9 in *Caesarea Maritima: A Retroperspective After Two Millennia*. Edited by Avner Raban, and Kenneth G. Holum. Leiden: Brill.

Jacobson, David M. 2001. Herod the Great Shows His True Colors. *Near Eastern Archaeology* 64(3):100–4.

Jacoby, Felix. 1926. *Die Fragmente der griechischen Historiker*. IIA. Berlin: Weidmannsche Buchhandlung.

Jensen, Morten Hørning. 2002a. Galilæa – arkæologi og historisk Jesus-forskning. Pages 41–55 in *Collegium Biblicum Årsskrift*. Edited by Ole Davidsen. København: Collegium Biblicum.

–, 2002b. *Galilæa på Jesu tid: En præsentation og vurdering af de sidste to årtiers Galilæa-forskning*. Aarhus: TeolTryk.

–, 2006. Josephus and Antipas: A Case Study of Josephus' Narratives on Herod Antipas. Pages 287–312 in *Making History: Josephus and Historical Method*. Edited by Zuleika Rodgers. Leiden: Brill.

–, Forthcoming. Message and Minting: The Coins of Herod Antipas in Their Second Temple Context As a Source for Understanding the Religio-Political and Socio-Economic Dynamics of Early First Century Galilee. In *Religion, Ethnicity and Identity in Ancient Galilee*. Edited by Jürgen Zangenberg, Harold Attridge, and Dale B. Martin. Tübingen: Mohr Siebeck.

Jervell, Jacob. 1960. Herodes Antipas og hans plass i evangelieoverleveringen. *Norsk Teologisk Tidsskrift* 61(1):28–40.

Jones, A.H.M. 1938. *The Herods of Judaea*. Oxford: Oxford at the Clarendon Press.

Kanael, Baruch. 1963. Ancient Jewish Coins and Their Historical Importance. *Biblical Archaeologist* 26:38–62.

Kelly, Morgan. Unpublished Article. Division of Labour in the Long Run: Evidence From Small Change.

Kindler, A. 1958. The Coinage of the Hasmonaean Dynasty. Pages 10–28 in *The Dating and Meaning of Ancient Jewish Coins and Symbols: Six Essays in Jewish Numismatics*. Tel-Aviv – Jerusalem: Schocken Publishing House.

–, 1961. *The Coins of Tiberias*. Israel: Hamei Tiberia.

Klimowsky, E.W. 1958. Symbols on Ancient Jewish Coins. Pages 81–97 in *The Dating and Meaning of Ancient Jewish Coins and Symbols: Six Essays in Jewish Numismatics*. Edited by L. Kadman et al. Tel-Aviv – Jerusalem: Schocken Publishing House.

Kloppenborg Verbin, John S. 2000. *Excavating Q: The History and Setting of the Sayings Gospel*. Minneapolis: Fortress Press.

Kokkinos, Nikos. 1998. *The Herodian Dynasty: Origins, Role in Society and Eclipse*. Journal for the Study of the Pseudepigrapha Supplement Series 30. Sheffield: Sheffield Academic Press.

Krieger, Klaus-Stefan. 1994. *Geschichtsschreibung als Apologetik bei Flavius Josephus*. Texte und Arbeiten zum neutestamentlichen Zeitalter 9. Tübingen: A. Francke Verlag.

–, 2000. A Synoptic Approach to *War* 2 §§ 117–283 and *Antiquities* 18–20. Paper presented at the SBL Annual Meeting. Toronto. November 19. [Cited May 2006]. Available from http://pace.cns.yorku.ca/York/york/josephus-ext.htm.

Lapin, Hayim. 2001. *Economy, Geography, and Provincial History in Later Roman Palestine*. Texts and Studies in Ancient Judaism 85. Tübingen: Mohr Siebeck.

Lämmer, Manfred. 1976. Griechische Wettkämpfe in Galiläa unter der Herrschaft des Herodes Antipas. *Kölner Beitrage zur Sportwissenschaft* 5:37–67.

Laughlin, John C.H. 1993. Capernaum: From Jesus' Time and After. *Biblical Archaeology Review* 19(5):54–61.

–, 2000. *Archaeology and the Bible*. Approaching the Ancient World. London : Routledge.

Lebram, J.C.H. 1973. Review of *Herod Antipas*, by Harald Hoehner. *Vigilae Christianae* 27(3):232–5.

Levine, Lee I. 1974. R. Simeon B. Yohai and the Purification of Tiberias: History and Tradition. *Hebrew Union College Annual* 49:134–85.

–, ed. 1992. *The Galilee in Late Antiquity*. New York: The Jewish Theological Seminary of America.

–, 1997. Archaeology and the Religious Ethos of Pre-70 Palestine. Pages 110–20 in *Hillel and Jesus: Comparative Studies of Two Major Religious Leaders*. Edited by James H. Charlesworth, and Loren L. Johns. Minneapolis: Fortress Press.

–, 2000. *The Ancient Synagogue: The First Thousand Years*. New Haven & London: Yale University Press.

Lichtenberger, Achim. 2003. *Kulte und Kultur der Dekapolis*. Abhandlungen des deutschen Palästina-Vereins 29. Wiesbaden: Harrassowitz Verlag.

Liversidge, Joan. 1983. Wall Painting and Stucco. Pages 97–115 in *A Handbook of Roman Art: A Survey of the Visual Arts of the Roman World*. Edited by Martin Henig. Oxford: Phaidon.

Loffreda, Stanislao. 1985. *Recovering Capharnaum*. Studium Biblicum Franciscanum Guides 1. Jerusalem: Custodia Terra Santa.

–, 1993. Capernaum. Pages 291–5 in vol. 1 of *The New Encyclopedia of Archaeological Excavations in the Holy Land*. Edited by Ephraim Stern. 4 vols. Jerusalem: The Israel Exploration Society & Carta.

–, 1997. Capernaum. Pages 416–9 in vol. 1 of *The Oxford Encyclopedia of Archaeology in the Near East*. Edited by Eric M. Meyers. 5 vols. New York, Oxford: Oxford University Press.

Loftus, Francis. 1974. A Note on Σύνταγμα τῶν γαλιλαίων B.J. Iv 558. *Jewish Quarterly Review* 65:182–83.

–, 1977–1978. The Anti-Roman Revolts of the Jews and the Galileans. *Jewish Quarterly Review* 68:78–98.

Longstaff, Thomas R.W., and Tristram C. Hussey. 1997. Palynology and Cultural Process: An Exercise in the New Archaeology. Pages 151–62 in *Archaeology and the Galilee: Texts and Contexts in the Graeco-Roman and Byzantine Periods*. Edited by Douglas R. Edwards, and C. Thomas McCollough. Vol. 143 of *South Florida Studies in the History of Judaism*. Atlanta, Georgia: Scholars Press.

Lovering, Eugene, H., Jr., ed. 1994. *Society of Biblical Literature 1994 Seminar Papers*. Society of Biblical Literature Seminar Paper Series 33. Atlanta, Georgia: Scholars Press.

Lull, David J., ed. 1988. *Society of Biblical Literature 1988 Seminar Papers*. Society of Biblical Literature Seminar Paper Series 27. Atlanta, Georgia: Scholars Press.

Mack, Burton L. 1988. *A Myth of Innocence: Mark and Christian Origins*. Philadelphia: Fortress Press.

–, 1993. *The Lost Gospel: The Book of Q & Christian Origins*. Shaftesbury, Dorset: Element.

–, 1997. Q and a Cynic-Like Jesus. Pages 25–36 in *Whose Historical Jesus?* Edited by William E. Arnal, and Michel Desjardins. Canada: Canadian Corporation for Studies in Religion.

Mackowski, Richard M. 1979. "Scholars' Qanah". *Biblische Zeitschrift* 23:278–84.

Madden, Frederic W. 1864. *History of Jewish Coinage and of Money in the Old and New Testament*. London: Bernard Quaritch.

Magness, Jodi. 2001. The Question of the Synagogue: The Problem of Typology. Pages 1–48 in *The Special Problem of the Synagogue*. Edited by Alan J. Avery-Peck, and Jacob Neusner. Vol. 4 of *Judaism in Late Antiquity. Part Three: Where We Stand: Issues and Debates in Ancient Judaism*. Leiden: Brill.

Malina, Bruce J. 1996. *The Social World of Jesus and the Gospels*. London and New York: Routledge.

–, 2001. *The New Testament World: Insights From Cultural Anthropology*. 3. (rev. & exp.) Louisville, Kentucky: Westminster John Knox Press.

Malitz, Jürgen. 2003. *Nikolaos von Damaskus: Leben des Kaisers Augustus*. Texte zur Forschung 80. Darmstadt: Wissenschaftliche Buchgesellschaft.

Manasseh, N. E. 1937. Architecture and Topography. Pages 1–16 in *Preliminary Report of the University of Michigan Excavations At Sepphoris, Palestine, In 1931*. Edited by Leroy Waterman. Ann Arbor: University of Michigan Press.

Marshall, John W. 1997. The *Gospel of Thomas* and the Cynic Jesus. Pages 37–60 in *Whose Historical Jesus?* Edited by William E. Arnal, and Michel Desjardins. Canada: Canadian Corporation for Studies in Religion.

Martin, Dale B. 1999. Social-Scientific Criticism. Pages 125–41 in *To Each Its Own Meaning: An Introduction to Biblical Criticisms and Their Application*. Edited by Steven L. McKenzie, and Sephen R. Haynes, 2nd ed. Louisville, London, Leiden: Westminster John Knox Press.

Mason, Steve. 1998. Should Any Wish to Enquire Further (*Ant.* 1.25): The Aim and Audience of Josephus's *Judean Antiquities/Life.* Pages 64–103 in *Understanding Josephus: Seven Perspectives.* Edited by Steve Mason. Vol. 32 of *Journal for the Study of the Pseudoepigrapha Supplement Series.* Sheffield: Sheffield Academic Press.

–, 2001. *Life of Josephus: Translation and Commentary.* Flavius Josephus: Translation and Commentary 9. Leiden: Brill.

–, 2003a. Contradiction or Counterpoint? Josephus and Historical Method. *Review of Rabbinic Judaism* 6(2–3):145–88.

–, 2003b. Flavius Josephus in Flavian Rome: Reading On and Between the Lines. Pages 559–89 in *Flavian Rome: Culture, Image, Text.* Edited by A.J. Boyle, and W.J. Dominik. Leiden: Brill.

–, 2003c. *Josephus and the New Testament.* 2nd rev. and enl. ed. Peabody, Massachusetts: Hendrickson Publisher, Inc.

–, 2005a. Figured Speech and Irony in Flavius Josephus. Pages 243–88 in *Flavius Josephus and Flavian Rome.* Edited by Jonathan Edmonson, Steve Mason, and James Rives. Oxford: Oxford University Press.

–, 2005b. Reading Josephus' *Bellum Iudaicum* in the Context of Flavian Audience. Pages 70–100 in *Josephus and Jewish History in Flavian Rome and Beyond.* Edited by Joseph Sievers, and Gaia Lembi. Vol. 104 of *Supplements to the Journal for the Study of Judaism.* Leiden: Brill.

McLaren, James S. 1998. *Turbulent Times? Josephus and Scholarship on Judaea in the First Century CE.* Journal for the Study of the Pseudoepigrapha Supplement Series 29. Sheffield: Sheffield Academic Press.

–, 2001. Would the real Judas please stand up? Paper presented at the SBL Annual Meeting. Denver. November 19. [Cited May 2006]. Available from http://pace.cns.yorku.ca/York/york/conference2001–ext.htm.

McRay, John. 1988. Excavation of Low-Level Settlement Sites. Pages 169–78 in *Benchmarks in Time and Culture: An Introduction to Palestinian Archaeology.* Edited by Joel F. Drinkard, Gerald L. Mattingly, and Maxwell J. Miller. Atlanta, Georgia: Scholars Press.

–, 1997. *Archeology & The New Testament.* 1991. Reprint. Grand Rapids, Michigan: Baker Book House.

Meier, John P. 1991. *A Marginal Jew: Rethinking the Historical Jesus.* Vol. 1. *The Roots of the Problem and the Person.* New York: Doubleday.

Meshorer, Ya'akov. 1967. *Jewish Coins of the Second Temple Period,* trans. I.H. Levine. Tel-Aviv: AM Hassefer Publishers Ltd.

–, 1982a. *Ancient Jewish Coinage. Volume I: Persian Period Through Hasmonaeans.* New York: Amphora Books.

–, 1982b. *Ancient Jewish Coinage. Volume II: Herod the Great Through Bar Kochba.* New York: Amphora Books.

–, 1985. *City-Coins of Eretz-Israel and the Decapolis in the Roman Period.* Jerusalem: The Israel Museum.

–, 1996. Market Weight. Pages 201 in *Sepphoris in Galilee: Crosscurrents of Culture.* Edited by Rebecca Martin Nagy. Raleigh: North Carolina Museum of Art.

–, 2001. *A Treasury of Jewish Coins: From the Persian Period to Bar Kokhba.* Jerusalem: Yad Ben-Zvi Press.

Meyers, Carol L., and Eric M. Meyers. 1997. Sepphoris. Pages 527–36 in vol. 4 of *The Oxford Encyclopedia of Archaeology in the Near East.* Edited by Eric M. Meyers. 5 vols. New York, Oxford: Oxford University Press.

Meyers, Carol L. et al. 1996. The Dionysos Mosaic. Pages 111–5 in *Sepphoris in Galilee: Crosscurrents of Culture*. Edited by Rebecca Martin Nagy. Raleigh: North Carolina Museum of Art.

Meyers, Eric M. 1976. Galilean Regionalism As a Factor in Historical Reconstruction. *Bulletin of the American Schools of Oriental Research* 221:92–102.

–, 1979. The Cultural Setting of Galilee: The Case of Regionalism and Early Judaism. Pages 686–702 in *Judentum: Allgemeines; Palästinisches Judentum*. Edited by Wolfgang Haase. Vol. 19-II-1 of *Aufstieg und Niedergang der römischen Welt*. Berlin – New York: Walter De Gruyter.

–, 1992a. The Challenge of Hellenism for Early Judaism and Christianity. *Biblical Archaeologist* 55:84–91.

–, 1992b. The Drawings of J. Robert Teringo in *Jesus and the Forgotten City*. *Biblical Archaeologist* 55:106–7.

–, 1992c. Roman Sepphoris in Light of New Archaeological Evidence and Recent Research. Pages 321–38 in *The Galilee in Late Antiquity*. Edited by Lee I. Levine. New York: The Jewish Theological Seminary of America.

–, 1997. Jesus and His Galilean Context. Pages 57–66 in *Archaeology and the Galilee: Texts and Contexts in the Graeco-Roman and Byzantine Periods*. Edited by Douglas R. Edwards, and C. Thomas McCollough. Vol. 143 of *South Florida Studies in the History of Judaism*. Atlanta, Georgia: Scholars Press.

–, 1998. The Early Roman Period At Sepphoris: Chronological, Archaeological, Literary, and Social Considerations. Pages 343–55 in *Hesed Ve-Emet: Studies in Honor of Ernest S. Frerichs*. Edited by Jodi Magness, and Seymour Gitin. Atlanta, Georgia: Scholars Press.

–, ed. 1999. *Galilee Through the Centuries: Confluence of Cultures*. Winona Lake, Indiana: Eisenbrauns.

Meyers, Eric M., and Mark A. Chancey. 2000. How Jewish Was Sepphoris in Jesus' Time? *Biblical Archaeology Review* 26(4):18–33.

Meyers, Eric M. et al. 1995. Second Temple Studies in the Light of Recent Archaeology: Part II: The Roman Period, A Bibliography. *Currents in Research: Biblical Studies* 3:129–52.

Meyers, Eric M., Carol L. Meyers, and Kenneth G. Hoglund. 1994. Sepphoris (Sippori), 1993. *Israel Exploration Journal* 44:247–50.

–, 1995. Sepphoris (Sippori), 1994*. *Israel Exploration Journal* 45:68–71.

–, 1997. Zippori (Sepphoris) – 1994. *Excavations and Surveys in Israel* 16:46–7.

Meyers, Eric M., Carol L. Meyers, and Ehud Netzer. 1985. Sepphoris (Sippori), 1985 (I). *Israel Exploration Journal* 35:295–7.

–, 1986. Sippori – 1985. *Excavations and Surveys in Israel* 5:101–4.

–, 1987. Artistry in Stone: The Mosaics of Ancient Sepphoris. *Biblical Archaeologist* 50:223–31.

–, 1987. Sepphoris (Sippori), 1986 (I) – Joint Sepphoris Project*. *Israel Exploration Journal* 37:275–8.

–, 1987–1988. Sippori (Sepphoris) – 1986: I. The Joint Sepphoris Project. *Excavations and Surveys in Israel* 6:95–7.

–, 1988–1989. Sippori (Sepphoris) – 1987/1988. *Excavations and Surveys in Israel* 7–8:169–73.

–, 1990. Sepphoris (Sippori), 1987 and 1988*. *Israel Exploration Journal* 40:219–22.

–, 1992. *Sepphoris*. Winona Lake: Eisenbrauns.

Meyers, Eric M., and James F. Strange. 1981. *Archaeology, The Rabbis, and Early Christianity*. Nashville, Tennessee: Parthenon Press.

Meyers, Eric M., James F. Strange, and Dennis E. Groh. 1978. The Meiron Excavation Project: Archaeological Survey in Galilee and Golan, 1976. *Bulletin of the American Schools of Oriental Research* 230:1–24.

Meyshan, Josef. 1954. The Coinage of Agrippa the First. *Israel Exploration Journal* 4:186–200.

–, 1958. The Coins of the Herodian Dynasty. Pages 29–41 in *The Dating and Meaning of Ancient Jewish Coins and Symbols: Six Essays in Jewish Numismatics*. Tel-Aviv – Jerusalem: Schocken Publishing House.

Miller, Stuart S. 1984. *Studies in the History and Traditions of Sepphoris*. Studies in Judaism in Late Antiquity 37. Leiden: Brill.

–, 1992. Sepphoris, the Well Remembered City. *Biblical Archaeologist* 55(June):74–83.

–, 1996. Hellenistic and Roman Sepphoris: The Historical Evidence. Pages 21–9 in *Sepphoris in Galilee: Crosscurrents of Culture*. Edited by Rebecca Martin Nagy. Raleigh: North Carolina Museum of Art.

Moorey, P.R.S. 1991. *A Century of Biblical Archaeology*. Cambridge: The Lutterworth Press.

Moreland, Milton. 2001. Q and the Economics of Early Roman Galilee. Pages 561–75 in *The Sayings Source Q and the Historical Jesus*. Edited by A. Lindemann. Leuven: Leuven University Press.

–, 2002a. Review of *Archaeology and the Galilean Jesus: A Re-Examination of the Evidence. Crossing Galilee: Architectures of Contact in the Occupied Land of Jesus. Jesus and the Village Scribes: Galilean Conflicts and the Setting of Q*, by Jonathan L. Reed, Marianne Sawicki, and William E. Arnal. *Journal of Biblical Literature* 121(4):757–66.

–, 2002b. Imagining the Peasant in Roman Galilee: Archaeology, Q, and the Modern Theorist. Paper presented at the SBL annual meeting 2002. Toronto.

–, 2004. The Galilean Response to Earliest Christianity: A Cross-Cultural Study of the Subsistence Ethic. Pages 37–48 in *Religion and Society in Roman Palestine: Old Questions, New Approaches*. Edited by Douglas R. Edwards. New York and London: Routledge.

–, Forthcoming. The Jesus Movement in the Villages of Roman Galilee: Archaeology, Q, and Modern Anthropological Theory. *Semeia*.

Moxnes, Halvor. 1998. Jesus' galilæiske kontekst: Den historiske Jesus i forhold til hus, landsby og by. Pages 103–36 in *Den historiske Jesus og hans betydning*. Edited by Troels Engberg-Pedersen. København: Gyldendal.

–, 2001a. The Construction of Galilee As a Place for the Historical Jesus – Part 2. *Biblical Theology Bulletin* 31(2):64–77.

–, 2001b. The Construction of Galilee As a Place for the Historical Jesus – Part 1. *Biblical Theology Bulletin* 31(1):26–37.

Mulholland, M. Robert. 2001. Sociological Criticism. Pages 170–86 in *Interpreting the New Testament: Essays on Methods and Issues*. Edited by David Alan Black, and David S. Dockery. Nashville Tennessee: Broadman & Holmen Publishers.

Müller, Karlheinz. 1979. Jesus vor Herodes. Eine redaktionsgeschichtliche Untersuchung. Pages 111–41 in *Zur Geschichte des Urchristentums*. Edited by Gerhard Dautzenberg, Helmut Merklein, and Müller Karlheinz. Freiburg: Herder.

Nagy, Rebecca Martin, ed. 1996. *Sepphoris in Galilee: Crosscurrents of Culture*. Raleigh: North Carolina Museum of Art.

Negev, Avraham, Antonio Frova, and M. Avi-Yonah. 1993. Caesarea: Excavations in the 1950s and 1960s. Pages 272–80 in vol. 1 of *The New Encyclopedia of Archaeological*

Excavations in the Holy Land. Edited by Ephraim Stern. 4 vols. Jerusalem: The Israel Exploration Society & Carta.

Netzer, Ehud. 1975. The Hasmonean and Herodian Winter Palaces At Jericho. *Israel Exploration Journal* 25:89–100.

–, 1977. The Winter Palaces of the Judean Kings At Jericho At the End of the Second Temple Period. *Bulletin of the American Schools of Oriental Research* 228:1–13.

–, 1996a. The Palaces Built by Herod – A Research Update. Pages 27–54 in *Judaea and the Greco-Roman World in the Time of Herod in the Light of Archaeological Evidence.* Edited by Klaus Fittschen, and Gideon Foerster. Göttingen: Vanderhoeck & Ruprecht.

–, 1996b. The Promomontory Palace. Pages 193–207 in *Caesarea Maritima: A Retroperspective After Two Millennia.* Edited by Avner Raban, and Kenneth G. Holum. Leiden: Brill.

–, 2001. *The Palaces of the Hasmoneans and Herod the Great.* Jerusalem: Israel Exploration Society.

Netzer, Ehud, and Lee I. Levine. 1993. Caesarea: Excavations in the 1970s. Pages 280–2 in vol. 1 of *The New Encyclopedia of Archaeological Excavations in the Holy Land.* Edited by Ephraim Stern. 4 vols. Jerusalem: The Israel Exploration Society & Carta.

Netzer, Ehud, and Zeev Weiss. 1993. Sepphoris (Sippori), 1991–1992. *Israel Exploration Journal* 43:190–6.

–, 1994. *Zippori.* Jerusalem: Israel Exploration Society.

–, 1997. Architectural Development of Sepphoris During the Roman and Byzantine Periods. Pages 117–29 in *Archaeology and the Galilee: Texts and Contexts in the Graeco-Roman and Byzantine Periods.* Edited by Douglas R. Edwards, and C. Thomas McCollough. Vol. 143 of *South Florida Studies in the History of Judaism.* Atlanta, Georgia: Scholars Press.

Nicolas Purcell. 1999. Strabo. Page 1447 in *The Oxford Classical Dictionary,* 3rd ed. Edited by Simon Hornblower, and Antony Spawforth. 1 vol. Oxford: Oxford University Press.

Niese, Benedictus, ed. 1955. *Flavii Iosephi Opera: Edidit Et Apparatu Critico Instruxit* 1885–1895. Reprint. Berlin: Weidmannsche Verlagsbuchhandlung.

Nolland, John. 1993. *Luke 18:35–24:53.* Word Biblical Commentary 35c. Dallas, Texas: Word Books.

Noy, David, Alexander Panayotov, and Hanswulf Bloedhorn. 2004. *Volume I: Eastern Europe.* In *Inscriptiones Judaicae Orientis.* Texts and Studies in Ancient Judaism 101. Tübingen: Mohr Siebeck.

Nun, Mendel. 1988. *Ancient Anchorages and Harbours Around the Sea of Galilee.* Ein Gev: Kibbutz Ein Gev.

–, 1989. *The Sea of Galilee and Its Fishermen in the New Testament.* Ein Gev: Kibbutz Ein Gev.

–, 1993a. *Ancient Stone Anchors and Net Sinkers From the Sea of Galilee.* Ein Gev: Kibbutz Ein Gev.

–, 1993b. Cast Your Net Upon the Waters: Fish and Fishermen in Jesus' Time. *Biblical Archaeology Review* 19(6):46–56.

–, 2001. *Der See Genezareth und die Evangelien: Archäologische Forschungen eines jüdischen Fischers.* Biblische Archäologie und Zeitgeschichte 10, trans. Rainer Riesner. Gießen: Brunnen Verlag.

Oakman, Douglas E. 1986. *Jesus and the Economic Questions of His Day.* Studies in the Bible and Early Christianity 8. Leiston-Queenston: The Edwin Mellen Press.

–, 1994. The Archaeology of First-Century Galilee and the Social Interpretation of the Historical Jesus. Pages 220–51 in *Society of Biblical Literature 1994 Seminar Papers.*

Edited by Eugene Lovering, H., Jr. Vol. 33 of *Society of Biblical Literature Seminar Paper Series*. Atlanta, Georgia: Scholars Press.

Osiek, Carolyn. 1989. The New Handmaid: The Bible and Social Sciences. *Theological Studies* 50(2):260–78.

–, 2003. The Social-Scientific Study of Women in Mediterranean Antiquity. Paper presented at The SBL Annual Meeting. Atlanta.

Oster, Richard E., Jr. 1993. Review of *Jesus and the Forgotten City: New Light on Sepphoris and the Urban World of Jesus*, by Richard A. Batey. *Critical Review of Books in Religion* 6:201–4.

Ostmeyer, Karl-Heinrich. 2005. Armenhaus und Räuberhöhle? Galiläa zur Zeit Jesu. *Zeitschrift für die neutestamentliche Wissenschaft* 96:147–70.

Otto, Walter. 1913. Herodes Antipas. Pages 167–91 in vol. Supplementband II of *Paulus Real-Encyclopädie der Classischen Altertumswissenschaft*. Edited by Georg Wissowa. Stuttgart: Alfred Druckenmüller Verlag.

Overman, J. Andrew. 1988. Who Were the First Urban Christians? Urbanization in Galilee in the First Century. Pages 160–8 in *Society of Biblical Literature 1988 Seminar Papers*. Edited by David J. Lull. Vol. 27 of *Society of Biblical Literature Seminar Paper Series*. Atlanta, Georgia: Scholars Press.

–, 1993. Recent Advances in the Archaeology of the Galilee in the Roman Period. *Currents in Research: Biblical Studies* 1:35–57.

–, 1997. Jesus of Galilee and the Historical Peasant. Pages 67–73 in *Archaeology and the Galilee: Texts and Contexts in the Graeco-Roman and Byzantine Periods*. Edited by Douglas R. Edwards, and C. Thomas McCollough. Vol. 143 of *South Florida Studies in the History of Judaism*. Atlanta, Georgia: Scholars Press.

Parker, Pierson. 1987. Herod Antipas and the Death of Jesus. Pages 197–208 in *Jesus, the Gospels, and the Church: Essays in Honor of William R. Farmer*. Edited by E.P. Sanders. USA: Mercer University Press.

Pastor, Jack. 1997. *Land and Economy in Ancient Palestine*. London: Routledge.

Patrich, Joseph. 2002. Herod's Hippodrome-Stadium At Caesarea and the Games Conducted Therein. Pages 29–70 in *What Has Athens to Do with Jerusalem: Studies in Honor of Gideon Foerster*. Edited by L. Rutgers. Vol. 1 of *Interdisciplinary Studies in Ancient Culture and Religion*. Leuven: Peeters.

Perowne, Stewart. 1958. *The Later Herods: The Political Background of The New Testament*. London: Hodder and Stoughton.

Pilch, John J., ed. 2001. *Social Scientific Models for Interpreting the Bible: Essays by the Context Group in Honor of Bruce J. Malina*. Leiden: Brill.

Porath, Y. 1995. Herod's Amphitheatre At Caesarea: A Multipurpose Entertainment Building. Pages 15–27 in *The Roman and Byzantine Near East: Some Recent Archaeological Research*. Edited by J.H. Humphrey. Vol. 14 of *Journal of Roman Archaeology Supplement Series*. Portsmouth: Journal of Roman Archaeology.

–, 1996. The Evolution of the Urban Plan of Caesarea's Southwest Zone: New Evidence From the Current Excavations. Pages 193–207 in *Caesarea Maritima: A Retroperspective After Two Millennia*. Edited by Avner Raban, and Kenneth G. Holum. Leiden: Brill.

Qedar, Shraga. 1986–1987. Two Lead Weights of Herod Antipas and Agrippa II and the Early History of Tiberias. *Israel Numismatic Journal* 9:29–35.

Raban, Avner. 1993. Maritime Caesarea. Pages 286–91 in vol. 1 of *The New Encyclopedia of Archaeological Excavations in the Holy Land*. Edited by Ephraim Stern. 4 vols. Jerusalem: The Israel Exploration Society & Carta.

Rajak, Tessa. 1973. Justus of Tiberias. *The Classical Quarterly* 23(2):345–68.

Rappaport, Uriel. 1984. Numismatics. Pages 25–59 in *The Cambridge History of Judaism: Introduction; The Persian Period*. Edited by W.D. Davies, and Louis Finkelstein. Vol. 1. Cambridge: Cambridge University Press.

–, 1994. Where Was Josephus Lying – In His *Life* or in the *War*. Pages 279–89 in *Josephus and the History of the Greco-Roman Period: Essays in Memory of Morton Smith*. Edited by Fausto Parente, and Joseph Sievers. Leiden: Brill.

Rast, Walter E. 1992. *Through the Ages in Palestinian Archaeology: An Introductory Handbook*. Philadelphia: Trinity Press International.

Reed, Jonathan L. 1992. *The Population of Capernaum*. The Institute for Antiquity and Christianity, Occasional Papers 24. Claremont: The Institute for Antiquity and Christianity.

–, 1994a. *Places in Early Christianity: Galilee, Archaeology, Urbanisation, and Q*. California: University of California at Claremont.

–, 1994b. Population Numbers, Urbanization, and the Economics: Galilean Archaeology and the Historical Jesus. Pages 203–19 in *Society of Biblical Literature 1994 Seminar Papers*. Edited by Eugene Lovering, H., Jr. Vol. 33 of *Society of Biblical Literature Seminar Paper Series*. Atlanta, Georgia: Scholars Press.

–, 1999. Galileans, "Israelite Village Communities," and the Sayings Gospel Q. Pages 87–108 in *Galilee Through the Centuries: Confluence of Cultures*. Edited by Eric M. Meyers. Winona Lake, Indiana: Eisenbrauns.

–, 2000. *Archaeology and the Galilean Jesus: A Re-Examination of the Evidence*. Harrisburg, Pennsylvania: Trinity Press International.

Reifenberg, A. 1969. *Ancient Jewish Coins*. 5 1947. Reprint. Jerusalem: Rubin Mass.

Renan, Ernest. 1991. *The Life of Jesus* (La vie de Jésus). New York: Prometheus Books.

Renfrew, Colin. 1984. *Approaches to Social Archaeology*. Edinburgh: Edinburgh University Press.

Renfrew, Colin, and Paul Bahn. 1991. *Archaeology: Theories, Methods and Practice*. London: Thames and Hudson Ltd.

Richard, Suzanne, ed. 2003. *Near Eastern Archaeology: A Reader*. Winona Lake, Ind.: Eisenbrauns.

Richardson, Peter. 1999. *Herod: King of the Jews and Friend of the Romans*. 1996. Reprint. Minneapolis: Fortress Press.

–, 2000. First-Century Houses and Q's Setting. Pages 63–83 in *Christology, Controversy and Community: New Testament Essays in Honour of David R. Catchpole*. Edited by David G. Horrell, and Christopher M. Tuckett. Vol. XCIX of *Supplements to Novum Testamentum*. Leiden: Brill.

–, 2002. What Has Cana to Do with Capernaum? *New Testament Studies* 48:314–31.

–, 2004. *Building Jewish in the Roman East*. Waco, Texas: Baylor University Press.

Richardson, Peter, and Douglas R. Edwards. 2002. Jesus and Palestinian Social Protest: Archaeological and Literary Perspectives. Pages 247–66 in *Handbook of Early Christianity: Social Science Approaches*. Edited by Anthony J. Blasi, Jean Duhaime, and Paul-André Turcotte. Walnut Creek: Altamira Press.

Rohrbaugh, Richard L., ed. 1996. *The Social Sciences and New Testament Interpretation*. Peabody, Massachusetts: Hendrickson Publisher, Inc.

Roth, Cecil. 1956. An Ordinance Against Images in Jerusalem, A.D. 66. *Harvard Theological Review* XLIX:169–77.

Rousseau, John J, and Rami Arav. 1995. *Jesus and His World*. Minneapolis: Fortress Press.

Rozenberg, Silvia. 1996. The Wall Paitings of the Herodian Palace At Jericho. Pages 121–38 in *Judaea and the Greco-Roman World in the Time of Herod in the Light of*

Archaeological Evidence. Edited by Klaus Fittschen, and Gideon Foerster. Göttingen: Vanderhoeck & Ruprecht.

Runesson, Anders. 2001. *The Origins of the Synagogue: A Socio-Historical Study.* Coniectanea Biblica 37. Stockholm: Almqvist & Wiksell.

–, 2002. Från integration till marginalisering: Arkeologi som text i analysen av tidlig diasporajudendom. *Svensk exegetisk årsbok* 67:121–44.

Rutgers, Leonard V. 1998. Some Reflections on the Archaeological Finds From the Domestic Quarter on the Acropolis of Sepphoris. Pages 179–93 in *Religious and Ethnic Communities in Later Roman Palestine.* Edited by Hayim Lapin. Vol. V of *Studies and Texts in Jewish History and Culture.* Maryland: University Press of Maryland.

Safrai, Ze'ev. 1992. The Roman Army in the Galilee. Pages 103–14 in *The Galilee in Late Antiquity.* Edited by Lee I. Levine. New York: The Jewish Theological Seminary of America.

–, 1994. *The Economy of Roman Palestine.* London: Routledge.

Sanders, E. P. 1993a. *The Historical Figure of Jesus.* London: Penguin.

–, 1993b. Jesus in Historical Context. *Theology Today* 50:429–48.

Savage, Carl. Forthcoming. Supporting Evidence for a First Century Bethsaida. In *Religion, Ethnicity and Identity in Ancient Galilee.* Edited by Jürgen Zangenberg, Harold Attridge, and Dale B. Martin. Tübingen: Mohr Siebeck.

Sawicki, Marianne. 1994. Archaeology As Space Technology: Digging for Gender and Class in Holy Land. *Method & Theory in the Study of Religion* 6:319–48.

–, 2000. *Crossing Galilee: Architectures of Contact in the Occupied Land of Jesus.* Harrisburg, Pennsylvania: Trinity Press International.

Schalit, Abraham. 1968. *Namenwörterbuch zu Flavius Josephus – Supplement 1.* A Complete Concordance to Flavius Josephus. Leidin: Brill.

Schiffman, Lawrence H. 1992. Review of *Jesus and the Forgotten City, New Light on Sepphoris and the Urban World of Jesus,* by Richard A. Batey. *Biblical Archaeologist* 55:105–6.

Schürer, Emil. 1901. 3rd ed. Vol. 1. *Geschichte des jüdischen Volkes im Zeitalter Jesu Christi – Erster Band.* Leipzig: J.C. Hinrichs'sche Buchhandlung

–, 1907. 4th ed. Vol. 2. *Geschichte des jüdischen Volkes im Zeitalter Jesu Christi.* Leipzig: J.C. Hinrichs'sche Buchhandlung.

–, 1973. Vol. 1. *The History of the Jewish People in the Age of Jesus Christi (175 B.C – A.D. 135)* (Geschichte des jüdischen Volkes im Zeitalter Jesu Christi), eds. Geza Vermes, and Fergus Millar. Edinburgh: T. & T. Clark Ltd.

–, 1979. Vol. 2. *The History of the Jewish People in the Age of Jesus Christ (175 B.C – A.D. 135)* (Geschichte des jüdischen Volkes im Zeitalter Jesu Christi), eds. Geza Vermes, Fergus Millar, and Matthew Black. Edinburgh: T. & T. Clark Ltd.

Schwartz, Daniel R. 1990. *Agrippa I: The Last King of Judaea.* Texts and Studies in Ancient Judaism 23. Tübingen: J.C.B. Mohr (Paul Siebeck) Tübingen.

Scott, James C. 1976. *The Moral Economy of the Peasant: Rebellion and Subsistence in Southeast Asia.* New Haven – London: Yale University Press.

Segal, Arthur. 1995. *Theatres in Roman Palestine and Provincia Arabia.* Leiden: Brill.

–, 1997. *From Function to Monument: Urban Landscapes of Roman Palestine, Syria and Provincia Arabia.* Oxbow Monograph 66. Oxford: Oxbow Books.

Segal, Arthur, et al. 2002. Hippos: Third Season of Excavations July 2002. Zinman Institute of Archaeology, University of Haifa. [Cited May 2006]. Available from http://hippos.haifa.ac.il/report.htm.

–, 2003. Hippos: Third Season of Excavations June-July 2003. Zinman Institute of Archaeology, University of Haifa. [Cited May 2006]. Available from http://hippos.haifa.ac.il/report.htm.

–, 2004. *Hippos - Sussita: Fifth Season of Excavations and Summary of All Five Seasons.* Haifa: University of Haifa.

Shanks, Michael, and Christopher Tilley. 1987. *Re-Constructing Archaeology: Theory and Practice.* Cambridge: Cambridge University Press.

Shepherd, Naomi. 1987. *The Zealous Intruders: The Western Rediscovery of Palestine.* London: Collins.

Singer, Suzanne, F. 1977. The Winter Palaces of Jericho. *Biblical Archaeology Review* 3(2):5–17.

Smallwood, E. Mary. 1961. *Philonis Alexandrini, Legatio Ad Gaium: Edited With an Introduction, Translation and Commentary.* Leiden: Brill.

Soards, Marion L. 1985a. The Silence of Jesus Before Herod: An Interpretative Suggestion. *Australian Biblical Review* 33:41–5.

–, 1985b. Tradition, Composition, and Theology in Luke's Account of Jesus Before Herod Antipas. *Biblica* 66:344–64.

Sperber, Daniel. 1998. *The City in Roman Palestine.* New York – Oxford: Oxford University Press.

Stacey, David. 2004. *Excavations At Tiberias, 1973–1974: The Early Islamic Periods.* IAA Reports 21. Jerusalem: Israel Antiquities Authority.

Stegemann, Wolfgang, Bruce J. Malina, and Gerd Theißen. 2002. *The Social Setting of Jesus and the Gospels.* Minneapolis: Fortress Press.

Stein, Alla. 1992. Gaius Julius, An Agonoramos From Tiberias. *Zeitschrift für Papyrologie und Epigraphik* 93:144–8.

Stern, M. 1974. *Greek and Latin Authors on Jews and Judaism.* Vol. 1. *From Herodotus to Plutarch.* Jerusalem: The Israel Academy of Sciences and Humanities.

Strange, James F. 1977. The Capernaum and Herodium Publications. *Bulletin of the American Schools of Oriental Research* 226:65–73.

–, 1984. Sepphoris (Sippori), 1983. *Israel Exploration Journal* 34:51–2.

–, 1991. Two Aspects of the Development of Universalism in Christianity: The First to the Fourth Centuries. Pages 35–46 in *Religion and Global Order.* Edited by William R. Gerrett. New York: Paragon House Publishers.

–, 1992a. Cana of Galilee. Pages 827 in vol. 1 of *The Anchor Bible Dictionary.* Edited by David Noel Freedman. 6 vols. New York: Doubleday.

–, 1992b. Six Campaigns At Sepphoris: The University of South Florida Excavations, 1983–1989. Pages 339–55 in *The Galilee in Late Antiquity.* Edited by Lee I. Levine. New York: The Jewish Theological Seminary of America.

–, 1992c. Some Implications of Archaeology for New Testament Studies. Pages 23–59 in *What Has Archaeology to Do With Faith?* Edited by James H. Charlesworth, and Walter P. Weaver. Philadelphia: Trinity Press International.

–, 1993. The University of South Florida Excavations at Sepphoris, Israel: Report of the Excavations: 1993. [Cited May 2006]. Available from http://www.colby.edu/rel/archaeology/Sep93.html.

–, 1994a. First-Century Galilee From Archaeology and From the Texts. Pages 81–90 in *Society of Biblical Literature 1994 Seminar Papers.* Edited by Eugene Lovering, H., Jr. Vol. 33 of *Society of Biblical Literature Seminar Paper Series.* Atlanta, Georgia: Scholars Press.

–, 1994b. The University of South Florida Excavations at Sepphoris, Israel: Report of the Excavations: 14 June-15 July, 1994. [Cited May 2006]. Available from http:// www.colby. edu/rel/archaeology/Sep94.html.

–, 1995. The University of South Florida Excavations at Sepphoris, Israel: Report of the Excavations: 1995. [Cited May 2006]. Available from http://www.colby.edu/- rel/archaeology/Sep95.html.

–, 1996a. The Eastern Basilical Building. Pages 117–21 in *Sepphoris in Galilee: Cross-currents of Culture*. Edited by Rebecca Martin Nagy. Raleigh: North Carolina Museum of Art.

–, 1996b. The University of South Florida Excavations at Sepphoris, Israel: Report of the Excavations: 10 June-12 July, 1996. [Cited May 2006]. Available from http:// www.colby.edu/rel/archaeology/Sep96.html.

–, 1997a. First Century Galilee From Archaeology and From the Texts. Pages 39–48 in *Archaeology and the Galilee: Texts and Contexts in the Graeco-Roman and Byzantine Periods*. Edited by Douglas R. Edwards, and C. Thomas McCollough. Vol. 143 of *South Florida Studies in the History of Judaism*. Atlanta, Georgia: Scholars Press.

–, 1997b. The Sayings of Jesus and Archaeology. Pages 291–305 in *Hillel and Jesus: Comparative Studies of Two Major Religious Leaders*. Edited by James H. Charlesworth, and Loren L. Johns. Minneapolis: Fortress Press.

–, 1997c. The University of South Florida Excavations at Sepphoris, Israel: Report of the Excavations: May 8–23, 1997. [Cited May 2006]. Available from http://www.colby. edu/rel/ archaeology/ Sep97.html.

–, 1998. The University of South Florida Excavations at Sepphoris, Israel: Report of the Excavations: May 11 – July 14, 1998. [Cited May 2006]. Available from http:// www.colby.edu/rel/archaeology/Sep98.html.

–, 1999. The Sepphoris Newsletter, 1999. [Cited May 2006]. Available from http:// www.colby.edu/rel/archaeology/.

–, 2000a. Galilee. Pages 391–8 in vol. 1 of *Dictionary of New Testament Background*. Edited by Craig A. Evans, and Stanley E. Porter. Downers Grove, Illinois: InterVarsity Press.

–, 2000b. The University of South Florida Excavations at Sepphoris, Israel: Report of the Excavations: May 11 – July 14, 2000. [Cited May 2006]. Available from http:// www.colby.edu/rel/archaeology/S00.htm.

–, 2000c. The USF Excavations at Sepphoris, the 2000 Season. [Cited May 2006]. Available from http://www.colby.edu/rel/archaeology/.

–, 2001. Sepphoris and Galilee in Josephus, *Vita*. Paper presented at the SBL Annual Meeting. Denver. November 19. [Cited May 2006]. Available from http://pace.cns. yorku.ca/York/york/conference2001–ext.htm.

Strange, James F., Dennis E Groh, and Thomas R. W. Longstaff. 1988. Sepphoris (Sippori), 1987*. *Israel Exploration Journal* 38:188–90.

–, 1999a. Sepphoris, 1996*. *Israel Exploration Journal* 49:122–3.

–, 1999b. Sepphoris, 1997*. *Israel Exploration Journal* 49:124–6.

–, 1999c. Sepphoris, 1998*. *Israel Exploration Journal* 49:126–8.

Strange, James F., and Thomas R. W. Longstaff. 1985a. Sepphoris (Sippori), 1985 (II)*. *Israel Exploration Journal* 35:297–9.

–, 1985b. Sippori – 1985. *Excavations and Surveys in Israel* 4:100–2.

–, 1987. Sepphoris (Sippori), 1986 (II)*. *Israel Exploration Journal* 37:278–80.

–, 1987–1988. Sippori (Sepphoris) – 1986: II. University of South Florida Expedition. *Excavations and Surveys in Israel* 6:97–8.

Strange, James F., Thomas R. W. Longstaff, and Dennis E Groh. 1989–1990. Sippori – 1988. *Excavations and Surveys in Israel* 9:19–20.

–, 1993. Zippori – 1991. *Excavations and Surveys in Israel* 13:29–31.

–, 2006. *Excavations At Sepphoris: Volume One: University of Florida Probes in the Citadel and Villa.* Leiden: Brill.

Strickert, Fred. 1995. The Coins of Philip. Pages 165–89 in *Bethsaida: A City by the North Shore of the Sea of Galilee.* Edited by Rami Arav, and Richard A. Freund. Kirksville, Missouri: Thomas Jefferson University Press.

Sussman, Varda. 1973. Early Jewish Iconoclasm on Pottery Lamps. *Israel Exploration Journal* 23:46–7.

Syon, Danny. 1992. Gamla: Portrait of a Rebellion. *Biblical Archaeology Review* 18(1):20–37.

–, 2004. *Tyre and Gamla: A Study in the Monetary Influence of Southern Phoenicia on Galilee and the Golan in the Hellenistic and Roman Periods.* Jerusalem: Unpublished PhD dissertation.

Syon, Danny, and Shlomit Nemlich. 2001. *Gamla.* Qazrin: Golan Archaeological Museum.

Syon, Danny, and Z. Yavor. 2002. Gamla 1997–2000. *Hadashot Arkheologiyot – Excavations and Surveys in Israel* 114:2*–5*.

–, 2005. Gamla 1997–2000. *'Atiqot* 50:1–35.

Theißen, Gerd. 1985. Das "schwankende Rohr" in Mt. 11,7 und die Gründungsmünzen von Tiberias. *Zeitschrift des deutschen Palästina-Vereins* 101:43–55.

–, 1992. *The Gospels in Context: Social and Political History in the Synoptic Tradition.* Edinburgh: T. & T. Clark Ltd.

Theißen, Gerd, and D. Winter. 1997. *Die Kriterienfrage in der Jesusforschung. Vom Differenzkriterium zum Plausibilitätskriterium.* Freiburg: Novum Testamentum et Orbis Antiquus 34.

Tsafrir, Yoram. 1998. The Fate of Pagan Cult Places in Palestine: The Archaeological Evidence with Emphasis on Bet Shean. Pages 197–218 in *Religious and Ethnic Communities in Later Roman Palestine.* Edited by Hayim Lapin. Vol. V of *Studies and Texts in Jewish History and Culture.* Maryland: University Press of Maryland.

Tsuk, Tsvika. 1996. The Aqueducts of Sepphoris. Pages 45–9 in *Sepphoris in Galilee: Crosscurrents of Culture.* Edited by Rebecca Martin Nagy. Raleigh: North Carolina Museum of Art.

–, 1999. The Aqueducts to Sepphoris. Pages 161–76 in *Galilee Through the Centuries: Confluence of Cultures.* Edited by Eric M. Meyers. *Duke Judaic Studies Series Volume 1.* Winona Lake, Indiana: Eisenbrauns.

–, 2000. Bringing Water to Sepphoris. *Biblical Archaeology Review* 26(4):34–41.

Turcotte, Paul-André. 2002. Major Social Scientific Theories: Origins, Development, and Contributions. Pages 29–60 in *Handbook of Early Christianity: Social Science Approaches.* Edited by Anthony J. Blasi, Jean Duhaime, and Paul-André Turcotte. Walnut Creek – Lanham – New York – Oxford: Altamira Press.

Tyson, Joseph B. 1960. Jesus and Herod Antipas. *Journal of Biblical Literature* 79:239–46.

Tzaferis, Vasillios. 1983. New Archaeological Evidence on Ancient Capernaum. *Biblical Archaeologist* 46:198–204.

–, 1990. Sussita Awaits the Spade. *Biblical Archaeology Review* 16(5):50–8.

–, 1993. Excavations in the Area of the Greek Orthodox Church. Pages 1464–70 in vol. 1 of *The New Encyclopedia of Archaeological Excavations in the Holy Land.* Edited by Ephraim Stern. 4 vols. Jerusalem: The Israel Exploration Society & Carta.

van Henten, Jan Willem. 2003. The Two Dreams At the End of Book 17 of Josephus' *Antiquities*. Pages 78–93 in *Internationales Josephus-Kolloquium Dortmund 2002*. Edited by Jürgen U. Kalms, and Folker Siegert. Vol. 14 of *Münsteraner Judaistische Studien*. Münster – Hamburg – London: LIT Verlag.

Vann, Lindley. 1983. News From the Field: Herod's Harbor Construction Recovered Underwater. *Biblical Archaeology Review* 9(3):10–4.

Vogel, Manuel. 1999. Vita 64–69, Das Bilderverbot und die Galiläapolitik des Josephus. *Journal for the Study of Judaism in the Persian, Hellenistic and Roman Period* 30(1):65–79.

Wacholder, Ben Zion. 1962. *Nicolaus of Damascus*. Berkeley: University of California Press.

Wachsmann, Shelley. 1997. Galilee Boat. Pages 377–9 in vol. 2 of *The Oxford Encyclopedia of Archaeology in the Near East*. Edited by Eric M. Meyers. 5 vols. New York, Oxford: Oxford University Press.

Wagner-Lux, Ute et al. 1993. Preliminary Report on the Excavations and Architectural Survey in Gadara (Umm Qeis) in Jordan, Area I (1992). *Annual of the Department of Antiquities of Jordan* 37:385–95.

Waterman, Leroy, et al. 1937. *Preliminary Report of the University of Michigan Excavations At Sepphoris, Palestine in 1931*. Ann Arbor: University of Michigan Press.

Weber, Thomas Maria. 1990. *Umm Qais: Gadara of the Decapolis – A Brief Guide to the Antiquities*. Amman: Al Kutba, Publishers.

–, 1991a. Gadara in der Dekapolis: Ausgrabungen in Umm Qais/Nordwestjordanien in den Jahren 1986 bis 1999. *Mitteilungen des Deutschen Archäologen-Verbandes e.V.* 22(1):16–22.

–, 1991b. Gadara of the Decapolis Preliminary Report on the 1990 Season At Umm Qeis. *Annual of the Department of Antiquities of Jordan* 35:223–63.

–, 2002. *Gadara – Umm Qes*, Gadara Decapolitana: Untersuchungen zur Topographie, Geschichte, Architektur und der Bildenden Kunst einer "Polis Hellenis" im Ostjordanland. Abhandlungen des deutschen Palästina-Vereins 30. Wiesbaden: Harrassowitz Verlag.

–, Forthcoming. Gadara and the Galilee. In *Religion, Ethnicity and Identity in Ancient Galilee*. Edited by Jürgen Zangenberg, Harold Attridge, and Dale B. Martin. Tübingen: Mohr Siebeck.

Weinstein, James M. 1988. Radiocarbon Dating. Pages 235–60 in *Benchmarks in Time and Culture: An Introduction to Palestinian Archaeology*. Edited by Joel F. Drinkard, Gerald L. Mattingly, and Maxwell J. Miller. Atlanta, Georgia: Scholars Press.

Weiss, Zeev. 1993. Sepphoris. Pages 1324–8 in vol. 4 of *The New Encyclopedia of Archaeological Excavations in the Holy Land*. Edited by Ephraim Stern. 4 vols. Jerusalem: The Israel Exploration Society & Carta.

–, 1996. The Jews and the Games in Roman Caesarea. Pages 443–53 in *Caesarea Maritima: A Retroperspective After Two Millennia*. Edited by Avner Raban, and Kenneth G. Holum. Leiden: Brill.

–, 1998. Buildings for Entertainment. Pages 77–102 in *The City in Roman Palestine*. Edited by Daniel Sperber. Oxford: Oxford University Press.

–, 1999a. Adopting a Novelty: The Jews and the Roman Games in Palestine. Pages 23–49 in *The Roman and Byzantine Near East – Some Recent Archaeological Research*. Edited by J. H. Humphrey. Vol. 2 of *Journal of Roman Archaeology – Supplementary Series*. Portsmouth: Journal of Roman Archaeology.

–, 1999b. Zippori – 1997. *Hadashot Arkheologiyot – Excavations and Surveys in Israel* 109:16*–18*.

–, 1999c. Zippori (Sepphoris) – 1998. *Hadashot Arkheologiyot – Excavations and Surveys in Israel* 110:20*–23*.

–, 2000. Zippori – 1998. *Hadashot Arkheologiyot – Excavations and Surveys in Israel* 111:21*–23*.

–, 2002. Zippori – 2001. *Hadashot Arkheologiyot – Excavations and Surveys in Israel* 114:23*24*.

–, 2003. Zippori – 2002. *Hadashot Arkheologiyot – Excavations and Surveys in Israel* 115:25*26*.

Weiss, Zeev, and Ehud Netzer. 1993. Zippori – 1990/1991. *Excavations and Surveys in Israel* 12:13–5.

–, 1994. Zippori – 1992/1993. *Excavations and Surveys in Israel* 14:40–6.

–, 1996a. Hellenistic and Roman Sepphoris: The Archaeological Evidence. Pages 29–37 in *Sepphoris in Galilee: Crosscurrents of Culture.* Edited by Rebecca Martin Nagy. Raleigh: North Carolina Museum of Art.

–, 1996b. The Mosaics of the Nile Festival Building. Pages 127–32 in *Sepphoris in Galilee: Crosscurrents of Culture.* Edited by Rebecca Martin Nagy. Raleigh: North Carolina Museum of Art.

–, 1996c. Sepphoris During the Byzantine Period. Pages 81–9 in *Sepphoris in Galilee: Crosscurrents of Culture.* Edited by Rebecca Martin Nagy. Raleigh: North Carolina Museum of Art.

–, 1998. Zippori – 1994–1995. *Excavations and Surveys in Israel* 18:22–7.

Welch, Katherine. 1998. Greek Stadia and Roman Spectacles: Asia, Athens, and the Tomb of Herodes Atticus. *Journal of Roman Archaeology* 11:117–45.

Whiston, William, A.M., Trans. 1995. *The Works of Josephus: Complete and Unabridged. New Updated Edition.* 11th ed.1987. Reprint. USA: Hendrickson Publisher, Inc.

Whitley, David S. 1998. *Reader in Archaeological Theory: Post-Processual and Cognitive Approaches.* Routledge Readers in Archaeology. London: Routledge.

Wilkinson, John. 1977. *Jerusalem Pilgrims Before the Crusades.* Warminster: Aris & Philips.

–, 1981. *Egeria's Travels to the Holy Land.* Jerusalem: Ariel.

Willert, Niels. 1989. *Pilatusbilledet i den antikke jødedom og kristendom.* Bibel og historie 11. Århus: Aarhus Universitetsforlag.

Willett, William M. 1866. *Herod Antipas.* New York.

Wirgin, W. 1968. A Note on the 'Reed' of Tiberias. *Israel Exploration Journal* 18:248–49.

Wright, N. T. 1996. *Jesus and the Victory of God.* Christian Origins and the Question of God 2. Minneapolis: Fortress Press, London: SPCK.

Yeivin, S. 1937. Historical and Archaeological Notes. Pages 17–34 in *Preliminary Report of the University of Michigan Excavations At Sepphoris, Palestine, In 1931.* Edited by Leroy Waterman. Ann Arbor: University of Michigan Press.

Zangenberg, Jürgen. 2001. *Magdala Am See Gennesaret.* Kleine Arbeiten Zum Alten Und Neuen Testament. Waltrop: Verlag Hartmut Spenner.

Zeitlin, Solomon. 1974. Who Were the Galileans? New Light on Josephus' Activities in Galilee. *Jewish Quarterly Review* 65:189–203.

Figures

Figure 1

Coin of Hadrian depicting the temple in Tiberias, the Hadrianeion, in a tetrastyle fashion. Obverse: The buste of Hadrian with a laurel. Reverse: Zeus in a temple with the legend in the left side reading, TIBEP. © David Hendin.

Figure 2

Map of ancient Tiberias. From Yizhar Hirschfeld, *A Guide to Antiquity Sites in Tiberias*, 1992. Courtesy of the Israel Antiquities Authority.

Figure 3

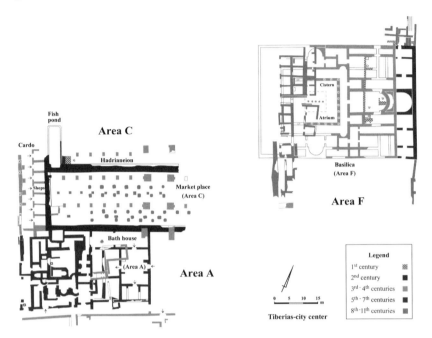

Map of the present excavations at Tiberias under the direction of Yizhar Hirschfeld. Drawing by Dov Porotsky. © Yizhar Hirschfeld.

Figure 4

The Southern Gate with the round towers and part of the cardo. From Yizhar Hirschfeld, *A Guide to Antiquity Sites in Tiberias*, 1992. Courtesy of the Israel Antiquities Authority.

Figure 5

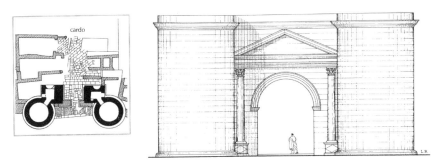

Suggested reconstruction of The Southern Gate with the round towers and part of the cardo. From Yizhar Hirschfeld, *A Guide to Antiquity Sites in Tiberias*, 1992. Courtesy of the Israel Antiquities Authority.

Figure 6

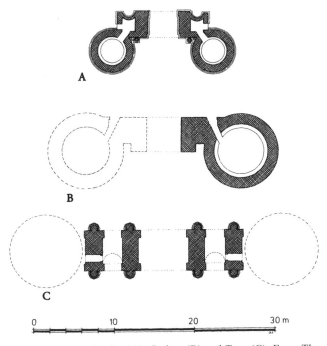

Comparison of the gates in Tiberias (A), Gadara (B) and Tyre (C). From Thomas Weber, *Gadara - Umm Qes, Gadara Decapolitana*, 2002.

Figure 7

Area C, square O-16, Wall no. 300-302. Notice the water installation on top of wall no. 302. Photo: Morten Hørning Jensen.

Figure 8

Artefacts found in locus 3018: a. Sample of white plaster. b. Reddish plaster with white pattern. c. Sample of imported marble. Photos: Morten Hørning Jensen.

Figure 9

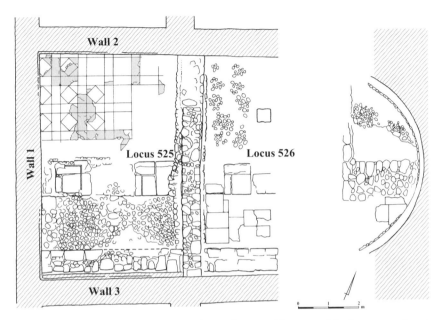

Map of locus 525 and 526, where portions of a magnificent marble floor were found. Drawing: Dov Porotsky. © Yizhar Hirschfeld.

Figure 10

Locus 525 (at the rear) and 526 (at the front). Photo: Morten Hørning Jensen.

Figure 11

Marble pieces collected in locus 525 from the magnificent *opus sectile* floor. Photo: Morten Hørning Jensen.

Figure 12

Black ash layer found in locus 526. Photo: Morten Hørning Jensen.

Figure 13

Section of wall 166 with fresco *in situ* (at the rear). Photo: Morten Hørning Jensen.

Figure 14

Section of the 9 m thick curved wall believed to part of the stadium. Photo: Jan Højland.

Figure 15

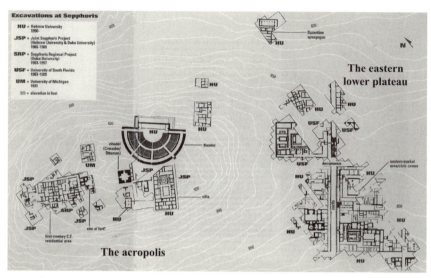

Map of the excavations in Sepphoris. © Eric M. Meyers and Mark A. Chancey.

Figure 16

The Western Summit. Photo: Morten Hørning Jensen.

Figure 17

The Roman theatre at Sepphoris with a splendid view across the Bet Netofa Valley. Photo: Morten Hørning Jensen.

Figure 18

Portion of the Dionysos mosaic in Sepphoris. Photo: Morten Hørning Jensen.

Figure 19

The colonnaded cardo in Sepphoris. Note the solid limestone slabs, heavily worn down after 500 hundred years of use. Photo: Morten Hørning Jensen.

Figure 20

Stones dressed in the "Herodian" fashion from the wall facing the cardo of the basilical building in field V of the USF dig. Photo: Morten Hørning Jensen.

Figure 21

The newly discovered coin believed to be the earliest known coin of Herod Antipas. Obverse: A grain of barley or wheat beside the legend TET PA_ _HC Δ. Reverse: A palm tree with seven branches and the legend HP W. © David Hendin.

Figure 22

Antipas' first series dated to his 24th regnal year. The largest denomination to the left, and the smallest to the right. Obverse: Date, LKΔ, 19/20 CE; floral plant (the reed); legend, HPWΔOY TETPAPXO (of Herod the Tetrarch, the smallest denomination abbreviated). Reverse: The legend, TIBE/PIAC within a wreath. © David Hendin.

Figure 23

Antipas' second series, dated to his 33rd regnal year. The largest denomination to the left, the second largest to the right, and the smallest denomination below. Obverse: Date, L ΛΓ, 28/29 CE; floral plant (palm branch); legend, HPWΔOY TETPAPXOY (of Herod the Tetrarch, abbreviated in the smallest denomination). Reverse: Same as figure 22. © David Hendin.

Figure 24

The largest denomination of Antipas' fifth series, dated to his 43rd regnal year. Obverse: Date, ETOC MΓ, 38/39 CE; floral plant (palm tree with seven branches and clusters of grapes); legend HRΩΔHC TETPAPXHC (Herod Antipas). Reverse: The legend ΓAIΩ KAICAPI ΓEPMA/NIKΩ within a wreath. © David Hendin.

Figure 25

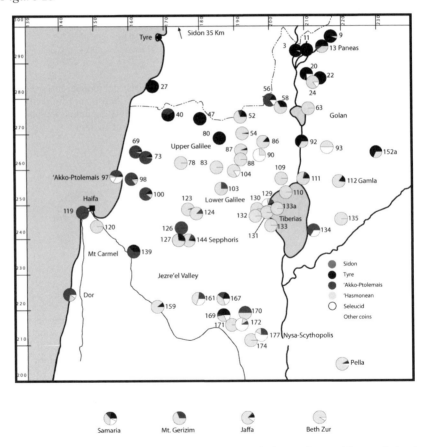

Map of the coinage distribution in the Hasmonean period, attesting a widespread circulation of Hasmonean coins in both Lower and Upper Galilee. © Danny Syon.

Figure 26

Period	Categories				
	Sidon	Tyre	'Akko-Ptolemais		Other
1. Ptolemaic (300-200 BCE)	Ptolemaic (8)	Ptolemaic (166)	Ptolemaic (5)		Other Ptolemaic mints, mainly Egypt and Cyprus (268) / Other coins, mainly Seleucid, Side and Aradus (19)
2. Seleucid (200-125 BCE)	Seleucid (35) / Civic (18)	Seleucid (1495)	Seleucid (309) / Civic (86)		Other Seleucid mints, mainly Antioch (397) / Other coins, mainly Ptolemaic, Side, Aradus (21)
3. Hasmonean (125-63 BCE)	Autonomous (192)	Autonomous (891)	Late Seleucid (44) / Civic/Autonomous (?) (304)	Hasmonean (5632)	Seleucid, Mainly Damascus and Antioch (217) / Other: mainly Nabatean, Iturean, Antioch, Ascalon, Cyprus (Ptolemy IX) (70)
4. Early Roman (63 BCE–70 CE)	Autonomous (83)	Autonomous (189)	Civic/Autonomous and colonial (104)	Jewish: Herodian dynasty, procurators, Roman administration and Great Revolt (723)	Others: mainly Nabatean and city coins (185) / Roman Imperial: denarii and bronze (39)
5. Middle Roman (70–256 CE)	Autonomous and colonial (81)	Autonomous (368) / Colonial (398)	Colonial (221)	Other city coins (1098)	Roman Imperial: denarii, provincial tetradrachms and bronze (135)

General figure revealing the coinage distribution attested in Danny Syon's survey. Note the small number of identified Herodian coins. © Danny Syon.

Figure 27

Site No.	Site	Paneas	Tiberias	J'lem, Samaria, Caesarea
3	Hagoshrim Avocado	3		13
6	Hagoshrim	1		1
8	Qal'at Bustra	1		
11	Dan-Dafna			1
12	Snir			1
13	Paneas	1	2	6
18	Tel Sheikh Yusuf			1
20	Tel Anafa	7		1
23	Kh. el-Beda	1		
24	Tel Yardinon			16
40	H. Karkara		1	
54	Gush Halav	1	10	15
58	Qeren Naftali	1		
60	H. Qazyon		1	
64	Makbarat Banat Yakub		1	
68	Kh. el-Shubeika			1
83	Rama			2
86	Nabratein	1	2	2
87	Meron	2	3	15
88	H. Shema'			2
90	Zefat			1
92	'Ateret			1
93	Qasrin		1	
94	Qseibeh			1
96	Yahudiya		1	
97	'Akko			5
100	Tel Keisan			1
103	H. Zalmon		2	
104	H. Beer Sheva		1	
106	Huqoq			1
107	H. Ravid		2	1
110	Capernaum			1
111	Betsaida	4	1	5
112	Gamla	54	68	197
113	H. Kanaf			3
123	Yodefat, Shifat	1	14	24
124	H. Qana			2
125	H. 'Ofrat			2
127	Shihin			10
129	Ginnosar boat site	1		
131	Migdal		4	13
132	Arbel		3	3
133	Tiberias		1	6
134	Hippos		2	
136	Sumaqa			2
139	Sha'ar Ha-'Amaqim	1	3	14
144	Sepphoris			38
147	Kh. El-Tirya	1		
148	Kafr Kanna			1
153a	Sha'ar Hagolan area			1
154	Umm el-Zinat			1
158	Midrakh 'Oz			1
159	Meggido	1		3
162	El Kader			1
164	H. Zafzafot			1
167	Giv'at Boleq			4
169	Giv'at Qumi		3	27
171	Tel Slawim			4
174	Tel Basul			24
175	Sede Nahum			1
177	Bet She'an			34

List of coins of Herod Antipas (Tiberias including later city-coins) with a known provenance according to Danny Syon. © Danny Syon.

Figure 28

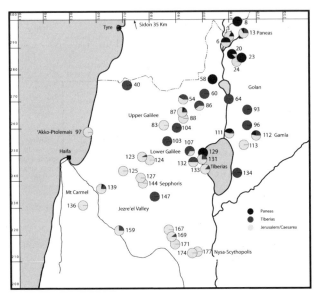

Map of the coinage distribution in Galilee and the Golan in the period 63 BCE-70 CE according to Danny Syon's survey. © Danny Syon.

Figure 29

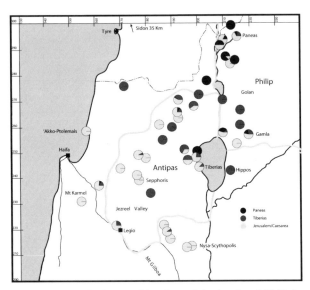

Same map as figure 28 with the imposed borders of Antipas' and Philip's tetrarchies. © Danny Syon.

Index of Ancient Sources

1. Old Testament

2. New Testament

3. Josephus

4. Other Greek and Latin Sources

5. Rabbinic Sources

Index of Modern Authors

Index of Subjects and Key Terms

Wissenschaftliche Untersuchungen zum Neuen Testament
Alphabetical Index of the First and Second Series

Böhlig, Alexander: Gnosis und Synkretismus. Volume 1 1989. *Volume 47* – Volume 2 1989. *Volume 48.*

Böhm, Martina: Samarien und die Samaritai bei Lukas. 1999. *Volume II/111.*

Böttrich, Christfried: Weltweisheit – Menschheitsethik – Urkult. 1992. *Volume II/50.*

Bolyki, János: Jesu Tischgemeinschaften. 1997. *Volume II/96.*

Bosman, Philip: Conscience in Philo and Paul. 2003. *Volume II/166.*

Bovon, François: Studies in Early Christianity. 2003. *Volume 161.*

Brocke, Christoph vom: Thessaloniki – Stadt des Kassander und Gemeinde des Paulus. 2001. *Volume II/125.*

Brunson, Andrew: Psalm 118 in the Gospel of John. 2003. *Volume II/158.*

Büchli, Jörg: Der Poimandres – ein paganisiertes Evangelium. 1987. *Volume II/27.*

Bühner, Jan A.: Der Gesandte und sein Weg im 4. Evangelium. 1977. *Volume II/2.*

Burchard, Christoph: Untersuchungen zu Joseph und Aseneth. 1965. *Volume 8.*

– Studien zur Theologie, Sprache und Umwelt des Neuen Testaments. Ed. by D. Sänger. 1998. *Volume 107.*

Burnett, Richard: Karl Barth's Theological Exegesis. 2001. *Volume II/145.*

Byron, John: Slavery Metaphors in Early Judaism and Pauline Christianity. 2003. *Volume II/162.*

Byrskog, Samuel: Story as History – History as Story. 2000. *Volume 123.*

Cancik, Hubert (Ed.): Markus-Philologie. 1984. *Volume 33.*

Capes, David B.: Old Testament Yaweh Texts in Paul's Christology. 1992. *Volume II/47.*

Caragounis, Chrys C.: The Development of Greek and the New Testament. 2004. *Volume 167.*

– The Son of Man. 1986. *Volume 38.*

– see *Fridrichsen, Anton.*

Carleton Paget, James: The Epistle of Barnabas. 1994. *Volume II/64.*

Carson, D.A., O'Brien, Peter T. and *Mark Seifrid* (Ed.): Justification and Variegated Nomism. Volume 1: The Complexities of Second Temple Judaism. 2001. *Volume II/140.* Volume 2: The Paradoxes of Paul. 2004. *Volume II/181.*

Ciampa, Roy E.: The Presence and Function of Scripture in Galatians 1 and 2. 1998. *Volume II/102.*

Classen, Carl Joachim: Rhetorical Criticsm of the New Testament. 2000. *Volume 128.*

Colpe, Carsten: Iranier – Aramäer – Hebräer – Hellenen. 2003. *Volume 154.*

Crump, David: Jesus the Intercessor. 1992. *Volume II/49.*

Dahl, Nils Alstrup: Studies in Ephesians. 2000. *Volume 131.*

Deines, Roland: Die Gerechtigkeit der Tora im Reich des Messias. 2004. *Volume 177.*

– Jüdische Steingefäße und pharisäische Frömmigkeit. 1993. *Volume II/52.*

– Die Pharisäer. 1997. *Volume 101.*

Deines, Roland and *Karl-Wilhelm Niebuhr* (Ed.): Philo und das Neue Testament. 2004. *Volume 172.*

Dettwiler, Andreas and *Jean Zumstein* (Ed.): Kreuzestheologie im Neuen Testament. 2002. *Volume 151.*

Dickson, John P.: Mission-Commitment in Ancient Judaism and in the Pauline Communities. 2003. *Volume II/159.*

Dietzfelbinger, Christian: Der Abschied des Kommenden. 1997. *Volume 95.*

Dimitrov, Ivan Z., James D.G. Dunn, Ulrich Luz and *Karl-Wilhelm Niebuhr* (Ed.): Das Alte Testament als christliche Bibel in orthodoxer und westlicher Sicht. 2004. *Volume 174.*

Dobbeler, Axel von: Glaube als Teilhabe. 1987. *Volume II/22.*

Dryden, J. de Waal: Theology and Ethics in 1 Peter. 2006. *Volume II/209.*

Du Toit, David S.: Theios Anthropos. 1997. *Volume II/91.*

Dübbers, Michael: Christologie und Existenz im Kolosserbrief. 2005. *Volume II/191.*

Dunn, James D.G.: The New Perspective on Paul. 2005. *Volume 185.*

Dunn , James D.G. (Ed.): Jews and Christians. 1992. *Volume 66.*

– Paul and the Mosaic Law. 1996. *Volume 89.*

– see *Dimitrov, Ivan Z.*

–, *Hans Klein, Ulrich Luz* and *Vasile Mihoc* (Ed.): Auslegung der Bibel in orthodoxer und westlicher Perspektive. 2000. *Volume 130.*

Ebel, Eva: Die Attraktivität früher christlicher Gemeinden. 2004. *Volume II/178.*

Ebertz, Michael N.: Das Charisma des Gekreuzigten. 1987. *Volume 45.*

Eckstein, Hans-Joachim: Der Begriff Syneidesis bei Paulus. 1983. *Volume II/10.*

– Verheißung und Gesetz. 1996. *Volume 86.*

Ego, Beate: Im Himmel wie auf Erden. 1989. *Volume II/34.*

Ego, Beate, Armin Lange and *Peter Pilhofer* *(Ed.):* Gemeinde ohne Tempel – Community without Temple. 1999. *Volume 118.*

– and *Helmut Merkel* (Ed.): Religiöses Lernen in der biblischen, frühjüdischen und früh-christlichen Überlieferung. 2005. *Volume 180.*

Eisen, Ute E.: see *Paulsen, Henning.*

Elledge, C.D.: Life after Death in Early Judaism. 2006. *Volume II/208.*

Ellis, E. Earle: Prophecy and Hermeneutic in Early Christianity. 1978. *Volume 18.*

– The Old Testament in Early Christianity. 1991. *Volume 54.*

Endo, Masanobu: Creation and Christology. 2002. *Volume 149.*

Ennulat, Andreas: Die 'Minor Agreements'. 1994. *Volume II/62.*

Ensor, Peter W.: Jesus and His 'Works'. 1996. *Volume II/85.*

Eskola, Timo: Messiah and the Throne. 2001. *Volume II/142.*

– Theodicy and Predestination in Pauline Soteriology. 1998. *Volume II/100.*

Fatehi, Mehrdad: The Spirit's Relation to the Risen Lord in Paul. 2000. *Volume II/128.*

Feldmeier, Reinhard: Die Krisis des Gottessohnes. 1987. *Volume II/21.*

– Die Christen als Fremde. 1992. *Volume 64.*

Feldmeier, Reinhard and *Ulrich Heckel* (Ed.): Die Heiden. 1994. *Volume 70.*

Fletcher-Louis, Crispin H.T.: Luke-Acts: Angels, Christology and Soteriology. 1997. *Volume II/94.*

Förster, Niclas: Marcus Magus. 1999. *Volume 114.*

Forbes, Christopher Brian: Prophecy and Inspired Speech in Early Christianity and its Hellenistic Environment. 1995. *Volume II/75.*

Fornberg, Tord: see *Fridrichsen, Anton.*

Fossum, Jarl E.: The Name of God and the Angel of the Lord. 1985. *Volume 36.*

Foster, Paul: Community, Law and Mission in Matthew's Gospel. *Volume II/177.*

Fotopoulos, John: Food Offered to Idols in Roman Corinth. 2003. *Volume II/151.*

Frenschkowski, Marco: Offenbarung und Epiphanie. Volume 1 1995. *Volume II/79* – Volume 2 1997. *Volume II/80.*

Frey, Jörg: Eugen Drewermann und die biblische Exegese. 1995. *Volume II/71.*

– Die johanneische Eschatologie. Volume I. 1997. *Volume 96.* – Volume II. 1998. *Volume 110.* – Volume III. 2000. *Volume 117.*

Frey, Jörg and *Udo Schnelle (Ed.):* Kontexte des Johannesevangeliums. 2004. *Volume 175.*

– and *Jens Schröter* (Ed.): Deutungen des Todes Jesu im Neuen Testament. 2005. *Volume 181.*

Freyne, Sean: Galilee and Gospel. 2000. *Volume 125.*

Fridrichsen, Anton: Exegetical Writings. Edited by C.C. Caragounis and T. Fornberg. 1994. *Volume 76.*

Gäbel, Georg: Die Kulttheologie des Hebräerbriefes. 2006. *Volume II/212.*

Gäckle, Volker: Die Starken und die Schwachen in Korinth und in Rom. 2005. *Volume 200.*

Garlington, Don B.: 'The Obedience of Faith'. 1991. *Volume II/38.*

– Faith, Obedience, and Perseverance. 1994. *Volume 79.*

Garnet, Paul: Salvation and Atonement in the Qumran Scrolls. 1977. *Volume II/3.*

Gemünden, Petra von (Ed.): see *Weissenrieder, Annette.*

Gese, Michael: Das Vermächtnis des Apostels. 1997. *Volume II/99.*

Gheorghita, Radu: The Role of the Septuagint in Hebrews. 2003. *Volume II/160.*

Gräbe, Petrus J.: The Power of God in Paul's Letters. 2000. *Volume II/123.*

Gräßer, Erich: Der Alte Bund im Neuen. 1985. *Volume 35.*

– Forschungen zur Apostelgeschichte. 2001. *Volume 137.*

Green, Joel B.: The Death of Jesus. 1988. *Volume II/33.*

Gregg, Brian Han: The Historical Jesus and the Final Judgment Sayings in Q. 2005. *Volume II/207.*

Gregory, Andrew: The Reception of Luke and Acts in the Period before Irenaeus. 2003. *Volume II/169.*

Grindheim, Sigurd: The Crux of Election. 2005. *Volume II/202.*

Gundry, Robert H.: The Old is Better. 2005. *Volume 178.*

Gundry Volf, Judith M.: Paul and Perseverance. 1990. *Volume II/37.*

Häußer, Detlef: Christusbekenntnis und Jesusüberlieferung bei Paulus. 2006. *Volume 210.*

Hafemann, Scott J.: Suffering and the Spirit. 1986. *Volume II/19.*

– Paul, Moses, and the History of Israel. 1995. *Volume 81.*

Hahn, Ferdinand: Studien zum Neuen Testament. Volume I: Grundsatzfragen, Jesusforschung, Evangelien. 2006. *Volume 191.* – Volume II: Bekenntnisbildung und Theologie in urchristlicher Zeit. 2006. *Volume 192.*

Hahn, Johannes (Ed.): Zerstörungen des Jerusalemer Tempels. 2002. *Volume 147.*

Hamid-Khani, Saeed: Relevation and Concealment of Christ. 2000. *Volume II/120.*

Hannah, Darrel D.: Michael and Christ. 1999. *Volume II/109.*

Harrison; James R.: Paul's Language of Grace in Its Graeco-Roman Context. 2003. *Volume II/172.*

Hartman, Lars: Text-Centered New Testament Studies. Ed. von D. Hellholm. 1997. *Volume 102.*

Hartog, Paul: Polycarp and the New Testament. 2001. *Volume II/134.*

Heckel, Theo K.: Der Innere Mensch. 1993. *Volume II/53.*

– Vom Evangelium des Markus zum viergestaltigen Evangelium. 1999. *Volume 120.*

Heckel, Ulrich: Kraft in Schwachheit. 1993. *Volume II/56.*

– Der Segen im Neuen Testament. 2002. *Volume 150.*

– see *Feldmeier, Reinhard.*
– see *Hengel, Martin.*
Heiligenthal, Roman: Werke als Zeichen. 1983. *Volume II/9.*
Hellholm, D.: see *Hartman, Lars.*
Hemer, Colin J.: The Book of Acts in the Setting of Hellenistic History. 1989. *Volume 49.*
Hengel, Martin: Judentum und Hellenismus. 1969, ³1988. *Volume 10.*
– Die johanneische Frage. 1993. *Volume 67.*
– Judaica et Hellenistica.
  Kleine Schriften I. 1996. *Volume 90.*
– Judaica, Hellenistica et Christiana.
  Kleine Schriften II. 1999. *Volume 109.*
– Paulus und Jakobus.
  Kleine Schriften III. 2002. *Volume 141.*
– and *Anna Maria Schwemer:* Paulus zwischen Damaskus und Antiochien. 1998. *Volume 108.*
– Der messianische Anspruch Jesu und die Anfänge der Christologie. 2001. *Volume 138.*
Hengel, Martin and *Ulrich Heckel* (Ed.): Paulus und das antike Judentum. 1991. *Volume 58.*
– and *Hermut Löhr* (Ed.): Schriftauslegung im antiken Judentum und im Urchristentum. 1994. *Volume 73.*
– and *Anna Maria Schwemer* (Ed.): Königsherrschaft Gottes und himm-lischer Kult. 1991. *Volume 55.*
– Die Septuaginta. 1994. *Volume 72.*
–, *Siegfried Mittmann* and *Anna Maria Schwemer* (Ed.): La Cité de Dieu / Die Stadt Gottes. 2000. *Volume 129.*
Herrenbrück, Fritz: Jesus und die Zöllner. 1990. *Volume II/41.*
Herzer, Jens: Paulus oder Petrus? 1998. *Volume 103.*
Hill, Charles E.: From the Lost Teaching of Polycarp. 2005. *Volume 186.*
Hoegen-Rohls, Christina: Der nachösterliche Johannes. 1996. *Volume II/84.*
Hoffmann, Matthias Reinhard: The Destroyer and the Lamb. 2005. *Volume II/203.*
Hofius, Otfried: Katapausis. 1970. *Volume 11.*
– Der Vorhang vor dem Thron Gottes. 1972. *Volume 14.*
– Der Christushymnus Philipper 2,6-11. 1976, ²1991. *Volume 17.*
– Paulusstudien. 1989, ²1994. *Volume 51.*
– Neutestamentliche Studien. 2000. *Volume 132.*
– Paulusstudien II. 2002. *Volume 143.*
– and *Hans-Christian Kammler:* Johannesstudien. 1996. *Volume 88.*
Holtz, Traugott: Geschichte und Theologie des Urchristentums. 1991. *Volume 57.*
Hommel, Hildebrecht: Sebasmata. Volume 1 1983. *Volume 31* – Volume 2 1984. *Volume 32.*

Horbury, William: Herodian Judaism and New Testament Study. 2006. *Volume 193.*
Horst, Pieter W. van der: Jews and Christians in Their Graeco-Roman Context. 2006. *Volume 196.*
Hvalvik, Reidar: The Struggle for Scripture and Covenant. 1996. *Volume II/82.*
Jauhiainen, Marko: The Use of Zechariah in Revelation. 2005. *Volume II/199.*
Jensen, Morten H.: Herod Antipas in Galilee. 2006. *Volume II/215.*
Johns, Loren L.: The Lamb Christology of the Apocalypse of John. 2003. *Volume II/167.*
Joubert, Stephan: Paul as Benefactor. 2000. *Volume II/124.*
Jungbauer, Harry: „Ehre Vater und Mutter". 2002. *Volume II/146.*
Kähler, Christoph: Jesu Gleichnisse als Poesie und Therapie. 1995. *Volume 78.*
Kamlah, Ehrhard: Die Form der katalogischen Paränese im Neuen Testament. 1964. *Volume 7.*
Kammler, Hans-Christian: Christologie und Eschatologie. 2000. *Volume 126.*
– Kreuz und Weisheit. 2003. *Volume 159.*
– see *Hofius, Otfried.*
Kelhoffer, James A.: The Diet of John the Baptist. 2005. *Volume 176.*
– Miracle and Mission. 1999. *Volume II/112.*
Kelley, Nicole: Knowledge and Religious Authority in the Pseudo-Clementines. 2006. *Volume II/213.*
Kieffer, René and *Jan Bergman (Ed.):* La Main de Dieu / Die Hand Gottes. 1997. *Volume 94.*
Kim, Seyoon: The Origin of Paul's Gospel. 1981, ²1984. *Volume II/4.*
– Paul and the New Perspective. 2002. *Volume 140.*
– "The 'Son of Man'" as the Son of God. 1983. *Volume 30.*
Klauck, Hans-Josef: Religion und Gesellschaft im frühen Christentum. 2003. *Volume 152.*
Klein, Hans: see *Dunn, James D.G.*
Kleinknecht, Karl Th.: Der leidende Gerechtfertigte. 1984, ²1988. *Volume II/13.*
Klinghardt, Matthias: Gesetz und Volk Gottes. 1988. *Volume II/32.*
Kloppenborg, John S.: The Tenants in the Vineyard. 2006. *Volume 195.*
Koch, Michael: Drachenkampf und Sonnenfrau. 2004. *Volume II/184.*
Koch, Stefan: Rechtliche Regelung von Konflikten im frühen Christentum. 2004. *Volume II/174.*
Köhler, Wolf-Dietrich: Rezeption des Matthäusevangeliums in der Zeit vor Irenäus. 1987. *Volume II/24.*
Köhn, Andreas: Der Neutestamentler Ernst Lohmeyer. 2004. *Volume II/180.*
Kooten, George H. van: Cosmic Christology in Paul and the Pauline School. 2003. *Volume II/171.*

Korn, Manfred: Die Geschichte Jesu in veränderter Zeit. 1993. *Volume II/51.*

Koskenniemi, Erkki: Apollonios von Tyana in
der neutestamentlichen Exegese. 1994.
Volume II/61.
– The Old Testament Miracle-Workers in
Early Judaism. 2005. *Volume II/206.*

Kraus, Thomas J.: Sprache, Stil und historischer Ort des zweiten Petrusbriefes. 2001.
Volume II/136.

Kraus, Wolfgang: Das Volk Gottes. 1996.
Volume 85.

Kraus, Wolfgang and *Karl-Wilhelm Niebuhr*
(Ed.): Frühjudentum und Neues Testament
im Horizont Biblischer Theologie. 2003.
Volume 162.
– see *Walter, Nikolaus.*

Kreplin, Matthias: Das Selbstverständnis Jesu.
2001. *Volume II/141.*

Kuhn, Karl G.: Achtzehngebet und Vaterunser
und der Reim. 1950. *Volume 1.*

Kvalbein, Hans: see *Ådna, Jostein.*

Kwon, Yon-Gyong: Eschatology in Galatians.
2004. *Volume II/183.*

Laansma, Jon: I Will Give You Rest. 1997.
Volume II/98.

Labahn, Michael: Offenbarung in Zeichen und
Wort. 2000. *Volume II/117.*

Lambers-Petry, Doris: see *Tomson, Peter J.*

Lange, Armin: see *Ego, Beate.*

Lampe, Peter: Die stadtrömischen Christen in
den ersten beiden Jahrhunderten. 1987,
²1989. *Volume II/18.*

Landmesser, Christof: Wahrheit als Grundbegriff neutestamentlicher Wissenschaft.
1999. *Volume 113.*
– Jüngerberufung und Zuwendung zu Gott.
2000. *Volume 133.*

Lau, Andrew: Manifest in Flesh. 1996.
Volume II/86.

Lawrence, Louise: An Ethnography of the
Gospel of Matthew. 2003. *Volume II/165.*

Lee, Aquila H.I.: From Messiah to Preexistent
Son. 2005. *Volume II/192.*

Lee, Pilchan: The New Jerusalem in the Book
of Relevation. 2000. *Volume II/129.*

Lichtenberger, Hermann: Das Ich Adams und
das Ich der Menschheit. 2004. *Volume 164.*
– see *Avemarie, Friedrich.*

Lierman, John: The New Testament Moses.
2004. *Volume II/173.*

Lieu, Samuel N.C.: Manichaeism in the Later
Roman Empire and Medieval China.
²1992. *Volume 63.*

Lindgård, Fredrik: Paul's Line of Thought in
2 Corinthians 4:16-5:10. 2004.
Volume II/189.

Loader, William R.G.: Jesus' Attitude Towards
the Law. 1997. *Volume II/97.*

Löhr, Gebhard: Verherrlichung Gottes durch
Philosophie. 1997. *Volume 97.*

Löhr, Hermut: Studien zum frühchristlichen
und frühjüdischen Gebet. 2003. *Volume 160.*
– see *Hengel, Martin.*

Löhr, Winrich Alfried: Basilides und seine Schule. 1995. *Volume 83.*

Luomanen, Petri: Entering the Kingdom of
Heaven. 1998. *Volume II/101.*

Luz, Ulrich: see *Dunn, James D.G.*

Mackay, Ian D.: John's Raltionship with
Mark. 2004. *Volume II/182.*

Maier, Gerhard: Mensch und freier Wille.
1971. *Volume 12.*
– Die Johannesoffenbarung und die Kirche.
1981. *Volume 25.*

Markschies, Christoph: Valentinus Gnosticus?
1992. *Volume 65.*

Marshall, Peter: Enmity in Corinth: Social
Conventions in Paul's Relations with the
Corinthians. 1987. *Volume II/23.*

Mayer, Annemarie: Sprache der Einheit im
Epheserbrief und in der Ökumene. 2002.
Volume II/150.

Mayordomo, Moisés: Argumentiert Paulus
logisch? 2005. *Volume 188.*

McDonough, Sean M.: YHWH at Patmos:
Rev. 1:4 in its Hellenistic and Early Jewish
Setting. 1999. *Volume II/107.*

McDowell, Markus: Prayers of Jewish
Women. 2006. *Volume II/211.*

McGlynn, Moyna: Divine Judgement and
Divine Benevolence in the Book of
Wisdom. 2001. *Volume II/139.*

Meade, David G.: Pseudonymity and Canon.
1986. *Volume 39.*

Meadors, Edward P.: Jesus the Messianic
Herald of Salvation. 1995. *Volume II/72.*

Meißner, Stefan: Die Heimholung des Ketzers.
1996. *Volume II/87.*

Mell, Ulrich: Die „anderen" Winzer. 1994.
Volume 77.

Mengel, Berthold: Studien zum Philipperbrief.
1982. *Volume II/8.*

Merkel, Helmut: Die Widersprüche zwischen
den Evangelien. 1971. *Volume 13.*
– see *Ego, Beate.*

Merklein, Helmut: Studien zu Jesus und Paulus.
Volume 1 1987. *Volume 43.* – Volume 2
1998. *Volume 105.*

Metzdorf, Christina: Die Tempelaktion Jesu.
2003. *Volume II/168.*

Metzler, Karin: Der griechische Begriff des Verzeihens. 1991. *Volume II/44.*

Metzner, Rainer: Die Rezeption des Matthäusevangeliums im 1. Petrusbrief. 1995.
Volume II/74.
– Das Verständnis der Sünde im Johannesevangelium. 2000. *Volume 122.*

Mihoc, Vasile: see *Dunn, James D.G..*

Mineshige, Kiyoshi: Besitzverzicht und Almosen bei Lukas. 2003. *Volume II/163.*

Mittmann, Siegfried: see *Hengel, Martin.*

Korn, Manfred: Die Geschichte Jesu in veränderter Zeit. 1993. *Volume II/51.*

Koskenniemi, Erkki: Apollonios von Tyana in der neutestamentlichen Exegese. 1994. *Volume II/61.*
- The Old Testament Miracle-Workers in Early Judaism. 2005. *Volume II/206.*

Kraus, Thomas J.: Sprache, Stil und historischer Ort des zweiten Petrusbriefes. 2001. *Volume II/136.*

Kraus, Wolfgang: Das Volk Gottes. 1996. *Volume 85.*

Kraus, Wolfgang and *Karl-Wilhelm Niebuhr* (Ed.): Frühjudentum und Neues Testament im Horizont Biblischer Theologie. 2003. *Volume 162.*
- see *Walter, Nikolaus.*

Kreplin, Matthias: Das Selbstverständnis Jesu. 2001. *Volume II/141.*

Kuhn, Karl G.: Achtzehngebet und Vaterunser und der Reim. 1950. *Volume 1.*

Kvalbein, Hans: see *Ådna, Jostein.*

Kwon, Yon-Gyong: Eschatology in Galatians. 2004. *Volume II/183.*

Laansma, Jon: I Will Give You Rest. 1997. *Volume II/98.*

Labahn, Michael: Offenbarung in Zeichen und Wort. 2000. *Volume II/117.*

Lambers-Petry, Doris: see *Tomson, Peter J.*

Lange, Armin: see *Ego, Beate.*

Lampe, Peter: Die stadtrömischen Christen in den ersten beiden Jahrhunderten. 1987, ²1989. *Volume II/18.*

Landmesser, Christof: Wahrheit als Grundbegriff neutestamentlicher Wissenschaft. 1999. *Volume 113.*
- Jüngerberufung und Zuwendung zu Gott. 2000. *Volume 133.*

Lau, Andrew: Manifest in Flesh. 1996. *Volume II/86.*

Lawrence, Louise: An Ethnography of the Gospel of Matthew. 2003. *Volume II/165.*

Lee, Aquila H.I.: From Messiah to Preexistent Son. 2005. *Volume II/192.*

Lee, Pilchan: The New Jerusalem in the Book of Relevation. 2000. *Volume II/129.*

Lichtenberger, Hermann: Das Ich Adams und das Ich der Menschheit. 2004. *Volume 164.*
- see *Avemarie, Friedrich.*

Lierman, John: The New Testament Moses. 2004. *Volume II/173.*

Lieu, Samuel N.C.: Manichaeism in the Later Roman Empire and Medieval China. ²1992. *Volume 63.*

Lindgård, Fredrik: Paul's Line of Thought in 2 Corinthians 4:16-5:10. 2004. *Volume II/189.*

Loader, William R.G.: Jesus' Attitude Towards the Law. 1997. *Volume II/97.*

Löhr, Gebhard: Verherrlichung Gottes durch Philosophie. 1997. *Volume 97.*

Löhr, Hermut: Studien zum frühchristlichen und frühjüdischen Gebet. 2003. *Volume 160.*
- see *Hengel, Martin.*

Löhr, Winrich Alfried: Basilides und seine Schule. 1995. *Volume 83.*

Luomanen, Petri: Entering the Kingdom of Heaven. 1998. *Volume II/101.*

Luz, Ulrich: see *Dunn, James D.G.*

Mackay, Ian D.: John's Raltionship with Mark. 2004. *Volume II/182.*

Maier, Gerhard: Mensch und freier Wille. 1971. *Volume 12.*
- Die Johannesoffenbarung und die Kirche. 1981. *Volume 25.*

Markschies, Christoph: Valentinus Gnosticus? 1992. *Volume 65.*

Marshall, Peter: Enmity in Corinth: Social Conventions in Paul's Relations with the Corinthians. 1987. *Volume II/23.*

Mayer, Annemarie: Sprache der Einheit im Epheserbrief und in der Ökumene. 2002. *Volume II/150.*

Mayordomo, Moisés: Argumentiert Paulus logisch? 2005. *Volume 188.*

McDonough, Sean M.: YHWH at Patmos: Rev. 1:4 in its Hellenistic and Early Jewish Setting. 1999. *Volume II/107.*

McDowell, Markus: Prayers of Jewish Women. 2006. *Volume II/211.*

McGlynn, Moyna: Divine Judgement and Divine Benevolence in the Book of Wisdom. 2001. *Volume II/139.*

Meade, David G.: Pseudonymity and Canon. 1986. *Volume 39.*

Meadors, Edward P.: Jesus the Messianic Herald of Salvation. 1995. *Volume II/72.*

Meißner, Stefan: Die Heimholung des Ketzers. 1996. *Volume II/87.*

Mell, Ulrich: Die „anderen" Winzer. 1994. *Volume 77.*

Mengel, Berthold: Studien zum Philipperbrief. 1982. *Volume II/8.*

Merkel, Helmut: Die Widersprüche zwischen den Evangelien. 1971. *Volume 13.*
- see *Ego, Beate.*

Merklein, Helmut: Studien zu Jesus und Paulus. Volume 1 1987. *Volume 43.* – Volume 2 1998. *Volume 105.*

Metzdorf, Christina: Die Tempelaktion Jesu. 2003. *Volume II/168.*

Metzler, Karin: Der griechische Begriff des Verzeihens. 1991. *Volume II/44.*

Metzner, Rainer: Die Rezeption des Matthäusevangeliums im 1. Petrusbrief. 1995. *Volume II/74.*
- Das Verständnis der Sünde im Johannesevangelium. 2000. *Volume 122.*

Mihoc, Vasile: see *Dunn, James D.G.*

Mineshige, Kiyoshi: Besitzverzicht und Almosen bei Lukas. 2003. *Volume II/163.*

Mittmann, Siegfried: see *Hengel, Martin.*

Twelftree, Graham H.: Jesus the Exorcist. 1993. *Volume II/54.*

Urban, Christina: Das Menschenbild nach dem Johannesevangelium. 2001. *Volume II/137.*

Visotzky, Burton L.: Fathers of the World. 1995. *Volume 80.*

Vollenweider, Samuel: Horizonte neutestamentlicher Christologie. 2002. *Volume 144.*

Vos, Johan S.: Die Kunst der Argumentation bei Paulus. 2002. *Volume 149.*

Wagener, Ulrike: Die Ordnung des „Hauses Gottes". 1994. *Volume II/65.*

Wahlen, Clinton: Jesus and the Impurity of Spirits in the Synoptic Gospels. 2004. *Volume II/185.*

Walker, Donald D.: Paul's Offer of Leniency (2 Cor 10:1). 2002. *Volume II/152.*

Walter, Nikolaus: Praeparatio Evangelica. Ed. von Wolfgang Kraus und Florian Wilk. 1997. *Volume 98.*

Wander, Bernd: Gottesfürchtige und Sympathisanten. 1998. *Volume 104.*

Watts, Rikki: Isaiah's New Exodus and Mark. 1997. *Volume II/88.*

Wedderburn, A.J.M.: Baptism and Resurrection. 1987. *Volume 44.*

Wegner, Uwe: Der Hauptmann von Kafarnaum. 1985. *Volume II/14.*

Weissenrieder, Annette: Images of Illness in the Gospel of Luke. 2003. Volume II/164.

–, *Friederike Wendt* and *Petra von Gemünden* (Ed.): Picturing the New Testament. 2005. *Volume II/193.*

Welck, Christian: Erzählte ‚Zeichen'. 1994. *Volume II/69.*

Wendt, Friederike (Ed.): see *Weissenrieder, Annette.*

Wiarda, Timothy: Peter in the Gospels. 2000. *Volume II/127.*

Wifstrand, Albert: Epochs and Styles. 2005. *Volume 179.*

Wilk, Florian: see *Walter, Nikolaus.*

Williams, Catrin H.: I am He. 2000. *Volume II/113.*

Wilson, Walter T.: Love without Pretense. 1991. *Volume II/46.*

Wischmeyer, Oda: Von Ben Sira zu Paulus. 2004. *Volume 173.*

Wisdom, Jeffrey: Blessing for the Nations and the Curse of the Law. 2001. *Volume II/133.*

Wold, Benjamin G.: Women, Men, and Angels. 2005. *Volume II/2001.*

Wright, Archie T.: The Origin of Evil Spirits. 2005. *Volume II/198.*

Wucherpfennig, Ansgar: Heracleon Philologus. 2002. *Volume 142.*

Yeung, Maureen: Faith in Jesus and Paul. 2002. *Volume II/147.*

Zimmermann, Alfred E.: Die urchristlichen Lehrer. 1984, ²1988. *Volume II/12.*

Zimmermann, Johannes: Messianische Texte aus Qumran. 1998. *Volume II/104.*

Zimmermann, Ruben: Christologie der Bilder im Johannesevangelium. 2004. *Volume 171.*

– Geschlechtermetaphorik und Gottesverhältnis. 2001. *Volume II/122.*

Zumstein, Jean: see *Dettwiler, Andreas*

Zwiep, Arie W.: Judas and the Choice of Matthias. 2004. *Volume II/187.*

*For a complete catalogue please write to the publisher
Mohr Siebeck • P.O. Box 2030 • D–72010 Tübingen/Germany
Up-to-date information on the internet at www.mohr.de*